DNA and the Criminal Justice System

Basic Bioethics
Glenn McGee and Arthur Caplan, editors

DNA and the Criminal Justice System
The Technology of Justice

Edited by David Lazer

The MIT Press
Cambridge, Massachusetts
London, England

MIT Press books may be purchased at special quantity discounts for business or sales promotional use. For information, please email special_sales@mitpress.mit.edu or write to Special Sales Department, The MIT Press, 5 Cambridge Center, Cambridge, MA 02142.

This book was set in Sabon by SNP Best-set Typesetter Ltd., Hong Kong, and was printed and bound in the United States of America.

Library of Congress Cataloging-in-Publication Data

DNA and the criminal justice system : the technology of justice / edited by David Lazer.
    p. cm. — (Basic bioethics)
Includes bibliographical references and index.
ISBN 0-262-12265-0 (alk. paper) — ISBN 0-262-62186-X (pbk. : alk. paper)
1. DNA fingerprinting—United States. 2. Forensic genetics—United States—Databases.
3. Criminal justice, Administration of—United States. I. Lazer, David. II. Series.

KF9666.5.D63 2004
345.73′067—dc22   2004042847

10 9 8 7 6 5 4 3 2 1

This book is dedicated to Lisa Bernt.

Contents

Series Foreword

We are pleased to present the twelfth book in the series Basic Bioethics. The series presents innovative works in bioethics to a broad audience and introduces seminal scholarly manuscripts, state-of-the-art reference works, and textbooks. Such broad areas as the philosophy of medicine, advancing genetics and biotechnology, end-of-life care, health and social policy, and the empirical study of biomedical life are engaged.

Glenn McGee
Arthur Caplan

Basic Bioethics Series Editorial Board
Tod S. Chambers
Susan Dorr Goold
Mark Kuczewski
Herman Saatkamp

Preface. DNA: Diviner of Guilt or Threat to Liberty?

The spring of 2003 was a desperate one in Baton Rouge, Louisiana. DNA had linked five brutal rape-murders in the Baton Rouge area to a single perpetrator. There was no obvious pattern in terms of geography or demography, and the police were bereft of useful leads, except for the observation by witnesses in several of the cases of the presence of a white GM pickup truck near the scene of the crime.

The tension broke abruptly on May 26, 2003, when DNA collected from Derrick Todd Lee, in the investigation of a seemingly unrelated case, matched the DNA collected from the five crime scenes. This match was followed by a brief manhunt, in which Lee was apprehended in Atlanta.

The Lee case is thus an unambiguous success of the use of DNA in the criminal justice system; without DNA Lee would not have been identified as a suspect. But underneath the surface it also unveils some potentially troubling details about the use of DNA in the criminal justice system. Consider the following:

Although Louisiana's criteria for inclusion in the state's convict DNA database are among the most expansive in the country, not a single investigation had been aided by that database, because the state had not allocated adequate resources to actually collect and process samples.[1]

All fifty states have passed laws creating DNA databases—one in each state for DNA profiles of individuals convicted (and sometimes, just arrested) for particular crimes, and one for profiles developed from DNA evidence left at the scenes of crimes. However, resources have been slow to follow the mandate to create these databases. Louisiana stands out in this respect because its ambitious criteria for inclusion create a large gap between theory and practice, but at that time six other states reported no investigations aided as a result of their DNA databases, and another ten states reported that ten or fewer investigations aided. In fact, the majority of investigations in the country that have been aided by state DNA databases come from just four states: Florida, New York, Virginia, and Illinois. It is unclear how many of these "investigations aided" provided leads that law enforcement energetically followed and that resulted in convictions.

After the publicity surrounding the case, Louisiana expanded the criteria for inclusion in its offender database to encompass all individuals convicted of felonies and all individuals arrested for felonies.

The criteria for inclusion in convict databases have grown progressively more expansive, with thirty states now mandating inclusion of all those with felony convictions in the database and some states including juveniles and some misdemeanors (see concluding chapter). Experience from states that have aggressively expanded their databases suggests that larger databases garner substantially more matches. It is clear, however, that expansion of the groups whose DNA goes into the databases exacerbates both resource allocation and civil-liberties issues.

Louisiana collected over 1,000 samples in its search for the serial killer—largely Caucasian men in their twenties (based on an FBI profile of the murderer), many in large part based on their possession of a white pickup truck.[2]

The first use of DNA in a criminal investigation involved a "DNA dragnet": to capture the aptly named Colin Pitchfork in 1987. DNA dragnets involve collecting DNA from a large set of people that collectively is more likely to contain the perpetrator—for example, from a town, or from owners of a GM pickup. By the very nature of DNA dragnets, there is little basis to suspect particular individuals. In the Louisiana case, the exclusion samples taken by police were in principle consensual. This consent was illusory, however. As the West Baton Rouge chief deputy stated: "Anybody that's been approached. . . , and [the officer] explains why—most of them say, 'Sure I'd be happy to.' " Refusal was considered potentially indicative of guilt: "A court order would be issued immediately . . . and they would be swabbed."[3] Further, upon exclusion of these individuals as sources of the DNA from the crime scene, the state has refused to return or destroy the DNA and records of that DNA—a common practice among law enforcement agencies.[4]

This is the first documented case in the United States in which crime scene DNA samples were analyzed to identify the race of the alleged perpetrator.[5]

This use of DNA is illustrative of the broader possibilities of employing DNA analysis to build profiles regarding unknown suspects. Perhaps more serious, from a privacy perspective, is the information that DNA collected from convicts, arrestees, and suspects might reveal about them (and their relatives) beyond what is necessary for crime investigation—everything from propensity to develop certain diseases to paternity.

The Lee case thus highlights the enigmatic character of DNA in the criminal justice system—as diviner of guilt, and as potential threat to liberty. This book is devoted to considering the implications of this collision between twenty-first-century technology and twentieth-century justice, and to examining the broad normative question of how the balance between individual interests in privacy and autonomy and the societal interest in security needs to be redrawn in the face of the technical possibilities that DNA offers. It is an outgrowth of a landmark conference cosponsored by the Department of Justice's National Commission on the Future of DNA Evidence and Harvard's John F. Kennedy School of Government, "DNA and the Criminal Justice System," in November 2000. This conference brought together the leading academics and policymakers involved in this area after a tumultuous decade in which DNA emerged out of nowhere as one of the stars of the criminal justice system, but one whose role in many ways was still emerging. The three years since the conference have been incredibly dynamic ones, with postconviction DNA testing laws expanding to cover most of the country, with the national DNA database system growing more than tenfold, and with the background of September 11 swinging the interests of society dramatically toward security. These years have not produced equivalent leaps in the clarity of the role DNA should play in the criminal justice system. This observation provides the rationale, then, to proceed with a book that brings together essays from many of the speakers at the 2000 conference.

The roadmap to the book is as follows. The first part of the book lays the conceptual, historical, legal, and scientific groundwork for the volume. The introductory chapter provides a thematic overlay. The key to understanding the response to DNA technology, in the end, may have little to do with its merits, but rather with the trust in the system to use the technology properly. Properly using DNA in the criminal justice system is thus a governance challenge that involves both adapting to and shaping the emerging technology.

Stephen Breyer (chapter 2) provides the motivation for the volume by outlining the role that the book plays in furthering the discourse on the role of technology in society. Frederick Bieber (chapter 3) then outlines the trajectory of DNA technology, examining how it has been used in the criminal justice system to the present, as well as directions the technology is likely to take in the near future. Simon Cole (chapter 4) provides a history of identification technologies in the criminal justice system, highlighting, somewhat ominously, how identifiers become imbued with greater significance than simply identification. Edward Imwinkelried (chapter 5) examines the impact DNA has had in the courtroom, arguing that DNA has rather neatly been integrated into courtroom procedures, but that the most interesting issues lie precourtroom (e.g., the development of DNA databases), and postcourtroom (i.e., postconviction). Margaret Berger (chapter 6) further develops the latter theme, discussing how the durability and probative power of DNA have undermined one of the fundamental tenets of the criminal justice system: finality.

George Annas (chapter 7) and R. Alta Charo (chapter 8) then establish the bioethical basis for precourtroom issues by examining the issues raised by the collection of DNA data. Barry Steinhardt (chapter 9), Amitai Etzioni (chapter 10), Viktor Mayer-Schönberger (chapter 11), and D. H. Kaye and Michael Smith (chapter 12) then turn to the question, what should be done when the state collects DNA data to fight crime? These four chapters offer starkly different answers to this question, with all of the chapters asserting the need for substantial control over the data, but with Steinhardt arguing that ultimately the only satisfactory control is for the databases to be as limited as possible; Kaye and Smith arguing that there should be a universal database; and Etzioni and Mayer-Schönberger arguing that the scope of the database should be determined by a balancing of individual and societal interests, with Etzioni emphasizing the latter, and Mayer-Schönberger the former.

Garland Allen (chapter 13) and Troy Duster (chapter 14) then turn to an issue that is a storm cloud just over the horizon: the use of arguments regarding the genetic bases of criminal behavior in the justice system (and society more broadly). Duster examines how the collection of DNA material on the basis of criminal behavior might be transformed into a research program on the genetic determinants of such behavior. Allen analyzes the rise of eugenics in the United States earlier this century and critiques both the science of behavioral genetics and, in particular, its popularization and use in society.

Finally, Sheila Jasanoff (chapter 15) and David Lazer and Michelle Meyer (chapter 16) turn to the role of democratic discourse in defining the use of DNA in the criminal justice system. Jasanoff examines what she labels the "identity crisis" of DNA—the many roles that DNA can play, as identifier, diagnostic, and property—and discusses the role that the National Commission on the Future of DNA Evidence played in defining the debates around the use of DNA in the criminal justice system. Lazer and Meyer conclude the book with a discussion of the current state of these debates, examining where a consensus has emerged and where there is still substantial division and debate within society.

The purpose of this book is thus not to provide the definitive answer to how DNA should be used in the criminal justice system—indeed, there are many disagreements among the authors as to that answer. Instead, our collective hope is to define the debate and to help anticipate the challenges that will arise in the coming decade.

Notes

1. FBI statistics available at http://www.fbi.gov/hq/lab/codis/aidedmap.htm.

2. Lee is African American; it is unclear whether he ever had a white pickup truck in his possession.

3. Glenn Wilson, "In Louisiana, Debate over DNA Dragnet," *Christian Science Monitor*, February 21, 2003.

4. This is particularly notable because in many crimes DNA is routinely collected from relatives and friends of the victim. Many states have informed-consent forms that indicate that the collected DNA will be saved and compared to that from other crimes. It is unclear what the consent form in Louisiana stated.

5. "Racial Profiling: Will a New DNA Test Shatter Serial Killer Myths?" ABCnews.com, June 13, 2003.

Acknowledgments

It is a truism that edited volumes are collective efforts; however, if there were a case of an "especially true" truism, this would be it. This volume grew out of the conference "DNA and the Criminal Justice System" that was held at the Kennedy School in November 2000. This conference was cosponsored by the National Commission on the Future of DNA Evidence of the National Institute of Justice and the Center for Business and Government (CBG) of Harvard's John F. Kennedy School of Government. The conference was a huge success, in significant part because of the personal investments of the executive director of the National Commission, Christopher Asplen, and the director of the CBG, Ira Jackson. The conference, in fact, grew out of a conversation that Chris and I had after one of the commission's meetings, and his involvement in the conference, and his work on the National Commission, was a truly a model of public service. Ira, in turn, immediately saw the intellectual and public value of the conference and this volume and was just extraordinarily supportive, and the conference and the volume are much the stronger as a result.

Edited volumes are only as strong as the engagement of their contributors. In this case, all of the contributors were extraordinarily engaged, both with the material and with each other, and I thank all of them for that. Among the contributors are two colleagues that were there from conception to choosing a publisher: Sheila Jasanoff and Frederick Bieber. Sheila is one of those rare colleagues who helps you to take an intellectual problem, turn it a little this way, and a little that way, until you have a completely new perspective on it. Fred is the model of a scientist who has ventured in the domain of public discourse, much to the benefit of both science and society. This volume has benefited greatly from their sage advice.

I also need to thank the team that helped me put this volume together: Elisabeth Palladino, who was there from the beginning, helping me conceive the overall structure of the project; Paul Hodge, who was my "master strategist" on the conference; Eugene Mar, who did yeoman's work on the research for my chapters; Michelle Meyer, who coauthored the concluding chapter and was extraordinary in her work in pushing the volume through its final stages; and Jason Scott, who most ably cut his teeth working at the Kennedy School on this project.

Finally, I dedicate this volume to my spouse and partner in life, Lisa Bernt. Lisa had to suffer through the usual hardships of the spouse of someone finishing a book, but she also contributed enormously on the creative side of the volume. In fact, my involvement in this area can be traced to a conversation I had with her years ago, when I was thinking new subjects for my research. Her suggestion: DNA and the criminal justice system. That fortuitous conversation has been followed by many others on the subject, and this volume is one of the results.

I

Laying the Groundwork

1

Introduction: DNA and the Criminal Justice System

David Lazer

Just a couple of weeks ago in New York City where I sit as a member of the [New York] Forensic Science Commission, it was brought to our attention that the New York City Medical Examiner's Office would like to create a similar laboratory which would be able to solve property crimes. And it was mentioned at that meeting by some of the people there, that in order to make that laboratory most effective in doing this, it would be critically important to include for elimination purposes biological samples that have come from the New York City Police Department.

Needless to say, the blood drained out of the face of some of the people who are [charged] with this particular responsibility, because they realize the problems they would have in effectuating it. Perhaps these New York police officers and perhaps their brethren in England realize that if you wanted to do some of these research studies, one of the studies you might wish to do is to find the gene for antisocial behavior. And if you were doing that, perhaps the first data set you'd like to study are law enforcement personnel.

Peter Neufeld, Innocence Project, November 20, 2000[1]

One attorney . . . had a position that thousands of innocent people are in jail because of DNA typing. That same attorney has this position—thousands of innocent people are in jail because of no DNA typing.

So how do we reconcile these, what seem to be, diametrically opposed positions? And the reality is, is that we have an adversary system. And that given certain situations, one will take one position versus another position. Even though the same practices, the same tools, the same interpretations are used, we can find this to occur.

Bruce Budowle, Federal Bureau of Investigation, November 19, 2000[2]

An earlier volume on the use of DNA in the criminal justice system was titled *DNA on Trial*.[3] In it, for example, Richard Lewontin and Daniel L. Hartl's influential early critique of the use of DNA evidence in criminal proceedings questioned whether the science of DNA testing was ready for the courtroom—whether, for instance, random-match probabilities produced by the population genetics of the early 1990s reflected the complexities of the distribution of DNA in the population.[4]

Today DNA technology is no longer on trial; in fact, it has now been rather neatly integrated into the courtroom. This, of course, does not mean that there are no controversial issues surrounding the use of DNA technology in criminal prosecution. What is striking is that the dominant controversies about DNA technology now revolve around the competence of the criminal justice system rather than the reliability of the technology itself. The very precision of DNA technology is, in fact, exhibit 1 in the current trial of the criminal justice system.

The O. J. Simpson case is a prime example of the relative roles of trust in DNA technology and trust in the system to use the technology. The Simpson case still dominates the public perception of the use of DNA in the criminal justice system. In fact, there was more media coverage of the DNA issues in the Simpson case than on *both* the development of a national DNA database *and* wrongful convictions uncovered as a result of DNA evidence *during the entire 1990s.*[5] Underlying the Simpson case was the issue of trust: not trust in DNA technology, but trust in the system. Did the Los Angeles Police Department handle the samples from Simpson properly? Might they have engaged in a conspiracy to frame Simpson? In the end, the technology was not a cure for distrust in the system.

The apparent paradox that the FBI's Bruce Budowle raises in his quote beginning the chapter—the fact that some individuals, such as the Innocence Project's Peter Neufeld, also quoted, question the reliability of DNA technology in one circumstance (e.g., in the Simpson trial) and use that technology to their advantage in other circumstances (e.g., postconviction exonerations)—is resolved when one considers the distrust of the criminal justice system evident in Neufeld's statement. The system, according to this view, wrongly convicts individuals because of racial biases, the underfunding of the defense, and unreliable police practices. DNA technology occasionally offers an ex post correction of these errors; however, the technology cannot be trusted in the hands of the system as the system is currently constructed. As discussed later in the chapter, issues regarding the trustworthiness of the U.S. criminal justice system are deeply embedded in current policy debates about the development of DNA databases and the use of DNA for postconviction reviews.

Trusting Justice

On May 1, 1990, Roy Criner was convicted of the 1986 murder and rape of Deanna Ogg and sentenced to ninety-nine years in prison. Seven years later, a DNA test conducted on the semen left on Ogg's body excluded Criner as its source. However, a state district court decision to grant Criner a new trial was overturned in a five-to-four decision by the Texas Court of Criminal Appeals, which offered the theory that Ogg might have had consensual intercourse prior to being raped by Criner and that Criner might have worn a condom or not ejaculated. Three years later, a cigarette butt from the crime scene was tested: It contained DNA from Ogg and the individual who was the source of the semen on Ogg's body—*not* Criner, thus undermining the appeals court's theory. In July 2000, the Texas Board of Pardons and Paroles, at the request of the prosecutor, recommended that Criner be set free.[6]

The Criner case highlights the potential of DNA to identify, postconviction, who did *not* commit a crime by demonstrating that crime scene evidence that is almost certainly from the perpetrator of the crime does not match the individual convicted of the crime. The area of postconviction exoneration has received far more press, but far less policy action, than the development of DNA databases.[7]

The over 140 convict exonerations in the United States that have resulted from postconviction DNA analysis since 1989 raise two serious questions about the U.S. criminal justice system. The first question is whether the system is receptive to evidence that it has erred in a particular case. The second is whether these exonerations highlight systematic fault lines in the system itself.

The Criner case is indicative of a lack of receptivity of the system to postconviction application of DNA analysis. This is likely in part because DNA evidence, in principle, can be incorporated into the normal process of appealing a guilty verdict. However, this is, at most, just part of the story. As Margaret Berger highlights in chapter 6, the "system" has always placed a high priority on finality and has created a set of barriers to the introduction of new evidence in a case. The importance of finality is at least partly a result of resource constraints, combined with the natural tendency of evidence to "depreciate" over time. Yet DNA evidence does not (necessarily) depreciate. Institutions built around this depreciation principle are thus a poor fit with DNA technology. The question, then, is how to recalibrate our institutions to match this powerful technology. This is the question that Berger takes up in detail.

The most prominent institution that has developed around the issue of postconviction DNA analysis has been the Innocence Project. Barry Scheck and Neufeld started the Innocence Projects in 1992 at the Cardoza School of Law. The success of the Cardoza program led to the founding of forty-one other Innocence Projects, most between 1999 and 2002. The success of the Innocence Projects has created pressure on public officials to sponsor review programs. Thirty-nine states have passed statutes to facilitate postconviction review based on DNA technologies, including a number of state programs to facilitate access. Also, a few district attorneys around the country have begun reviews of convictions that were returned prior to access to DNA technology; the first to initiate such a review was Paul Pfingst of San Diego in 2000. Strikingly, although increased statutory rights of convicts to access to DNA evidence have facilitated postconviction review, none of the exonerations to date has been the result of either a state-run or DA-run postconviction review program.

This troubling observation raises two obvious questions: (1) Why has the use of DNA to exonerate convicts been slow to spread? and (2) why, where there have been proactive government-sponsored programs, have virtually no convicts been exonerated?

The most obvious explanation is that resources are limited. Simply because the technology allows something to be done does not mean that it should, since there will be opportunity costs to any use of resources. Notably, though, as Berger points out, existing government programs have not been resource-intensive; furthermore, exonerations actually save resources because of the cost of taking care of prisoners. A more plausible explanation is that there are no powerful constituencies within government who are in favor of reviewing old cases. In fact, postconviction review is dangerous to incumbent officials because of the possibility that it will reveal errors by individuals and the system. It is perhaps unsurprising, therefore, that those review programs that have sprung up were started with a significant lag after DNA evidence became routinely available in the courtroom (about 1993).

DNA Databases: The Architecture of Security and Trust

On March 3, 1986, Debbie Smith was abducted from her home in Williamsburg, Virginia, robbed, and raped. The subsequent police investigation reached a dead end, until a sudden breakthrough on July 26, 1995: the newly-entered DNA profile of a prisoner, Norman Jimmerson, matched the semen collected from the rape kit. Jimmerson was subsequently convicted and sentenced to two life sentences plus 25 years with no chance of parole. As Debbie Smith testified:

For the first time in six and a half years, I could feel myself breathe. . . . Finally, I could quit looking over my shoulder. No longer did I have to drive around in circles hoping a neighbor would drive by so I could get the courage to get out of my car to go into my own front door if no one else was home. Unfamiliar noises no longer left me panic-stricken. I no longer scanned faces in a crowd to see if he was following me. Suicide was no longer a consideration. And finally, my husband is grateful that I don't wake him up anymore in the middle of the night with the ear-piercing screams.[8]

In 1984, 13-year-old Heidi Marie Fredette's body was found dumped by the side of Highway 36 in Tehama County. She had been strangled, stabbed and sexually assaulted.

Fifteen years later, evidence taken at the time of her death was analyzed as part of the state Department of Justice's "old and cold" program. A DNA fingerprint of the rapist was completed and compared against the DNA databank of known felons in Berkeley.

A cold hit was made to David James McIntosh, 53, whose genetic profile was in the databank because of a conviction for kidnapping, rape and assault with intent to commit rape. McIntosh was just days away from being released from Folsom State Prison, but he is now being prosecuted for murder, kidnapping and murder by torture of Heidi, and will be eligible for the death penalty.[9]

The development of a national DNA database, starting in 1990 and accelerating in 1994 with the DNA Identification Act, has created a scenario in law enforcement in which perpetrators of crimes may be ensnared by minute biological traces they have left behind at the scenes of their crimes, as Jimmerson and McIntosh were. In fact, according to the FBI, through March 2004, 16,100 crime investigations in the United States had been aided through convict DNA databases.[10] This likely represents a tiny fraction of the potential investigative potential of the national DNA database: the United Kingdom (with a fifth of the population of the United States), which developed a national database earlier than the United States, claims to have seven to eight hundred investigations aided per week—a rate that, every six months, exceeds the total hits in the *history* of the U.S. program![11]

These numbers, in fact, understate the potential value produced by DNA databases, because they do not count (1) the number of cases in which likely suspects have been excluded (saving both the potential suspect some distress and the police investigative resources); (2) investigative resources saved because of the shortened investigations resulting from cold hits; (3) societal costs from additional crimes committed by perpetrators who either would not otherwise have been caught or would have been caught later; and (4) the deterrent effect of a DNA database. Given these potential public benefits from DNA databases, it is unsurprising that DNA database laws authorizing the creation of DNA databases rapidly spread through all fifty, states during the 1990s. Perhaps because of the rapid spread, there are substantial state-to-state variation's in DNA database laws with respect to (1) resources devoted to the databases; (2) criteria for inclusion in the database; and (3) regulation of privacy-related issues.

The variation among states in resources devoted to DNA databases is reflected in an enormous state-to-state variation in database effectiveness. In fact, most of the investigations aided by the database through the end of 2003 were in four states:

Virginia, Florida, New York, and Illinois.[12] In contrast, Louisiana, with the widest statutory mandate for inclusion in the database in the country, as of the end of 2003 had not aided a single investigation (largely because of a lack of resources devoted to actually placing samples in the database).[13]

The categories of criminals are included (in principle) in the database also varies substantially from state to state. As the concluding chapter discusses, some states at one end of the spectrum include only very narrow categories of offenders (typically those convicted of felony sex crimes) in the database, whereas those with broader criteria allow for the inclusion of all individuals arrested for a felony. There has been a strong trend in recent years toward broader inclusion, such that most recent laws designate all felons for inclusion in the database.

These trends presents some interesting puzzles, particularly: (1) Why has database legislation spread so rapidly (as compared to postconviction relief)?; and (2) why, in contrast, has the allocation of resources to databases moved more slowly? These questions are addressed, in part, by the following story by Christopher Asplen, who was executive director of the National Commission on the Future of DNA Evidence at the time he told it:

> I was speaking to the National Conference of State Legislatures on this particular issue, and I was giving it to them very strongly. I was really sticking to them the issue that, hey folks, it's very clear. This saves lives.
>
> I gave them the whole tangible implication speech. I gave them the Debbie Smith story. I laid it out all for them, and I said what you've done is you have done what is often done in state legislation—you've created an unfunded mandate, and the effect of that is that we're going to lose lives, et cetera, et cetera.
>
> One of the legislators raises his hands, stands up at the end of the question-and-answer period and he says, wait a minute. He says, let me explain to you how this works. He says we're all pro–law enforcement. But let me tell you how we have to deal with the allocation of limited resources. Law enforcement comes to us and they say here's our list of the top things that we want funded, and we go and we give law enforcement their top three. As soon as your issue gets into the top three, your issue will get funded, but don't tell us we're doing something wrong here until law enforcement is telling us they really need it.[14]

The symbolic value of DNA databases is pretty clear: They are about monitoring dangerous criminals. The cost of legislation that simply authorizes—but does not fund—a DNA database is zero. It is when resources are to be allocated to databases that could go elsewhere that the system pushes back: The same resources could be used to cut taxes, improve schools, and so on. In fact, the key constituency for directing resources toward databases is law enforcement—and as Asplen's anecdote makes clear, the opportunity cost of resources spent on a database is borne largely by law enforcement. Requests for funds for creation, support, or expansion of a database will displace something else that law enforcement puts on its list of legislative funding priorities, and these are often items that have stronger advocates embedded within the law enforcement community. For many states, therefore, the key impetus for the expansion of their databases has been federal funding.

The success of DNA databases at identifying perpetrators of crimes has at this point created a self-reinforcing dynamic for the growth of these databases, which has been exponential in the last three years. Ironically, although the expansion of state DNA databases creates an incentive to invest further resources into the system, it also puts greater burdens on the long-run political-ethical calculus undergirding the system. As reiterated throughout this volume, DNA is revealing. It may reveal where you have been. It may reveal what you look like. It may reveal your propensity for getting a particular disease. It reveals who you are related to and may reveal your relatives' propensity for getting a particular disease. As the database expands, it may prompt some people to push back against the database, as well as to protect the data that have already been collected, particularly as the database begins to include individuals not convicted of any crime, like arrestees and suspects. The backlash is likely to be even greater if law enforcement includes in the databases samples collected from potential suspects of crimes who were subsequently excluded from having contributed the crime scene samples and samples collected in "DNA dragnets." It can be expected to be especially strong if the system begins to search for "near misses" to identify close relatives of those in the databases, the number of which could considerably exceed the number of individuals "officially" in the databases. The design imperative of DNA databases will necessarily shift from providing security, for which it has been optimized up to this point, to ensuring the trust of the public, which will increasingly find itself directly or indirectly included in the database. It is this balance of security and trust that Barry Steinhardt (chapter 9), Amitai Etzioni (chapter 10), Viktor Mayer-Schönberger (chapter 11), and D. H. Kaye and Michael Smith (chapter 12) address.

Trusting Science

Barry Scheck: One question. Would it make any difference if you started the research the other way and you said, all right, let's look at pedophiles which is a particularly troubling kind of crime? We even have the United States Supreme Court Opinion and a number of statutes that say that Courts can permanently incarcerate people who have been convicted of pedophilia if they find they have an inherent—and you can easily read into that term "genetic"—basis for the disorder. And please also bear in mind that what might be interesting information in the abstract to geneticists, please remember we as lawyers and judges in the system, we will take the smallest association and use it for release decisions, for guilt or innocence determinations because in many ways it looks like and arguably could be better than a lot of the data that comes into Court or might seem that way.

So would you have any inherent, Dr. Watson, ethical objections to just saying let's take all the convicted pedophiles and study those blood samples?

James Watson: If you could find something, I don't see necessarily the harm. As a scientist, you have to ask, well, are you wasting your time. But I think you're more or less saying we shouldn't get knowledge because the legal and judicial system is bad, and lawyers get off people. So I mean it seems to me that the failure of the legal system shouldn't be that we shouldn't find out the basis of behavior which is pretty scary.[15]

The final institution that developments in the use of DNA technology in criminal justice challenge is science. What are the boundaries that science should erect between itself and the criminal justice system? The goal of maximizing scientific knowledge may, at times, be inconsistent with the needs of the criminal justice system. And the ethical limits that science constructs in its search for knowledge (see chapters 7 and 8) may also be inconsistent with the needs of the criminal justice system. How, in turn, will science be shaped by its encounter with the justice system? The dynamite question is, will genetics offer insight into bases of criminal behavior? If so, how will the criminal justice system use that information? Should "genetically determined predispositions" enter into decisions about guilt and innocence (my genes made me do it)? Might genetic tests be the basis of preemptive incarceration? Might genetic tests offer a road map for preventing antisocial behavior?

Garland Allen documents, in chapter 13, repeated (and generally unsuccessful) efforts to understand the genetic bases of behavior. In chapter 4, Simon Cole discusses serious endeavors to connect physical attributes to criminal behavior (e.g., whether particular "swirl patterns" in fingerprints are correlated with criminal behavior). There is a much broader and deeper scientific consensus that our genetic makeup is related to our behavior (even if, as Allen argues, the relationship between the two is too complicated to untangle) than there has ever been with respect to the relationship between swirl patterns and criminality. There is thus a critical conjunction of scientific consensus (regarding the connection between behavior and genetics) and the criminal justice system (collecting genetic material from individuals who have been convicted of particular criminal behavior). This conjunction connects directly to the issue, mentioned earlier in the chapter, searching DNA databases for near misses: Broad swaths of our society may find themselves under "genetic surveillance" because they share genes with someone who has been convicted of a crime. The ideology of genetic determinism readily supports such scrutiny: Those who share genes with criminals are at higher risk for engaging in criminal behavior. In chapter 14, Troy Duster connects views about genetic determinism to racial imbalances in the U.S. criminal justice system: If crime is viewed as genetically determined, and certain racial groups are disproportionately detained in criminal investigations and convicted of crimes, then it might be a small and dangerous leap to explain this disparity as genetically determined.

Closely following this issue is that of trusting science in the criminal justice system. The laboratory capacities that the criminal justice system has developed are often dependent on, and controlled by, the law enforcement community, which typically has a stake in the results of the analyses conducted by those laboratories. Academic scientists have developed a sophisticated (if not always successful) set of safeguards to buffer researchers from the demands of those with stakes in the outcomes of their research. The criminal justice system has little in the way of such buffers; it instead leans heavily on the adversarial processes of the courtroom to bring to light any biases or flaws in the science. Such reliance is problematic, however, especially where resources on the defense side are not available to critically examine the science underlying the prosecution's case.

Conclusion

The thoughtful incorporation of technology into our society requires the act of imagining the obvious. It requires an active evaluation of our values as a society, of how our society can and should be reshaped by the technology, and of how the technology should be shaped by our society. These are acts of imagination, because they require conjecture upon conjecture as to how social institutions and technology co-adapt, the plausible alternatives for which are countless. They are acts of imagining the obvious, because after the future plays out, the path we have taken will seem obvious and inevitable. However, in fact, there is a set of alternative paths before us. The role of public discourse (as Stephen Breyer and Sheila Jasanoff discuss in chapters 2 and 15, respectively), and of a volume such as this, is to help define these alternative visions.

Notes

1. Peter Neufeld, statement, roundtable on "Privacy: Processes and Structures" ("DNA and the Criminal Justice System" conference, John F. Kennedy School of Government, Harvard University, Cambridge, Mass., November 21, 2000). The proceedings of the conference are available online at www.dnapolicy.net.

2. Bruce Bodowle, statement, roundtable on "Development of DNA Technology: What It Makes Possible, What It Will Make Possible" ("DNA and the Criminal Justice System" conference, John F. Kennedy School of Government, Cambridge, Mass., November 20, 2000).

3. Paul R. Billings, ed., *DNA on Trial: Genetic Identification and Criminal Justice* (Woodbury, N.Y.: Cold Spring Harbor Laboratory Press, 1992).

4. Richard C. Lewontin and Daniel L. Hartl, "Population Genetics in Forensic DNA Typing," *Science* 254 (1991). A 1996 National Research Council report's assessment that adequate methodologies existed to deal with population substructure reflects the current scientific consensus. See National Research Council, Committee on DNA Technology in Forensic Science: An Update, *The Evaluation of Forensic DNA Evidence* (Washington, D.C.: National Academies Press, 1996).

5. David Lazer, "The Diffusion of DNA Databases" (working paper, National Center for Digital Government, John F. Kennedy School of Government, Cambridge, Mass., 2004).

6. Bob Burtman, "Free at Last," *Houston Press*, August 3, 2000.

7. David Lazer, "The Diffusion of DNA Databases" (working paper, National Center for Digital Government, John F. Kennedy School of Government, Cambridge, Mass., 2004).

8. Debbie Smith, testimony before the Subcommittee on Government Efficiency, Financial Management and Intergovernmental Relations, *How Effectively Are State and Federal Agencies Working Together to Implement the Use of New DNA Technologies?* 107th Cong., 1st Sess., June 12, 2001.

9. Charlie Goodyear and Erin Hallissy, "State Boosts Felon's DNA Database; Crime-Fighting Cache Becomes Largest in U.S.," *San Francisco Chronicle*, June 25, 2001.

10. See www.fbi.gov/hq/lab/codis/aidedmap.htm.

11. See www.forensic.gov.uk/forensic/entry.htm.

12. See www.fbi.gov/hq/lab/codis/aidedmap.htm.

13. There has been a dramatic increase in resources devoted to Louisiana's DNA database since early 2002 as a result of a serial killer who left DNA at each of the scenes of his crimes; the database was initially of no use in tracking down the killer because of the lack of samples in it. This provided an impetus to the state legislature to allocate resources to the database.

14. Christopher Asplen, statement, roundtable on "Public Deliberation of Complex Issues: DNA in the Criminal Justice System as a Case Study" ("DNA and the Criminal Justice System" conference, John F. Kennedy School of Government, Harvard University, Cambridge, Mass., November 21, 2000).

15. James Watson, testimony before the National Commission on the Future of DNA Evidence ("DNA and the Criminal Justice System" conference, John, F. Kennedy School of Government, Harvard University, Cambridge, Mass., November 19, 2000).

2
Furthering the Conversation about Science and Society

Stephen Breyer

Vaclav Havel recently said that the best in contemporary America includes both "the fantastic development of science and technology, generating more welfare," and also the "profundity of civil liberty and the strength of its democratic institutions."[1] We will continue to warrant that praise only if we who work in law, in science, and in public policy increasingly understand one another and work together. I should like to focus here on a related question: How can legal institutions—which must give answers—interact with science, which so often poses difficult questions? What I want to emphasize is the importance of making difficult science-related choices only when there has been extensive, informed development of the relevant legal and policy issues *prior* to decision. To act coherently, we in the law must be able to have a sense of the likely social and economic impact of our choices *before* we act—so that our decisions are grounded in realistic predictions of what science will do, and not fanciful predictions of what science might do. If we make decisions about scientifically related matters before their time, we do so in a vacuum. Throughout this chapter, I shall use examples that illustrate both how scientific/legal interaction works in the Supreme Court and why extensive earlier interaction is often necessary before either the Court or a legislature can reach sound policy determinations.

Keep several background circumstances in mind. First, the current U.S. Supreme Court, on which I serve, consists of nine judges, seven men and two women, appointed for life. We are a court of last resort. We receive about eight thousand requests for hearing annually (out of several hundred thousand cases decided each year across the country). We hear and decide eighty to one hundred of those cases, each involving a difficult, typically open question of federal law: regulations, statutes, or provisions of the federal Constitution. Four of us were law teachers, eight of us were appellate court judges, and seven of us were previously in private practice. None of us has a background in the natural sciences.

Second, genetic research promises not a few, but many, changes in many different fields of the law. In the field of genetics, every month seems to bring a new discovery or new implementations of earlier discoveries. Changes in our understanding and ability to make use of the genetic code already promise to affect criminal law; family law; patent law; the laws protecting privacy; and our regulation of safety, the environment, health care, insurance, and employment. And we are only at the beginning.

Third, law itself is complex, not only because it comprises all these different fields, but also because it relies upon a variety of different mechanisms. The many forms of law relevant to genetics range from professional rules of ethics governing, say, research or hospital care, to local, state, or federal regulatory rules, to jury-administered civil standards, to judge-administered common law, to civil and criminal statutes, to federal and state Constitutions. Legislative enactments and judicial decisions are only two of the several ways in which law reflects changes in social policy in light of scientific developments.

Fourth, legal institutions react slowly. Change in the law ordinarily takes place after the event, in light of known circumstances, rather than in anticipation of what is to come. The principle of restraint is built into nearly every aspect of the American legal system. The Supreme Court's powers, for example, are limited by the fact that we can only act on live controversies brought before us. Congress, in turn, is limited by our review, by the president's veto, and by many other aspects of our political system. In borrowed scientific terms, American legal institutions require an enormous amount of "activation energy" before anything happens.

Given these background circumstances, one might well ask how our Court's judges, nine laymen and -women, considering any one of many possible different scientifically significant legal issues in various fields of law, can obtain a proper understanding of the relevant science and its significance. Of course, traditionally some have believed that we need not know science but only law to make decisions. This view is increasingly unrealistic. Since the implications of our legal decisions in the real world often can and should play a role in those decisions, the clearer our understanding of the relevant science, the better. But I repeat: We are not scientists; hence the dilemma.

The ordinary way we learn the details of relevant technical subject matter is through "briefs"—that is, the legal papers filed by the parties and other interested groups in cases that come before our Court. When four years ago we considered whether the Constitution provided a right of a terminally ill patient to physician-assisted suicide, we received about seventy briefs, including numerous *amicus curiae* (friend of the court) briefs, each twenty to thirty pages, submitted by groups who were not parties to the case. These groups included medical associations, psychiatrists, nurses, representatives of the physically and mentally disabled, hospice workers, religious associations, scientific organizations, law professors, and others. Sometimes a group would split, with different parts taking different sides of the case.

This is not the only way we can learn. In our first major Internet case, for example, our library prepared demonstrations that helped assure each of us that we knew how to use the Net and understood the technical matters at issue. And of course justices do not live in a vacuum; we read newspapers or magazines or books just like any citizen. But briefs are more directed to the precise questions we face. And in my view, briefing of the relevant medical features of the "right to die" case worked well. Seventy briefs, though requiring a week or so to read, is not too many, at least if we receive that number only on rare occasions. The *amicus* briefs were not repetitive. At their most useful, they told us *not* about the law, which the parties to the case discussed, but how our decision, along with the relevant medical practices, might affect the groups (for example, of doctors, nurses, or hospice workers) whose experience they reflected. They presented the kind of predictions of consequence that, in my view, we need.

But most important was the timing. The "right to die" issue did not come to us at the first sign of controversy. It came after many groups and individuals had reflected carefully upon the implications and impact of the legal issue. The relevant public-policy issues, including our decision's likely social impact, had already been debated at length, in various public forums, often by representatives of many of the same groups that had submitted briefs. In such cases our Court rides the coattails of an existing public debate. A select committee of the House of Lords in Britain had previously written a thorough report about the "right to die," after extensive hearings in which evidence, including empirical evidence, had been presented. A New York state commission had done the same. The matter had been debated in Australia and in Oregon as well as in the Netherlands. The result of the earlier discussion and debate was not agreement about the proper result; but it was agreement about the nature of the question and upon many of the relevant parameters.

This kind of agreement—the kind that focuses issues and excludes unreasonable possibilities—is critically important. When asked whether a certain scientific paper was wrong, the physicist Wolfgang Pauli replied, "Certainly not. That paper is not good enough to be wrong."[2] Those are the papers that this kind of preparation can, and must, exclude. The upshot will not always be the "correct" judicial decision; but it will normally be a reasonable decision; and I would defend our Court's "right to die" decision on that basis. Our Court was adequately informed and prepared for that decision, thanks mainly to an existing, and mature, public debate.

By way of contrast, three sets of issues, arising from developments in genetics, may not yet have been subject to the kind of public discussion and debate that help to ensure the soundness of a public-policy decision. The first set consists of those discussed in this volume: DNA and the criminal process. DNA evidence promises not only to make future criminal trials more reliable, but also to permit the reevaluation of past convictions, perhaps convictions that were secured many years ago. When should those convictions be reexamined? Are present reopening procedures adequate, in light both of the added certainty that DNA evidence can provide and of the numbers of closed cases in which potentially determinative DNA evidence might be obtained? Must the boundaries of preexisting legal rights be reshaped better to avoid the risk of imprisoning a defendant who is in fact innocent? Are new statutes needed?[3] Similarly, DNA identification may raise privacy concerns. Suppose a check of a convict DNA database reveals a near miss, thereby implicating a relative who has no record of conviction and was consequently not included in the bank.[4] What kind of legal rules should apply? To answer these questions intelligently, one must understand DNA, law, the nature of criminal investigations, the mix of prison populations, and potential costs. Obviously informed conversations among those who understand different parts of the problem—prior to judicial or legislative decision making—will help produce better public policy.

A second set of examples arises out of genetic discoveries that permit doctors to forecast an increased likelihood that certain individuals will develop cancer. For several years now a handful of genetic tests have been available that predict an individual's likelihood (and in a few cases certainty) of developing diseases such as cystic fibrosis, Tay-Sachs, Huntington's disease, familial Alzheimer's, and certain forms of familial cancers. But this list is about to grow exponentially. An international consortium of scientists is currently sequencing the twenty-four chromosomes of the human genome. Chromosome 14, which in January 2003 became the fourth chromosome to be fully mapped and is the longest piece of contiguous DNA to be sequenced to date, is the site of two clusters of genes that are vital for the functioning of the immune system as well as more than sixty disease genes, including those for a form of spastic paraplegia that strikes young children; for missing teeth, a condition called oligodontia; for several kinds of vision and hearing impairments; and for early-onset Alzheimer's. With every sequenced chromosome come numerous genetic links to diseases, and with these, in turn, comes the potential to test individuals in advance for predispositions to these diseases. The implications for public policy are widespread.

We are not truly used to the idea of knowing, in advance, who will and who will not develop a deadly disease like Alzheimer's or cancer. Where the risks are so great, accuracy is important; family information may be helpful; but relevant medical records are private. So there is a sense that some people should have a chance to get at private medical records. But on the other hand, when the results of genetic testing can mean so much, people want, more than ever, to keep that information private. To what extent will modification of privacy policies prove desirable? And in which direction should protection of genetic privacy go? And who will provide for, and pay for, the psychological and family counseling that would often seem necessary? The diagnostic revolution may transform the existing public-policy debate about environmental contributors to disease—contributors like diet or exposure to carcinogenic substances. Law has not made, and could not make, our environment free of carcinogens. Instead, we tolerate the presence of carcinogenic chemicals in numerous products that are useful to everyday modern life, such as gasoline, pesticides, and barbecued foods. We do so because the risks are relatively small and difficult to eliminate in their entirety, and we do not know in advance who will succumb to them. But what will happen if certain of those products create large risks for a few individuals whom we can identify in advance? How can we, how should we, selectively regulate their exposure?

Our greater ability to predict disease at the individual level poses especially difficult questions for legal regimes that rely upon our inability to do so. Our laws typically permit insurance rates to reflect comparative individual risks of death or disease. Often the man who has suffered three heart attacks already must pay more for insurance; and does a new employer does not always have to hire him. Will the law continue to permit this kind of selectivity when genetic testing permits more accurate and long-range predictions of disease risk? Should the law forbid some, or all, such discrimination? Does it make sense, as some states have already done, to create a new category of "genetic discrimination" and treat it like discrimination based upon race or gender?

For the law, these questions are difficult to answer, and not simply because they demand specialized interdisciplinary knowledge. In addition, their answers depend upon social consequences that are not yet certain. We are a little like late Victorians asked to predict the social consequences of the automobile. And the science itself, say, in respect to cancer and its causes, continuously changes, which changes, in turn, pose new policy questions or demand new answers. We are asked to hit a moving target.

Not surprisingly, policy change so far seems to have occurred primarily in those areas of law in which change itself is more easily revised or reversed—for example, rules governing funding, professional responsibility, or ethics, and administrative regulations or executive orders, all of which embody a degree of necessary flexibility. The question for the future is whether these "disease-related" problems will require the kind of statutory change, or judicial interpretation of important statutes or even the Constitution, that carries with it a degree of legal permanence.

Let me turn to a third, more purely legal area in which rapid developments in genetic research have led to calls for legal change, namely, patent law. If an inventor creates a product or process that is "useful," "novel," and "nonobvious" and does not simply consist of "laws of nature, natural phenomena or abstract ideas," then the patent law, in return for disclosure, grants the inventor a twenty-year monopoly over that product or process. This patent law approach is a one-size-fits-all approach. The question is, does it fit the world of genetic research?

The Supreme Court has held that that patent law does not distinguish between "living and inanimate things, but between products of nature, whether living or not, and human-made inventions."[5] In principle, "anything under the sun that is made by man" can be patented—if it meets the four (and a few other) requirements.[6] But that is just the beginning.

We have seen scientists obtain patents for isolating, through hard work and considerable financial investment, a previously unknown sequence of DNA useful, say, in agriculture or medicine. An example is the BRCA1 gene, which is linked to certain familial cancers, and its mutant forms. But what about granting patents on a mere gene fragment whose utility is only as a probe for finding the gene itself? What about patents for the isolation of cell membrane receptors?

The most difficult question is deciding when these or other products of genetic research reflect only discovery of an existing aspect of nature, like Einstein's discovery of the principles of relativity, and when they amount to a protectable invention or useful device. Should it matter if the more apt description of the scientist's work is the "discovery" of how a part of the body functions, rather than the "invention" of how to use that part of the body to perform a useful, say, diagnostic, task? This latter question will sometimes seem unanswerable. Cloning a previously unknown DNA sequence is a little like the "discovery" of a preexisting part of the human body; it is also something like the expensive, time-consuming, and novel isolation of a previously unknown molecule.

It might be more helpful to ask instead how well patent law's subclassifications and precedents here fit patent law's basic job. That job is developing financial incentives that, as they operate in the marketplace, will encourage useful discovery and disclosure without unduly restricting the dissemination of those discoveries, hindering the circulation of important scientific ideas, or scattering ownership to the point at which it inhibits use of the underlying genetic advance. And—if patent law's legal categories do not well match that law's basic objectives where genetic research is at issue—how should the law be changed?

This basic question leads to others. Do these problems reflect misapplication of the law's existing categories in lower courts? If so, could higher courts revise those decisions, say, with the help of guidance of the sort I have already described? Should Congress revise the patent statutes, altering categories or creating special forms of protection? How do we strike a proper balance between the resulting legal complexity and the simplicity promised by a "one size fits all" law of patents?

I raise these questions to point out that what might seem a more purely legal question nonetheless calls for the expertise not only of lawyers, but also of economists, scientists, the biotechnology industry, and those familiar with the operation of capital markets. The best answers will arise when the legal issue is focused by previous conversations between science, business, economics, and law. Neither courts nor legislatures may yet find wise answers in the absence of such earlier interaction.

Why have I contrasted the "right to die" case on the one hand with forensic DNA analysis, genetic links to disease, and patent law on the other? Because through that contrast I hope to distinguish what is often a more helpful, from a less helpful, way for scientists, courts, and legislatures to interact.

The less helpful, but traditional, model of interaction looks at the policymaking process as if it consisted of powerful decision makers limited to the choice of permitting or forbidding certain conduct. Interested parties, in this traditional lobbying model, submit information urging the decision maker to support or not to support, to ban or not to ban, a scientific development or activity based upon its potential for further benefit or harm. This model is clear. It sometimes works well: Remember Albert Einstein writing to Franklin Roosevelt about the need to develop atomic energy. But I do not believe that obtaining the ear of an elected official, even a president, is as critical as sometimes is believed.

The approach the traditional lobbying model suggests is not always helpful where genetic research is at issue. In the early 1970s some individuals, including some highly informed scientists, believed that developments in genetic engineering entailed serious social risks. Following the traditional lobbying model, they presented their views to Congress; and they asked for the imposition of moratoriums on, or prohibitions of, certain genetic research. They did not succeed in obtaining the legislation they advocated. And one can easily imagine the harmful consequences to which bans of the proposed type might have led. Genetic research so far has not led to the creation of the "mosquito-man," nor does cloning seem likely to produce multiple carbon copies of General Francisco Franco, as once was feared. Rather, that research has led to enormously beneficial discoveries related to our health and well-being. That is not surprising. History suggests that government efforts to direct or control free thought and research impose major social costs. With hindsight, one might say that the effort to obtain legislation significantly limiting or banning research was misplaced, in respect to both its timing and its approach.

My contrast suggests the virtues of a different model. In this model scientists, other experts, lawyers, legislators, perhaps judges, too, engage in an ongoing extended policy-oriented conversation—outside legislative or judicial forums. It is a conversation that takes place in writing or at conferences, in articles or at lectures, likely prior to, though perhaps contemporaneously with, direct consideration by courts or by legislatures of major statutory changes. It helps to inform the public debate that inevitably surrounds legislative change, in part by diminishing the likelihood that the public will react to "outlier" examples, say, mosquito-men or carbon copies of General Franco.

As an example, consider the seminar on the regulation of electricity, the Harvard Electric Policy Group, sponsored by Harvard's Kennedy School of Government and attended not only by professors of economics and government, but also by regulators, industry executives, representatives of consumer and environmental groups, lawyers, and even an occasional judge. Since 1993 the seminar has provided (and continues to provide) a forum, not for negotiating, but for the discovery of common approaches to the facts, identification of the relevant unknowns, and the creation of areas of agreement and disagreement. This kind of development, I believe, has helped major change in public policy respecting electricity generation to proceed on a reasonably informed basis.

The conversational metaphor is not new. I want only to reaffirm its value as an aid to bringing about sensible legal reactions to scientific and technical change. It foresees a mature interaction between reasonable parties and an institutional relationship in which law neither ignores science nor reacts like a scold. It potentially includes within its interactive scope not just scientists or just scientists and policy-makers, but all significantly affected groups. It suggests that judges or legislatures may wait to see what consequences, good or bad, actually result. It looks to readily revisable kinds of legal change when the need for immediate legal action is pressing. It recognizes the difficulty of predicting what effects major scientific advances may have. And it aptly describes how law best develops in a democratic society—not imposed from on high, but bubbling up out of interactions among informed, interested groups and eventually with the public at large.

The courts cannot lead such conversations, though sometimes judges may participate in them. Rather, courts are more likely ultimately to determine the statutory or constitutional "reasonableness" of solutions proposed by others. And the courts work best when they are well informed. Judges are at ease when they can rely upon what has come before.

Michael Oakeshott, in describing liberal education, better explained what I have in mind. "The pursuit of learning," he said, "is not a race in which the competitors jockey for the best place, it is not even an argument or a symposium; it is a conversation. . . . [E]ach study appear[s] as a voice whose tone is neither tyrannous nor plangent, but humble and conversable. . . . Its integration is not superimposed but springs from the quality of the voices which speak, and its value lies in the relics it leaves behind in the mind of those who participate."[7]

My basic point is that a dialogue with the courts, judges, and lawyers depends for its success upon earlier, or ongoing, conversations with many other groups as well. This volume is an example of such a conversation. The task—that of creating a generalist voice that will speak for an age of specialization—is difficult to accomplish, but it is important to try. I am pleased to have had an opportunity to participate in that effort.

Notes

1. Vaclav Havel, remarks upon receipt of the 1997 Fulbright Prize for International Understanding.

2. P. W. Huber, in *Galileo's Revenge* (New York: Harper Collins, 1991), 54.

3. For a discussion of these and other issues related to postconviction DNA testing, see chapter 6 of this volume.

4. See chapter 16 of this volume and "Lower-Stringency Searching and The Matter of Siblings" in chapter 3 of this volume.

5. *Diamond v. Chakrabarty*, 447 U.S. 303, 313 (1980).

6. Ibid., at 309.

7. Michael Oakeshott, *The Voice of Liberal Learning* (New Haven, Conn.: Yale University Press, 1989), 109–110.

3

Science and Technology of Forensic DNA Profiling: Current Use and Future Directions

Frederick R. Bieber

DNA-Based Human Identity Testing and Its Forensic Applications

Introduction

Although DNA-based genetic analysis has long-standing and important roles in research, medical diagnostics, and patient care, the central role of DNA typing in forensic investigations has been emphasized in the aftermath of the September 11, 2001, attacks on the United States. DNA-based genetic profiling has been a key tool for direct and indirect identification of hundreds of victims from these attacks. In addition, typing of relatives of suspected terrorist operatives has been suggested as a method to assist in the indirect identification of recovered remains of such suspects. Study of microbial DNA allows the tracing of strain-specific origins of infectious agents, including weaponized pathogens. These events bring home the wider application of modern DNA technology to assist not only in criminal investigations and humanitarian aims, but also in matters pertaining to military intelligence and national security.

Because of its utility, forensic genetic profiling, based on inherited DNA variation, has now gained universal acceptance as a forensic tool that is crucial to the proper and complete investigation of many civil and criminal matters. Civil conflicts such as patient sample or nursery mix-ups and paternity testing, as well as probate and immigration disputes, have been resolved using DNA from known reference sources. Crime scene DNA evidence compared to known samples from victims or suspects has proven fundamental in the resolution of felony crimes and has also, in many cases, served as a powerful exculpatory or exclusionary tool. Indeed, as of this writing, in the United States 140 individuals have had their criminal convictions vacated based on the results of DNA testing. These DNA exclusions occurred years or even decades after the original convictions, which were based primarily on circumstantial evidence or faulty eyewitness identifications. Furthermore, identities of missing persons and unknown soldiers have been determined through the study of DNA from close relatives, providing an indirect method of assigning identity to recovered remains that would otherwise be unidentifiable. Lastly, genetic data banks of biological samples and databases of computerized DNA profiles are now in widespread use for a variety of forensic applications, including identification of possible suspects and missing persons.

This chapter provides background technical information on current DNA-based laboratory methods used in human identity testing and an overview of computerized searching of forensic DNA databases. Application of current and future DNA-based genetic technologies offers exciting opportunities as well as some potentially troubling dilemmas and challenges. Practitioners and society must consider how DNA technology and genetic data sharing should be utilized while remaining mindful of the need to balance the interests of public safety against those of individual privacy.

History of Forensic Identity Testing

Human forensic identity testing can trace its modern origins to the late nineteenth century, when several individuals in Argentina and Europe recognized the utility of fingerprint ridge pattern analysis for forensic use (see Chapter 4). The British geneticist Sir Francis Galton, a cousin of Charles Darwin, was an early Mendelist who recognized that digital fingerprint analysis could be used for identification.[1] Galton's own studies of the various fingerprint ridge patterns on the volar surfaces of the distal phalanges revealed that even monozygotic twins, who are derived from the same fertilized egg and therefore genetically identical, have distinctive patterns. Hence, the use of fingertip ridge analysis, inaugurated by the French and British police, gained widespread adoption in Europe and Latin America in the late nineteenth century, and such analysis rapidly spread to other police and investigative agencies around the world.[2]

During the first decades of the twentieth century, laboratory methods were developed to identify heritable variation in human blood types determined by genetic variation in red blood cell surface antigens. The central importance to medicine of these discoveries became clear with their use for serotyping those needing blood transfusions as a result of illness or injury or during surgery, especially in times of war or other armed conflicts. Related serological typing techniques were subsequently used for other applications such as typing and cross-matching suitable donors of bone marrow and whole organs for transplantation. The human blood groups, as well as inherited variants in blood cell enzymes or serum proteins, were quickly recognized as useful for research in population genetics and evolution. The implications of this research for forensic purposes (e.g., paternity testing, nursery mix-ups) were widely appreciated. Applications of these techniques to other tissues and body fluids from both evidentiary samples obtained at crime scenes and known samples from suspects or victims have been introduced into courtrooms throughout the world.[3] While extremely useful even today for elimination or exclusion purposes, these older methods of blood typing are rather nonspecific for purposes of individualized identification because there are relatively few types within a particular blood group system (e.g., in the ABO system, there are only four major serologically defined types, and only two in the Rh system).[4]

Not until the mid-1970s were methods for detecting genetic variation at the DNA level introduced to medicine, research, and forensics. These laboratory methods include techniques for DNA isolation and amplification, fragment separation, and direct sequencing. Genetic testing is now a routine part of prenatal diagnostics, of newborn screening, and of diagnostic protocols for patients with cancer and many common chronic adult-onset diseases.[5] The study of population group differences in certain regions of the genome has increased our understanding of plant and animal origins and relatedness.[6] Applications of modern molecular biology, dependent on DNA technology, have increased understanding of embryonic development, control of the cell cycle, and cell-to-cell communication.

Genetic Variation at the DNA Level and Its Utility as a Biological Identifier

DNA is the genetic material that determines, in part, individual characteristics that are faithfully transmitted from parent to offspring. DNA is divided and packaged into chromosomes that reside in the nucleus of individual cells. During each cell division these chromosomes replicate and divide, ensuring that the two daughter cells receive DNA content identical to that of the parent cell. During gametogenesis (formation of sperm and egg) half of the parent chromosomes (and DNA) are transmitted to each offspring, as revealed in the nineteenth-century discoveries of Gregor Mendel. In addition to genetic material inherited from both parents, some forms of DNA are inherited only from fathers or from mothers. For example, DNA on the human Y chromosome is transmitted directly from fathers only to their sons. In a different way, DNA within organelles known as mitochondria is transmitted only in the cytoplasm of the mother's egg cell to all of her sons and daughters. The manner in which DNA is inherited is useful for establishing parentage (mother-father-child combinations) and for tracing maternal and paternal lineages. Similarly, in microbes, genetic studies of DNA sequences allow comparison of strain differences in infectious pathogens.

A wide variety of animal and microbial genomes are now completely known, and modern robotic technology will allow sequencing of many additional organisms in the coming decade. The genome of any organism includes both coding and noncoding domains. Coding regions contain specific DNA sequences that can be translated into RNA or protein sequences, whereas noncoding regions do not.[7] Current estimates suggest that the three billion base pairs of DNA in each human cell encode approximately thirty thousand genes that produce an even greater number of functional gene products through a regulated process called alternative splicing. These gene products, in turn, govern most other chemical and physiological processes. Mutations and other genetic variants occur commonly in the functional genes. Whereas many of these genetic alterations in coding regions have no known effect, others form the basis for certain heritable diseases, or conversely, advantageous traits, depending on the specific nature of the DNA alteration, the organism's other repertoire of genes, and the environmental condition of the organism.

In addition to DNA sequences that encode functional gene products, a large proportion of many animal and plant genomes contain noncoding regions that do not appear to encode functional genes and may have other functions. Geneticists have documented that 98 percent of the human genome shows little, if any, sequence variation within the population. That is, only 2 percent of the genome has sufficient variation in DNA sequence to be useful for forensic distinctions. Ample variation exists in the noncoding regions of nuclear genes to allow DNA profiling for forensic analysis.[8] This inherited genetic variation (polymorphism) allows comparison of the similarities and differences among members of the same (or different) species. Variation in specific regions of the genome (genetic loci) is analyzed to identify the variant DNA lengths or sequences (known as alleles) present in a particular DNA sample. In humans, variant regions of forensic interest exist in the noncoding DNA comprising the autosomes (twenty-two pairs in humans), the so-called sex chromosomes (a single XX pair in females, a single XY pair in males) and in the DNA of the cellular pool of mitochondrial chromosomes (mtDNA). As in the case of coding DNA variation, DNA sequence differences in the noncoding regions may have no functional importance that confers selective advantage or disadvantage to the individual organism.

Contemporary Forensic Profiling for Individual Identification

The first major publicly recognized forensic use of DNA-based genetic profiling involved the study of DNA size variations (RFLPs, or Restriction Fragment Length Polymorphism) in crime scene evidence in England in the mid-1980s.[9] Alec Jeffries, a professor at the University of Leicester, utilized multilocus DNA probes (i.e., probes to several distinct regions of the genome) to study evidence from two separate crime scenes (rape kit swabs from two teenage rape/homicide victims). He compared the DNA hybridization patterns from the evidence samples to those of a confessor to one of these two crimes. Jeffries' laboratory findings excluded the (false) confessor as a source of the DNA found at both crime scenes.[10] In addition to excluding the false confessor, Jeffries documented the apparent genetic similarity of the hybridization patterns in the evidence from the two victims, indicating a single source (i.e., a possible serial killer). The search for the true perpetrator of these two sexual homicides involved comparison of DNA profiles from the samples taken from the two crime scenes to those collected from known individuals (adult males living in the region, who were encouraged to come forward for voluntary blood donation).[11] This process eventually identified the single perpetrator of both murders. This dramatic use of modern DNA-based methods for forensic testing led to replacement of the older serological blood typing methods in virtually all laboratories in developed countries by the late 1990s. It also drew attention to the exculpatory power of DNA typing and to the possibility of typing large numbers of individuals for elimination as suspects, and raised the idea of computerized storage of the DNA profiles of large numbers of individuals for use in investigations of unsolved crimes.

In the United States, perhaps the first forensic use of polymerase chain reaction (PCR)–based DNA typing was to assist a Pennsylvania court in a 1986 case in determination of whether two autopsy samples were derived from the same person.[12] The first appellate decision after a DNA-based conviction was handed down in 1990 in the matter of *Kansas v. Searles*,[13] involving a conviction on charges of sexual assault. Admission of DNA evidence had not been opposed prior to trial, and the issue of admissibility was not raised on appeal. The first death penalty cases based on PCR-based DNA evidence were *Texas v. Fuller*[14] and that of Timothy Spencer, who had brutally raped and murdered many women in Virginia.[15]

In current practice, even minimal trace evidentiary biological samples, including single hairs, decomposed tissue, and charred remains, can be used for highly discriminating DNA profiling.[16] There are obviously many uses for such forensic profiling. In addition to the well-known use of forensic-profiling techniques in murder and sexual assault investigations, in which DNA is extracted from crime scene evidence, profiles are developed, and the DNA profiles are then compared to those obtained from known individuals (i.e., victims or suspects), all of the methods and procedures described in this chapter can be utilized in humanitarian identification of bodies from natural disasters or accidents (e.g., identification of plane crash and other victims from the September, 11, 2001, attacks on the United States), identification of war crime victims (e.g., in Kosovo and Bosnia), reunification of family members separated by war, natural disaster, or political oppression (e.g., in Argentina), and identification of recovered remains from "unknown soldiers." Other applications include animal forensics (e.g., in poaching and bird-smuggling cases and endangered-species identification) and the study of human origins via population genetics.[17]

In addition to highlighting its value as a tool for biological identification that can include and thereby implicate an individual suspect, it is important to underscore the role of DNA-based genetic identity testing as an exculpatory tool (see chapter 6). Similarly, DNA-based forensic testing of biological evidence frequently excludes males named as fathers in civil paternity matters, as well as a sizable proportion of suspects, defendants in criminal investigations, and convicted persons. As noted previously, already in the United States, as of the writing of this chapter, 140 individuals have been released, postconviction, based on results of DNA typing that was performed many months or years after conviction. A fair number of these individuals whose convictions were overturned, vacated, or remanded for retrial based on such postconviction DNA profiling were death row inmates.[18]

Although some seem assured that the majority of cases worthy of reexamination based on DNA evidence have been processed, in fact, the next wave of postconviction reviews has already commenced, as contemporary DNA-based studies reveal that a fair proportion of purported microscopic human-hair matches do not concur with results of nuclear and mtDNA comparisons.[19]

Current Methods for Forensic DNA Analysis

Many of the methods used in forensic analysis are similar, and in some cases identical, to those used for research and for clinical diagnostic protocols.[20] What is notable about their use in forensic identity testing is the application of the high discriminatory power of the profiling systems for genetic exclusions or individualization.[21] Scientists interested in genetic variation at the DNA level in animal and plant populations employ a number of methods for study of biological samples. First, chemical and physical extraction methods are capable of removing intact DNA molecules from various tissues, even those compromised by environmental or storage conditions.[22] The chemical methods use detergents to remove other cellular or chemical components of the tissue or fluid sample, whereas the physical methods utilize special synthetic membranes to physically bind to the membrane DNA molecules from individual samples. Second, the PCR allows amplification of trace amounts of extracted DNA into a quantity sufficient for analysis.[23] Third, automated methods for direct determination of the base-pair sequence of DNA are now available, and a variety of laboratory methods allow detection and comparison of length differences in certain defined regions of the genome that are known to exhibit stable inherited variation.[24] Finally, in cases involving human DNA specifically, computerized digital storage of the resulting DNA profile (i.e., the specific length or sequence of DNA identified at one or more loci) allows rapid comparison of sample profiles from evidence or from individuals whose profiles have been stored in a central database.[25]

The Polymerase Chain Reaction

Once intact DNA has been extracted from a known or evidentiary source, most current laboratory methods for forensic DNA analysis take advantage of the PCR. PCR is used for amplification (or copying) of specific regions of the genome and can be initiated from even trace amounts of DNA. The PCR process mimics the normal cellular processes used in the replication of DNA molecules in living cells and organisms. After twenty-five to thirty-five cycles of PCR-based DNA amplification, millions of copies of the original source DNA molecules have been created, yielding sufficient PCR product to allow detection of variation in DNA sequence or length from the original biological sample. The PCR process does not amplify all of the DNA in a sample, just the short sequences specifically targeted using well-designed primers (which are like bookends to the region of interest).

Current validated PCR-based methods detect genetic variation as either sequence polymorphisms or length polymorphisms.[26] PCR analysis can be performed simultaneously on several distinct genetic loci (multiplexing), which is more efficient than performing separate PCR amplifications of each locus. PCR methodology amplifies even minimal amounts of DNA efficiently. As little as 0.25 nanograms of DNA can be typed using this method (e.g., forty to fifty cells from a single hair root or a single drop of blood). The sensitivity of the process requires great care to reduce the chance of introducing extraneous DNA from other sources into the process. A separate area of the laboratory is therefore typically reserved for the preamplification and post-amplification steps of the PCR process to prevent introduction of contaminant DNA.[27]

Indirect Detection of PCR-Amplified DNA Sequence Variation: The Reverse Dot-Blot Method

An important laboratory procedure developed in the late 1980s and used widely since the early 1990s detects DNA sequence polymorphisms using an indirect method referred to as the "reverse dot-blot" system. In this system, DNA molecules are labeled with chemical tags during PCR amplification.[28] These tagged PCR products are then hybridized to a membrane containing fixed probes that recognize specific DNA sequences (alleles) present in a biological sample. This method was developed for the human leukocyte antigen (HLA) DQ locus first by scientists at the Cetus Corporation and then by Roche Molecular Systems.[29] With a commercially available kit (PolyMarker, from Applied Biosystems), it is possible to amplify alleles at five additional distinct genetic loci simultaneously in a single multiplex reaction.[30] The DQ and PM (Polymarker) kits contain all the necessary reagents, including primers for PCR, and the typing strips. Although this commercial reverse dot-blot system, widely used in the recent past, continues to serve as a useful technique, especially for exclusion screening, it lacks the discriminating power of current methods. Also, because there are few alleles at these particular DQ and PM loci in the population, these loci are less useful for the study of DNA mixtures.

Direct Methods for Detection of DNA Sequence Variation: Detection of Single-Nucleotide Polymorphisms

Other methods are now in use for more rapid and direct detection of genetic variation at the level of the individual DNA base pair. Such genetic variation is commonly referred to as single-nucleotide polymorphism (SNP, pronounced "snip"). Laboratory methods have been developed that permit simultaneous detection of the specific nucleotide bases present at hundreds of distinct sites in the genome using microarrays or microchips.[31] These methods for SNP detection will undoubtedly join other methods in many forensic laboratories.

In addition to its use to study mtDNA and for SNP detection in human samples, DNA sequencing technology has compelling forensic use in other organisms as well. For example, the complete DNA sequences of over forty microbial genomes are already known. Direct sequencing of microbial genomes has allowed the evolutionary relationships of related strains to be studied by comparison of the base-pair sequences of organisms, including infectious pathogens, that may be weaponized and used in terrorist or other criminal acts.[32] Databases of these DNA sequences will be vital components of criminal investigations of illicit use of microbial pathogens and of national and international biodefense strategies.[33]

Detection of Length Variation in PCR-Amplified DNA Products

Throughout the 1990s, PCR-based systems were continuously developed and improved to detect inherited differences in the length of certain DNA repeats in the genomes of plants and animals.[34] These methods identify size or length differences in specific DNA sequences that are repeated side by side (i.e., in tandem) in various noncoding regions of the genome.[35] At a given locus, the specific number of these repeat units varies in the population, making these markers useful for forensic purposes.[36] Some of these loci are termed *variable number of tandem repeats* (VNTRs), and much smaller repeat units (two to seven Watson-Crick base-pair repeats) are termed *short tandem repeats* (STRs).[37] VNTRs and STRs are stable and inherited as Mendelian traits. PCR primers can be designed to amplify STRs in such a way that the amplified PCR products can be separated and their size determined. At loci on the nonsex chromosomes, any individual can have one or two STR alleles, depending on whether he or she inherited the same- or different-sized repeat units from each parent. Each allele designation refers to the specific number of STRs amplified by a given primer set. For example, at any given locus, an individual could have inherited eleven repeats from each parent and would therefore be referred to as an 11,11 homozygote. However, his sister might have inherited 11 repeats from one parent and 14 from the other and be referred to as an 11,14 heterozygote at that locus. At any genetic locus there can be ten or more alleles in a population, yet a single individual can have only one or two alleles, as stated in Mendel's first and second laws.[38] STR typing results can be recorded in a digitized format, allowing direct comparison with stored database information.

Detection of STR Variants on the Human Y Chromosome

Recent work has revealed genetic variation at STR loci on the human Y chromosome, transmitted from fathers to sons.[39] These Y-chromosome-specific markers reside in the nonrecombining region of the Y chromosome and are therefore transmitted intact, barring mutation, from father to son. Collaborative efforts have allowed construction of Y-chromosome STR (Y-STR) population databases that are useful in forensics.[40] The Y chromosome in males is transmitted only to sons, and Y-chromosome STRs can be detected using the PCR-based methods previously described. After many such Y-linked STR loci are typed, a so-called haplotype can be identified that would be similar in all male descendents of a particular man.[41] Because males have only one Y chromosome they have a single allele at each Y chromosome locus.[42] Thus, the Y-specific DNA is transmitted basically intact from fathers to sons, generation after generation.

Depending on the circumstances of a forensic investigation, Y-chromosome STR analysis can be a useful adjunct to the standard panel of autosomal loci normally used in forensic analysis.[43] For example, in mass-disaster investigations, Y-STR analysis can determine whether an unidentified body (i.e., the source of a particular DNA sample) should be excluded or included as a possible relative (e.g., son, father, brother) of a surviving or deceased male whose DNA reference source is available.

Study of Mitochondrial DNA Inherited by Sons and Daughters from Mothers

In addition to DNA in the cell nucleus, there is another source of cellular DNA relevant to medicine, research and forensics, namely, mitochondrial DNA (mtDNA). Many copies of mitochondria (intracytoplasmic organelles essential for cellular energy production) are present in each cell. They replicate and segregate during each cell division, ensuring that the resulting daughter cells each contain multiple mitochondria. Because each individual mitochondrion contains many copies of a circular mitochondrial chromosome, there are many copies of the mitochondrial genome in each cell.

Mitochondrial genetic material (mtDNA) is transmitted almost exclusively by mothers to their offspring in the mitochondrial chromosomes contained within the cytoplasm of the egg cell. Diseases are known that result from deletion or mutation of the mtDNA. DNA sequence variation in the mitochondrial chromosome is extremely useful in population migration and evolutionary studies and for forensic profiling. This variation is detected by direct sequencing of the DNA base pairs in variable regions (the "control regions") of the mitochondrial chromosome.[44] There is a phenomenon known as heteroplasmy in which distinct populations of mtDNA can exist together in the same cell or in different tissues from a single individual. This observation may have implications for interpretation of mtDNA sequencing results.[45]

In special circumstances, mtDNA profiling is especially useful for kinship analysis or for victim identification when a known comparison sample for a decedent is unavailable for study but a sample from a sibling or mother is available.[46] Because mtDNA is maternally inherited, matrilineal relatives will typically have the same mtDNA profiles.[47] Thus, although mtDNA sequencing enables certain types of family reconstruction to be accomplished, the results of mtDNA sequencing, by itself, cannot distinguish among children born to the same mother.[48]

Which Methods to Use?

Decisions about which of the various DNA profiling methods to use in a given instance depend in part on the nature and purpose of the particular investigation, whether DNA mixtures are suspected,[49] and the level of degradation expected in the samples. For example, typing of additional loci would be needed to distinguish the DNA profiles of close relatives, as they are more likely to share common profiles than are unrelated individuals. DNA mixtures might demand Y-chromosome haplotype analysis using Y-chromosome STR variation.[50] Complex family or kinship reconstruction might require mtDNA analysis. These are just a few of the considerations applied to such analytical decisions.

The older PCR-based reverse dot-blot tests (i.e., the DQ and PM kits) are the least technically demanding to perform both in terms of experience and equipment requirements. A reasonably high throughput is possible (fifty samples can be amplified and hybridized in a day by a single technologist), and the equipment requirements are minimal. These factors, together with the test's relatively high power of discrimination,[51] previously made the commercial reverse dot-blot test kits particularly suitable for screening large numbers of samples, especially for exclusion purposes. PCR-based products also perform well on samples in which the DNA is degraded (and in which, therefore, only short pieces of DNA may remain), a very common occurrence in forensic samples. However, as mentioned earlier, these particular loci are not ideal for analysis of complex DNA mixtures, and the current STR-based systems are both more amenable to automation and much more useful in analysis of complex forensic mixtures. Also, STR-based systems have increased power of discrimination over previously used dot-blot systems and greater multiplexing capability.

As the demand for greater volume of testing increases, newer technology, along with use of robotics, has been incorporated into many forensic laboratories. STR systems have replaced the dot-blot systems in all laboratories in the United States, Canada, and Europe. The PCR process, because of its ability to amplify trace amounts of DNA, increases the sensitivity of detection of all alleles present in a sample but does not necessarily lead to conclusive identity determination, especially when the biological evidence contains complex DNA mixtures. Typing a larger number of loci increases the test's power of discrimination, thereby increasing the possibility of excluding a falsely accused donor of a forensic sample, while also making estimates of combined match probabilities more probative when there is a match at all typed loci.

Y-STR haplotyping and mtDNA sequencing (see earlier discussion), along with routine nuclear-DNA profiling, can be used alone or in combination. Thus, for some compromised biological-crime scene or disaster scene evidence, mtDNA analysis is possible, whereas traditional nuclear-DNA analysis is not. This is especially relevant when nuclear DNA is compromised as a result of postmortem decay or of other detrimental environmental effects on nuclear DNA, or when recovered remains or evidence includes only bone and hair, which often contain ample mtDNA but insufficient nuclear DNA for testing. In particular, Y-chromosome profiling is useful in cases involving sexual assault in which a DNA mixture of a female victim and one or more male contributors is found, as it targets only the male cells (containing the Y chromosome).

Sequence-based mtDNA typing or automated SNP analysis of autosomal and Y-chromosome loci play an increasingly important part in certain types of investigations. DNA mixtures are often identified in forensic evidence, and the interpretation of such mixtures may be complicated.[52] Evidentiary samples may also contain certain nonhuman DNA (e.g., bacterial or plant DNA), and these samples must be analyzed using other methods than those described herein if the nonhuman DNA is probative.[53] Decisions about which of the various laboratory methods to use depend largely upon the nature, source, condition, an number of the samples to be analyzed. Other methods (not described herein) are used in the case of suspected bioterrorism to identify strain differences in microorganisms and to individualize nonhuman biological samples[54] and for drug interdiction programs.[55]

Statistical Interpretation of DNA Profiling Results and Phenotype Prediction

Statistical Interpretation of Results   The simple objective of PCR-based forensic DNA profiling is to compare the alleles representing the genetic types present in the

DNA extracted from evidence to those found in blood or tissue from known samples. After careful laboratory analysis of single-source samples, usually one of the three following interpretations applies:

▪ *Inclusion*: Known or reference standard sample alleles are present in the evidentiary or questioned sample.

▪ *Exclusion*: Known or reference standard sample alleles are not present in the evidentiary or questioned sample.

▪ *Inconclusive*: No conclusion can be reached as to the source of the DNA extracted from the questioned sample.

When an interpretation of DNA inclusion is made,[56] the "finders of fact" (i.e., members of the jury) must be provided with an estimate of how common or how rare the particular DNA profile identified from the sample is.[57] Most statistical calculations of such estimates use the so-called product rule, which involves multiplication of the estimates of the expected frequency of the identified DNA profile at each locus to produce a final estimate known as the *point estimate of the combined match probability*. These frequency estimates vary according to differences in frequencies of alleles in different populations and can even differ within populations as a result of population substructure.[58] Composition and size of the reference population databases are important considerations in computing DNA profile frequency estimates.[59]

Thus a particular multilocus DNA profile found in biological evidence would be expected to be found less frequently in a randomly selected individual if there are rare alleles in the DNA profile than if there are common alleles; thus in cases in which a multilocus DNA profile is found in both biological evidence from a particular crime and a suspect in the investigation of that crime, the match is less likely (i.e., more significant and better evidence of a link) the rarer are the alleles involved. Similarly any given thirteen-locus DNA profile would be observed far less frequently (if ever) in an person unrelated to the source of the sample than a five- or six-locus profile from the same source. Simply put: The less common the allele(s) identified in a profile, and the larger the number of loci typed, the smaller the chance statistically of observing that particular DNA profile in a randomly selected individual unrelated to the source of the DNA from which the profile was drawn.

For example, if the DNA profile in a sample is the same as that in a particular individual at only two loci, and if the allele combination observed at each locus occurs with a frequency of one in ten individuals in the population, then the calculated combined random-match probability (i.e., the expected chance of observing the same DNA profile in the sample and in a randomly selected person unrelated to the sample source) for the two independent loci would be one in one hundred. In contrast, if the calculation were based on thirteen loci, and the allele combination observed at each locus occurred with a frequency of one in ten individuals, the calculated random-match probability would be one in ten trillion. Actual estimates generated can range anywhere from one chance in ten for a single-locus profile to one chance in seven hundred quintillion or less for a sixteen-locus profile with uncommon alleles. Because of the multiplication step using the product rule, each additional independent locus for which profile results are available dramatically changes the frequency estimates from the thousands to the billions, the quadrillions, or even the quintillions.

Statistical calculations differ for mtDNA and for Y-STR data because their genetic transmission differs from that of the autosomal alleles. They also differ for complex mixtures, paternity testing, and kinship analysis of missing persons identification by family reconstruction.[60] For example, a set of Y-chromosome STR data is considered as a single haplotype, and its frequency is assessed based on studies of relevant populations. Mutation rates for Y-STRs are comparable to those of autosomal STRs.[61] In forensic cases involving DNA mixtures, statistical interpretation requires methods that involve computation of likelihood ratios or exclusion probabilities.[62]

It is imperative to note that calculation of the probability of a random DNA match between crime scene evidence and a given suspect does not constitute a calculation of the probability of the suspect's guilt or innocence.[63] Such statistical calculations simply provide an estimate of the expected frequency of observing a particular profile in a randomly selected individual unrelated to the source of the DNA from which the profile was developed. Like that of any other facts or opinions presented under oath, the probative value of statistical interpretations of DNA evidence varies depending on other circumstances of the instant case.[64]

DNA Analysis for Prediction of Traits of Unknown Suspects, Victims or Missing Persons: Gender, Specific Traits, Age, Race, and Ethnicity

Medical examiners, forensic scientists, and criminal investigators frequently deal with human remains, body tissues, or bodily fluids from unidentified victims or suspects and wish to use biomarkers to predict some useful physical characteristics of the source of the tissue, in attempts to identify him or her. For example, recovered remains or body fluids from mass disasters or crime scenes may need to be identified using DNA analysis. A number of methods, described in this section, either already exist or are in development that could be used for prediction of physically distinguishing characteristics.

Amelogenin typing predicts the gender profile of the contributor of a single-source DNA sample, as PCR analysis of samples derived from females (XX) and males (XY) yields different profiles.[65] Several research groups have used genetic variation at the melanocortin receptor (MCR1) locus to predict hair color.[66] A related melanocortin receptor (MCR4) predicts obesity.[67] Several age-related changes in human DNA could, in theory, be useful forensic biomarkers in predicting the approximate age of the individual from whom DNA a particular sample was isolated.[68] For example, loss of repeated telomeric DNA sequences (TTAGGG) from human chromosomes as well as the accumulation of certain mtDNA mutations has been associated with increasing age. In addition, the methylation status of CpG islands (gene-associated stretches of DNA that are normally unmethylated) also changes with age.[69] Practical methods for forensic detection of age-related loss of telomeric DNA sequence length are not currently available or in use.

Several research groups and commercial ventures have attempted to identify genetic markers that can be used to predict the racial or ethnic ancestry of the source of a DNA sample.[70] One of these companies (DNA Print Genomics) currently uses SNP markers and a mathematical-likelihood analysis and claims to be able to identify DNA samples belonging to one of four major groups; sub-Saharan African, Indo-European, Native American Indian, and East Asian.[71] Their analyses also report admixture estimates when appropriate.[72] The reliability and utility of such DNA profiling for ethnicity prediction would be expected to be limited to the degree to which population admixture exists in the reference population groups. Use of searching algorithms to predict physical traits from SNP profiles is likely to be of considerable interest to researchers, genealogists, and law enforcement and public safety personnel.[73] Use of such DNA profiling for forensic prediction of race or ethnicity could become a matter of considerable debate if it leads to fears that DNA-based ethnic or racial group prediction or profiling could be used for inappropriate purposes, including outright genetic discrimination. DNA ancestry computations may not translate into a predictable phenotype, especially in admixture situations. For example, an individual male may be largely Caucasian but have a Y-chromosome haplotype common in another population group if a distant direct male progenitor was from that group. At the time of this writing, DNA-based ancestry predictions of the type just described had actually been used successfully by law enforcement in search of possible suspects in a high-profile case in Louisiana, as discussed in the preface to this volume.

Critical Scientific Parameters for Reliable Forensic DNA Analysis

Competent and honest scientific analysis is crucial for promoting public confidence in the results of forensic DNA profiling.[74] Issues relating to public confidence in crime laboratories were much in the news in the spring of 2003, as the press was reporting that Houston, Texas, Police Chief C. O. Bradford had asked the Texas Department of Public Safety to purge from its forensic DNA database all cases examined by the Houston Police Department (HPD) crime laboratory. He reportedly made this request after serious questions arose about the accuracy of certain HPD crime laboratory DNA test results that had been introduced into trials resulting in jury convictions, as subsequent retesting had shown different results.[75] In other cases, reversals of convictions have been based on appeals court determinations of overzealous prosecution, erroneous forensic-expert testimony, and improper forensic-expert opinion.[76] Even the FBI laboratory has not escaped criticism and agreed to adopt forty major recommendations of the Office of the Inspector General to improve laboratory policies and procedures. These recommendations followed an eighteen-month review that focused on three units of the laboratory.[77] Although the Office of the Inspector General's review found no instances of evidence tampering, perjury, or systematic contamination of evidence, it did, according to the FBI, highlight needed improvements in forensic laboratory practices.

At this writing, dozens of previously adjudicated criminal cases involving DNA analysis were reportedly under review and scrutiny in the United States, as a police laboratory in Fort Worth, Texas, was facing an inquiry over allegations of improper DNA procedures,[78] a U.S. Department of Justice review was examining past cases after an allegation that an FBI laboratory technician failed to follow proper laboratory procedures,[79] and an Orlando, Florida, crime laboratory worker's case files were under review.[80]

To what extent these publicized retrospective reviews of forensic-laboratory practices will uncover serious laboratory or personnel deficiencies or result in any significant changes in interpretation of results is not yet known. Nevertheless it is clear that any fair justice system will benefit from, and therefore must remain continuously open to, outside scrutiny. This should include regular systematic review of forensic-laboratory practices, procedures, and protocols using external scientific oversight committees, internal and external audits, and accreditation by proper professional agencies.[81] Validation studies are important in this process, as are inter-laboratory comparison studies.[82]

Two National Research Council reports,[83] several sets of FBI DNA Advisory Board (DAB) guidelines,[84] and numerous independent validation studies[85] have detailed the general scientific practices necessary for sound forensic DNA analysis. The FBI DAB guidelines, as well as subsequent recommendations of the Scientific Working Group on DNA Analysis Methods (SWGDAM),[86] along with the experience of the individual laboratories and analysts, form the basis for current guidelines on the use and interpretation of forensic DNA evidence.

Validation Studies and Population Studies   Adherence to high standards and use of quality equipment and reagents are clearly essential for forensic investigations.[87] Careful validation studies of the reagents and commercially available kits used in forensic genetic typing performed by a number of research groups have indicated that the results of such typing, when performed correctly, according to appropriate protocols, are reliable and trustworthy.[88] Results of forensic DNA typing of specific genetic loci must, therefore, behave in accordance with known biological rules (e.g., Mendel's laws, Hardy–Weinberg equilibrium), and the loci must segregate independently of one another if the product rule is used for statistical estimation of expected profile frequencies.[89] The two National Research Council reports mentioned previously make recommendations in regard to the laboratory and population-genetic aspects of forensic testing and data analysis. Journal literature on these subjects is also abundant.[90]

General Laboratory Issues   Sample collection, chain of custody, quality control, quality assurance, and care in sample handling and transport are particularly relevant in forensic investigations and require careful attention to detail.[91] The challenges of identifying small samples and sample mixtures, occasionally present in human-genetics research and in diagnostic genetics, are often the rule in DNA-based forensic testing. As a general rule, no forensic sample should be processed unless the technologies to be used in the processing have been validated and performed according to the FBI DAB or SWGDAM recommendations,[92] using standard control reference material supplied by or traceable to the National Institute of Standards and Technology (NIST). Other laboratory considerations include maintenance and calibration of equipment, assay of the quantity of DNA amplified, employment of methods to ascertain that DNA amplification has occurred, and use of appropriate controls.[93]

Laboratory and Personnel Accreditation and Quality Assurance   A number of professional agencies have been involved in accreditation and certification of laboratories and personnel involved in genetic testing and human identity testing. These include the American Board of Medical Genetics, the American Board of Pathology, American Association of Blood Banks, the American Board of Criminalistics, and the American Society of Crime Laboratory Directors. Several proficiency-testing programs are available for practitioners of DNA-based forensic and paternity testing, including those administered by several commercial laboratories and by the College of American Pathologists. In the early 1990s, forensic laboratories in the United States followed guidelines promulgated by the Technical Working Group on DNA Analysis Methods (TWGDAM). In late 1995, in accordance with the legislatively mandated requirements of the Federal DNA Identification Act of 1994, the FBI director appointed the initial members of the DAB and charged them with promulgation of updated recommendations and policies on quality assurance standards for laboratories conducting forensic DNA testing. The DAB made several recommendations during its tenure, approved by the FBI director, that define minimum quality assurance standards and place specific requirements on forensic laboratories that handle DNA testing and their personnel. Once approved by the director, implementation of these policies is mandatory for receipt of federal funding and for participation in the Combined DNA Index System (CODIS).[94] The DAB guidelines also addressed quality control and proficiency testing, including minimum education and training requirements for laboratory personnel. Since the DAB's final meeting in November 2000, SWGDAM (which evolved from TWGDAM) has continued to meet regularly and has taken on the responsibility of updating the DAB's guidelines and recommendations to the forensic community. SWGDAM has held several meetings each year and has created guidelines for training of forensic laboratory personnel.[95]

Caveats in the Interpretation of Forensic DNA Testing Results

Laboratory forensic geneticists are in a unique position in the search for truth in cases involving the results of genetic identity testing results. Whereas attorneys for the prosecution and the defense are clearly advocates both for justice and for their clients ("the people" and "the defendant," respectively), the scientist/DNA analyst called as an expert witness has a distinct and important role as an educator to the judge in the pretrial hearings and to the finders of fact in a jury trial. As an expert witness, the forensic scientist is asked to offer factual testimony as well as opinion testimony. This is a special role in the adversarial justice system and should be exercised in a cautious and conservative fashion.

Several examples underscore the importance of understanding the caveats in interpretation of DNA evidence and the role of the expert witness as an unbiased participant in forensic casework. In a number of cases, DNA results have linked an individual suspect or victim who happens to be a monozygotic twin (i.e., an "identical twin") to a person who is the source of crime scene evidence. Clearly, routine analysis of nuclear DNA polymorphisms cannot distinguish between monozygotic twins (triplets, quadruplets, and so on). Thus, a so-called DNA match, although inclusionary, is not necessarily probative. Similarly, DNA patterns from close relatives (especially those from small, isolated populations or from those conceived by consanguineous parents) have a greater chance of matching than do those from randomly selected, unrelated individuals, and this is often important to consider in statistical analyses of DNA testing results.[96] Conversely, a nonmatch (or apparent exclusion) could be misleading to the finders of fact. For example, patterns and alleles identified through DNA typing of blood samples obtained from suspects or victims who were bone marrow recipients after the time evidence was collected from a particular crime scene will not match the patterns and alleles identified from DNA extracted from the evidence, even if the DNA extracted did in fact come from the suspect or victim in question. Buccal epithelial or other nonmyeloid tissue would be needed to make the appropriate DNA profile comparison in such a case. Most geneticists recognize that DNA typing cannot determine, ipso facto, when or how specific biological evidence was deposited at a particular location. Hopefully this is also made apparent to, and considered carefully by, the judge, lawyers, and members of the jury in any trial involving DNA evidence, as well as the interested public.[97] Conversely, not finding a particular DNA profile at a given crime scene does not demonstrate conclusively that the source of that profile was not at the scene and involved in the crime. It therefore follows that the interpretation of postconviction DNA exclusions can be difficult and equivocal. In many postconviction cases, it is implied or argued that once a DNA profile from biological evidence excludes (i.e., does not match) a previously convicted individual, he is therefore exonerated, ipse dixit. Such assertions are not necessarily justified in cases in which the convicted individual could have been party to the criminal conduct without necessarily leaving biological evidence.

Compiling and Searching of Tissue Banks and DNA Databases for Medical, Research, and Forensic Uses

In a practical sense, banking of DNA samples and DNA profiles existed before the operation of contemporary forensic DNA registries. In the United States, repositories of human tissue or DNA that predate DNA registries include heel-stick blood spot cards obtained in the first days of life from all live-born infants. Newborn blood spot cards are collected for genetic-disease screening by local departments of health to allow prompt identification and timely care of severe but treatable inherited metabolic and genetic diseases. How long these newborn blood spot cards are stored by individual states likely varies, as do regulations regarding access to them for purposes other than the original one.

Furthermore, hospital pathology departments around the world routinely archive paraffin-embedded tissues from surgical biopsies and autopsy studies conducted for prognostic and diagnostic testing. These hospital archives have literally millions of stored human tissues samples. Once stored, these tissue blocks can be retrieved for DNA extraction if needed for additional review, new diagnostic testing, or approved research. The Center for Pathology Informatics at the University of Pittsburgh Medical Center has proposed a system to acquire, from its existing system of patient records, pathology lab data on tissues (from patients) stored in its tissue bank collection as well as clinical data to allow researchers studying prostate cancer to query and visualize the data set for tissue annotated with specific parameters.[98]

In the UK Biobank project, the Medical Research Council (MRC) and the Wellcome Trust biomedical research charity have funded an effort to collect DNA samples and medical and personal data on up to five hundred thousand individuals 45–69 years of age for research on the genetic and environmental factors leading to common ailments, including cancer, heart disease, diabetes, and Alzheimer's disease.[99] In the United States, the DNA Sciences Gene Trust Project has similarly registered more than ten thousand participants from all fifty U.S. states in a research study to identify links between genes and common disease. The focus is on serious common diseases like breast cancer, type 2 diabetes, colon cancer, multiple sclerosis, and psoriasis. DNA sequencing will be performed on samples from these individuals to examine DNA variation that may be linked to disease propensity.[100] IBM and the Mayo Clinic have announced plans to develop "information-based medicine," a system to integrate genealogy and population data. Physicians, pharmaceutical companies, and researchers will electronically the clinic's patient information databases, which may be the largest in the world.[101]

The use of confidential medical records for criminal investigations involving DNA raises some compelling policy issues. For example, in Scotland, police obtained, via warrant, confidential medical data on an inmate at the Glenochil prison in Glasgow, Stephen Kelly, as a result of a blood sample Kelly had voluntarily given for medical research as part of a molecular epidemiological investigation into an outbreak of HIV through needle sharing.[102] Results of this epidemiological study had been published in the *British Medical Journal* in 1997. As a result of DNA sequence similarities in the virus that had infected Kelly's girlfriend and that which caused the outbreak in the Glenochil prison, identified through the blood sample Kelly had given, Kelly was charged with, and convicted of, culpable and reckless behavior for having sex with his girlfriend without telling her that he was infected with HIV.

Creation and Searching of Forensic DNA Databases

History and Current Practice   In addition to the medically related storage of DNA or tissues described above, various forensically related biological tissue banks or DNA databases have been created in a growing number of countries. These include those containing biological tissue or computerized DNA profiles from mass-disaster victims and their genetically related family members, from missing persons, and from active-duty, reserve, and retired military personnel, and finally, DNA registries of convicted offenders and crime scene samples.[103] Several states have offered parents the opportunity to prepare and keep potential sources of DNA from their children, storing a blood spot on filter paper or a lock of hair in a way that allows future DNA testing should the child be lost, run away, or be otherwise displaced.[104]

Mass Collections of DNA from U.S. Military Personnel   In the United States, all uniformed military personnel, since the early 1990s, have been required to provide reference blood samples, suitable for DNA extraction, upon entrance into the military or prior to deployment. The blood is preserved on special blood spot cards, which are stored as the modern equivalent of "dog tags" for use in identification in the event that the individual is killed or missing in action. These blood spot cards, intended exclusively for human-remains identification, have allowed such identification in the case of fallen soldiers in both foreign and domestic arenas.

Department of Defense (DOD) regulations have always allowed, under federal or military judicial order, access to these stored military blood spot cards for DNA profiling as part of certain criminal investigations. These DOD regulations were recently codified as an amendment to the 2003 Defense Authorization Act, signed into law by President George W. Bush on December 2, 2002. Although the means for doing so is now codified in federal law, it is not widely appreciated that DNA profiles of current and former military members could be obtained from these stored blood cards for use in investigations of suspected criminal activity. Nevertheless, under DOD regulations and now as federal law, such a DNA search or screen would not be different, de facto, from searching computerized records of digital fingerprints taken from all military members, virtually all sworn law enforcement officers, and many other individuals employed in sensitive positions involving security clearances.

The current reality in the United States is that the blood spot cards stored in a DNA bank by the DOD can be interrogated, by order of the courts, for forensic investigations in a manner quite different from the original humanitarian intent of the collection. This is, to many, a disturbing example of the so-called slippery slope, and such "morphing" of the use of DNA collection hits at the very heart of concern over matters of genetic privacy and constitutional freedoms. Not surprisingly, some have expressed concern that DNA profiling and database searching of such data might be used for a mass search (or "sweep"); the concern is expressed even in regard to cases in which an unnamed military person is a suspect in a crime. Judicial approval for such broad searches would be expected to be more difficult to obtain or undoubtedly would be challenged in the military courts in regard to due process. Nevertheless, it must be remembered that the very first major forensic case to use DNA profiling (*R. v. Pitchfork* in Britain)[105] utilized a mass DNA collection from hundreds of males (although these nonmilitary "DNA sweeps" are, in principle, "consensual," there is undoubtedly pressure to supply a DNA sample). Such mass bloodings for DNA collection also have occurred in several other countries, with some involving crimes on or near military bases. Thus it is yet untested in many state, federal, and military courts precisely what criteria would determine whether the government had probable cause, beyond an individualized search, for DNA extraction and subsequent profile search on a larger number of individuals. An interesting question arises as to whether military blood spot cards would be considered part of a soldier's medical record and therefore be protected as confidential and private as a matter of existing medical privacy protections (for example, the 1996 Health Insurance Portability and Accountability Act).

Offender DNA Registries In addition to the above databases, all fifty U.S. states have statutes providing for obligatory DNA banking of blood or saliva samples from those convicted of certain felony crimes. Similar federal legislation is in force covering those convicted of specified offenses in the District of Columbia and other U.S. federal territories and property and members of the U.S. military while on active duty. Many other countries, including Canada and Great Britain, have regional or national DNA databases containing the computerized DNA profiles of certain convicted offenders or of crime scene evidence. Some of these DNA registries also accommodate computerized DNA profiles from missing persons or from mass-disaster victims and family members for reference and kinship reconstruction. Such profiles are kept separate from the offender registry, to assist in the identification of discovered decomposed or skeletal remains that might be linked to those reported missing (e.g., after mass casualties or disasters).

Under the provisions of the enacted federal and state legislation, blood or other tissue samples are obtained from those covered for DNA extraction and multiple genetic loci are typed. The number of loci typed in such cases varies among countries; in the United States, thirteen STR loci are typed. Typing results (multilocus DNA profiles) are stored in a computerized database for future comparison to DNA profiles from evidentiary samples from unsolved crimes (crime scene index samples). Similarly, profiles from evidentiary samples from unsolved crimes can be compared to those in the databank of known offenders (offender index). In the United States, individual states search their data against those in either a local or a central national index, CODIS, maintained by the FBI. CODIS is designed to link offenders or unsolved cases to one another and thus can identify possible suspects in jurisdictions other than that in which a particular unsolved crime was committed.[106] Interagency agreements between the U.S. and foreign governments, assisted by INTERPOL, allow sharing of DNA profiles among nations for purposes of forensic investigations.

Legal criteria for inclusion in convicted-offender registries vary considerably from state to state, with some registries limited to those convicted of homicide and sexual assaults, whereas others include all convicted felons. Some have advocated inclusion of all arrestees after pilot studies by law enforcement agencies suggested that entering DNA profiles from those arrested for property crimes may be helpful in identifying serial perpetrators whose criminal careers may escalate from property crimes to felony assaults. Federal financial support to the states has made it possible for thousands of cases involving unsolved sexual assaults to be reopened, allowing DNA extraction and profiling of sexual assault rape kits from cases in which no suspect was identified by other means.

Since the inception of CODIS and the various state-operated DNA databases, hundreds of case-to-case or case-to-suspect hits (i.e., DNA matches) have been reported, with one state (Florida) now obtaining several new hits each week. Given the well-known high degree of criminal recidivism, particularly in sexual-assault cases, DNA databases hold promise for identification of many more perpetrators than would be possible without such coordinated efforts.[107]

There appears to be some jurisdictional variation in disposition of DNA samples once criminal cases have been adjudicated. Crime victims' profiles are not ordinarily kept in the databases, but it is not clear on the whole what happens to the DNA profiles of those who were arrested or charged, but against whom charges were later dropped, or of those who were acquitted at trial of all charges. Although some statutes allow a person acquitted of a crime to request removal of his DNA profile from the forensic DNA database, this does not necessarily protect him from a database search of his profile before it is actually removed. An interesting recent case provides an example. In Indiana, on March 26, 1997, a woman was raped, and authorities later identified the DNA profile of the perpetrator, but no attacker was identified initially. Six months later, Damon Smith was arrested and charged with rape in an unrelated case and under court order provided tissues for DNA analysis and comparison. On July 28, 1998, Smith was tried on this rape charge but was acquitted by the trial jury based on a consent defense. Also in July 1998, the Indianapolis–Marion County Forensic Services Agency compared Smith's DNA profile to those from unsolved cases, according to normal procedures, and found a tentative match with the profile of the assailant in the earlier rape. Smith was then charged with rape, robbery, and burglary in connection with the previous case. He then moved to suppress the DNA evidence, and the trial court denied his motion. The Supreme Court of Indiana subsequently affirmed the lower trial court's denial of the defendant's motion to suppress.[108] Although the courts have supported the concept of CODIS databases for convicted offenders, a recent federal case is of interest, as it relates to the question of whether those on probation after serving many years for crimes predating CODIS legislation will also have to submit DNA samples.[109]

The U.S. 9th Circuit Court of Appeals ruled, in October 2003, that the collection of DNA from parolees violates the 4th amendment (*Kincade v. U.S.*). In March

2004, the 9th Circuit Court, sitting en banc, heard additional arguments on this matter. In consideration of the effectiveness of DNA database searching in the criminal justice system, it is important that the benefits of DNA databases be measured not simply by the number of matches or hits in criminal investigations, but also by the number of DNA eliminations often leading to exonerations. Indeed, the elimination of suspects based on DNA profiling and database searching can relieve uninvolved parties from unnecessary intrusions from law enforcement personnel and, as an added benefit, can save time and money by averting countless hours of wasted investigative time.

Lower-Stringency Searching and the Matter of Siblings   Genetically related siblings typically share one or both parents. Thus it would be expected full siblings would share DNA profiles much more commonly than would unrelated persons. This expectation is supported by data collected on sibling and nonsibling DNA profiles in the United States. Upon comparison, the DNA profiles of full siblings show the expected higher degree of allele sharing and locus identity than those of unrelated individuals.[110] My data demonstrate that full siblings born to unrelated parents have identical STR profiles at an average of four of the thirteen CODIS core loci, compared to, on average, identity at less than a single locus among unrelated individuals. My data set included a sibling pair with identity at nine of the thirteen CODIS loci. A colleague has informed me of the discovery, in a quality control search of a DNA database, of a pair of closely related (i.e., incestuously conceived) inmate brothers who reportedly share identical DNA profiles at ten of thirteen STR CODIS core loci,[111] and another colleague has informed us of an eleven-locus match in a brother and sister.[112] Also, it can be noted that siblings with the same mother would be expected to share mtDNA profiles and that brothers with the same father would have identical Y-chromosome STR haplotypes.

These observations in siblings have important implications for forensic geneticists, as it becomes important to consider the matter of siblings (typically brothers) in cases in which complete multilocus DNA profiles are not obtained (e.g., because of DNA degradation). Also, in a search of a DNA data bank, a high degree of allele sharing can provide an important investigative lead (i.e., possibly implicating a sibling, parent, or child) even in the absence of a complete-profile match of crime scene evidence against a registry of convicted offenders. Thus, it is important for DNA data bank administrators to have a carefully considered policy about when to notify law enforcement when a high degree of allele sharing is found in a computer search, even if it does not involve a complete match at all loci. In reality, sibling issues are the exception rather than the rule in forensic investigations, and low-stringency database searches using the current thirteen-locus STR analysis would be expected to lead to too many partial-profile hits to be of any practical use in the majority of investigations, because many alleles are very common in the population and would be shared by large numbers of individuals. However, if SNP technology comes into use, large numbers of loci could be tested, and some SNPs are extremely rare in some populations and universal in others. Thus searching for certain key SNP alleles could allow low-stringency searches to be quite effective.

Direct and Indirect Forensic Kinship Analysis for Human-Remains Identification
DNA profiling has been a key tool for direct and indirect identification of hundreds of victims from the September 11, 2001, terrorist attacks, as well as from many other acts of war, air crashes, and mass disasters. It is often the only method that will allow unequivocal identification and has enabled the U.S. military to retrospectively identify hundreds of fallen soldiers whose remains were recovered years after they were lost in combat (e.g., from World War II and the Korean and Vietnam conflicts). The simple objective of forensic DNA profiling in these types of cases is to compare the STR profile or mtDNA sequence in DNA extracted from human remains to that found in DNA extracted from a known (or reference) blood or tissue sample. In cases in which a known reference DNA sample is available and the recovered remains sample can be analyzed completely, such a comparison is straightforward. Also, in closed systems, like air crashes, the passenger manifest or some other definitive accounting of the number of victims and their identities allows investigators to make contact with relatives to obtain known reference samples from the victims' personal items or clothing for direct DNA comparison with profiles from remains at the crash site or crime scene. Most uniformed U.S. military personnel have blood spot cards on file for just this purpose. Through these blood spot records and the passenger list for the flight, remains from almost all of those lost on September 11, 2001, at the Somerset, Pennsylvania, and Pentagon crash sites were identified by members of the Armed Forces DNA Identification Laboratory, which has a contract with the FAA—many only by use of DNA profile comparisons.

In contrast to DNA identification of remains in closed systems, that involving open systems, like those of the World Trade Center twin towers or the mass graves in the former Yugoslavia, is more complicated, because all of the names and the precise number of individuals who perished are not necessarily known, and reference DNA samples from these victims often are not available for direct DNA profile comparison. Therefore, close family members and more distant relatives must come forward to provide a DNA sample if victim identification is to occur using DNA. Databases are needed to compare the thousands of DNA profiles from recovered human remains with those of known living relatives. This process requires sophisticated software to perform complex mathematical-likelihood ratio analysis for these indirect identifications.[113]

By mid-2003 the remains of almost half of the nearly 2,800 World Trade Center victims had been identified using a combination of forensic methods, including DNA profiling. One of the 343 firefighters who died at the WTC was initially identified (incorrectly) as someone who turned out to be a fallen comrade from the same fire company. The initial identification had relied on the uniform, an amulet around his neck, and the presence of a cervical spine anomaly. The correct identity was discovered only after DNA typing results were available, allowing his remains to be given to the appropriate family. Amazingly, both men had worn identical uniforms and amulets, and both had a similar cervical spine anomaly. Hopefully, DNA analysis will allow recovery efforts to be successful in identification of a fair proportion of the remaining unidentified bodies or samples recovered from the World Trade Center towers. Such identification is not always straightforward, however. For example, in the former Yugoslavia, many of the surviving family members of those buried in the mass graves, who would be useful for identification of the dead, are wandering or confined as refugees, displaced from their homes and villages, and therefore separated from their families, making such kindred reconstruction impossible.[114]

Surname Searching as a Forensic Tool?   Interestingly, males generally "inherit" yet another enduring trait from their fathers beyond their nuclear or Y-chromosome DNA profile: their family name or surname. Thus database searching of surnames could be considered in an investigative search of possible criminal suspects, once a particular Y-chromosome DNA haplotype profile is identified in forensic evidence.[115] For example, in a hypothetical investigation, once a specific Y-chromosome DNA haplotype is identified in key forensic evidence, a database search might identify a haplotype as one commonly found in males named "Adamsky," or "Baker," or "Smiley." Individuals with the same or similar surnames might then be targeted for investigation or questioning, or even for court-mandated DNA profiling. There would certainly be constitutional, privacy, and civil-liberties concerns about this concept, as any involuntary DNA profiling based only on the circumstance of having a certain last name would lack the element of individualized suspicion the judicial system has held to be a requisite. Although surname searching based on Y-chromosome haplotype DNA profiling might seem an implausible idea, in theory it could be a highly efficient search strategy in cases of very rare DNA profiles associated with uncommon surnames.

Conclusion: DNA, the Silent Eyewitness

The utility of DNA-based genetic analysis has been amply demonstrated during the past decade. Applications of such analysis include civil paternity testing, medical diagnostics, and forensic testing, as well identification of victims from war and mass casualties. Use of DNA profiling as an exculpatory tool and as powerful inclusionary evidence cannot be underemphasized as it provides, in some cases, the make-or-break evidence freeing incarcerated inmates or sealing the fate of defendants in jury trials.[116] Moreover, the powerful exculpatory potential of DNA profiling and the possibility of exoneration as a result remind us of the need not to ignore those cases in which DNA profiling was never performed.

Inferences about certain specific individual traits (e.g., hair or eye colour) can be made based on DNA analysis of specific genes. Ethnic differences markers (EDMs) have been identified from alleles that have large frequency differences among certain populations. These EDMs have been used in study of ethnic admixture to map complex genetic diseases.[117] Therefore, predictions about the ethnic, regional, or geographical ancestry of human remains or recovered biological evidence could theoretically be made if sufficient loci are typed. It is too soon to predict whether such DNA-based ethnic or racial profiling would be useful in searches for suspects or in humanitarian identification of recovered remains and whether such predictions, as a basis for probable cause, would withstand scrutiny by the courts. Caveats include the probabilistic nature of such predictions and the dependence on typing loci not ordinarily used in forensic work.

Storage of evidence and protocols for retrospective DNA profiling of previously adjudicated cases will continue, sine die, to challenge the courts and the manpower of personnel in the criminal justice system. Despite the remarkable capabilities of modern crime laboratories, fiscal imperatives often prevent optimal use of forensic DNA profiling or searching of the existing databanks. For example, in individual cases, funding shortages typically limit the number of evidentiary exemplars examined. What effect this has on the result of individual cases is unknown. In old, unsolved cases, lack of DNA extraction obviously precludes the DNA profiles from being entered into the crime scene index, and this undoubtedly allows some violent serial offenders to remain undiscovered in the community. Because of these funding shortages and also staff shortages, DNA profiles in current or ongoing cases often cannot be searched promptly against the profiles obtained from other solved or unsolved cases or against the profiles of known offenders. Thus, many unsolved or cold cases languish in the archives of crime labs, waiting for that tenacious investigator, committed forensic scientist, concerned family member, or the media to reactivate the case. Fortunately, in the United States, federal funding has made it possible to reduce the backlog somewhat, but other factors prevent such reduction in many cases. This is indeed unfortunate in light of the recidivistic nature of many offenders.

Several practical matters account for the tremendous backlog in working old, unsolved cases that might benefit from modern DNA analysis.[118] The first is a shortage of qualified examiners in the crime labs. Lack of sufficient qualified personnel or funding will continue to require crime laboratories to send out overflow samples to commercial contractors. Even though advances in computer robotics and sample-tracking software have eliminated many hours of tedium in the handling and processing of samples, the initial examination of evidence, the selection of which exemplars to test, and the interpretation of results requires highly skilled individuals whose work and interpretations will be scrutinized in the courts. The second is difficulties with proper evidence storage, which may prevent successful extraction of DNA years later. While a case is being adjudicated, crime scene evidence involved in the case is very often stored properly in crime labs or police storage facilities under carefully controlled conditions. However, once the adjudication process is complete, storage practices are highly variable, and sadly, key evidence that may have been untested may be more haphazardly stored under less-than-ideal conditions or even discarded, preventing current or future technologies from being applied in retrospective analysis. Very recently, legislative proposals have been offered in several states to require that all evidence obtained in criminal investigations that might contain biological evidence be stored indefinitely. In California, victims of sexual assault have the right under pending legislation to learn the status and whereabouts of the rape kits compiled as evidence in investigation of their cases.[119]

New methods, along with development of miniaturized crime scene field kits, have led some to speculate about applications of forensic DNA profiling for use in the field. Indeed, we may not be far away from the time when such miniaturized kits could permit DNA extraction, analysis, and computer database searching at the crime scene. Although possible, it is unclear whether such on-the-spot assessment would be desirable or sensible, or whether such field applications would conform to DAB or SWGDAM requirements for standardized protocols in laboratories.

Novel methods will continue to improve the array of laboratory methods used for forensic profiling of human and nonhuman DNA. Interpretational challenges involving complex DNA mixtures will continue to require the help of impartial academic and private-sector experts, as well as qualified forensic scientists. The forensic community has invested considerable effort and expense in validating the methods for STR typing of the thirteen core CODIS loci, and these will predictably remain the methods of choice for the foreseeable future. Many investigations will be augmented by mtDNA sequencing and Y-chromosome STR profiling. The future promises to bring increased use of SNP assays, of microarrays for mass screening of hundreds of loci, and of robotics to improve efficiency in sample handling. This will reduce the costs in time and labor needed to perform testing. Additional technical advances will allow DNA extraction, DNA profiling, and searching a DNA database of known offenders without the long delays now encountered in some jurisdictions.

Major questions remain about the collection and storage of DNA samples from volunteers, patients, relatives of missing persons, and military personnel. Society must assess the benefits and risks of such collections as it weighs the gains in public safety against the costs of diminished privacy.

Notes

This chapter is dedicated to the memory of the late David Bing, a superb scientist, enthusiastic mentor, and loyal friend.

The author gratefully acknowledges Norman Gahn (Milwaukee district attorney's office), Lisa Kahn (Los Angeles County district attorney's office), Col. Brion Smith (AFDIL/U.S. DOD), Ed Blake (Forensic Science Associates), Heather Miller Coyle (Connecticut State Police Forensic Science Laboratory), Harvard Medical School students Michelle Lee and Mireya Nadal, and David Lazer (John F. Kennedy School of Government, Harvard University) for useful comments and discussions.

The author, a member of the Faculty of Medicine at Harvard University, serves as medical geneticist at Brigham and Women's Hospital (Boston) and as a commissioned officer in the

U.S. Army Reserve. Statements herein are not made to represent the opinions or positions of any of the institutions or organizations with which he is affiliated.

1. F. Galton, *Fingerprints* (London: MacMillan, 1892); S. Cole, *Suspect Identities: A History of Fingerprinting and Criminal Identification* (Cambridge, Mass.: Harvard University Press, 2001).

2. F. R. Bieber, "Overview of Human Identity Testing and Forensic Genetics," *Current Protocols in Human Genetics*, unit 14.1 (1997).

3. R. Saferstein, *Criminalistics*, 8th ed. (Englewood Cliffs, N.J.: Prentice Hall, 2004).

4. R. R. Race and R. Sanger, *The Blood Groups of Man*, 6th ed. (Oxford: Blackwell Scientific, 1975).

5. B. Richards et al., "Multiplex PCR Amplification from the CFTR Gene Using DNA Prepared from Buccal Brushes/Swabs," *Human Molecular Genetics* 2 (1993): 159–163; A. P. Shuber et al., "Efficient 12-Mutation Testing in the CFTR Gene: A General Model for Complex Mutation Analysis," *Human Molecular Genetics* 2 (1993): 153–158.

6. N. O. Bianchi et al., "Characterization of Ancestral and Derived Y-Chromosome Haplotypes of New World Native Populations," *American Journal of Human Genetics* 63, no. 6 (1998); F. Calafell et al., "Short Tandem Repeat Polymorphism Evolution in Humans," *European Journal of Human Genetics* 6, no. 1 (1998).

7. A. J. F. Griffiths et al., *An Introduction to Genetic Analysis*, 7th ed. (San Francisco: Freeman, 2000).

8. See E. S. Lander, L. M. Linton, and B. Birren, "Initial Sequencing and Analysis of the Human Genome," *Nature* 409, no. 6822 (2001): 860–921; J. C. Venter et al., "The Sequence of the Human Genome," *Science* 291, no. 5507 (2001): 1304–1351.

9. P. Gill, A. J. Jeffreys, and D. J. Werrett, "Forensic Application of DNA 'Fingerprints,'" *Nature* 316, no. 6023 (1985): 76–79; A. J. Jeffreys, J. F. Brookfield, and R. Semeonoff, "Positive Identification of an Immigration Test-Case Using Human DNA Fingerprints," *Nature* 317, no. 6040 (October 31–November 6, 1985); A. J. Jeffreys, V. Wilson, and S. L. Thein, "Individual-Specific 'Fingerprints' of Human DNA," *Nature* 318, no. 6046 (December 12–18, 1985): 577–579.

10. The exclusionary power of DNA typing has tremendous utility in forensics, and thus DNA typing should always be considered, even when a suspect has confessed.

11. See J. Wambaugh, *The Blooding* (New York: Morrow, 1989).

12. *Commonwealth v. Pestinikas*, 617A.2d 1339, 1343 (PA Super. 1992).

13. *State v. Searles*, 246 Kan. 567 (1990).

14. *Tyrone Fuller v. State of Texas*, 827 S.W.2d 919 (1992).

15. *Spencer v. Commonwealth*, 393 S.E.2d 609 VA (1990).

16. B. Budowle, ed., *DNA Typing Protocols: Molecular Biology and Forensic Analysis* (Natick, Mass.: Eaton, 2000); J. M. Butler, *Forensic DNA Typing: Biology and Technology behind STR Markers* (New York: Academic Press, 2001).

17. T. Balazs et al., "Human Population Genetic Studies of Five Hypervariable DNA Loci," *American Journal of Human Genetics* 44 (1989): 182–190; R. Helmuth et al., "HLA-DQα

Allele and Genotype Frequencies in Various Human Populations, Determined by Using Enzymatic Amplification and Oligonucleotide Probes," *American Journal of Human Genetics* 47 (1990): 515–523; C. T. Comey and B. Budowle, "Validation Studies on the Analysis of the HLA-DQα Locus Using the Polymerase Chain Reaction," *Journal of Forensic Science* 36 (1991): 1633–1648; H. A. Hammond et al., "Evaluation of 13 Short Tandem Repeat Loci for Use in Personal Identification Applications," *American Journal of Human Genetics* 55 (1994): 175–189; C. Kimpton et al., "Evaluation of an Automated DNA Profiling System Employing Multiplex Amplification of Four Tetrameric STR Loci," *International Journal of Legal Medicine* 106 (1994): 302–311; J. Replogle et al., "Identification of Host DNA by Amplified Fragment Length Polymorphism Analysis: Preliminary Analysis of Human Crab Louse (*Anoplura Pediculidae*) Excreta," *Journal of Medical Entomology* 31 (1994); M. N. Hochmeister et al., "Swiss Population Data and Forensic Efficiency Values on 3 Tetrameric Short Tandem Repeat Loci HUMTH01, TPOX, and CSF1PO Derived Using a STR Multiplex System," *International Journal of Legal Medicine* 107 (1995): 246–249; G. Sensabaugh and D. H. Kaye, "Non-human DNA Evidence," *Jurimetrics Journal* 38 (1998): 1–16; H. Miller Coyle et al., "The Green Revolution: Botanical Contributions to Forensics and Drug Enforcement," *Croatian Medical Journal* 42, no. 3 (2001); H. Miller Coyle et al., "A Simple DNA Extraction Method for Marijuana Samples Used in Amplified Fragment Length Polymorphism (AFLP) Analysis," *Journal of Forensic Science* 48 (2003).

18. See E. Connors et al., *Convicted by Juries, Exonerated by Science: Case Studies in the Use of DNA Evidence to Establish Innocence after Trial* (Washington, D.C.: National Institute of Justice, 1996).

19. John Stewart, personal communication.

20. See Griffiths et al., *Introduction to Genetic Analysis*; Lander, Linton, and Birren, "Initial Sequencing and Analysis of the Human Genome"; Venter et al., "Sequence of the Human Genome."

21. R. Wyman and R. White, "A Highly Polymorphic Locus in Human DNA," *Proceedings of the National Academy of Sciences U.S.A.* 77 (1980): 6754–6758; G. Herrin, "Probability of Matching RFLP Patterns from Unrelated Individuals," *American Journal of Human Genetics* 52 (1993): 491–497; B. Budowle et al., "Analysis of the Variable Number of Tandem Repeats Locus D1S80 by the Polymerase Chain Reaction Followed by High Resolution Polyacrylamide Gel Electrophoresis," *American Journal of Human Genetics* 48 (1992); National Research Council, Committee on DNA Technology in Forensic Science, *DNA Technology in Forensic Science* (Washington, D.C.: National Academies Press, 1992); National Research Council, Committee on DNA Technology in Forensic Science: An Update, *The Evaluation of Forensic DNA Evidence* (Washington, D.C.: National Academies Press, 1996).

22. See D. H. Bing et al., "Isolation of DNA from Forensic Evidence," *Current Protocols in Human Genetics*, unit 14.3 (2000); D. H. Bing and F. R. Bieber, "Collecting and Handling Samples for Parentage and Forensics DNA-Based Genetic Testing," *Current Protocols in Human Genetics*, unit 14.2 (1997); J. S. Waye et al., "A Simple Method for Quantifying Human Genomic DNA in Forensic Specimen Extracts," *BioTechniques* 7, no. 8 (1989); H. C. Lee, T. Palmbach, and M. T. Miller, *Henry Lee's Crime Scene Handbook* (New York: Academic Press, 2001).

23. C. J. Word, T. M. Sawosik, and D. H. Bing, "Summary of Validation Studies from Twenty-Six Laboratories in the United States and Canada on the Use of the AmpliType PM

PCR," *Journal of Forensic Science* 42 (1997): 39–48; M. N. Hochmeister et al., "Typing of DNA Extracted from Compact Bone Tissue from Human Remains," *Journal of Forensic Science* 36, no. 6 (1991); R. Allen et al., "Analysis of the VNTR Locus AmpliFLP D1S80 by the PCR Followed by High-Resolution PAGE," *American Journal of Human Genetics* 48 (1991): 137–144; D. H. Bing and F. R. Bieber, "Manual Methods for PCR-Based Forensic DNA Analysis," *Current Protocols in Human Genetics*, unit 14.6 (1999); Butler, *Forensic DNA Typing*; Miller Coyle et al., "A Simple DNA Extraction Method."

24. Butler, *Forensic DNA Typing*.

25. P. Gill et al., "Databases, Quality Control and Interpretation of DNA Profiling in the Home Office Forensic Science Service," *Electrophoresis* 12 (1991): 204–209; Federal Bureau of Investigation, "State DNA Database Laws: Outline of Provisions" (Washington, D.C.: U. S. Department of Justice, 1996); Federal Bureau of Investigation, DNA Advisory Board, "Quality Assurance Standards for Convicted Offender DNA Databasing Laboratories" (Washington, D.C.: U.S. Department of Justice, 1999), available at www.fbi.gov.

26. C. J. Sprecher et al., "A General Approach to Analysis of Polymorphic Short Tandem Repeat Loci," *BioTechniques* 20 (1996): 206–276; Word, Sawosik, and Bing, "Summary of Validation Studies from Twenty-Six Laboratories."

27. See D. H. Bing and F. R. Bieber, "Isolation of DNA for Forensic Evidence," *Current Protocols in Human Genetics*, unit 14.3 (1998).

28. C. T. Comey et al., "PCR Amplification and Typing of the HLA-DQα Gene in Forensic Samples," *Journal of Forensic Science* 38 (1993): 239–249; B. Budowle, B. W. Koons, and T. R. Moretti, "Subtyping of the HLA-DQA1 Locus and Independence Testing with PM and STR/VNTR Loci," *Journal of Forensic Science* 43, no. 3 (1998): 657–660.

29. R. K. Saiki, T. L. Bugawan, G. T. Horn, K. B. Mullis, and H. A. Erlich, "Analysis of Enzymatically Amplified B-globin and HLA-DQa DNA with Allele-Specific Oligonucleotide Probes," *Nature* 324, no. 6093 (1986): 163–166; R. Reynolds et al., "Analysis of Genetic Markers in Forensic DNA Samples Using the Polymerase Chain Reaction," *Anal. Chem.* 63 (1991): 2–15.

30. C. A. Crouse, V. Vincek, and B. K. Caraballo, "Analysis and Interpretation of the HLA DQα '1.1 Weak-Signal' Observed during the PCR-Based Typing Method," *Journal of Forensic Science* 39 (1994): 41–51; C. A. Crouse, D. C. Nippes, and E. L. Ritzline, "Confirmation of PM Typing Protocols for Consistent and Reliable Results," *Journal of Forensic Science* 41 (1996): 493–496.

31. C. H. Brenner and B. S. Weir, "Issues and Strategies in the DNA Identification of World Trade Center Victims," *Theoretical Population Biology* 63 (2003); J. Whitfield, "World Trade Center Forensics Break New Ground," *Nature Science Update* 23 (April 2003).

32. P. Keim et al., "Multiple-Locus Variable-Number Tandem Repeat Analysis Reveals Genetic Relationships with *Bacillus anthracis*," *Journal of Bacteriology* 182 (2000); A. R. Hoffmaster et al., "Molecular Subtyping of *Bacillus anthracis* and the 2001 Bioterrorism-Associated Anthrax Outbreak, United States," *Emerging Infectious Diseases* 8 (2002).

33. National Research Council, *Countering Bioterrorism: The Role of Science and Technology* (Washington, D.C.: National Academies Press, 2002).

34. B. Budowle et al., "Fixed Bin Analysis for Statistical Evaluation of Continuous Distributions of Allelic Data from VNTR Loci for Use in Forensic Comparisons," *American Journal*

of Human Genetics 48 (1991): 841–855; B. Budowle et al., "Validation Studies of the CTT STR Multiplex System," *Journal of Forensic Science* 42, no. 4 (1997); G. F. Sensabaugh and E. T. Blake, "DNA Analysis in Biological Evidence: Applications of the Polymerase Chain Reaction," in *Forensic Science Handbook*, vol. 3, ed. R. Saferstein (Englewood Cliffs, N.J.: Reagents/Prentice Hall, 1993): 416–452; Hammond, "Evaluation of 13 Short Tandem Repeat Loci, 175–189"; Sensabaugh and Kaye, "Non-human DNA Evidence"; C. J. Fregeau, K. L. Bowen, and R. M. Forney, "Validation of Highly Polymorphic Fluorescent Multiplex Short Tandem Repeat Systems Using Two Generations of DNA Sequencers," *Journal of Forensic Science* 44, no. 1 (1999); K. A. Micka et al., "Validation of Multiplex Polymorphic STR Amplification Sets Developed for Personal Identification Applications," *Journal of Forensic Science* 41 (1996): 582–590.

35. K. Y. Kasai, Y. Nakamura, and R. White, "Amplification of a Variable Number of Tandem Repeats (VNTR) Locus (pMCT118) by the Polymerase Chain Reaction (PCR) and Its Application to Forensic Science," *Journal of Forensic Science* 35 (1990): 1196–1200.

36. Griffiths et al., *An Introduction to Genetic Analysis*.

37. A. Mannucci et al., "Forensic Application of a Rapid and Quantitative DNA Sex Test by Amplification of the X-Y Homologous Gene Amelogenin," *International Journal of Legal Medicine* 106 (1994): 190–193; A. Akane, "Sex Determination by PCR Analysis of the X-Y Amelogenenin Gene," *Methods in Molecular Biology* 98 (1998); A. M. Lins et al., "Multiplex Set for Amplification of Polymorphic Short Tandem Repeat Loci: Silver Stain and Fluorescent Detection," *BioTechniques* 20 (1996): 882–889; A. M. Lins et al., "Development and Population Study of an Eight-Locus Short Tandem Repeat (STR) Multiplex System," *Journal of Forensic Science* 43, no. 6 (1998); K. A. Micka et al., "TWGDAM Validation of a Nine-Locus and a Four-Locus Fluorescent STR Multiplex System," *Journal of Forensic Science* 44 (1999): 1243–1257; Butler, *Forensic DNA Typing*.

38. C. A. Crouse and J. Schumm, "Investigation of Species Specificity Using Nine PCR-Based Human STR Systems," *Journal of Forensic Science* 40 (1995): 952–956; Budowle, *DNA Typing Protocols*; Butler, *Forensic DNA Typing*; C. L. Holt et al., "TWGDAM Validation of AmpFlSTR PCR Amplification Kits for Forensic DNA Casework," *Journal of Forensic Science* 47 (2002); J. M. Wallin et al., "Constructing Universal Multiplex PCR Systems for Comparative Genotyping," *Journal of Forensic Science* 47 (2002).

39. See M. Prinz et al., "Multiplexing of Y-Chromosome-Specific STRs and Performance for Mixed Samples," *Forensic Science International* 85 (1997): 209–218; M. Kayser et al., "Evaluation of Y-Chromosomal STRs; A Multicenter Study," *International Journal of Legal Medicine* 110 (1997): 125–133, 141–149; M. Kayser et al., "Online Y-Chromosome Short Tandem Repeat Haplotype Reference Database (YHRD) for U.S. Populations," *Journal of Forensic Science* 47, no. 3 (2002): 510–513; Butler, *Forensic DNA Typing*.

40. See www.ystr.org; www.ystr.org/usa; and www.ystr.org/asia.

41. See Butler, *Forensic DNA Typing*; S. K. Sinha et al., "Development and Validation of a Multiplexed Y-Chromosome STR Genotyping System, Y-PLEX 6, for Forensic Casework," *Journal of Forensic Science* 48, no. 1 (2003).

42. Occasional reports of two or even three Y-chromosome alleles have been made in individual males—probably representing locus duplication in these individuals.

43. See www.promega.com and www.reliagene.org.

44. S. Anderson et al., "Sequence and Organization of the Human Mitochondrial Genomes," *Nature* 290, no. 5806 (1981): 457–465; Budowle et al., 2000; M. R. Wilson et al., "Extraction, PCR Amplification, and Sequencing of Mitochondrial DNA from Human Hair Shafts," *BioTechniques* 18 (1995); M. R. Wilson et al., "Validation of Mitochondrial DNA Sequencing for Forensic Casework Analysis," *International Journal of Legal Medicine* 108 (1995); M. R. Wilson et al., "A Family Exhibiting Heteroplasmy in the Human Mitochondrial DNA Control Region Reveals Both Somatic Mosaicism and Pronounced Segregation of Mitotypes," *Human Genetics* 100 (1997); M. M. Holland and T. J. Parsons, "Mitochondrial DNA Sequence Analysis—Validation and Use for Forensic Casework," *Forensic Science Review* 11 (1999): 21–50; K. W. P. Miller and B. Budowle, "A Compendium of Human Mitochondrial DNA Control Region: Development of an International Standard Forensic Database," *Croatian Medical Journal* 42, no. 3 (2001).

45. P. E. Coskun, E. Ruiz-Pesini, and D. C. Wallace, "Control Region mtDNA Variants: Longevity, Climatic Adaptation, and a Forensic Conundrum," *Proceedings of the National Academy of Sciences* 100, no. 5 (2003).

46. R. M. Fourney, "Mitochondrial DNA and Forensic Analysis—A Primer for Law Enforcement," *Canadian Society of Forensic Science Journal* 31, no. 1 (1998): 45–53.

47. Brenner and Weir, "Issues and Strategies."

48. E. Huffine et al., "Mass Identification of Persons Missing from the Break-Up of the Former Yugoslavia; Structure, Function, and the Role of the International Commission on Missing Persons," *Croatian Medical Journal* 42, no. 3 (2001); F. R. Bieber, "Reckoning with the Dead," *Harvard Medical Alumni Bulletin* 76, no. 2 (2002).

49. S. Banaschak, K. Moller, and H. Pfeiffer, "Potential DNA Mixtures Introduced through Kissing," *International Journal of Legal Medicine* 111, no. 5 (1998); C. Ladd et al., "Interpretation of Complex Forensic DNA Mixtures," *Croatian Medical Journal* 42, no. 3 (2001).

50. J. G. Shewale et al., "DNA Profiling of Azoospermic Semen Samples from Vasectomized Males by Using Y-PLEX 6 Amplification Kit," *Journal of Forensic Science* 48, no. 1 (2003).

51. Sensabaugh and Blake, "DNA Analysis in Biological Evidence."

52. See Ladd et al., "Interpretation of Complex Forensic DNA Mixtures."

53. See Sensabaugh and Kaye, "Non-human DNA Evidence"; Miller Coyle et al., "A Simple DNA Extraction Method."

54. Keim et al., "Multiple-Locus Variable-Number Tandem Repeat Analysis."

55. Miller Coyle et al., "A Simple DNA Extraction Method."

56. C. G. G. Aitken, *Statistics and the Evaluation of Evidence for Forensic Scientists* (Chichester, England: Wiley, 1995); H. Harding and R. Swanson, "DNA Database Size," *Journal of Forensic Science* 43, no. 1 (1998): 248–249; National Research Council, Committee on DNA Technology in Forensic Science: An Update, *The Evaluation of Forensic DNA Evidence*; B. S. Weir, *Genetic Data Analysis II* (Sunderland, Mass.: Sinauer, 1996); I. W. Evett and B. S. Weir, *Interpreting DNA Evidence: Statistical Genetics for Forensic Scientists* (Sunderland, Mass.: Sinauer, 1998).

57. Budowle, *DNA Typing Protocols*; Federal Bureau of Investigation, U. S. Department of Justice, DNA Advisory Board, "Statistical and Population Genetics Issues Affecting the

Evaluation of the Frequency of Occurrence of DNA Profiles Calculated from Pertinent Population Databases," *Forensic Science Communications* 2, no. 3 (July 2000).

58. C. J. Fregeau et al., "Population Genetic Characteristics of the STR Loci D21S11 and FGA in Eight Diverse Human Populations," *Human Biology* 70, no. 5 (1998); B. Budowle and R. Chakraborty, "Population Variation at the CODIS Core Short Tandem Repeat Loci in Europeans," *Legal Medicine* 3, no. 1 (2001); B. Budowle et al., "United States Population Data on the Multiplex Short Tandem Repeat Loci—HUMTHO1, TPOX, and CSF1PO—and the Variable Number Tandem Repeat Locus D1S80," *Journal of Forensic Science* 42, no. 5 (1997): 846–849; B. Budowle, K. L. Monson, and R. Chakraborty, "Estimating Minimum Allele Frequencies for DNA Profile Frequency Estimates for PCR-Based Loci," *International Journal of Legal Medicine* 108 (1996); E. M. Steinberger, L. D. Thompson, and J. M. Hartmann, "On the Use of Excess Homozygosity for Subpopulation Detection" (letter), *American Journal of Human Genetics* 52 (1993): 1275–1277.

59. R. Chakraborty, "Sample Size Requirements for Addressing the Population Genetic Issues of Forensic Use of DNA Typing," *Human Biology* 64 (1992); R. Chakraborty et al., "Nondetectability of Restriction Fragments and Independence of DNA Fragment Sizes within and between Loci in RFLP Typing of DNA," *American Journal of Human Genetics* 55 (1994); R. Chakraborty et al., "The Utility of STR Loci beyond Human Identification: Implications for the Development of New DNA Typing Systems," *Electrophoresis* 20 (1999).

60. A. Sozer, C. Kelly, and D. Demers, "Molecular Analysis of Paternity," *Current Protocols in Human Genetics*, unit 14.4 (1998); Ladd et al., "Interpretation of Complex Forensic DNA Mixtures"; Brenner and Weir, "Issues and Strategies."

61. These mutation rates are about 2.8×10^3. See Kayser et al., "Evaluation of Y-Chromosomal STRs"; M. Kayser and A. Sajantila, "Mutations at Y-STR Loci: Implications for Paternity Testing and Forensic Analysis," *Forensic Science International* 118 (2001).

62. See Ladd et al., "Interpretation of Complex Forensic DNA Mixtures"; Federal Bureau of Investigation, "Statistical and Population Genetics Issues."

63. J. J. Koehler, "The Psychology of Numbers in the Courtroom: How to Make DNA Match Statistics Seem Impressive or Insufficient," *Southern California Law Review* 74 (2001); "Why DNA Likelihood Ratios Should Account for Error (Even When a National Research Council Report Says They Should Not)," *Jurimetrics Journal* 37 (1997); "One in Millions, Billions and Trillions: Lessons from People v. Collins (1968) for People v. Simpson (1995)," *Journal of Legal Education* 47 (1997); "When Are People Persuaded by DNA Match Statistics?" *Law and Human Behavior* 25 (2001).

64. L. Tribe, "Trial by Mathematics: Precision and Ritual in the Legal Process," *Harvard Law Review* 84 (April 1971); D. H. Kaye, "Clarifying Burdens of Persuasion: What Bayesian Decision Rules Do and Do Not Do," *International Journal of Evidence and Proof* 3, no. 1 (1999); J. L. Gastwirth, ed., *Statistical Science in the Courtroom* (New York: Springer Verlag, 2000).

With regard to statistical interpretation of DNA evidence, the reader should be aware that several court rulings have addressed this issue in some detail. In its ruling in *Minnesota v. Kromah et al.* (C8-02-1034), the high court encourage[d] district courts to be mindful of the impact of quantitative probability statistics on DNA analysis. In *State v. Joon Kyu Kim*, we disallowed the admission of quantitative statistical probability evidence, recognizing the danger that a jury may equate such evidence with the likelihood that the defendant was guilty (398 N.W.2d 544, 548–49 [Minn. 1987]). Thus, courts need to be fully cognizant of the potentially prejudicial nature of the statistical probability evidence and ensure that DNA identification evidence is not presented in a misleading or unfairly prejudicial way (*Bloom v. State*, 516 N.W. 2d 159 [Minn. 1994]).

65. See D. Neeser and S. Liechti-Gallati, "Sex Determination of Forensic Samples by Simultaneous PCR Amplification of Alpha-Satellite DNA from Both the X and Y Chromosomes." *Journal of Forensic Science* 40 (1995): 239–241.

66. N. Flanagan et al., "Pleiotropic Effects of the Melanocortin 1 Receptor (MC1R) Gene on Human Pigmentation," *Human Molecular Genetics* 9, no. 17 (2000).

67. J. F. List and J. F. Habener, "Defective Melanocortin 4 Receptors in Hyperphagia and Morbid Obesity," *New England J. Med.* 348, no. 12 (2003): 1085–1095.

68. C. B. Harley, A. B. Futcher, and C. W. Greider, "Telomeres Shorten during Ageing of Human Fibroblasts," *Nature* 345 (1990); H. Vaziri et al., "Loss of Telomeric DNA during Aging of Normal and Trisomy 21 Human Lymphocytes," *American Journal of Human Genetics* 52 (1993).

69. A. Baumer et al., "Age-Related Human MtDNA Mutations: A Heterogeneous Set of Deletions Arising at a Single Pair of Directly Repeated Sequences," *American Journal of Human Genetics* 54 (1994); J. Tra et al., "Infrequent Occurrence of Age-Dependent Changes in CpG Island Methylation as Detected by Restriction Landmark Genome Scanning," *Mechanics of Ageing and Development* 123 (2002).

70. M. D. Shriver et al., "Ethnic Affiliation Estimation Using Population-Specific DNA Markers," *American Journal of Human Genetics* 60 (1997).

71. See www.ancestrybydna.com.

72. Matt Thomas, DNA Print Genomics, personal communication, April 16, 2003.

73. H. E. Collins-Schramm et al., "Ethnic-Difference Markers for Use in Mapping by Admixture Linkage Disequilibrium," *American Journal of Human Genetics* 70 (2002).

74. See H. C. Lee and C. Ladd, "Criminal Justice: An Unraveling of Trust?" *Public Perspective* 8 (1997): 6–7.

75. K. Axtman, "Bungles in Texas Crime Lab Stir Doubt over DNA," *Christian Science Monitor*, April 18, 2003; A. Bernstein, "Crime Lab Scandal Leaves Prosecutor Feeling Betrayed," *Houston Chronicle*, March 16, 2003.

76. See *McCarty v. State*, OK CR 271, 765 P.2d 1215 (1998).

77. See U.S. Department of Justice, Office of the Inspector General, *Special Report: The FBI Laboratory; An Investigation into Laboratory Practices and Alleged Misconduct in Explosives-Related and Other Cases* (Washington, D.C.: U.S. Department of Justice, 1997).

78. D. Boyd, "Crime Lab Subject of Criminal Investigation," *Fort Worth Star Telegram*, April 13, 2003.

79. J. Solomon, "Probe of F.B.I.'s DNA Lab Practices Widens," Associated Press, April 28, 2003.

80. R. Stutzman, "Judge Rips FDLE Silence in Lab Flap," *Orlando Sentinel*, August 3, 2002.

81. Lee and Ladd, "Criminal Justice"; F. R. Bieber and D. Lazer, "Lessons Learned from a Miscarriage of Justice," *Boston Globe*, April 12, 2003.

82. D. L. Duewer et al., "NIST Mixed Stain Studies #1 and #2: Interlaboratory Comparison of DNA Quantification Practice and Short Tandem Repeat Multiplex Performance with Multiple-Source Samples," *Journal of Forensic Science* 46 (2001): 1199–1210; Word, Sawosik, and Bing, "Summary of Validation Studies from Twenty-Six Laboratories"; B. E. Krenke et al., "Validation of a 16-Locus Fluorescent Multiplex System," *Journal of Forensic Science* 47, no. 4 (2002); N. Fildes and R. Reynolds, "Consistency and Reproducibility of AmpliType PM Results between Seven Laboratories: Field Trial Results," *Journal of Forensic Science* 40 (1995): 279–286.

83. National Research Council, Committee on DNA Technology in Forensic Science, *DNA Technology in Forensic Science*; National Research Council, Committee on DNA Technology in Forensic Science: An Update, *The Evaluation of Forensic DNA Evidence*.

84. See Technical Working Group on DNA Analysis Methods (TWGDAM), "Guidelines for a Quality Assurance Program for DNA Analysis," *Federal Bureau of Investigation Crime Laboratory Digest* 22 (1995): 21–50; Federal Bureau of Investigation, "State DNA Database Laws." Federal Bureau of Investigation, DNA Advisory Board, "Quality Assurance Standards for Forensic DNA Testing Laboratories" (Washington, D.C.: U.S. Department of Justice, 1998); Federal Bureau of Investigation, DNA Advisory Board, "Quality Assurance Standards for Convicted Offender DNA Databasing Laboratories"; Federal Bureau of Investigation, DNA Advisory Board, "Statistical and Population Genetics Issues," available at www.fbi.gov.

85. See Word, Sawosik, and Bing, "Summary of Validation Studies from Twenty-Six Laboratories."

86. SWGDAM, "Short Tandem Repeat (STR) Interpretation Guidelines," *Forensic Science Communications* 2, no. 3 (2003); "Training Guidelines for Forensic Laboratories," *Forensic Science Communications* 3, no. 4 (2001).

87. D. H. Bing and F. R. Bieber, "RFLP Analysis of Forensic DNA Samples with Single-Locus VNTR Genetic Markers," *Current Protocols in Human Genetics*, unit 14.5 (1998); "Manual Methods for PCR-Based Forensic DNA Analysis."

88. R. W. Cotton, L. Forman, and C. J. Word, "Research on DNA Typing Validated in the Literature," *American Journal of Human Genetics* 49 (1991): 898–899; Budowle et al., "Analysis of the Variable Number of Tandem Repeats Locus D1S80"; E. S. Lander and B. Budowle, "DNA Fingerprinting Dispute Laid to Rest," *Nature* 371 (1994): 735–738; B. Budowle et al., "Validation and Population Studies of the Loci LDLR, GYPA, HBGG, D7S8, and Gc (PM Loci), and HLA-DQα Using a Multiplex Amplification and Typing Procedure," *Journal of Forensic Science* 40, no. 1 (1995): 45–54; J. M. Wallin et al., "TWGDAM Validation of the AmpFlSTR Blue PCR Amplification Kit for Forensic Casework Analysis," *Journal of Forensic Science* 43, no. 3 (1998): 66–96.

89. National Research Council, Committee on DNA Technology in Forensic Science, *DNA Technology in Forensic Science*; National Research Council, Committee on DNA Technology in Forensic Science: An Update, *The Evaluation of Forensic DNA Evidence*.

90. E. S. Lander, "DNA Fingerprinting on Trial," *Nature* 339 (1989): 501–505; I. W. Evett and P. Gill, "A Discussion of the Robustness of Methods for Assessing the Evidential Value of DNA Single Locus Profiles in Crime Investigations," *Electrophoresis* 12 (1991): 226–230; Gill et al., "Databases, Quality Control and Interpretation of DNA Profiling"; A. Edwards et al., "Genetic Variation at Five Trimeric and Tetrameric Tandem Repeat Loci in Four Human Population Groups," *Genomics* 12 (1992): 241–253; R. C. Lewontin, "Which Population?" (letter), *American Journal of Human Genetics* 52 (1993): 205; Richards et al., "Multiplex PCR Amplification"; Neeser and Liechti-Gallati, "Sex Determination of Forensic Samples"; I. W. Evett et al., "Establishing the Robustness of Short-Tandem-Repeat Statistics for the Forensic Applications," *American Journal of Human Genetics* 58 (1996): 398–407; Micka et al., "Validation of Multiplex Polymorphic STR Amplification Sets"; P. Gill, "Role of Short Tandem Repeat DNA in Forensic Casework in the UK—Past, Present, and Future Perspectives," *BioTechniques* 32 (2002): 366–368.

91. H. C. Lee et al., "Guidelines for the Collection and Preservation of DNA Evidence" (Washington, D.C.: U.S. Department of Justice, 1993); H. C. Lee et al., "Forensic Applications of DNA Typing, Collection and Preservation of DNA Evidence," *American Journal of Forensic Medicine and Pathology* 19 (1998); Lee, Palmbach, and Miller, *Henry Lee's Crime Scene Handbook*; Federal Bureau of Investigation, DNA Advisory Board, "Quality Assurance Standards for Convicted Offender DNA Databasing Laboratories"; C. A. Scherczinger et al., "A Systematic Analysis of PCR Contamination," *Journal of Forensic Sciences* 44 (1999): 1270–1272; T. Toledano et al., "An Assessment of DNA Contamination Risks in New York City Medical Examiner Facilities," *Journal of Forensic Science* 42, no. 4 (1997): 721–724.

92. SWGDAM, "Short Tandem Repeat (STR) Interpretation Guidelines"; "Training Guidelines."

93. National Research Council, Committee on DNA Technology in Forensic Science: An Update, *The Evaluation of Forensic DNA Evidence*; Federal Bureau of Investigation, DNA Advisory Board, "Quality Assurance Standards for Convicted Offender DNA Databasing Laboratories."

94. Federal Bureau of Investigation, DNA Advisory Board, "Quality Assurance Standards for Forensic DNA Testing Laboratories."

95. SWGDAM, "Training Guidelines."

96. M. T. Bourke et al., "Sib Pair Identity at Multiple STR Loci: Implications for Interpretation of Forensic DNA Casework" (paper presented at the American Academy of Forensic Sciences annual meeting, Reno, Nev., February 6, 2000); Ladd et al., "Interpretation of Complex Forensic DNA Mixtures."

97. C. Ladd et al., "A Systematic Analysis of Secondary DNA Transfer," *Journal of Forensic Sciences* 44 (1999): 1270–1272.

98. See http://path.upmc.edu/cpi/ab-cap2.htm.

99. See www.mrc.ac.uk.

100. See www.dna.com.

101. N. Weil, "IT Is Pushing Medical Care to a New Era, IBM Exec Says," *InfoWorld*, March 26, 2003.

102. C. Dyer, "Use of Confidential HIV Data Helps Convict Former Prisoner," *British Medical Journal* 322 (March 17, 2001): 633; S. M. Bird and A. J. L. Brown, "Criminalisation of HIV Transmission: Implications for Public Health in Scotland," *British Medical Journal* 323 (November 17, 2001): 1174–1177.

103. Gill et al., "Databases, Quality Control and Interpretation of DNA Profiling"; J. E. McEwen and P. R. Reilly, "A Review of State Legislation on DNA Forensic Data Banking," *American Journal of Human Genetics* 54 (1994): 941–958; J. McEwen, "Forensic DNA Data Banking by State Crime Laboratories," *American Journal of Human Genetics* 56 (1995): 1487–1492.

104. Child Trace International, Inc., offers, for a "suggested donation" of $15, a LifePrint DNA Management Kit containing an "FBI compatible" applicator swab used to transfer a buccal mucosa sample for storage at home. See www.yeswi.org/dna.html.

105. See Wambaugh, *The Blooding*.

106. Federal Bureau of Investigation, "State DNA Database Laws."

107. McEwen and Reilly, "A Review of State Legislation;" Scheck, "DNA Data Banking"; McEwen, "Forensic DNA Data Banking."

108. 744 N.E.2d 437; 2001 Ind. LEXIS 273 (1998).

109. U.S. District Judge William B. Shubb found in that case that forcing probationers to submit blood for entry into CODIS violates the Fourth Amendment's prohibition of "suspicionless" searches. He wrote, "Because the act authorizes suspicionless searches primarily for general law enforcement purposes, it is unconstitutional." A challenge to the California CODIS statute was brought by the federal defender's office on behalf of Danny Miles, age fifty-three, who was on parole after conviction of armed bank robbery in 1974. The court ruled that "after three decades, the government would not be able to use that offense as justification for invading his bodily integrity and obtaining his identifying information without some individualized suspicion of criminal wrongdoing." D. Walsh, "Judge Rejects Forced DNA Tests on Probationers," *Sacramento Bee*, November 7, 2002.

110. Bourke et al., "Sib Pair Identity at Multiple STR Loci."

111. C. Tomsey, personal communication, April 16, 2003.

112. D. Coffman, personal communication, April 16, 2003.

113. See Brenner and Weir, "Issues and Strategies."

114. Huffine et al., "Mass Identification of Persons Missing"; Bieber, "Reckoning with the Dead."

115. See Kayser et al., "Online Y-Chromosome."

116. F. Bieber, "Forensic Genetics: Challenges and Opportunities Ahead" (paper presented at FBI International Symposium on Setting Quality Standards for the Forensic Community, San Antonio, Tex., May 3–7, 1999, available at www.fbi.gov/programs/lab/fsc; *Forensic Science Communications* 1, no. 2 [July 1999]).

117. Collins-Schramm et al., "Ethnic-Difference Markers."

118. See National Institute of Justice, *Report to the Attorney General on Delays in Forensic DNA Analysis* (Washington, D.C.: U.S. Department of Justice, 2003).

119. Lisa Kahn, personal communication, February 10, 2003.

4

Fingerprint Identification and the Criminal Justice System: Historical Lessons for the DNA Debate

Simon A. Cole

There is a great deal of debate these days about the impact of the newest identification technology, DNA typing, on the criminal justice system. The introduction and rapid diffusion of this powerful technique over the past two decades or so has raised a host of important questions:

- How accurate, discriminating, and reliable is DNA, and how do we measure these attributes?
- How do we police the application of DNA typing to minimize errors?
- How inclusive should DNA databases be?
- What kind of threat do they pose to individual privacy and to civil liberties?
- What is the relationship between the criminal justice application of DNA typing and other applications in areas like health care, immigration control, and scientific research?
- Do genetic databases raise the specter of a resurgence of eugenics?

Although there has been extensive debate over many of these issues for at least a decade now, much of this debate has been—and still is—conducted as if these issues have been raised anew by DNA typing. In fact, biometric systems of criminal identification have been with us for more than a century and half. Although other identification technologies are important, I am chiefly referring here to fingerprint identification, which has reigned as the world's dominant method of criminal identification since around the 1920s. Many of the most urgent issues now being debated with reference to DNA have been debated before with reference to fingerprinting. Indeed, our current discourse over DNA typing in many ways uncannily echoes the discourse in the early twentieth century, when fingerprinting was a powerful new criminal identification technology sweeping the world. To the extent that our historical experience with fingerprint identification has been cited in the

DNA debate, it has largely been based on a superficial, and largely mythical, understanding of the history of fingerprinting. The current debate will be better informed if we dig a bit more deeply into our past experiences with other biometric technologies of criminal identification.

A Brief History of Criminal Identification

To assess the impact of criminal identification databases on criminal justice systems, it is first necessary to have some understanding of why biometric criminal identification databases were built in the first place. Contrary to the popular image of fingerprinting as a tool for forensic investigation, fingerprint identification was developed for purposes of criminal record keeping, rather than forensics. Specifically, fingerprinting was developed to facilitate the storage and retrieval of criminal histories by the state.

The impetus behind the development of biometric criminal identification technologies in the late nineteenth century was complex, including such factors as rapid urbanization; the increasing anonymity of urban life, and the dissolving of local networks of familiarity in which individuals were "known" by their neighbors; growing migration of individuals from city to city, country to country, and continent to continent; and the necessity of governing imperial possessions populated by large numbers of people whom it was necessary to monitor, control, and identify. Perhaps most important, however, was the shift in the philosophy of punishment, documented most famously by the French historian Michel Foucault, from classical to reformist jurisprudence.[1] Under classical jurisprudence, punishments were meted out in strict proportion to the severity of the crime of which the offender had been convicted. Criminal histories were largely irrelevant under classical jurisprudence: A robbery was punished the same whether it was the offender's first or his fifth. Reformist jurisprudence, in contrast, sought to tailor punishment to the character of the offender. Under reformist jurisprudence, therefore, a criminal history was desirable—crucial, even—because it enabled the state to draw sharp distinctions between first-time offenders and what were variously known as "habitual criminals," "incorrigibles," "repeat offenders," or "recidivists," a term coined in both English and French in the late nineteenth century.

Attempts to retrieve criminal histories filed according to names could be evaded by the simple expedient of adopting an alias. Beginning in the 1880s, two new technologies emerged that promised to solve the problem of aliases by linking criminal records not to names, but to some representation of the criminal's body. Such a system required that criminal records be filed according to some bodily property rather than by name. One of these systems, fingerprinting, is familiar to us today. The other, anthropometry—the measurement of the human body—has largely been forgotten. Nonetheless, the two systems battled for dominance until well into the 1920s.

The chief architect of anthropometric identification was Alphonse Bertillon, an official at the Paris police prefecture. Bertillon's father was a demographer, and Alphonse was familiar with anthropometry as a social scientific tool. In Bertillon's system, developed during the 1880s, eleven anthropometric measurements were taken using specially calibrated calipers and rulers, and the results were recorded on a printed card. Based on empirical data, Bertillon devised three equally populated categories for each measurement: small, medium, and large. Cards were filed according to which category they fell into for all eleven measurements. Faced with a suspect, Bertillon's operators could record all eleven measurements and search the existing criminal records for a card containing very similar measurements. If operators suspected a match, they confirmed it by reference to "peculiar marks," such as birthmarks, scars, and tattoos. The dimensions, locations, orientations, and descriptions of these peculiar marks were also recorded on the Bertillon card.

Though it sounds cumbersome to our ears, by contemporary accounts, the system was extraordinarily effective. Bertillon awed visitors to the Paris police department with his ability to retrieve matching cards in minutes from a vast archive containing tens of thousands of criminal records. Meanwhile, government bureaucrats in colonial India, Japan, and the United States were experimenting with using inked impressions of the papillary ridges on the tip of the finger for the *less* challenging task of *authenticating* identity—that is, of verifying that an individual was indeed who he claimed to be. The use of fingerprints for indexing criminal records, however, was stymied by the lack of a system for filing identification cards according to fingerprint patterns. By the 1890s, anthropometric identification was rapidly being adopted by prisons and police departments worldwide.

Today, of course, anthropometric identification, with its meticulous skull measurements and attention to body size, evokes the pseudosciences of phrenology, craniometry, and somatotyping and their contributions to racist science. What is less known, however, is that both identification systems—fingerprinting as well as anthropometry—were closely tied to biologically determinist efforts to find bodily markers of character traits like intelligence and criminality. Cesare Lombroso, the founder of criminal anthropology, a discipline that purported to read signs of criminality in skull sizes and shapes, facial features, and body types, called the Bertillon system "an ark of salvation" for the nascent field, although Bertillon himself maintained an agnostic stance toward the use of anthropometric data to diagnose criminal propensity.[2] And though it is now largely forgotten, a thriving research program that began in the 1890s and has extended (albeit in greatly diminished and increasingly marginalized form) through the present day seeks to correlate fingerprint pattern types with race, ethnicity, and character traits, such as insanity and criminality.

To the late-nineteenth-century scientific mind, it seemed obvious that fingerprint patterns were probably inherited and therefore should correlate with race, ethnicity, disease propensity, abilities, and various behavioral characteristics. Indeed, one of the pioneers of the modern system of fingerprint identification was Sir Francis Galton, who is better known as the statistician who founded the "eugenics" movement (and coined the term). The convergence of fingerprinting and eugenics in the person of Galton is often treated as a mere coincidence, but in fact Galton's ideas about eugenics were closely bound up in the development of criminal identification.[3] Indeed, Galton's chief contribution to the development of the fingerprint system— his tripartite classification scheme for sorting all fingerprint patterns into three groups: arches, loops, and whorls—was devised chiefly for the purpose of using fingerprint patterns as bodily markers of heredity and character.

In his landmark book *Finger Prints*, Galton published a study of the frequency with which these three pattern types appeared among various races. He was disappointed, however, to find almost no significant variations, other than slightly fewer arches among Jews.[4] This was what the anthropologist Paul Rabinow has called "Galton's regret" in his provocative essay of that title.[5] Despite Galton's regret, however, a scientific research program arose beginning in the 1890s that *did* attach biological significance to Galton's three pattern types. In 1892, the same year Galton published his results, the French medico-legalist René Forgeot found an overrepresentation of arch patterns among prisoners at the Bologne penal colony.[6] The following year, the French psychiatrist Charles Féré found more arches among both epileptics (epilepsy was thought to be a manifestation of evolutionary "degeneration," which also caused madness, disease, and criminality) and monkeys.[7] Similarly, David Hepburn, an Irish anthropologist, found more loops and whorls among "higher" primate species like chimpanzees and orangutans than in the "lower" monkeys.[8] "Degeneration theory," a gloss on human evolution fashionable at the time, explained these results intuitively: The arch was the simplest pattern and therefore the least evolved.[9] However, there was also a rival school of thought. In the United States, the Smith College anatomist Harris Wilder and his assistant (and later wife) Inez Whipple argued that the arch was the *most* evolved pattern because it was *least* functional as a tread for swinging from tree branches. Thus, the arch denoted the greatest distance from our primate ancestors.[10]

This sort of research continued well into the 1920s. In Galton's laboratory, researchers studied the inheritance of fingerprint patterns.[11] Other researchers measured the frequency with which pattern types appeared in different ethnic groups.[12] The most ambitious study of this kind, published by the Norwegian biologist Kristine Bonnevie in 1924, found that Asians had a higher proportion of whorls, and fewer arches, than Europeans.[13] In 1922, the *New York Times* reported that a German professor, Heinrich Poll, predicted that life insurance companies would soon be able to "tell from finger prints what will be the insured's career."[14] This type of research never died out completely. The most recent publication claiming to be able to diagnose criminality from fingerprint pattern types dates from 1991.[15]

In short, the discourse surrounding fingerprinting in the early part of this century was strikingly similar to the discourse surrounding DNA today. It was widely assumed that pattern types appeared with different frequencies among different racial and ethnic populations, that heredity could be traced using fingerprint patterns (there was even the occasional paternity case in which fingerprint patterns were introduced as evidence), and that fingerprint patterns contained information that would soon be able to predict individuals' propensity for certain diseases and even their behavioral characteristics, including criminal propensity.[16]

Paradoxically, Galton's fingerprint research had a much greater impact in an area, criminal record keeping, that he would have viewed as far less important than hereditary research. Galton's tripartite division of fingerprint patterns into arches, loops, and whorls provided the foundation for the creation of a system for using fingerprint patterns to index criminal records in a manner similar to Bertillon's system based on measurements. The earliest workable fingerprint classification systems were developed almost simultaneously during the mid-1890s by Juan Vucetich, a police official in La Plata, Argentina, and Edward Henry, Azizul Haque, and Chandra Bose of the British colonial police in the Bengal province of India. The crucial inventive steps consisted of extending Galton's tripartite classification system by subdividing loops by means of "ridge counting" (measuring the number of intervening ridges between the "delta," the point at which the transverse ridges separated to flow around the central pattern, and the center of the print) and whorls by means of "ridge tracing" (following a ridge from the delta and determining whether it passed inside or outside the center of the print). In this way, loops and whorls could be assigned to subcategories. By classifying each individual according to the pattern types and subtypes on *all ten fingers*, fingerprint classifiers could, like Bertillon operators, sort even very large collections of identification cards into relatively small groups. Examiners could classify the fingerprints of an unknown suspect and refer to a small number of potentially matching cards. They could then determine whether all the detail between the two sets of fingerprints was consistent.

The two rival fingerprint classification systems, the Argentine "Vucetich system" and the British Indian "Henry system," diffused during the 1900s and began to compete with anthropometric identification systems. Although it seems counterintuitive to us today, the prevailing wisdom at the time held that anthropometry was the scientifically superior system because it had a basis in mainstream academic sciences (anthropology and ethnology). The chief advantages of fingerprinting were practical: It was cheaper and faster than anthropometry, and crucially, the *recording* of data—the taking of inked finger impressions—required only minimal training. (The *filing* of fingerprint patterns still required substantial training in the arcana of Vucetich's or Henry's rules of classification.) The quality and consistency of anthropometric data, in contrast, depended greatly on the diligence with which operators adhered to specified procedures for taking measurements. Obtaining consistent measurements required thorough training, supervision, and disciplining of operators.

Contrary to what we might think today, the potential forensic application of fingerprinting exerted only minimal influence over identification bureau chiefs choosing between fingerprinting and anthropometry. Bloody or "latent" fingerprints (invisible finger impressions made visible by "dusting" with powder) had been used to investigate crimes as early as 1892 in Argentina, 1897 in India, and 1903 in Britain (as well as, forgotten to history, in the late 1850s in Albany, New York). Although these cases did attract some favorable publicity for fingerprinting, they did not necessarily convince identification bureau chiefs to discard their anthropometric identification files. Identification bureaus could stick with anthropometric identification systems and still use fingerprinting for forensic investigation, as Bertillon himself did in a 1902 murder case. Fingerprints could be used as a check on anthropometric identification, and space for fingerprints was added to the bottom of anthropometric identification cards, even in France. The Bertillon system, meanwhile, had its own bonus application that could assist in the investigation of crime: the *portrait parlé*, or "spoken likeness," a system of codes, suitable for transmission via telegraph, for describing the physical appearance of a suspect so that officials in another city could apprehend a suspect even without a photograph. Although it sounds fanciful to us today, at the time the *portrait parlé* was viewed as a crime-fighting tool equal in utility to latent fingerprint identification. In any case, identification bureau chiefs were more concerned with maintaining systems of criminal records that would expose recidivists and help remove them from society than with solving specific crimes.

Although there were rare reported cases in which fingerprint evidence exonerated someone who has been inculpated by other means, there was nothing analogous to the recent spate of postconviction exonerations generated by forensic DNA evidence (see chapter 6). One example was one of the earliest forensic fingerprint cases, the Rojas case in Argentina in 1892. The initial suspect in the murder of two young children in the village of Necochea was the mother's suitor, one Velasquez. Standard tactics, including torture and forcing Velasquez to sleep with the corpses, failed to elicit a confession. Only then did detectives, familiar with Vucetich's work with fingerprints, examine a bloody fingerprint found at the crime scene. This print matched not Velasquez, but the victims' mother, Francesca Rojas. Confronted with this evidence, Rojas confessed to the crime. Although Velasquez had not yet been convicted when the fingerprint evidence was discovered, one might reasonably infer that, as the prime suspect in the grisly murder of two young children, he would have been. At the same time, the bloody fingerprint did not definitively prove that Rojas committed the crime, as she might have touched the corpses postmortem.[17]

In early criminal trials, fingerprint classifiers were qualified to testify as experts in the analysis and interpretation of fingerprint patterns. They testified as to the identity of latent fingerprint impressions by matching "minutiae" or "Galton details" or "points of similarity"—generally ridge endings or bifurcations—between the latent print and the inked print of the suspect. Based on these similarities, they proffered testimony that the latent print and the suspect's inked print were "identical" and that it was a "fact" that they came from the same source finger, to the exclusion of all other fingerprints in the world.[18] This extraordinarily strong conclusion was justified on the basis that "there are no two fingerprints alike." This fundamentally unprovable assertion was in turn justified by reference to treatises in the field that declared it to be so and by the fact that identification bureaus had not yet discovered any identical fingerprint patterns on two different fingers. Occasional reference was also made to an unspecified law of nature that "nature never repeats" or to a statistical calculation by Galton that held that the probability of two different complete fingerprints being exactly alike was 1 in 64 billion.

None of these arguments shed much light on the validity or reliability of what it was these expert witnesses were claiming to be able to do: use similarities of detail between two fingerprint impressions to substantiate the conclusion that the two must come from a common source finger, to the exclusion of all other fingers in the world. This would have required some sort of measurement of how much corresponding detail warranted such a conclusion and of how accurate fingerprint experts were at making the interpretive decisions they claimed to make with absolute certainty. The arguments that no two fingers contained exactly identical papillary ridge formations begged the question of whether different fingers might contain areas of ridge detail similar enough that they might leave latent impressions that might give a fingerprint examiner a false impression of identicality. Forensic fingerprint identification's lone informed critic, the Scottish physician Henry Faulds, meanwhile, pointed out that identification bureaus' failure to find any identical fingerprints from two different fingers was hardly surprising considering that their records were filed according to the aggregate patterns on *all ten fingers*.[19]

Although in early cases some trial judges and some juries expressed skepticism about warranting a criminal conviction on the basis of a single fingerprint match (while expressing confidence in the system by which criminal histories were authenticated by reference to the full set of ten prints), case law worldwide quickly ratified the scientific nature of forensic fingerprint evidence and the legitimacy of fingerprint classifiers to testify as expert witness and to declare matches in terms of virtual certainty.[20] Neither the courts nor the defense bar imposed on fingerprint examiners the kind of demands that forensic DNA experts faced during the "DNA wars" of the late 1980s and 1990s (see chapter 5). Whereas DNA experts would later be required to verify their protocols through testing, fingerprint examiners were never asked to measure how accurately they could match latent fingerprint impressions with source fingers. Whereas two National Research Council panels would fiercely debate the niceties of the random-match probabilities that DNA experts should be allowed to use before juries, fingerprint examiners were permitted to eschew probabilities altogether and phrase forensic fingerprint matches as virtual certainties or "facts." Nonetheless, courts went on to ratify fingerprint identification as a science and as reliable evidence.[21] Eventually, American courts went so far as to reverse the burden of proof, demanding that the defense produce two identical fingerprints from different fingers, an impossible burden and one that was not necessary to support a defense argument that impressions from two different fingers might yet be similar *enough* to fool a fingerprint examiner.[22]

Although these legal decisions certainly helped boost fingerprinting's scientific credentials, they still did not tip the balance in favor of the fingerprint system. Thus for the first two decades of the twentieth century, most prison identification bureaus outside Argentina, India, and Britain (which were actively proselytizing fingerprinting) relied on anthropometry for the identification of felons. Fingerprint identification found other applications, such as *authenticating* the identity of military personnel, civil service applicants, or immigrants. Eventually, fingerprinting found a niche in police departments and courts charged with processing petty offenders, such as prostitutes, drunk-and-disorderlies, and vagrants. In these applications, the consequences of a potential error were less drastic, and the lower cost and greater speed of fingerprinting held great appeal.

The Will West case at the U.S. Penitentiary in Leavenworth, Kansas in 1903 has been touted by the FBI and by numerous popular and scholarly accounts as having dramatically demonstrated the superiority of fingerprinting to anthropometry. William and Will West were two African American convicts discovered at Leavenworth who supposedly coincided in their Bertillon measurements and possessed "a facial resemblance like that of twin brothers." Only when the identification clerks fingerprinted them were they able to tell them apart, thus exposing at once the fallibility of identification by name, photography, and anthropometry.[23] In fact, the Wests' anthropometric measurements did *not* match, and they were not fingerprinted either, at least not in 1903. They were fingerprinted sometime after that, and the dramatic story was concocted by fingerprint advocates to give fingerprinting an appealing creation myth. The transition from anthropometry to fingerprinting was a more gradual process, the racial dimensions of which are suggested by the construction of the Will West case around two supposedly indistinguishable African Americans.[24]

Only after the First World War did the eventual triumph of fingerprinting over anthropometry become assured. Fingerprinting upon arrest became standard procedure in law enforcement agencies large and small, and police departments' collections of fingerprint cards began to outstrip prisons' collection of Bertillon cards. Although early legal decisions split on the question of whether the recording of fingerprints upon arrest was constitutional, the weight of legal opinion eventually supported the practice. Courts also allowed law enforcement agencies to retain fingerprint records even when the individual was not convicted or even acquitted, except in cases of illegal arrests. Although the bulk of fingerprint collection took place at the local level, in 1924, the newly founded Federal Bureau of Investigation created an Identification Division, positioned as a national repository of fingerprint cards, although the original cards were still retained by local law enforcement agencies. At the same time, the FBI also established a civil fingerprint file that included the prints of civil servants and immigrants. Although there are specific federal statues that forbid the use in criminal investigations of fingerprints taken for immigration or motor vehicle purposes, courts have otherwise upheld the searching of civil fingerprint files for criminal investigations.[25]

Proponents of fingerprinting hoped to extend the civil use of fingerprinting even further, calling for "universal identification" of all citizens. As with DNA today,[26] identification entrepreneurs exploited parents' fears of kidnapping by offering, for a modest fee, to record their children's fingerprints in a private file.[27] As with DNA today, proponents of fingerprinting noted that a universal fingerprint database would enable the authorities to identify disaster victims. They cited the 1904 Slocum ship fire, the deadliest American maritime disaster of the twentieth century, much in the way that DNA proponents today cite the use of DNA to identify the victims of the crash of TWA Flight 800 and the bombings of the World Trade Center and Pentagon.[28] (A key difference, of course, is that by obtaining samples from family members, officials can use DNA to identify disaster victims even if the victim does not have a DNA sample on file in a database. Humanitarian use of fingerprints requires that the victim's fingerprints have previously been recorded and stored in a database unless an authenticated latent print can be recovered from the victim's home.)

In the 1930s, the FBI and a variety of conservative civic organization like the American Legion, the American Coalition, the Daughters of the American Revolution, the Merchants' Association, and various chambers of commerce got involved in the drive for universal fingerprinting. Local police departments and chambers of commerce jointly organized fingerprint drives to urge citizens to voluntarily submit their fingerprints. Hundreds of thousands of American citizens volunteered their—and their children's—fingerprints in these drives.[29]

Although a universal civilian identifier could have proven extremely useful in many applications, both criminal and civil, the stigma that the public already associated with fingerprinting—that being fingerprinted was tantamount to being treated like a criminal—and privacy and civil-liberties concerns conspired to doom the universal fingerprint movement. The movement's ultimate death can be dated to the period 1935–1943, during which three different bills proposing universal fingerprinting or attaching a fingerprint to the newly created social security card failed to pass Congress.[30]

Despite the FBI's enthusiasm for universal fingerprinting, it is unlikely that the FBI or anyone else really had the technical capability in the postwar period to actually handle a universal fingerprint database, even had there been the political will to create one. In fact, fingerprint databases were far from the omniscient surveillance systems early identification pioneers had hoped they would become. The panoptic power of fingerprint databases was limited by several factors: First, the Henry and Vucetich systems had multiplied into a profusion of different systems. Each nation—and in some countries each jurisdiction—had modified the Henry or Vucetich system slightly to accord with local preferences. Thus fingerprint classifications were not compatible across national and jurisdictional boundaries. An effort to search for a matching fingerprint record outside the local jurisdiction, therefore, required copying the fingerprint card and sending a separate copy to each neighboring agency. Efforts to develop universal telegraph codes for fingerprint patterns or to utilize facsimile technology to send fingerprint images to neighboring agencies foundered mainly on lack of cooperation between stubbornly local law enforcement agencies. Second, ten-print filing systems were of limited utility for searching latent prints, since cards were filed according to the aggregate patterns on *all ten fingers*. A manual search of a fingerprint database for a single latent print would therefore require multiple searches based on educated guesses about what finger the latent derived from and the pattern types on the absent nine digits. Numerous single-print filing systems devised to remedy this problem proved cumbersome and complicated. The problem of manually searching latent prints was exacerbated by the rapidly increasing size of fingerprint databases. The larger a fingerprint file grew, the more daunting the process of conducting a manual search. Thus for most of this century, fingerprint databases were useful primarily for determining whether a suspect had a criminal record locally. Inquiry could also be made to the FBI, but the response time was slow: usually a matter of weeks. Latent-print analysis was useful primarily when a suspect or a set of suspects had been selected by other means and their prints could be compared to the latent. Cracking of crimes solely through latent-fingerprint evidence was relatively rare.

Only with the advent of computerized fingerprint identification has routine searching of unidentified latent prints and instantaneous national searching become realistic. Data-processing technology was used to sort fingerprint cards as early as the 1940s, and research into computer imaging of fingerprints began in the 1960s. During the 1970s the FBI developed an automated search-and-retrieval system. Not until the mid-1980s, however, were Automated Fingerprint Identification Systems (AFIS) mature enough for local law enforcement agencies to begin investing in them. Instead of using ink, AFIS record prints using an optical scanner and store them as digital images. Technicians can enter an unidentified latent print into AFIS, and the systems will search their files and produce a list of candidate matches. A trained examiner then compares the latent with the candidates and determines whether any of them warrants a conclusion of identity. AFIS are good at winnowing a large database into a small number of likely candidates, but relatively poor at choosing the matching print: the "true" match is often *not* ranked first.

Optical scanning, digital storage, and computerized search and retrieval now give fingerprinting the potential to at last live up to its popular image, in which crime scene technicians can routinely solve crimes lacking suspects by searching latent prints against a large database. Such matches, called "cold hits," provided anecdotal justification for the procurement of AFIS. Thus the investigative application of fingerprint technology is just now beginning to catch up to the archival application. This development has already prompted calls to further extend the scope of fingerprint databases. The logic was exemplified by New York City's campaign against "quality of life" offenses. By arresting, booking, and fingerprinting offenders who would previously have been released with a warning or a court date, the New York Police Department (NYPD) intentionally sought to get as many potential offenders "into the system" as possible. The argument was that quality-of-life offenders were the same individuals that commit more serious crimes. This argument was borne out anecdotally in the John Royster case, in which the NYPD cracked a string of linked rapes and a homicide by entering a latent print found at the homicide scene into their AFIS. The print matched a stored print taken from a man named John Royster on the occasion of an arrest for subway fare evasion.[31] The case seemed to reverse the principle that had long held for fingerprint databases: The larger the database, the more difficult it was to search it. Now, with searches dependent on computer processing power rather than more costly human resources, the larger the database, the greater the chance of success. It appears that this logic is being borne out by "cold-case squads" that, using AFIS, are now able to search unidentified latent prints against much larger databases (such as the FBI's) than they were originally searched against. In Los Angeles this recently led to the arrest of a man for the killing of a police officer based on forty-five-year-old unidentified latent prints.[32]

Digitization also holds great promise for networking disparate local databases into a single national or international database, a long-deferred dream of identification advocates. At present, this effort has been hindered by incompatibilities among vendors of different AFIS, but the FBI and the National Institute of Standards and Technology are developing a universal standard for exchanging fingerprint information. The recent sniper case in the Washington, D.C., area, in which it took weeks for the unidentified latent print from a *murder* scene—which eventually helped hone in on a suspect in the sniper murders—to be run against the FBI database, demonstrates that we still do not have a seamless national fingerprint system.[33] This technology, combined with fingerprint-scanning devices located in police cars and wirelessly linked to a networked database, has the potential to turn the fingerprint system into the kind of omniscient global surveillance network envisioned by identification pioneers nearly a century ago (and warned of three decades ago in Ira Levin's dystopian novel *The Perfect Day*).[34] This vision is now achievable. Whether it is desirable is the subject of the remainder of this chapter.

Lesson of the Past No. 1: Eugenics

One of the most frequent objections raised to DNA databases is the threat of eugenics. The eugenics argument is based on what George Annas calls "genetic exceptionalism": distinguishing genetic identification from supposedly harmless biometric identification technologies like fingerprinting (see chapter 7). The argument is that genes, unlike fingerprint patterns, contain information about individuals' racial and ethnic heritage, disease susceptibility, and even behavioral propensities. In chapter 9, Barry Steinhardt sums up this argument most clearly:

Let me start with a point that I hope we can all agree on. Drawing a DNA sample is simply not the same as taking a fingerprint. Fingerprints are two-dimensional representations of the physical attributes of our fingertips. They are useful *only as a form of identification*. DNA profiling may be used for identification purposes, but the DNA itself represents far more than a fingerprint. Indeed, it trivializes DNA data banking to call it a genetic fingerprint.[35]

Steinhardt and other opponents of DNA databases argue that DNA samples contain sensitive information about race, ethnicity, paternity, disease susceptibility, and possibly behavioral propensities that might be (indeed, inevitably *will* be) abused in a number of ways (chapter 14, for example, echoes these concerns).

Insurance companies, employers, or other government agencies might raid the data for health-related information, leading to genetic discrimination against individuals or groups. Behavioral researchers will not be able to resist a database of convicted criminals, and most states' current laws do not bar them from accessing this data. Shoddy researchers may easily turn the skewed racial composition of our prisons into supposedly "scientific" evidence of links between crime and race. Most ominously of all, state-controlled DNA databases give the state the means to quickly identify members of racial or ethnic groups or individuals with certain diseases or possibly behavioral propensities. A genetic database in the hands of the Nazis, it is argued, would have made the Holocaust easier to execute.

In contrast, Amitai Etzioni responds in chapter 10 that the threat of eugenics is political, not technological, and that our best defense against a eugenic state is to strengthen democratic institutions, rather than to ban technologies with *potential* eugenic applications. Although I do not share Etzioni's easy confidence in the ability of American democratic institutions to resist eugenic impulses—and history suggests as well that they lack this ability[36]—Steinhardt's well-intentioned critique mistakenly locates the threat of eugenics in technology, rather than in ideology. As I described earlier in the chapter, the assumption that fingerprint patterns do not contain information that could be used for eugenic purposes is the product of a superficial understanding of history, based primarily on Rabinow's essay "Galton's Regret," which took on great significance because it represented the historical contribution to one of the earliest volumes that attempted to wrestle with the ethical and policy issues surrounding genetic identification, Paul Billings's *DNA on Trial*.[37]

Rabinow took Galton's failure to find convincing correlations between fingerprint patterns and race (a failure not shared by his colleagues in France, Germany, Ireland, and the United States) to mean that fingerprint patterns do not *in fact* correlate with race, disease, or behavioral propensity. Fingerprint patterns, he asserts, "tell us nothing about individual character or group affiliation."[38] In fact, the most recent studies have confirmed that racial and ethnic patterns in the distribution of fingerprint pattern types do exist, and they are just as Bonnevie described in 1924: more whorls among Asians.[39] Similarly, a 1982 article in a reputable scientific journal concludes that fingerprint patterns are indeed to some extent inherited.[40] As for behavioral propensities, the search continues: As recently as 1994, another reputable scientific journal published a study correlating certain fingerprint pattern types with homosexuality.[41] This research is questionable, of course, but no more so than the genetic research on homosexuality.

Rather than concluding that it is not possible to correlate fingerprint patterns with race, ethnicity, disease, or behavior, it would be more accurate to say that the scientific research program that sought to do so did not thrive. The reasons for the decline of the diagnostic fingerprint research program can be found in history, not in nature. First, biologists found new biological markers to examine, including, of course, the gene, which was rediscovered around 1900. Second, law enforcement officials, who became an increasingly dominant force within the community of people interested in fingerprints, found it more convenient to treat fingerprint patterns as meaningless information. This kept the identification process focused solely on individuals and uncluttered with distracting theories about whether race, inheritance, or criminal propensity might also be legible in fingerprint patterns. The law enforcement officials who dominated the fingerprint community after the First World War had an interest in erasing the history of diagnostic fingerprint research and muting discussion of the issue. By transforming fingerprint patterns from potentially significant biological markers into merely individualizing information, "used only for identification," law enforcement officials bestowed a "purity" or "neutrality" on fingerprint identification that augmented its credibility as an identification technique among both the general public and the courts. Thus diagnostic research into fingerprint patterns was marginalized from both sides. Had even a fraction of the scientific resources devoted to researching links between *genes* and disease, race, and behavior been devoted to researching links between fingerprint patterns and disease, race, and behavior, the latter might seem as significant to us as the former. The conception of fingerprints as useful only for identification is not a natural fact but a historical achievement.

I share the concerns about the potential resurgence of eugenics in the genetic age. Garland Allen clearly shows in chapter 13 that the media and a few misguided or unscrupulous researchers are laying the groundwork for the gene to become the latest biological marker to be enlisted in the eugenic program, despite the protests of most geneticists. I do believe, however, that a careful reading of the history of eugenics makes it clear that eugenics is an ideological, not a technological, phenomenon.[42] The pernicious aspect of eugenics is the stubborn belief that complex phenomena like race, health, behavior, and ability can be explained by looking at biological markers. The choice of biological marker—whether skull size or shape, fingerprint pattern, or a gene—is less important than the irrational faith that is invested in it. The correlations between biological marker and race, disease, or behavior do not need to be "real" to be viewed as significant by large numbers of otherwise intelligent people. In fact, it matters little whether they are real or not. This, after all, is the lesson of the craniometry episode, related famously by Stephen Jay Gould.[43] Similarly Troy Duster demonstrates in chapter 14 how easily genetic *markers* can be conflated with genetic *causes* of race, disease, or behavioral traits. The lesson to be learned from fingerprint identification is not that some biological markers keep us safe from eugenics and others are dangerous, but rather that society can attribute a bogus significance to any biological marker if it chooses to do so. Thus DNA is not any more dangerous than fingerprinting because the correlation of a single gene with Huntington's disease is "real." What is dangerous is allowing—and indeed encouraging—people to make the leap from Huntington's to more complex phenomena like schizophrenia, homosexuality, or criminality. Media speculation about genetic causes of such slippery phenomena as shyness, aggressiveness, thrill seeking, altruism, alcoholism, intelligence, and sexual orientation has drowned out the cautions of professional geneticists that single genes are unlikely to be the cause of any of these behavioral characteristics, or even of very many diseases. More voices need to be added to the few (such as Allen in chapter 13) that are trying to defuse the media hype surrounding genetics.[44] Whereas civil libertarians worry that equating DNA to fingerprints "trivializes" DNA, I worry that genetic exceptionalism dangerously *exaggerates* the causal power of DNA. The libertarian opposition to DNA databases inadvertently fuels the hype surrounding DNA, lending credence to simplistic assumptions (which these same critics abhor) that genes determine race, disease propensity, and even behavioral characteristics.

In short, I would argue that the principal contribution of genetics to a resurgence of eugenics remains metaphorical, rather than technological. The threat is less that government officials will actually be able to use genetic databases to weed potential lawbreakers out of the population, or target racial minorities in the effort to do so, than that the gene's enormous cultural resonance will serve as a powerful metaphor for convincing a gullible public that complex social behaviors like criminality have biological causes. The amply documented history of what Nicole Rafter calls "eugenic criminology" in this country and in Europe gives some indication of what comes next: the stigmatization of individuals with criminal records as "born criminals," the lifetime warehousing of them as irredeemable, involuntary sterilization, and the fueling of racial and ethnic prejudice (see chapter 13).[45] Our best defense against this kind of future remains defusing the cultural power of the gene to fuel the resurgence of simplistic biological determinism, rather than principled opposition to the technology of genetic identification.

Lesson of the Past No. 2: Ensuring the Reliability of Forensic Evidence

The overhasty anointing of forensic fingerprint identification as reliable evidence deterred all relevant actors from scrutinizing fingerprint evidence. Aside from a handful, "hard" scientists, like anatomists, statisticians, and forensic scientists with biological and mathematical training, did not view fingerprinting as a sexy research problem. Judges relied on a chain of citations, founded on the faulty logic that demonstrating that there are no two fingerprint patterns exactly alike establishes the reliability of forensic fingerprint identification, that expressed no doubt about the absolute reliability of fingerprint evidence. The practices of the defense bar are more difficult to gauge, but anecdotal evidence suggests that defense attorneys treated fingerprints unassailable evidence that did not merit the expenditure of scarce resources.[46] Fingerprint examiners themselves, by their own admission, ceased all research into the foundations of their science.[47] The result was that the criminal justice system as a whole treated forensic fingerprint evidence as a black box whose outputs were scientific, unassailable, unproblematic, and error free. Forensic fingerprint identification evolved into a practice wholly in the capture of law enforcement agencies—there were virtually no fingerprint experts who were not present or former employees of law enforcement or other government agencies, like the military—entirely lacking external oversight, regulation, quality control, or proficiency testing. Fingerprint examiners were left in the position of having their opinions treated as gospel. Perhaps the most damning anecdotal evidence that the adversarial system was not up to the task of testing fingerprint examiners' conclusions was the New York state trooper evidence-tampering scandal of the 1990s, in which five state troopers pled guilty to fabricating fingerprint evidence in around forty cases over eight years, securing numerous criminal convictions, including homicide convictions. Despite the fact that many of these fabrications were crude and easily detectable, in none of these cases did the defense even hire a defense expert or challenge the fingerprint evidence.[48]

When forensic fingerprint evidence was put under intensified scrutiny by the defense bar in the late 1990s, serious problems were exposed. Fingerprint evidence was implicated in several cases of false conviction.[49] Proficiency testing of latent print examiners revealed shockingly high error rates.[50] And the lack of any scientific measurement of the accuracy of forensic fingerprint identification suggested that forensic fingerprint evidence might fail to meet the Supreme Court's standards for scientific and technical evidence.[51] If nothing else, these developments revealed the blasé and gullible attitude that the criminal justice system had adopted toward fingerprint evidence.

As the "DNA wars" subside, we need to guard against treating forensic DNA evidence with the same complacence with which forensic fingerprint evidence was treated for most of the last century. In particular, we should be concerned about allowing law enforcement to monopolize expertise in the area of forensic DNA typing. Serious consideration should also be given to removing forensic scientists from the employ of law enforcement agencies or finding other ways of combating conscious and unconscious pro-prosecution bias; to providing for external oversight, regulation, and proficiency testing of forensic laboratories; and to providing resources to defense counsel for truly independent evaluations of forensic evidence and the scientific foundation of forensic techniques.[52] Again, history teaches that no forensic technique is foolproof or error free. Indeed, if ever there was a technique that claimed to be foolproof, it was fingerprint evidence. Recent history demonstrates that DNA evidence, like other types of forensic evidence, is subject to laboratory error, pro-prosecution bias, and overstatement of the scientific certainty of conclusions.[53] Precautions should be taken to ensure that forensic DNA evidence receives ongoing scrutiny from the courts, the defense bar, and the scientific community and is not turned into a black box whose conclusions are treated as unassailable, error-free gospel.

Lesson of the Past No. 3: Breadth of Databases

Perhaps the most pressing question about the future of genetic identification is how broadly databases will, or should, expand. Should genetic criminal identification databases be restricted to violent felons, to felons, or to everyone convicted of a crime, no matter how petty? Should DNA samples be taken upon arrest or indictment? Should these samples be retained by the police, even in cases of dismissal, acquittal, or failure to prosecute? What about a universal database including all citizens or DNA typing at birth, as some, including most recently DNA typing's inventor, Sir Alec Jeffreys, have suggested, and as Kuwait, apparently, has begun implementing?[54] If the innocent have nothing to fear from DNA typing, as its advocates contend, why not include everyone in the database?

History shows that each advance in the technology of criminal identification has resulted in a broadening of criminal identification databases. Anthropometric identification, relatively slow and expensive, was used primarily in prisons on felons convicted of crimes serious enough to warrant prison terms. Fingerprinting shifted the locus of identification from the prison to the police department, from conviction to arrest. It broadened criminal identification databases to include individuals guilty of petty crimes that did not ordinarily merit prison sentences. The result was that a much larger segment of the population was included in criminal identification databases; many of those included, however, were not violent criminals but urban poor, racial minorities, and immigrants who were particularly vulnerable to arrest for petty crimes (what today would be called quality-of-life offenses) like vagrancy, public drunkenness, and prostitution.

There was an important consequence of combining expanded criminal identification databases with reformist jurisprudence, which emphasized the importance of recidivism as an indicator of propensity to crime and therefore future dangerousness. With expanded criminal identification databases, petty criminals, not violent felons, were most likely to accrue the requisite number of convictions to be adjudged "recidivists," not least because petty offenders, who served little, if any, prison time, would be released sooner and therefore have greater opportunity for rearrest. Thus, the weight of special punishments for recidivists tended to fall not on violent felons, but on repeat petty offenders.[55] The inevitable consequence of the combination of laws targeting recidivists—and there was a wave of such laws, called "Baumes laws," analogous to our "three-strikes-and-you're-out" laws, in the 1920s—and comprehensive criminal identification databases was to disproportionately punish *petty* offenders, a result we recently experienced anew with the most recent wave of "three-strikes" laws in this country.[56]

Essentially, the effect of fingerprint databases was to substitute recidivism, as vouched for by fingerprint records, for the definitive biological marker of criminality that criminologists had thus far failed to locate. Thus recidivists were treated as "born criminals" and subjected to all the special measures that criminologists had spent decades concocting, in anticipation of finding that elusive marker of criminality, such as longer, sometimes indefinite prison sentences, even for relatively minor offenses.

This perverse consequence of expanding criminal identification databases was little noticed at the time. Indeed, bigger fingerprint databases were widely viewed as a social good. As we have seen, however, in the 1930s and 1940s, Americans stopped short at the idea of a universal fingerprint database. Fingerprint databases were permitted to expand to include anyone convicted of a crime, no matter how petty. Civil databases including various special groups such as civil servants, schoolteachers, military personnel, and immigrants were permitted. But an identification-free zone was created for citizens who did not fall into these special categories and managed to avoid encounters with the criminal justice system.

In the midcentury debate over the scope of databases, the resolution was to legislate away the privacy rights of those labeled "criminals" while preserving a modicum of privacy for most of those labeled "law-abiding." As we begin the debate over the extent of DNA database, the most likely outcome seems to be that a similar bargain will be struck: "Tough on crime" politicians will win votes by legislating the expansion of DNA databases to include ever-larger categories of offenders. Indeed, this appears to already be occurring (see chapter 1), although it should be noted that legislators appear to be broadening the legal scope of DNA databases far more enthusiastically than they appropriate funds to actually implement the expansion.[57] Given the widespread popular view of DNA as "genetic blueprint" and distrust of government, however, these same politicians will be reluctant to support a universal genetic database. Thus DNA databases can be expected to include everyone designated "criminal" but not "law-abiding" citizens. In chapter 10, Etzioni offers an example of the kind of utilitarian analysis that could support this compromise; he argues that if an individual has been convicted of—or even suspected of—breaking the law once, the benefits to society of storing his or her DNA in a database outweigh his or her individual privacy rights. If, however, an individual is not a convict or a suspect, the balance tips the other way.

The history of fingerprint identification teaches that our primary concern about such a "creeping" database, as Steinhardt calls it in chapter 9, is that it threatens to inscribe race, class, or geographic inequities in arrest patterns, police practices, or criminal justice outcomes into the database. Criminal histories are not merely objective representations of individuals' antisocial behavior or of their potential dangerousness to society. They also reflect arrest patterns, policing practices, and biases in judicial outcomes and as such are likely to reflect race, class, and geographic inequities (see chapters 12 and 14). Once inscribed into the database, these inequities take on a seemingly neutral authority of their own: They appear to be pure, objective information, when in fact they may reflect the prejudices of police or judicial practitioners. In the case of fingerprinting, the criminal record, linked to the body by fingerprints, took on a life of its own, appearing to convey with objective authority the degree of recidivism—and thus the degree of potential dangerousness—of the offender. The potential for such skewing of the information contained in criminal histories remains significant today, not least because of the prevalence of plea bargaining and deal making in exchange for testimony. These practices ensure that the conviction that is officially inscribed into the criminal record is usually either lesser or greater than the offense actually committed, if indeed one was actually committed.

In short, an arrestee database, although probably the most politically, financially, and constitutionally palatable alternative, will inevitably reflect the race, class, and geographic biases embedded in police and judicial practices. One need only look to the recent scandals over racial profiling, the appalling racial composition of our prisons, drug task forces in Texas, or the differential application of the death penalty (and presumably, therefore, of all criminal sentencing) depending on the racial dimensions of the perpetrator-victim dyad to conclude that these biases, despite decades of effort to eradicate them, remain significant.[58] After passing through a DNA database, however, the biased information contained in criminal records will have essentially been "laundered," and it will be treated as objective information imbued with the considerable authority of science.

There remains, however, one crucial difference between today and the late 1930s, when citizens and law enforcement first struck a bargain over biometric identification. In the 1930s, the primary application of criminal identification databases was archival: linking individual suspects to their "true" criminal histories so that they could be adjudicated with the highest degree of fairness (for them) and safety (for society). Today, the justification for both fingerprint and DNA databases has shifted more toward the investigative rather than the adjudicative: The purpose of DNA databases, especially, is to solve crimes, not to determine proper punishments for those convicted. Cold searching, a novelty in the past, is becoming the principal function of—and justification for—criminal identification databases.[59] This brings us back to the inexorable logic of the criminal identification database in the computer age: The effectiveness of the database is wholly dependent on its size. Although one might reasonably conclude that society stands to gain more by entering a serial rapist into a genetic database than a "law-abiding" citizen, one nonetheless cannot deny that a universal DNA database could solve more crimes than one restricted to convicted criminals. If criminals, especially violent ones, leave their DNA at crime scenes, why wait for them to be caught and convicted before having the ability to solve those crimes? The incredible forensic power of DNA forces us to consider much more seriously the Swiftian "modest proposal" of a universal DNA database.

Aside from enhanced crime solving, the chief benefit of a universal database would be its equitability. David Kaye and Michael Smith (see chapter 12) and Edward

Imwinkelried suggest that a universal database would overcome the race, class, and geographic inequities inevitable in a broad convict or arrestee database.[60] Moreover, from a Rawlsian viewpoint, including everyone's DNA in a single database might be the most promising way to ensure proper oversight over the database. If everyone is a potential victim of an erroneous or fabricated DNA match, of an insurance company pillaging information from a government database, or of state-sponsored eugenics, then the politicians who fund the regulatory agencies, watchdog committees, and public defenders who protect us against such events may be more likely to maintain adequate funding over the long term, even as forensic DNA profiling inevitably ceases to be a hot issue and fades into the woodwork of police practice. It is on these grounds that Jeffreys recently came out in favor of a universal database. Viewing the suspect database that is currently developing in Britain as "discriminatory," Jeffreys contends that the only fair solution is to put everyone "in exactly the same boat." Then, Jeffreys argues, "the issue of discrimination disappears."[61] Duster, however, makes a compelling case in chapter 14 that although a universal database may not *perpetuate* the race, class, and geographic inequities embedded in police practices and the criminal justice system, neither will it *erase* them. The criminal behavior of individuals stigmatized by race, class, or geography will still be *documented* at a higher rate than that of the privileged.

Conclusion

As Duster's analysis suggests, the problems of injustice, determinism, and abuse of power override the technological systems in which they are embedded. History teaches that all three of the principal dangers posed by genetic identification—eugenics, wrongful conviction, and prejudiced databases—have root causes that run deeper than the choice of any particular identification technology. If we avoid being mesmerized by the momentous technological changes that are rapidly and inevitably approaching, the DNA debate—and especially the historic opportunity afforded by postconviction DNA testing—can be an occasion for probing more deeply into the root causes that continue to make our criminal justice system racist, classist, error prone, and too often a vehicle for state power rather than a champion of the citizen.

Notes

I am very grateful to Sheila Jasanoff and David Lazer for their roles in facilitating this chapter.

1. Michel Foucault, *Discipline and Punish: The Birth of the Prison*, trans. Alan Sheridan (New York: Vintage, 1979).

2. Quoted in David G. Horn, *Social Bodies: Science, Reproduction, and Italian Modernity* (Princeton: Princeton University Press, 1994), 30; Alphonse Bertillon, *Signaletic Instructions: Including the Theory and Practice of Anthropometrical Identification* (Chicago: University of Chicago Press, 1896), 202.

3. For more on this, see Simon A. Cole, *Suspect Identities: A History of Fingerprinting and Criminal Identification* (Cambridge, Mass.: Harvard University Press, 2001), 60–96.

4. Francis Galton, *Finger Prints* (London: Macmillan, 1892), 195.

5. Paul Rabinow, "Galton's Regret: Of Types and Individuals," in *DNA on Trial: Genetic Identification and Criminal Justice*, ed. Paul R. Billings (Woodbury, N.Y.: Cold Spring Harbor Laboratory Press, 1992), 5–18.

6. René Forgeot, *Des empreintes digitales étudiées au point de vue medico-judiciaire* (Lyon: A. Storck, 1892), 61–66.

7. Charles Féré, "Les empreintes des doigts et des orteils," *Journal de l'anatomie et de la physiologie normales et pathologiques de l'homme et des animaux* 29 (1893): 232–234; Charles Féré, "Notes sur les mains et les empreintes digitales de quelques singes," *Journal de l'anatomie et de la physiologie normales et pathologiques de l'homme et des animaux* 36 (1900): 255–267.

8. David Hepburn, "The Papillary Ridges on the Hands and Feet of Monkeys and Men," *Scientific Transactions of the Royal Dublin Society* 5 (1895): 532–535.

9. Daniel Pick, *Faces of Degeneration: A European Disorder, c. 1848–c. 1918* (Cambridge: Cambridge University Press, 1989).

10. Inez L. Whipple, "The Ventral Surface of Mammalian Chiridium with Special Reference to the Conditions Found in Man," *Zeitschrift für Morphologie und Anthropologie* 7 (1904): 261–368.

11. H. Waite, "Association of Finger-Prints," *Biometrika* 10 (1915): 421–478; Ethel M. Elderton, "On the Inheritance of the Finger-Print," *Biometrika* 13 (1920): 57–91.

12. L. W. LaChard, "Finger-Print Characteristics," *Journal of the American Institute of Criminal Law and Criminology* 10 (1919): 195–201.

13. Kristine Bonnevie, "Studies on Papillary Patterns of Human Fingers," *Journal of Genetics* 15 (1924): 1–112.

14. Quoted in *Finger Print and Identification Magazine* 4, (November 1922): 16.

15. Paul Gabriel Tesla, *Crime and Mental Disease in the Hand: A Proven Guide for the Identification and Pre-identification of Criminality, Psychosis and Mental Defectiveness* (Lakeland, Fla.: Osiris, 1991).

16. Harold Cummins and Charles Midlo, *Finger Prints, Palms and Soles: An Introduction to Dermatoglyphics* (Philadelphia: Blakiston, 1943), 210–213.

17. Julia E. Rodriguez, "Encoding the Criminal: Criminology and the Science of 'Social Defense' in Modernizing Argentina (1881–1920)" (Ph.D. diss., Columbia University, 2000).

18. *People v. Crispi* (New York 1911), trial transcript; *People v. Jennings* (Illinois 1910), trial transcript.

19. Henry Faulds, *Guide to Finger-Print Identification* (Hanley, U.K.: Wood Mitchell, 1905), 45–46.

20. *Emperor v. Sahdeo*, 3 Nagpur Law Reports 1 (India 1904); In re *Castelton's Case*, 3 Crim. App. 74 (U.K. 1909); *People v. Jennings*, 96 N.E. 1077 (Illinois 1911); *Parker v. Rex*, 14 C.L.R. 681 (Australia 1912).

21. *State v. Lapan*, 141 A. 685 (Vt. 1928).

22. *Grice v. State*, 151 S.W.2d 211 (Tex. 1941).

23. Identification Division, FBI, *A Brief Outline of the History, Services, and Operating Techniques of the World's Largest Repository of Fingerprints* (Washington, D.C.: Federal Bureau of Investigation, 1991), 7.

24. For more detail, see Cole, *Suspect Identities*, 140–167.

25. SEARCH Group, *Legal and Policy Issues Relating to Biometric Identification Technologies* (Washington, D.C.: Bureau of Justice Statistics, U.S. Department of Justice, 1990), 43–66; Pamela Sankar, "State Power and Record-Keeping: The History of Individualized Surveillance in the United States, 1790–1935" (Ph.D. diss., University of Pennsylvania, 1992), 279–290.

26. Diane Knich, "A Drive for Child Safety; Car Dealers' DNA Events Draw Vigilant Parents," *Washington Post*, April 2, 2002. Ashley E. Broughton, "Businesses Hand Out DNA Kits; Police Say Cotton Swabs May Help Them Find a Person Who Has Been Abducted," *Salt Lake City Tribune*, June 11, 2002.

27. Edward H. Murphy and James E. Murphy, *Finger Prints for Commercial and Personal Identification* (Detroit: International Title Recording and Identification Bureau, 1922). Child fingerprinting programs still exist today.

28. Frederick Kuhne, "The Origin, Classification and Uses of Finger Prints: An Ideal System of Identification for the General Public," *Scientific American* 114 (1916): 357–366.

29. Donald Dilworth, ed., *Identification Wanted: Development of the American Criminal Identification System, 1893–1943* (Gaithersburg, Md.: International Association of Chiefs of Police, 1977), 214–221; Richard L. Tobin, "Law-Abiding Americans Find Fingerprinting a Useful Fad Aiding Themselves and Police," *New York Herald Tribune*, May 1, 1935; Samuel Walker, *A Critical History of Police Reform: The Emergence of Professionalism* (Lanham, Md.: Lexington, 1977), 158.

30. American Civil Liberties Union, *Thumbs Down! The Fingerprint Menace to Civil Liberties* (1938); Dilworth, *Identification Wanted*, 228.

31. David Firestone, "For Giuliani, a Day of Police Praise and Policy Vindication," *New York Times*, June 15, 1996, 25.

32. Richard Winton and Mitchell Landesberg, "45 Years Later, Fingerprint Points to a Suspect in Case That Shocked the City," *Los Angeles Times*, January 30, 2003; Ken Ellingwood and Richard Winton, "Arrest Sheds Genial Image Decades in the Making," *Los Angeles Times*, January 31, 2003, A1; Andrew Blankstein, "Print Comparisons from 6,000 Slayings Languish," *Los Angeles Times*, February 10, 2003, B1.

33. David M. Halbfinger, "Sniper Clue Sat for Weeks in Crime Lab in Alabama," *New York Times*, October 26, 2002, A14.

34. Ira Levin, *This Perfect Day* (New York: Random House, 1970).

35. Chapter 9 of this volume, p. 173, emphasis added.

36. Daniel J. Kevles, *In the Name of Eugenics: Genetics and the Uses of Human Heredity* (Berkeley and Los Angeles: University of California Press, 1985).

37. Rabinow, "Galton's Regret"; Paul R. Billings, ed., *DNA on Trial: Genetic Information and Criminal Justice* (Woodbury, N.Y.: Cold Spring Harbor Laboratory Press, 1992).

38. Ibid., 7.

39. John Berry, "Race Relationships," *Fingerprint World* 2 (1977): 48–50. In a recent newsgroup posting, André Moenssens, a prominent professor of scientific evidence law, confirmed the view that there are racial variations in fingerprint pattern type frequency, the most notable being the lower proportion of arches and higher proportion of whorls among Asians. André Moenssens, electronic communication to Forensic Newsgroup, April 4, 2001.

40. C. H. Lin et al., "Fingerprint Comparison: I; Similarity of Fingerprints," *Journal of Forensic Science* 27 (1982): 290–304.

41. J. A. Hall and D. Kimura, "Dermatoglyphic Asymmetry and Sexual Orientation in Men," *Behavioral Neuroscience* 10 (1994): 1203–1206.

42. See, for example, Daniel J. Kevles, "On Eugenics and Criminology," in *In the Name of Eugenics*; see also Nicole H. Rafter, *Creating Born Criminals: Biological Theories of Crime and Eugenics* (Urbana: University of Illinois Press, 1997).

43. Stephen Jay Gould, *The Mismeasure of Man* (New York: Norton, 1981). Gould shows that racist craniometric researchers saw correlations between race and skull size, even when such correlations were not present in their own data.

44. For critiques of the simplistic understanding of single-gene causality, see Michael Morange, *The Misunderstood Gene*, trans. Matthew Cobb (Cambridge, Mass.: Harvard University Press, 2001); Richard C. Lewontin, *The Triple Helix: Gene, Organism, and Environment* (Cambridge, Mass.: Harvard University Press, 2000); Steven Rose, *Lifelines: Biology beyond Determinism* (Oxford: Oxford University Press, 1997).

45. Kevles, *In the Name of Eugenics*; Rafter, *Creating Born Criminals*.

46. See, for example, *Finger Print and Identificatoin Magazine*, September 1924, 2.

47. David Ashbaugh, *Quantitative-Qualitative Friction Ridge Analysis: An Introduction to Basic and Advanced Ridgeology* (Boca Raton, Fla.: CRC Press, 1999), 1–6.

48. Nelson E. Roth, *The New York State Police Evidence Tampering Investigation* (Confidential Report to the Governor of New York, Ithaca, N.Y., 1997).

49. James E. Starrs, "A Miscue in Fingerprint Identification: Causes and Concerns," *Journal of Police Science and Administration* 12 (1984): 287–296; "New Doubts over Fingerprint Evidence," *BBC News*, May 16, 2000; Anne Barnard, "Convicted in Slaying, Man Wins Freedom," *Philadelphia Inquirer*, December 24, 1999, B1; Stephen Grey, "Yard in Fingerprint Blunder," *London Times*, April 6, 1997; Michael Specter, "Do Fingerprints Lie?" *New Yorker*, May 27, 2002, 96–105.

50. Collaborative Testing Services, "Forensic Laboratory Testing Program Proficiency Testing Program: Latent Prints Examination," Report No. 9508, Sterling, Va.

51. David A. Stoney, "Fingerprint Identification," in *Modern Scientific Evidence*, ed. David L. Faigman et al. (St. Paul: West, 2001); Michael Saks, "Merlin and Solomon: Lessons from the Law's Formative Encounters with Forensic Identification Science," *Hastings Law Review* 49 (1998): 1069–1141; Robert Epstein, "Fingerprints Meet Daubert: The Myth of Fingerprint 'Science' Is Revealed," *Southern California Law Review* 75 (2002): 605–657; Simon A. Cole, "The Myth of Fingerprints: A Forensic Science Stands Trial," *Lingua Franca* 10 (2000): 54–62. So far, however, fingerprinting has survived legal challenges.

52. Michael D. Risinger et al., "The Daubert/Kumho Implications of Observer Effects in Forensic Science: Hidden Problems of Expectation and Suggestion," *California Law Review* 90 (2002): 1–56.

53. William C. Thompson, Franco Taroni, and Colin G. G. Aitken, "How the Probability of a False Positive Affects the Value of DNA Evidence," *Journal of Forensic Science* 48 (2003): 47–54; William C. Thompson, "Accepting Lower Standards: The National Research Council's Second Report on Forensic DNA Evidence," *Jurimetrics Journal* 37 (1997): 405–424; Will Hodgkinson, "DNA in the Dock," *Observer* (London), November 30, 2002; Peggy O'Hare, "H.P.D. to Review Crime Lab's Work; Investigation by Channel 11 Questioned Whether Errors Led to Jailing of Innocent," *Houston Chronicle*, November 16, 2002; Peggy O'Hare, "H.P.D. Retesting Falls Short, Critic Says," *Houston Chronicle*, January 19, 2003.

54. Bruce Lambert, "Giuliani Backs DNA Testing of Newborns for Identification," *New York Times*, December 17, 1998, B5; Frank Lombardi, "Test Tot DNA, Sez Rudi," *New York Daily News*, December 17, 1998, 33; "Florida Tries DNA Sampling to Protect Children," *New York Times*, January 27, 1999, A14; Simon Bevilacqua, "Fears over Call to Expand Database," *Sunday Tasmanian* (Hobart, Australia), December 9, 2001; Jen Kelly, "Shock DNA Sample Idea," *Herald Sun* (Melbourne, Australia), August 8, 2002; Julia Hartley-Brewer, "Ex–Police Chief Says Samples Should Be Taken from Every Baby to Net Future Serial Attackers, but Ministers Refuse to Foot the Bill; DNA Database Could Have Trapped the Trophy Rapist within Hours," *Sunday Express* (London), November 10, 2002; "Police Chief Wants Everyone on DNA File," *Herald* (Glasgow, Scotland), June 25, 2001; Stephen Robinson, "A Free Country," *Daily Telegraph* (London), September 13, 2002.

55. See, for example, Rafter, *Creating Born Criminals*.

56. George K. Brown, "Recidivism: A Socio-legal Survey of Its Definition, Incidence and Treatment in the United States" (Ph.D. diss., University of Pennsylvania, 1947); David Schichor and Dale K. Sechrest, *Three Strikes and You're Out: Vengeance as Public Policy* (Thousand Oaks, Calif.: Sage, 1996); Franklin E. Zimring, Gordon Hawkins, and Sam Kamin, *Three Strikes and You're Out in California* (New York: Oxford University Press, 2001).

57. Anna Gorman, "Murder Victims' Relative Seeks Wider State DNA Database," *Los Angeles Times*, December 22, 2003, B1. Maria Glod, "Va. to Begin Taking DNA after Arrests for Felonies; Prosecutors, Rights Activists Split on Database Expansion," *Washington Post*, January 1, 2003; Kevin Blanchard, "DNA Test Program to Expand," *Morning Advocate* (Baton Rouge, La.), November 23, 2002; Harold J. Krent, "DNA Testing Erodes Privacy,"

Chicago Sun-Times, March 13, 2002; "Iberia Parish to Take DNA of All Arrested," Associated Press State & Local Wire, June 2, 2002.

58. David Cole, *No Equal Justice: Race and Class in the American Criminal Justice System* (New York: New Press, 1999), 1–62.

59. Imwinkelried, chapter 5 of this volume. Maria Sanminiatelli, "Virginia's DNA Database Averaging One Cold Hit a Day," Associated Press State & Local Wire, April 29, 2001; Brooke A. Masters, "Killer in Landmark DNA Case Executed in Va.," *Washington Post*, March 15, 2002; Michael D. Shear, "DNA Database Touted by Police, Prosecutors," *Washington Post*, November 21, 2002; Erin Hallissy, "Baffling Rapes, Slayings Solved; Federal 'Cold Hit' DNA Database Links Old Evidence to Felons," *San Francisco Chronicle*, December 9, 2002; "Geraldine Palk Trial: 20-Year-Old Sample Led to Conviction of Killer," *South Wales Echo*, November 4, 2002; Claire Booth and Karl Fischer, "DNA Tests Lead Prosecutors to Inmate in 23-Year-Old Murder," *Contra Costa Times*, December 4, 2002.

60. Michael E. Smith, David H. Kaye, and Edward J. Imwinkelried, "DNA Data from Everyone Would Combat Crime, Racism," *USA Today*, July 26, 2001, 15A.

61. "Privacy Fears over DNA Database," *BBC News*, September 12, 2002; "Scientist Backs Universal DNA Bank," *BBC News*, February 18, 2001.

5

The Relative Priority that Should Be Assigned to Trial Stage DNA Issues

Edward J. Imwinkelried

When Paul Giannelli and I released the first edition of *Scientific Evidence* in 1986, we devoted a single subsection to DNA typing.[1] In that edition, we speculated that researchers "could conceivably develop forensic applications for their techniques. The genetic laboratories now researching DNA may ultimately advance genetic marker analysis far beyond the status quo."[2] For once, we were right. We are now well into the era of DNA evidence. The DNA Legal Assistance Unit of the American Prosecutors Research Institute periodically publishes an update on DNA case law. One such update, released in 2000, lists hundreds of published opinions.[3] The update reports the cases both by technology and by jurisdiction. According to the update, there are now 135 RFLP decisions rendered by state courts of last resort. The category of DNA decisions handed down by state intermediate appellate courts is even larger, numbering 165. Not only has there been a large volume of litigation; at times, the litigation has also been contentious. The literature abounds with frequent references to the "DNA wars."[4] The United States certainly has extensive experience with DNA evidence in the litigation system. It seems an appropriate time to pause, reflect on the developments in DNA analysis since 1986, and consider establishing national priorities for future utilization of DNA technology.

In doing so, it is tempting to leap to the conclusion that priority should be given to the issues related to the use of DNA evidence at the trial phase, which is the high-visibility phase of the litigation process. After all, DNA evidence played a prominent role in the "trial of the century," the 1995 prosecution of O. J. Simpson for murder.[5] Moreover, we now get a steady diet of DNA evidence in both real trials on *Court TV* and fictional trials in print and on the screen. At least at first blush, the trial forum appears to be the very battlefield on which the DNA wars are being waged.

However, the thesis of this chapter is that the trial phase should not be the future priority in use of DNA technology. In the late 1980s, some authorities predicted that the advent of forensic DNA testing would have a revolutionary impact on the justice system.[6] The advent of DNA typing was said to be the "second coming" of fingerprinting.[7] Although those assertions have turned out to be somewhat overstated, it is true that the use of DNA evidence has prompted the development of novel practices, resulted in the creation of some new institutions, and posed certain new legal issues.[8] However, on close scrutiny, it becomes clear that those developments have occurred largely in the pretrial and posttrial stages of the litigation process. For the most part, DNA evidence has had only a modest impact on the trial phase.

The first part of this chapter surveys the effects of DNA evidence on the pretrial and posttrial stages of criminal prosecution. As that part demonstrates, DNA evidence has wrought novel practices, institutions, and legal issues in those phases. The second part of the chapter contrasts the effects DNA technology has had on those phases with its effect on the trial stage. That part points out that with a single exception, DNA has not produced the same type of fundamental change at the trial phase. Rather, the second part of the chapter argues that at the trial stage, the principal impact of DNA evidence has been a better understanding of two issues—the importance of test procedure and the statistical evaluation of forensic evidence—that antedated DNA technology. Though it would certainly be a mistake to understate the impact that DNA technology has had at the trial stage, the impact at that stage has been much more limited than that on the earlier and later stages in the trial process. If the question is, on which stage of the process of handling DNA evidence should the legal system concentrate its reform efforts, the thesis of this chapter is that the answer should not be the trial phase.

The Impact of DNA Technology on the Pretrial and Posttrial Stages of the Litigation Process

The unique effects of DNA evidence on criminal prosecutions are largely attributable to two of DNA's characteristics. One is the durability of DNA. Although many types of trace evidence are evanescent, DNA lasts. It can be extracted, for instance, from skeletal remains,[9] even remains that have been badly burned.[10] DNA testing can be conducted decades after the relevant crime occurred.[11] Compared to the analysis of other genetic markers, DNA typing has a superior ability to analyze aged samples.[12] Indeed, DNA has been successfully extracted from Egyptian mummies.[13]

The other characteristic is the high degree of polymorphism of DNA types.[14] Contrast DNA typing with more traditional blood-grouping analysis. If the analyst relied solely on the latter type of testing, the only finding might be that the source of the sample falls into the H group, which includes 43 percent (i.e., almost half) of the human population.[15] Compare the FBI's analysis of the semen stain found on Monica Lewinsky's dress. The FBI Laboratory concluded that the chance that the semen was "not the President's is one in 7.87 trillion"[16]—a figure exceeding both the present world population and the number of human beings who have ever populated the world.

The combination of these two characteristics has led to the proliferation of new practices, institutions, and issues in the pretrial and posttrial stages of the litigation process.

The Pretrial Stage

Postconviction testing, exonerating wrongfully convicted defendants, has highlighted some old pretrial problems such as abusive interrogation tactics. The five teenagers previously convicted in the infamous Central Park jogger rape case were recently vindicated in part as a result of DNA testing.[17] There are now allegations that the police employed intense interrogation techniques to coerce the confessions that originally led to the convictions. However, DNA technology has done more than remind us of old problems in the criminal justice system; the technology has prompted innovations in pretrial procedures.

One effect of DNA technology at the pretrial stage has been the establishment of DNA databases. In addition to CODIS, maintained by the FBI,[18] every state has its own DNA database.[19] CODIS includes data about hundreds of thousands of DNA samples.[20] To be sure, the present size of even the largest extant DNA database pales in comparison to the FBI library of over 198 million fingerprint cards.[21] However, for the first time, large databases are being constructed for an identifying characteristic other than fingerprints. The explanation, of course, is the combination of the durability of DNA and the ability of DNA typing to yield low random-match probabilities. Those factors have made it worthwhile to establish the databases. The cost-benefit analysis did not justify creating a database for HLA markers because white cells are less durable than DNA,[22] and albeit more probative than red blood cell tests,[23] even HLA tests are less discriminating than DNA typing.

Not only has the advent of DNA technology led to the creation of new databases in laboratories, it has also prompted the creation of new "cold hit" units in police departments.[24] Prior to the availability of DNA typing, it was largely a waste of time to allocate police resources to a unit with the exclusive mission of investigating old crimes, even serious ones. Given the evanescent nature of the most common types of incriminating physical evidence, if the police did not locate inculpatory evidence shortly after the commission of the crime, it was highly unlikely that such evidence would materialize later. Unless there was an unexpected "break" in the form of a suspect's confession or an accomplice's report, it made little sense to continue to investigate old offenses. There was no need for a unit designated to conduct such investigations; if an unexpected break occurred in a particular case, the police could assign investigators to that case on an ad hoc basis. However, all that changed with DNA. Even old DNA samples can be tested against and compared with samples obtained from new suspects. As in the case of DNA databases, DNA technology has radically changed the benefit component of the cost-benefit analysis for cold-hit police units. Virginia is now averaging one cold hit per day,[25] and California's cold-hit program has recently achieved a similar success rate.

In addition, DNA technology has prompted several states to either extend the period covered by their statutes of limitations[26] or fashion a new exception to those statutes in sexual-assault cases.[27] The argument runs that DNA testing can identify a perpetrator with a high degree of probability and that that degree of probability effectively removes the doubt that ordinarily surrounds the prosecution of an old crime. The U.S. Supreme Court has acknowledged that the primary rationale for statutes of limitation is to protect the accused against "overly stale criminal charges."[28] If the accusatory pleading shows on its face that the period of limitations has already passed, the defendant has ordinarily been able to move successfully to dismiss the charge before trial. However, in the jurisdictions that have recognized these new exceptions, the prosecution can respond to such a motion by invoking the exception. Many jurisdictions are now considering legislation codifying such an exception.[29]

Finally, even without the benefit of such legislation, prosecutors in several states (California, Missouri, New York, Texas, Utah, and Wisconsin) have attempted to toll the statute of limitations by filing criminal complaints identifying offenders by their DNA profile.[30] In a case pending in Sacramento, California, the caption of the warrant read:

The People of the State of California v. JOHN DOE, unknown male with Short Tandem Repeat (STR) Deoxyribonucleic Acid (DNA) Profile at the following Genetic Locations, using the Cofiler and Profiler Plus Polymerase Chain Reaction (PCR) amplification kits: D3S1358 (15,15), D16S539 (9,10), THO1 (7,7), TPOX (6,9), CSF1PO (10,11), D7S820 (8,11), vWA (18,19), FGA (22,24), D8S818 (8,13), D13S317 (10,11), with said Genetic Profile being unique, occurring in approximately 1 in 21 sextillion of the Caucasian population, 1 in 650 quadrillion of the African American population, 1 in 420 sextillion of the Hispanic population Defendant(s).[31]

The Sacramento warrant was the first of its kind to lead to an arrest,[32] and in February 2001 a California Superior Court judge upheld the legality of the warrant and resulting arrest.[33] In July 2001, a judge in Milwaukee County, Wisconsin, upheld a similar warrant, and such warrants have now been filed in California, Kansas, New York, and Utah as well.[34]

These institutions and practices raise substantial novel questions. For example, in the case of DNA databases, the most obvious question is how inclusive the database ought to be. Should it be limited to persons convicted of sex offenses, ought it to include all persons convicted of felonies, or should it extend to arrestees? All the state databases currently cover convictions for sexual assault, half apply to homicide, and approximately a third extend to some juvenile offenses.[35] Thirteen states generally include all felons in their databases.[36] Louisiana requires all arrestees to contribute a sample to its database.[37] For that matter, there have been serious proposals for a universal database.[38] Another troublesome issue is who should have access to the database. Should its use be strictly confined to identification in criminal investigations, or ought certain types of scientists be permitted to use the data contained in the database in their research? If so, what types of research should be sanctioned?[39] Like DNA databases, the new DNA exceptions to the statutes of limitation pose significant questions. DNA evidence could be virtually conclusive in a case in which the only issue is the perpetrator's identity. However, it may be difficult to identify cases that fall into that category. Can the defendant defeat the exception simply by arguing that there are other lively issues in the case such as the *mens rea* with which the *actus reus* was committed? The task of drafting a statute that clearly specifies the category of target cases may prove to be a more difficult challenge than many have assumed. DNA complaints raise a host of issues, including whether the complaints satisfy the particular description requirement of rule 4(c)(1) of the *Federal Rules of Criminal Procedure*[40] and comport with the Fourth Amendment.[41] In short, the new institutions and practices have brought with them a host of as-yet unresolved policy and legal issues.

The Posttrial Stage

DNA technology cuts two ways. Just as DNA technology has given rise to the argument that we should lift the bar of the statute of limitations in certain cases to permit the prosecution of old crimes, DNA testing conducted long after a prisoner's conviction may make it possible to establish the prisoner's innocence.[42] In its report on postconviction relief, one of the working groups of the National Commission on the Future of DNA Evidence, the Working Group on Postconviction Issues, commented that DNA testing has a "remarkable" potential to exonerate long after a wrongful conviction.[43] In the working group's words, the advances in DNA testing "now make[] it possible to obtain conclusive [exculpatory] results in cases in which previous [non-DNA] testing had been inconclusive."[44] This development is attributable to the same two characteristics of DNA technology that prompted the pretrial developments, namely, the polymorphism of DNA systems and the durability of DNA. The durability of DNA permits the testing of samples recovered at the scene of crimes committed years before; and the polymorphism of DNA greatly increases the probability that if an accused has been wrongfully convicted, the result of DNA testing will be exculpatory.

However, like the recent pretrial developments, this posttrial development raises a myriad of new issues. That is the very reason why the commission established a separate working group devoted to the topic of postconviction relief. The working group's final report addresses such questions as how judges can retroactively determine whether the real issues at the prior trial were such that a subsequent DNA test result conclusively establishes innocence. In a late 2000 decision, the intermediate appellate court in Illinois struggled with that very question.[45] As the working group notes, if the prior trial turned on questions of the victim's or accused's state of mind, the DNA test might be largely irrelevant. The working group adds that in some cases possibly involving persons other than the victim and the accused, "reasonable persons might disagree as to whether the results are exonerative."[46] When multiple persons may have participated in a particular crime, the test might "not afford a clear elimination."[47] Other questions relate to how long the police should be required to retain crime scene evidence samples,[48] when the state ought to fund postconviction DNA testing,[49] and how any surviving victim of a particular crime should be notified that the case involving that crime is being reopened.[50] The last question can be especially sensitive if, as a result of the trauma resulting from the crime, the victim has developed "severe depression or suicidal ideation."[51] In short, as in the pretrial phase, at the posttrial stage the advent of

DNA technology has had the twin impacts of generating new practices and raising novel issues.

The Impact of DNA Technology on the Trial Stage of the Litigation Process

To gauge the impact of DNA typing on the trial stage of the litigation process, we must distinguish between two issues: the influence that DNA evidence can have on the trier of fact's ultimate decision and the extent to which, as in the pre- and post-trial stages, the advent of DNA technology has prompted the development of new practices or posed novel issues.

The Influence of DNA Evidence on the Trier of Fact's Decision

It is commonly assumed that DNA evidence can have a substantial influence on the ultimate decision of the trier of fact in a criminal case. That assumption accounts for some of the pre- and posttrial developments discussed earlier in the chapter. Laboratories would not be willing to invest the resources necessary to operate DNA databases and police departments would not establish cold-hit units devoted to the investigation of old crimes unless they assumed that triers of fact often find DNA evidence convincing. Likewise, it would be a waste of time to devise new procedures for postconviction DNA testing and relief unless the judges and clemency authorities adjudicating requests for such relief found DNA evidence persuasive.

Common sense suggests that a rational trier of fact would treat testimony about a random-match probability of one in 7.87 trillion as highly probative, if not dispositive. Moreover, there is certainly anecdotal evidence that in the typical case, testimony about a low random-match probability can be highly influential on juries and judges. However, there is little evidence that this type of testimony overwhelms the average lay juror, much less the typical judge presiding at a bench trial. To be sure, there have been only a limited number of studies of the impact of statistical evidence of this nature on triers of fact. However, most of the studies have yielded the finding that lay jurors are inclined to underutilize this type of evidence.[52] Two of the leading students of statistical evidence, David Kaye and Jonathan Koehler, have remarked that "[t]he clearest and most consistent finding" in the studies conducted to date is that laypersons undervalue expert testimony of a statistical nature, such as testimony about random-match probabilities in DNA cases.[53] In short, the influence of DNA evidence on triers of fact may be more modest than some anecdotes suggest.

The Extent to Which DNA Evidence Has Generated Novel Practices and Issues at Trial

It is true that the DNA era has witnessed a number of significant changes in the evidence law governing the admissibility of scientific testimony. The changes have taken the form of both important decisions by the U.S. Supreme Court and amendments to the controlling provisions of the *Federal Rules of Evidence*. During the 1990s, for example, the Supreme Court rendered a trilogy of noteworthy expert testimony decisions, *Daubert v. Merrell Dow Pharmaceuticals, Inc.*,[54] *General Electric Co. v. Joiner*,[55] and finally *Kumho Tire Co., Ltd. v. Carmichael*.[56] However, none of these cases involved DNA evidence. For that matter, none of the opinions even mentioned lower-court DNA decisions. Effective December 1, 2000, several amendments to the federal rules took effect. The amendments include changes to rules 702 and 703, the principal statutory provisions regulating the admission of expert testimony. Those changes do not include any special procedures or standards for DNA cases. Moreover, like the three Supreme Court decisions, the new Federal Rules of Evidence Advisory Committee notes accompanying the amendments make no mention of DNA evidence. The upshot is that although there have been major changes in the law governing expert testimony during the past decade, those changes were not driven by the advent of DNA testing.

Although DNA technology has posed novel issues in the pre- and posttrial stages of the litigation process, as a general proposition the technology has not had that impact on the trial stage. As Margaret Berger, the former reporter for the Federal Rules of Evidence Advisory Committee, has pointed out, the judicial opinions have generally not singled out DNA for special treatment.[57] The cases have neither announced peculiar admissibility rules for DNA evidence[58] nor carved out special DNA exceptions to existing general rules.[59] In truth, with the single exception of the question of whether laboratory error rates should be included in the computation of random-match probabilities,[60] the issues that have been litigated in DNA cases are questions that have arisen previously in non-DNA cases.[61]

The real impact of DNA typing at the trial stage has not been to revolutionize either procedures or substantive admissibility standards. Rather, the effect has been to help the bench and bar develop a better understanding of two critical issues concerning the weight of scientific testimony: the importance of proper scientific test procedure and the necessity of understanding the real significance of any probability cited to the trier of fact.

The Importance of Proper Scientific Test Procedure

It has long been the traditional view in many jurisdictions that the required foundation for a proffer of evidence resulting from scientific testing must include a showing that the expert followed the correct procedure in conducting the test and applying it to the facts of the instant case. However, even in those jurisdictions, the topic had been largely neglected prior to the DNA era:

Many leading treatises on scientific evidence concentrate[d] on the foundational element of proof of the general trustworthiness of the scientific technique while slighting the question of whether the analyst properly applied the technique in the instant case. The treatises that addressed[ed] the question typically ma[d]e short shrift of it.[62]

DNA cases have changed that. Two decisions, *People v. Castro*[63] and *State v. Scwhartz*,[64] have been especially influential. In those cases, the courts acknowledged the general reliability of DNA typing. However, in both cases the courts excluded the prosecution's DNA evidence for the stated reason that the analyst had not complied with correct scientific procedure in conducting the DNA test. The decisions attracted national publicity because they were the first major setbacks for DNA evidence in the courtroom. The decisions raised the visibility of the question of the importance of sound test protocols.[65] DNA cases may have indirectly provided an impetus for the December 1, 2000, amendment to rule 702 of the *Federal Rules of Evidence*, which now requires the proponent of expert testimony to show that "the witness has applied the principles and methods reliably to the facts of the case."[66] More broadly, DNA cases have made the bench and bar aware that an attack on the procedure used to test DNA for evidentiary purposes can be an effective challenge to the weight of any DNA evidence admitted.[67]

The Necessity of Understanding the Real Significance of Any Probability Cited to the Trier of Fact

A proponent of DNA evidence in a criminal trial is rarely content to elicit testimony from an expert that the defendant's DNA markers match those found in a crime scene sample. Ordinarily, the proponent goes farther and proffers a statistical evaluation of the match. The proponent wants the trier of fact to appreciate the extent to which the DNA match individuates the defendant as the source of the crime scene sample. The proper method of computing random-match probabilities was one of the primary foci of two National Research Council reports on forensic DNA in the 1990s.[68] Both reports addressed the dispute that had arisen over the admissibility of random-match probabilities.

The dispute over the admissibility of random-match probabilities not only forced the bench and bar to develop a better understanding of the assumptions behind and restrictions on the computation of random-match probabilities; eventually, the dispute broadened, with the desirable result that today there is a better appreciation of the differences among a random-match probability, a source probability,[69] and finally a guilt probability.[70] The clarification of the distinctions among these probabilities is an important step forward. In closing argument, out of ignorance, counsel sometimes mischaracterize the probability admitted. If counsel and the judge comprehend the pertinent distinctions, the closing arguments are more likely to properly describe the probability; and if counsel properly describe the probability during closing, the jury is more likely to treat the probability appropriately during deliberations.

Conclusion

It would be a mistake to understate the importance of the impact of DNA typing on the trial stage of the litigation process. As previously stated, at trial the trier of fact may give testimony about DNA evidence great, if not dispositive, weight. Moreover, the issues that DNA cases have refined are critical ones that are not confined to DNA cases.

It is vital that practitioners and judges realize the importance of the requirement for a showing of correct test procedure. If the requirement is understood to mandate proof that the analyst monitor the same variables controlled in the earlier research validating the scientific technique, the requirement is an "essential guarantee of the trustworthiness of scientific evidence."[71] In experiments conducted prior to any technique's acceptance as an evidentiary tool, researchers have validated the hypothesis of the trustworthiness of the particular technique by controlling certain variables.[72] In later forensic tests, the analyst must duplicate the conditions that obtained during the prior research; he or she must follow correct protocol at least to the extent of accounting for the same variables: "No matter how impressive the validity rates achieved in the earlier research, the experiments do not afford any assurance of the trustworthiness of the instant forensic test unless the forensic scientist"[73] replicates the conditions and controls the identical variables. Moreover, the proficiency studies conducted to date document that one of the most common causes of erroneous test results is sloppy test procedure.[74] The concern about proper test procedure, manifest in the DNA cases, should apply across the board to all types of scientific evidence.

Similarly, DNA cases have made a major contribution by highlighting the question of the true significance of any probabilities cited to the trier of fact. Like concerns about correct test procedure, the question of the true significance of a probability admitted at trial is by no means confined to DNA cases. According to Koehler, "The use of statistical testimony at trial has increased dramatically during the past two decades."[75] Throughout the domain of forensic science, there has been a decided trend toward offering statistical evaluations to quantify the probative value of any scientific analysis submitted to the trier of fact.[76] In the words of Judge Jack Weinstein,

Today, complex statistical evidence is being introduced in American courts in a wide variety of both civil and criminal matters. [A] LEXIS search of district court opinions using the words "statistic," "statistics," or "statistical" turned up 608 examples in the years 1960 to 1969; 2,786 cases from 1970 to 1979; 4,364 cases from 1980 to 1989; and 3,015 from 1990 through July 31, 1995.[77]

Despite these impacts of DNA evidence on the trial stage, I submit that in the future, the focus of reformers should not be on that phase of the litigation process. Although the trial stage is the high-visibility phase of the process, it is not the stage that has witnessed the promulgation of new practices, the creation of new institutions, or the emergence of truly novel issues. For the most part, those developments have occurred in the pre- and posttrial phases. Those are the stages that deserve the closest attention and the most concerted reform efforts. We are far enough into the DNA era that it is an appropriate time to pause, reflect, and set future national priorities regarding DNA use in law enforcement and the judicial system. Simply stated, the use of DNA at the trial stage should not be one of those priorities.

Notes

1. Paul C. Giannelli and Edward J. Imwinkelried, *Scientific Evidence* (Charlottesville, Va.: Michie, 1986), § 17-8(E).

2. Ibid., 603.

3. American Prosecutors Research Institute, DNA Legal Assistance Unit, *Reported Forensic DNA Cases* (Alexandria, Va., 2000).

4. Jonathan J. Koehler, "On Conveying the Probative Value of DNA Evidence: Frequencies, Likelihood Ratios, and Error Rates," *University of Colorado Law Review* 67 (1996): 884, n65; William C. Thompson, "Evaluating the Admissibility of New Genetic Identification Tests: Lessons from the DNA War," *Journal of Criminal Law and Criminology* 84 (1993).

5. Christopher B. Mueller, "Introduction: O. J. Simpson and the Criminal Justice System on Trial," *University of Colorado Law Review* 67 (1996): 732; William C. Thompson, "DNA Evidence in the O.J. Simpson Trial," *University of Colorado Law Review* 67 (1996): 826.

6. New York State Forensic DNA Analysis Panel, *Report i, 1* (1989); K. K. F. Kelly, J. J. Rankin, and R. C. Wink, "Method and Applications of DNA Fingerprinting: A Guide for the Non-scientist," *Criminal Law Review* (1987): 105 ("enormous potential"); Rorie Sherman, "DNA Evidence Dispute Escalates," *National Law Journal*, January 20, 1992, 3 ("the revolutionary forensic tool of DNA testing").

7. James E. Starrs, "The Dawning of DNA in the Legal World: A Red Sky in the Morning?" Testimony on March 15, 1989. Reported in *DNA Identification*, Hearings of the Subcommittee on the Constitution, Committee on the Judiciary, U.S. Senate, 101st Cong., 1st session 4-40 (Washington, D.C.: U.S. Government Printing Office). The irony is that fingerprinting testimony is now under attack. See Paul C. Giannelli and Edward J. Imwinkelried, "Forensic Science: Fingerprints," *Criminal Law Bulletin* 38 (2002): 642.

8. See Edward J. Imwinkelried and David H. Kaye, "DNA Typing: Emerging or Neglected Issues," *Washington Law Review* 76 (2001): 413.

9. Jamao Yamamoto et al., "Maternal Identification from Skeletal Remains of an Infant Kept by the Alleged Mother for 16 Years with DNA Typing," *Journal of Forensic Science* 43 (1998): 701.

10. Charles M. Strom and Svetlana Rechitsky, "Use of Nested PCR to Identify Charred Human Remains and Minute Amounts of Blood," *Journal of Forensic Science* 43 (1998).

11. Cristina Cattaneo et al., "Comparison of Three DNA Extraction Methods on Bone and Blood Stains up to 43 Years Old and Amplification of Three Different Gene Sequences," *Journal of Forensic Science* 42 (1998): 1126.

12. Debra Cassens Moss, "DNA—The New Fingerprints," *American Bar Association Journal* 74 (1988): 66.

13. K. K. F. Kelly, J. J. Rankin, and R. C. Wink, "Method and Applications of DNA Fingerprinting: A Guide for the Non-scientist," *Criminal Law Review* (1987): 105.

14. David L. Faigman et al., eds., *Modern Scientific Evidence: The Law and Science of Expert Testimony*, 2 vols. (St. Paul, Minn.: West, 1997), § 17-2.1.B2.3.2.

15. Andre A. Moenssens et al., *Scientific Evidence in Civil and Criminal Cases*, 4th ed. (Mineola, N.Y.: Foundation, 1995), § 13.10, at 778.

16. "A New DNA Policy: Statistics Are Out: A Qualified Certainty Is In," *Scientific Sleuthing Review* 22 (1998): 13. The report is available online at cnn.com/icreport/report/volume6/volume6247.html.

17. Jim Dwyer and Kevin Flynn, "New Light on Jogger's Rape Calls Evidence into Question," *New York Times*, December 1, 2002; Dakota Smith, "Rights: Suspects' DNA Ignored

in Central Park Jogger Case," Inter Press Service, December 12, 2002; "A Central Park Injustice," *San Francisco Chronicle*, December 11, 2002.

18. Peter Donnelly and Richard Friedman, "DNA Databases and the Legal Consumption of Scientific Evidence," *Michigan Law Review* 97 (1999): 939–940.

19. Ibid., 939.

20. Ibid., 940.

21. Paul C. Giannelli and Edward J. Imwinkelried, *Scientific Evidence*, 3rd ed. (Charlottesville, Va.: LEXIS Law Publishing, 1999), § 16-6, at 756.

22. "Human Leukocyte Antigen Testing: Technology versus Policy in Cases of Disputed Parentage," *Vanderbilt Law Review* 36 (1983): 1592.

23. Joel S. Kolko, "Admissibility of HLA Test Results to Determine Paternity," *Family Law Reporter (BNA)* 9 (1983): 4009–4019.

24. David E. Rovella, "Heating Up Cold Crime Squads," *National Law Journal*, March 8, 1999, A1.

25. Maria Sanminiatelli, "Virginia's DNA Database Averaging One Cold Hit a Day," Associated Press State & Local Wire, April 29, 2001.

26. For the most part, these statutes condition the extension on the availability of DNA evidence of the perpetrator's identity. Such legislation has been enacted in jurisdictions such as Colorado, Florida, Indiana, Michigan, Nevada, New Jersey, and New York.

27. "Drafting a Fair DNA Exception to the Statute of Limitations in Sexual Assault Cases," *Jurimetrics Journal* 39 (1999), 431; David Heckelman, "Senate OKs Bill Extending Limits on Prosecuting Some Sex Crimes," *Chicago Daily Law Bulletin*, May 8, 1998.

28. *United States v. Marion*, 404 U.S. 307, 321 (1971).

29. Issues of the *DNA Legislative and Media Report* (published weekly and posted online at docs.appliedbiosystems.com/hid.taf) for January 12 and 26, 2001, and February 9, 16, and 23, 2001, report that the following state legislatures are considering bills that would recognize the exception: Alabama, Colorado, Idaho, Indiana, Kansas, Massachusetts, Michigan, Nevada, New Jersey, New York, Oregon, Pennsylvania, and Texas.

30. Laurie L. Levenson, "Criminal Law: Stopping the Clock," *National Law Journal*, December 11, 2000, A15 (California, New York, Texas, and Wisconsin); James E. Starrs, "The John Doe DNA Profile Warrant," *Scientific Sleuthing Review* 24 (2000): 4 (California, Kansas, New York, and Wisconsin). The January 26, 2001, *DNA Legislative and Media Report* states that "a [grand] jury in Missouri has indicted the genetic profiles of two unknown rapists." See docs.appliedbiosystems.com/hid.taf.

31. Starrs, "The John Doe DNA Profile Warrant," 4.

32. Ibid.

33. M. S. Enkoji, "Judge Oks Use of DNA," *Sacramento Bee*, February 24, 2001, B1, B3 ("The use of DNA evidence cleared an unprecedented legal hurdle Friday when a Sacramento County Superior Court judge ruled that the biological marker alone is enough to identify a suspect in a 1994 rape. A warrant for the unnamed assailant identified only by genetic code from the seven-year-old crime is legal, even though the suspect's name was discovered after

the statute of limitations had expired, Superior Court Judge Tani G. Cantil-Sakauye said; the defendant in question is Paul Eugene Robinson; Robinson's attorney, Johnny Griffin, said that . . . [h]e is appealing the decision").

34. Melissa McCord, "Investigators Relying More on DNA to Solve Crime," Associated Press State & Local Wire, December 3, 2001; "Grand Jury Amends DNA Indictment after Rape Suspect Identified," Associated Press State & Local Wire, October 29, 2002.

35. "National DNA Evidence Commission Begins Work on Recommendations Sought by Justice Department," *United States Law Week (BNA)* 66 (1998): 2593.

36. John Branton, "Inmates' DNA Taken for Crime Database," *The Columbian* (Clark County, Wash.), July 22, 2002. See also chapter 1. Lazer notes that most of the recent proposed amendments to DNA legislation extend the legislation to all felons.

37. La.Rev.Stat.Ann. 15:609(A); "Iberia parish to take DNA of all arrested," Associated Press State & Local Wire, June 2, 2002; David H. Kaye, "The Constitutionality of DNA Sampling on Arrest," *Cornell Journal of Law and Public Policy* 10 (2001): 455; Martha L. Lawson, "Note: Personal Does Not Always Equal 'Private'; The Constitutionality of Requiring DNA Samples from Convicted Felons and Arrestees," *William & Mary Bill of Rights Journal* 9 (2001): 645; Aaron P. Stevens, "Arresting Crime: Expanding the Scope of DNA Databases in America," *Texas Law Review* 79 (March 2001), 921. See also David H. Kaye, Michael E. Smith, and Edward J. Imwinkelried, "Is a DNA Identification Database in Your Future?," *Criminal Justice* 16, no. 4 (Fall 2001). With one major exception, the courts have uniformly upheld the constitutionality of legislation mandating that persons such as convicts supply DNA samples. Paul C. Giannelli and Edward J. Imwinkelried, *Civil and Criminal Cases*, 3rd ed. (Charlottesville, Va.: LEXIS Law Publishing, 1999). *Scientific Evidence* §18-5(A), at 57–58. The notable exception is *U.S. v. Kincade*, 345 F.3d 1095 (9th Cir. 2003). Notwithstanding *U.S. v. Kincade*, the trend elsewhere is to uphold such legislation against constitutional attack. See, for example, *U.S. v. Plotts*, 347 F.3d 873 (10th Cir. 2003); *Vore v. U.S. Dept. of Justice*, 281 F. Supp.2d 1129 (D.Ariz. 2003).

38. Akhil Reed Amar, "The Government Should Require a DNA Sample, but Keep It Private," *Fulton County (Georgia) Daily Report*, June 21, 2001; Akhil Reed Amar, "With Safeguards, DNA Database Would Improve Justice System," *Seattle Post-Intelligencer*, May 12, 2002, F9; David H. Kaye, Michael E. Smith, and Edward J. Imwinkelried, "Is a DNA Identification Database in Your Future?" *Criminal Justice* 16 (2001): 44.

39. David Korn, "Genetic Privacy, Medical Information Privacy, and the Use of Human Tissue Specimens in Research," in *Genetic Testing and the Use of Information*, ed. Clarisa Long (Washington, D.C.: American Enterprise Press, 1999), 30; E. W. Clayton et al., "Informed Consent for Genetic Research on Stored Tissue Samples," *Journal of the American Medical Association* 274 (1995): 1786; John Harris, "Ethical Genetic Research on Human Subjects," *Jurimetrics Journal* 40 (1999): 77.

40. Fed.R.Crim.P. 4, 18 U.S.C.A.; Starrs, "The John Doe DNA Profile Warrant," *Scientific Sleuthing Review* 1, no. 3 (Fall 2000): 24.

41. Levenson, "Criminal Law," at A15. ("Given that most of us do not know our DNA composition, it is difficult to see how a DNA indictment gives notice to defendants that they face criminal charges and should promptly move to resolve those charges. If . . . it will take

long periods of time to identify the DNA defendants, there is a strong likelihood that memories will fade or evidence will be lost between the time of the indictment and the time the defendant is actually called to face the charges. Certainly in those cases in which the defendant claims that the sexual encounter was consensual, the delayed revelation of the DNA charges will make it more difficult to mount a defense"). See also Veronica Valdivieso, "DNA Warrants: A Panacea for Old, Cold Rape Cases?" *Georgetown Law Journal* 90 (2002): 1009; "Beyond Fingerprinting: Indicting DNA Threatens Criminal Defendant's Constitutional and Statutory Rights" (comment), *American University Law Review* 50 (2001): 979.

42. See Edward Connors et al., *Convicted by Juries, Exonerated by Science: Case Studies in the Use of DNA Evidence to Establish Innocence after Trial* (Washington, D.C.: National Institute of Justice, U.S. Department of Justice, 1996).

43. National Commission on the Future of DNA Evidence, *Postconviction DNA Testing: Recommendations for Handling Requests* (Washington, D.C.: National Institute of Justice, U.S. Department of Justice, 1999), 2.

44. Ibid. See also Jennifer Boemer, "Other Rising Legal Issues: In the Interest of Justice; Granting Post-conviction Deoxyribonucleic Acid (DNA) Testing to Inmates," *William Mitchell Law Review* 27 (2001); Rochelle L. Haller, "The Innocence Protection Act: Why Federal Measures Requiring Post-conviction DNA Testing and Preservation of Evidence Are Needed in Order to Reduce the Risk of Wrongful Executions," *New York Law School Journal of Human Rights* 18 (2001): 101; Frank Green, "Lawyer Stresses Power of DNA; Tests Clear Even Some Who 'Confess,'" *Richmond Times-Dispatch*, July 17, 2001, A1.

45. *People v. Urioste*, 736 N.E.2d 706, 249 Ill.Dec. 512 (App. 2000).

46. National Commission on the Future of DNA Evidence, *Postconviction DNA Testing*, 5.

47. Ibid., 40.

48. Ibid., 7.

49. Ibid., 49.

50. Ibid., 55–58.

51. Ibid., 55.

52. Joe S. Cecil, Valerie P. Hans, and Elizabeth C. Wiggins, "Citizen Comprehension of Difficult Issues: Lessons from Civil Jury Trials," *American University Law Review* 40 (1991): 744–745, 751, 754, 758; David Faigman and A. J. Baglioni, "Bayes' Theorem in the Trial Process: Instructing Jurors on the Value of Statistical Evidence," *Law & Human Behavior* 12 (1988): 13–16; Jane Goodman, "Jurors' Comprehension and Assessment of Probabilistic Evidence," *American Journal of Trial Advocacy* 16 (1992): 386 ("final judgments of guilt tended to be significantly lower than a Bayesian analysis suggests they should have been"); Jason Schklar and Shari Seidman Diamond, "Juror Reactions to DNA Evidence: Errors and Expectancies," *Law & Human Behavior* 23 (1999): 159 ("participants in our study afforded probabilistic evidence less weight than would be expected."); David Thompson, "Are Juries Competent to Evaluate Statistical Evidence?" *Law & Contemporary Problems* 52 (1989); William C. Thompson and Edward C. Schumann, "Interpretation of Statistical Evidence in Criminal Trials: The Prosecutor's Fallacy and the Defense Attorney's Fallacy," *Law & Contemporary Problems* 11 (1987): 183.

53. David H. Kaye and Jonathan Koehler, "Can Jurors Understand Probabilistic Evidence?" *Journal of the Royal Statistical Society* 154 (1991): 79–80; Jonathan Koehler, "The Psychology of Numbers in the Courtroom: How to Make DNA-Match Statistics Seem Impressive or Insufficient," *Southern California Law Review* 74 (2001): 1275.

54. 509 U.S. 579 (1993).

55. 522 U.S. 136 (1997).

56. 526 U.S. 137 (1999).

57. Margaret A. Berger, "Laboratory Error Seen through the Lens of Science and Policy," *U. C. Davis Law Review* 30 (1997): 1096, 1081.

58. Ibid., 1102.

59. Ibid.

60. Ibid.; Koehler, "On Conveying the Probative Value of DNA Evidence"; William C. Thompson, "Accepting Lower Standards: The National Research Council's Second Report on Forensic DNA Evidence," *Jurimetrics Journal* 37 (1997): 405.

61. For example, the question of whether the defense in a criminal trial can inform the jury of error rates disclosed by proficiency tests is not novel. The very same question arose during the 1970s when the Law Enforcement Assistance Administration released the results of the Laboratory Proficiency Testing Program. See "Introduction," in Edward J. Imwinkelried, *Scientific and Expert Evidence* (New York: Practicing Law Institute, 1981), 3–4. I can recall discussing that very question with defense counsel such as Ephraim Margolin of San Francisco shortly after the release of the report about the testing program, which attracted a fair measure of public attention at the time of its release. "Crime Labs' Credibility Questioned," *Trial* 15 (1978); "Forensic Failures: Evidence Tests Stump Labs," *Law Enforcement Assistance Administration Newsletter* 7, no. 7 (1978). John Ackerman, then dean of the National College of Criminal Defense Lawyers and Public Defenders, raised the possibility of using the proficiency test results as defense evidence. John Ackerman, "LEAA-Funded Study Casts Doubts on Reliability of Crime Lab Reports," *Trial Diplomacy Journal* 1 (1978).

62. Edward J. Imwinkelried, "The Debate in the DNA Cases over the Foundation for the Admission of Scientific Evidence: The Importance of Human Error as a Cause of Forensic Misanalysis," *Washington University Law Quarterly* 69 (1991): 32.

63. 545 N.Y.S.2d 985 (N.Y.Sup.Ct. 1989).

64. 447 N.W.2d 422 (Minn. 1989).

65. Rockne Harmon, "How Has DNA Evidence Fared? Beauty Is in the Eye of the Beholder," *Expert Evidence Report* 1 (1990): 149.

66. Fed.R.Evid. 702(3), 28 U.S.C.A.

67. Edward J. Imwinkelried, *The Methods of Attacking Scientific Evidence*, 3rd ed. (Charlottesville, Va.: Michie, 1997), chap. 12.

68. Committee on DNA Technology in Forensic Science: An Update, *The Evaluation of Forensic DNA Evidence* (Washington, D.C.: National Academies Press, 1996); Committee on DNA Technology in Forensic Science, *DNA Technology in Forensic Science* (Washington, D.C.: National Academies Press, 1992).

69. Koehler, "On Conveying the Probative Value of DNA Evidence," 862–863, 865, 878; Jonathan Koehler, "Error and Exaggeration in the Presentation of DNA Evidence at Trial," *Jurimetrics Journal* 34 (1993): 27–28.

70. Koehler, "Error and Exaggeration," 31–32; Jonathan Koehler, "DNA Matches and Statistics: Important Questions, Surprising Answers," *Judicature* 76 (1993): 224.

71. Imwinkelried, "The Debate in the DNA Cases," 29.

72. Ernest E. Snyder, *History of the Physical Sciences* (Columbus, Ohio: Charles E. Merrill, 1969), 38; Bert Black, "A Unified Theory of Scientific Evidence," *Fordham Law Review* 56 (1988): 595, 621, 623–624.

73. Imwinkelried, "The Debate in the DNA Cases," 29–30.

74. Joseph L. Peterson et al., *Crime Laboratory Proficiency Testing Research Program* (Washington, D.C.: U.S. Government Printing Office, 1978), 203–206, 223, 230, 239, 258; Hugh J. Hansen, Samuel P. Caudill, and Joe Boone, "Crisis in Drug Testing: Results of CDC Blind Study," *Journal of the American Medical Association* 253 (1985): 2382; Morton F. Mason, "Some Realities and Results of Proficiency Testing of Laboratories Performing Toxicological Analyses," *Journal of Analytical Toxicology* 5 (1981): 201; Naresh C. Jain, Thomas C. Sneath, and Robert D. Budd, "Blind Proficiency Testing in Urine Drug Screening: The Need for an Effective Quality Control Program," *Journal of Analytical Toxicology* 1 (1977): 142; M. Jeffrey Shoemaker, Martha Klein, and Leonard Sideman, "Drug Abuse Proficiency Testing in Pennsylvania 1972–1976," *Journal of Analytical Toxicology* 1 (1977): 130.

75. Jonathan J. Koehler, "The Probity-Policy Distinction in the Statistical Evidence Debate," *Tulane Law Review* 66 (1991): 141.

76. David McCord, "A Primer for the Nonmathematically Inclined on Mathematical Evidence in Criminal Trials: *People v. Collins* and Beyond," *Washington & Lee Law Review* 47 (1990): 793, 800–806; Louis J. Braun, "Quantitative Analysis and the Law: Probability Theory as a Tool of Evidence in Criminal Trials," *Utah Law Review* 4 (1982); "Foreword," *Law & Contemporary Problems* 46 (1983).

77. *United States v. Shonubi*, 895 F.Supp. 460, 514, 517–519 (E.D.N.Y. 1995) (Weinstein, J.), vacated, 103 F.3d 1085 (2d Cir. 1997).

6

Lessons from DNA: Restriking the Balance between Finality and Justice

Margaret A. Berger

One of the remarkable features of DNA testing is that not only does it suffice to convict, but it also serves to exonerate. To date, upwards of 140 convictions have been vacated as a consequence of postconviction DNA testing.[1] This number would undoubtedly be considerably higher had it been possible to test in the many cases in which crime scene evidence was inadvertently lost or routinely destroyed. It has been estimated that no evidence can be found in about 75 percent of the cases in which inmates seek DNA postconviction testing.[2]

These vacated convictions require us to rethink how our criminal justice system operates. They suggest the need to reassess the value of finality in criminal proceedings and to strike a new balance between the benefits of repose and the demands of justice. In this chapter, I first examine the assumptions buttressing our traditional approach to finality and how they have been challenged by DNA testing. I then turn to factors that need to be balanced in considering when postconviction DNA testing should be allowed. Finally, I discuss some lessons of enduring importance that we ought to remember once the demand for postconviction DNA testing dwindles, as it undoubtedly will. Postconviction testing will gradually become passé as DNA testing is routinely done prior to trial and as DNA technology reaches the point at which future retesting will not provide any more definitive answers when initial results are inconclusive. Nevertheless, even though in the long run the proper handling of postconviction requests for DNA testing may turn out to be a fleeting concern, this interim problem has highlighted flawed assumptions and failings in our criminal justice system that will continue to require attention.

The Case for Finality

The law has always recognized the need for finality in judicial proceedings, and especially in criminal proceedings. Indeed at common law, a motion for a new trial could be granted only during the term of the court in which the final judgment of conviction was entered.[3] Although over time, many states extended the period in which relief could be sought from a perceived erroneous judgment, the window in which this could be done remained quite narrow, rarely extending beyond a year.[4]

Why did the legal system seek to ensure the finality of most convictions? A number of strong beliefs converged to produce this result.

The Presumption of Correctness

First of all, there was a firmly embraced presumption that a jury of one's peers would render a correct verdict after a trial at which the accused was accorded a full panoply of constitutional guarantees, including the right to counsel. And the system provided, in addition, for appellate review and included mechanisms for correcting grave constitutional errors. Allowing verdicts to be reopened implied that this system did not always work and detracted from the majesty of the law. It seemed more palatable to suggest that in the rare instance of an erroneous verdict, executive clemency rather than judicial attention would adequately rectify the mistake.[5]

Evidence Becomes Less Reliable over Time

Second, there was a fear—a genuine and well-based fear—that vacating a criminal judgment would lead to a second trial in which the result was less likely to be accurate than the original verdict, because criminal proceedings often hinged on testimonial proof offered by eyewitnesses and other fact witnesses. Over time, we know that some of these witnesses will die or vanish; we live in a highly mobile society in which persons often relocate and then cannot be found. Even when a witness is available for a second trial, we know that memories fade with the passage of time. Furthermore, we suspect that perjury will flourish as witnesses become unavailable or fail to remember.

In *Herrera v. Collins*, the Supreme Court categorically stated that "the passage of time only diminishes the reliability of criminal adjudications."[6] The facts of *Herrera* certainly supported this conclusion. Ten years after his conviction, the petitioner claimed for the first time that his brother, who had died six years previously, was the actual killer. To prove this claim, petitioner offered a number of affidavits, which were inconsistent with one another, and with defendant's version of the events. The proof at trial had been extensive, including some traditional serological evidence and a letter signed by the petitioner in which he confessed his guilt.[7]

The Value of Closure

Finality also promoted needed closure for victims and their families and for participants in the legal proceedings: witnesses, judicial officers, prosecutors, victims' rights advocates, and law enforcement personnel. Finality meant that all these individuals could get on with their lives, because the case was over. Because some closure was undoubtedly a first step toward emotional healing, finality had value in contributing to better mental health.[8]

The Floodgates Argument

Judicial resources have always been strained. Finality conserved scarce judicial time by not opening the floodgates to meritless and costly claims. Furthermore, by freeing judges to handle cases in which there as yet had been no adjudication, finality served the presumption of innocence by providing an accused with a speedier opportunity to prove his innocence and emerge from the shadow of the state's accusation.

The Impact of DNA Testing on Arguments for Finality

Many of the assumptions on which the case for finality rested have been significantly undercut by the advent of DNA profiling. We now know that eyewitnesses may be mistaken, that traditional forensic evidence does not always produce accurate results, that DNA evidence actually gets better over time as technology improves, and that greatly expanded databases may enable the true culprit to be identified if postconviction DNA testing is done. It also remains true, however, that courts are hard put to handle their current dockets and that judicial budgets are as strained as ever. Furthermore, DNA testing has imposed tremendous costs in money and time on forensic laboratories as they struggle to handle current case work, to reassess unsolved cases, and to deal with enormous backlogs of samples collected for databanks. What has been the impact of these changes on the arguments for finality?

DNA Testing Rebuts the Presumption of Accuracy

Undoubtedly, the demonstration that numerous defendants were wrongfully convicted has made the most dramatic inroad into the case for finality, especially as a significant percentage of the convictions that have been vacated related to inmates who were on death row.[9] As yet, we know of no case in which someone was executed who would have been exonerated by DNA testing, but the possibility is real and is being investigated in a number of cases.[10]

For the first time, we have irrefutable proof of the fallibility of eyewitness testimony. Of course, the reliability of eyewitness identifications has been suspect for years.[11] The Supreme Court evinced an interest in reducing the suggestiveness of lineups as long ago as the 1960s[12] but shortly thereafter retreated from doing anything further to improve the accuracy of pretrial identifications.[13] Extensive psychological research that began in the 1970s—before DNA entered the courtroom—seemed to demonstrate convincingly the failings of eyewitness testimony.[14] Of necessity, however, the social science studies that documented the inaccuracies of witnesses' accounts were based almost exclusively on data derived through simulations. Skeptics questioned whether witnesses in real life would perform as poorly as the participants in a staged or scripted event who lacked the same incentives to make a correct identification and who were not as actively engaged in the event as a witness to a real crime.[15]

But the more than 140 convictions that have now been vacated on the basis of postconviction DNA testing offer unquestionable and systematic proof of the unreliability of eyewitness testimony. It has now become possible to analyze what went wrong in the proceedings that led to these convictions. Almost every one of these cases rested almost exclusively on an erroneous identification.[16] Furthermore, we know that even an intelligent witness who consciously sought to study her assailant's face could make an incorrect identification and, in addition, fail to recognize the true perpetrator.[17]

Moreover, the advent of DNA testing has done more than expose the fallacies of eyewitness testimony. It has also illuminated other errors. In many of the cases in which convictions have been overturned on the basis of DNA testing, the prosecution had relied on expert testimony about matching hair in addition to eyewitness testimony.[18] Mitochondrial DNA testing has now established the inaccuracy of microscopic hair comparisons that courts had previously admitted.[19]

DNA has also had a revolutionary impact on forensic-laboratory practices. Critics had for decades protested the sorry state of many U.S. crime laboratories.[20] Both committees formed by the National Research Council in the 1990s to study the forensic use of DNA stressed the need for strict laboratory standards to minimize the risk of error.[21] Under the leadership of the FBI, guidelines were developed for quality control and quality assurance programs in DNA laboratories,[22] and by 1999, a report by the National Institute of Justice reported progress in forensic DNA laboratories with regard to implementing such programs.[23] The report also recognized the need to tailor quality control and quality assurance programs for other types of forensic laboratories as well. The consequence has been a heightened awareness of the importance of credible laboratory performance and the realization that faulty or sloppy laboratory analyses may result in wrongful convictions.[24]

Obviously, the presumption that jury verdicts are correct takes a battering when we see indisputable proof of the weakness of eyewitness testimony, the worthlessness of some traditional forensic techniques, and the woefully deficient standards that exist in some crime laboratories.

DNA Evidence Becomes More Reliable over Time

One assumption on which the belief in finality rests—that the passage of time will undermine the accuracy of a criminal adjudication[25]—is completely refuted by DNA testing.[26] The cases in which convictions have been vacated demonstrate that a far more accurate result is sometimes obtainable by means of DNA testing, even though many years, often more than a decade, have elapsed since the original verdict.

Unlike the memory of witnesses, DNA does not fade away.[27] Furthermore, ever since forensic DNA first entered the courtroom, technological advances have steadily enhanced the discriminating power of DNA to identify correctly the source of biological samples. Additional progress is expected in the near future.[28]

DNA Testing May Lead to Closure in Unsolved Cases

The argument that finality provides closure for those emotionally involved is powerful. Reopening a case may be traumatic, especially for victims and their families, who thought that they had finally put what are often prolonged legal proceedings behind them. When DNA testing results in the exclusion of an inmate, the victim will suffer great guilt if his or her erroneous eyewitness testimony was responsible for the conviction,[29] and the victim may, in addition, be terrified that the real perpetrator will return, as he may have threatened to do.

Despite these compelling reasons for acknowledging the value of closure, the argument that finality is essential to psychological health has also become less convincing since the appearance of postconviction DNA testing. Testing may lead to new and different benefits for the victim that must be considered in evaluating the value of finality. For instance, if an inmate's identity as the perpetrator is confirmed— as it is in a significant percentage of cases[30]—the victim can be reassured that this result decreases the possibility that the assailant will be released on probation or parole. Furthermore, the inmate's DNA may be added to the federal or state data- bases, which may result in his being implicated in unsolved crimes.[31] If the testing results in an exclusion of the inmate, running the crime scene sample against DNA from other suspects or against a data bank may lead to the identification of the true culprit.[32] Although the victim may be left with regrets about her role in the original trial, she will finally have true closure, because attempts to reopen the original case will cease. In addition, she will have the satisfaction of knowing that others will be safer. If the perpetrator was not in prison at the time he was identified, he now will be, and if he was imprisoned, he will be much less likely to be released.

In cases of exclusion in which the identity of the true perpetrator is not immedi- ately revealed, running the crime scene sample against samples from unsolved crimes may prove helpful. If there is a match, further investigation may reveal other links between the cases that will serve to identify the perpetrator. Putting the sample into the database may also help to solve crimes in the future. Here, too, the linking of the cases may provide crucial investigative leads. Furthermore, as databases grow, there is a possibility that an unidentified sample will match a new entry. In sum, postconviction DNA testing may lead to resolutions beyond the particular pro- ceeding in question and provide closure in cases that would otherwise remain unsolved.

The Availability of Postconviction Testing Does Not Unloose Floodgates, Although It May Impose Some Costs

The floodgates argument has been in the news of late in connection with new legislation that would permit prisoners to seek access to DNA testing.[33] Until very recently, only two states, New York in 1994 and Illinois in 1998, had enacted special statutes that specifically authorize post-conviction access to DNA testing. This is changing rapidly. Spurred by growing public pressure to acknowledge the problem of wrongful convictions,[34] legislatures in many jurisdictions began to consider a host of new proposals. By January 1, 2004, thirty-seven states, including New York and Illinois, had enacted legislation authorizing inmates to seek DNA testing under spec- ified circumstances,[35] and legislation was pending in other states[36] and in Congress.[37]

Although critics voice apprehension that prisoners' petitions for DNA testing will have an adverse impact on the legal system,[38] the empirical evidence suggests that fears of an avalanche of requests are vastly overblown. For instance, the California attorney-general's office asked for $1.8 million in 2001 to respond to the four hundred petitions it expects to receive each year under California's statute, which took effect on January 1, 2001.[39] However, New York had a total of only about one hundred applications in the first seven years during which its statute has been in effect.[40] This is remarkably low considering the large population of New York, the extremely liberal standard in the New York statute,[41] and the fact that New York is the home of the Innocence Project, which far more than any other group has been involved in postconviction DNA proceedings. Furthermore, California's actual experience seems far more consistent with New York's than with the California attorney-general's office's prediction. In 2000, even before there was a statute, the district attorney's office for the County of San Diego, which has a population of three million, on its own initiative, began to review all convictions of persons still incarcerated that were obtained prior to 1993, the year when DNA casework began. With about 75 percent of the work completed, only three cases had been identified in which DNA testing might have made a difference in the outcome of the original trial, but in only one was there a possibility that testing would be done. One of the three inmates rejected the opportunity to be tested, and in a second case, no biological evidence that could be tested was preserved.[42]

That there may be considerably fewer requests for postconviction DNA testing than some envision does not, of course, mean that there are no costs associated with such requests. Aside from the expense of investigating, screening, and perhaps ultimately testing, the cases in which convictions have been vacated demonstrate that complex issues arise that command considerable judicial and prosecutorial attention before they are resolved. And certainly it is to be expected that the new statutes authorizing access to DNA testing will raise numerous questions of interpretation when they initially go into effect. In addition, as will be discussed later in the chapter, the right to postconviction testing will be meaningless unless the petitioner is afforded assistance in explaining the significance of an exclusionary result, and this aid will add to the cost of the proceedings. The scarce-resources argument therefore continues to have some strength, even though the more extreme predictions about the judicial system's being swamped by motions for postconviction DNA testing can be discounted.

The advent of DNA testing has clearly reduced the persuasiveness of traditional arguments that urge finality in criminal judicial proceedings. This inroad against the value of finality is a reality that more and more jurisdictions have become willing to accept—in at least some situations. For at a minimum, the new statutes that authorize postconviction DNA testing acknowledge that it is inconsistent with justice to deprive all wrongfully convicted persons of a meaningful opportunity to set aside their convictions in a judicial proceeding. These statutes vary considerably, however, in setting out the conditions under which access to DNA testing will be available and illustrate a variety of policy choices in striking a new balance between finality and justice.

Restriking the Balance between Finality and Justice

This section first considers and critiques three sets of policy choices that enter into determining when postconviction DNA testing will be made available. It then discusses procedural choices that also need to be made.

When Should DNA Testing Be Available?

Proof of Innocence versus a Lesser Standard   A fundamental choice that faces legislatures and courts is whether DNA testing should be available only when an exclusionary result could be determinative of the innocence of the petitioner seeking testing[43] or should be extended to situations in which proof of an exclusion might have a lesser effect.[44] For instance, testing could be limited to cases in which the result might raise a reasonable doubt,[45] or allowed if an exclusionary result at trial would probably have led to a more favorable verdict or sentence.[46] Determining the standard that exclusionary results must meet is the point at which striking an appropriate balance between the competing interests of finality and justice becomes most acute.

Sometimes the exonerative effect of an exclusion will be obvious, as when the petitioner was convicted of raping a sexually inactive child. At other times exoneration may depend on the facts of the case. If, for instance, the petitioner was convicted of raping a woman who reported that two men had raped her, and that she had not had consensual sex in the relevant period preceding the rape, testing will exonerate the petitioner only if the results reveal two separate DNA profiles, neither of which is the petitioner's.

There are also cases in which the effect of an exclusionary result will be in dispute. One such scenario occurs when the rape victim is dead and the prosecution argues that an exclusionary result does not prove the petitioner's innocence because if the victim had consensual sex before her death the crime scene DNA profile might be that of her partner rather than that of her assailant. Such an argument was made in the case of Roy Criner in Texas, in which the petitioner's conviction was reinstated by the reviewing court after it had been vacated on the basis of an exclusionary result. The petitioner was finally pardoned after a DNA test of a cigarette butt found near the victim's body was found to contain both the victim's DNA and DNA that matched the donor of the semen.[47]

In cases such as these it might be fairer to place the burden of proof on the prosecution to show the likelihood of the victim's having had consensual sex, rather than requiring the petitioner to rebut the possibility. If the petitioner is innocent, he is unlikely to have any information about the victim's life, but the prosecution will have conducted a full investigation into the victim's last few days in searching for her killer. The law often shifts the burden of establishing a fact to the party who has peculiar knowledge as to the matter.[48] Other evidentiary mechanisms, such as drawing inferences from the failure to produce evidence, might be needed to deal with other fact patterns. Suppose, for instance, that a victim admits to consensual sex at the relevant time, but his or her partner refuses to provide a sample, or has vanished, or is dead, all real possibilities given the time that may have elapsed between the conviction and the request for testing. As yet there is virtually no law on obtaining elimination samples from third persons, or on the consequences of such a sample's not being available.[49]

In some cases an exclusionary result will not be determinative of innocence. It might, however, raise a reasonable doubt about guilt or might likely have produced a more favorable result at the petitioner's trial, or it might simply be helpful to the petitioner, as when the conviction was used to enhance sentencing for a different crime. Determining precisely what effect the lack of DNA testing had on a trial's outcome may be extremely speculative. What, for instance, would have happened at the defendant's trial if the prosecutor had not continuously and suggestively waved a bloody shirt found at the defendant's house? Even if DNA testing proves that the bloodstains on the shirt are not the victim's, that does not prove that the defendant is not a murderer. But it might mean that defendant had a very unfair trial. Should we spend scarce resources on looking at that kind of case?

The new statutes contain a variety of different standards that run along the spectrum from requiring an exclusion to establish actual innocence[50] to no standard at all.[51] It is too soon to determine what a majority of the states are doing, because so many bills are pending, and the appellate courts have not as yet had an adequate opportunity to interpret the statutes that have gone into effect.[52]

Limiting Testing to Inmates with the Most Severe Sentences versus All Inmates
Some states have enacted statutes that tie access to postconviction testing to the severity of the petitioner's sentence. Tennessee and Kentucky allow petitions only by inmates who were convicted of first-degree murder and sentenced to death.[53] Washington similarly permits petitions by inmates on death row but also allows requests from persons sentenced to "life imprisonment without possibility of release or parole."[54]

Although it is perhaps understandable why a state might ration its resources by limiting postconviction DNA testing to cases in which exclusionary results would most likely have produced a different outcome, it is difficult to fathom why an inmate who never had an opportunity to establish his innocence through DNA testing should rot behind prison bars even when an exclusion would be exonerative.[55]

Insisting on a Continuous Claim of Innocence versus Treating Guilty Pleas and Confessions as Factors to Take into Account   We know from the work of the Innocence Projects that a high percentage of those whose convictions were ultimately vacated had confessed (or had allegedly confessed) to the crimes of which they were convicted.[56] We also know from other sources that false confessions are not a rarity.[57] Recently, the phenomenon received much attention in connection with the 1989 Central Park jogger rape case, in which five young men, then fourteen to sixteen years old, were convicted after they confessed to a particularly heinous gang rape in which the victim was left for dead. Twelve years later, an inmate imprisoned for a series of rapes confessed to the crime, and his DNA was found to match the Central Park crime scene sample.[58] The convictions were vacated.

The failure to assert a continuous claim of innocence should not, therefore, be treated as a conclusive factor weighing against a request for testing.

Procedural Issues
Another way of allocating resources is to provide varying benefits for petitioners depending on how likely it is that an exclusionary result would result in proof of

actual innocence. For instance, the state might pay for testing in certain categories of cases if the petitioner is indigent but not in others, though it would still permit testing if the inmate could arrange for funding.

Payment for counsel is, however, essential in the case of all requests. As the preceding discussion about the varying significance of an exclusionary result should indicate, far more is involved in postconviction DNA applications than simply asking for testing of the biological crime scene evidence. The viability of the inmate's claim cannot be assessed without a thorough investigation of the case. This means evaluating trial transcripts and laboratory and police reports, as well as trial and appellate briefs. It is highly unlikely that this can be done without the assistance of counsel, whose help is also essential in presenting the petitioner's request to the court ruling on the petition[59] and in identifying and locating the biological evidence that was collected and that might be testable if it still exists.

There is no constitutional right to counsel at the postconviction stage. While the new Arizona, California, Indiana, New Jersey, North Carolina, Oklahoma, and Wisconsin statutes contain specific provisions authorizing the court to appoint counsel for indigent petitioners seeking postconviction testing,[60] other statutes are silent on this issue. Since it is impossible to categorize the nature of a claim without counsel's assistance, the need for counsel for all indigent petitioners should be acknowledged in all jurisdictions, and some sort of funding mechanism should be established.[61] Otherwise the would-be petitioner might be thwarted in his efforts to obtain testing unless he manages to obtain the assistance of an organization like the Innocence Project or is referred to appropriate pro bono counsel by a sympathetic prosecutor or judge. Such an ad hoc approach does not deal adequately with the gravity of wrongfully obtained convictions. Funds for paying experts should be available as well, as defense counsel require assistance in assessing DNA evidence.[62]

Where Should the Responsibility for Assessing Postconviction Relief Lie?

Aside from spurring legislative action, the current interest in postconviction issues has had another effect: It has convinced some prosecutors to review convictions in their jurisdictions to determine whether inmates should be offered postconviction DNA testing even though they have not made a request for it. At first glance, this looks like a wonderful development. Prosecutorial review promises an evenhanded approach that would benefit all inmates and not just those who are particularly resourceful, or who have persistent lawyers, relatives, or friends who can find and persuade a court or prosecutor to allow access to DNA testing. But there is another side to this coin. We have ample evidence from other professions and from the law enforcement community itself that institutions frequently resist exposing errors committed by their constituents for fear of jeopardizing relationships with fellow members.[63] Unfortunately we know of quite a few long-standing failures to uncover mistakes in the criminal justice system. Prosecutors have been reluctant to report possible failings in the laboratory,[64] in police departments,[65] or within the prosecutorial office itself.[66] This institutional reluctance to acknowledge mistakes poses the risk that prosecutorial review, rather than uncovering instances in which postconviction testing should be done, will instead whitewash the system and make it harder to secure testing in any individual case.[67] As the foregoing discussion indicates, there is not always a bright line that instantly distinguishes a case in which testing is justified from one in which it is not. Institutional biases may blind prosecutors who are reviewing cases en masse from recognizing meritorious cases.

Is there anything that can be done to ensure that deserving candidates for postconviction DNA testing will not be overlooked? One possibility would be not to leave the initial protocol that sets out criteria for reviewing cases solely to the discretion of a prosecutorial office. Instead, the protocol should be designed by a joint committee that includes representatives of the defense bar, such as public defenders, and members of the judiciary who are familiar with DNA issues. A second possible safeguard would be to have the actual review of the convictions audited by an outside group, perhaps by sampling the cases that are being considered. Bar groups or law school clinics might be able to undertake some of this work pro bono. Finally, as has long been urged by the Innocence Project, we need a commission or commissions, like Britain has, to investigate all convictions that are vacated to determine what went wrong. Such a commission could look beyond the facts of a particular case to determine whether systemic problems in the jurisdiction produced the erroneous verdict. A finding of serious flaws in the operation of any component of law enforcement should trigger an independent review of inmate convictions with regard to the viability of postconviction DNA testing.[68]

Lessons for the Future

Requests for postconviction DNA testing may soon disappear. Indeed, some of the new statutes have inserted dates after which testing requests will be automatically denied in the absence of exceptional circumstances.[69] But although the need for postconviction DNA testing is undoubtedly a temporary phenomenon, one that will be relegated to a footnote in some treatise of the future, we will be making a terrible mistake if we do not extract some enduring lessons from this experience:

- We must develop protocols for preserving evidence after a conviction. We will never know how many persons remain in prison who could have been cleared by DNA testing, if only there had been something to test. At the very least we need guidelines on where and in what form evidence should be retained, and for how long, and we need provisions as to how available evidence should be inventoried. The countless hours spent in searching for evidence to test could certainly be put to better use. It may be that other technological innovations may occur in the future, raising the same need to reexamine evidence as existed with DNA. Furthermore, we know that evidence may have to be reexamined for many reasons. At this moment, there is an ongoing investigation of the police in Los Angeles as well as other cities, and investigations of forensic laboratories are being conducted in a number of states. The possibility of moratoriums on the death penalty is being explored. Overturning wrongfully obtained convictions in these jurisdictions and others may hinge on finding evidence in the files of the cases being reexamined.

- We must pay more attention to what constitutes good science. Many of the convictions that have been vacated on the basis of DNA evidence hinged on forensic science that should and could have been attacked at trial, either because the underlying science had not been validated, or because the laboratory procedures used were so deficient. Bad forensic science cannot be eliminated unless funding for studies and educating the defense bar is provided.

- We must improve the quality of defense counsel representing indigents. Many of the cases in which convictions have been vacated demonstrate that the defendant might well not have been convicted if he had been provided with adequate representation.

- The postconviction DNA testing cases clearly point to the ugly effect of racism on our criminal justice system. The Innocence Project found that 40 percent of the cases in which it was successful in having a conviction vacated involved a black inmate and white victims, even though only 15 percent of sex murders had these characteristics.

The postconviction DNA testing cases provide us with a window through which to view our criminal justice system. The landscape that we glimpse clearly corresponds with other contemporaneous accounts of the sorry state of criminal justice in the United States.[70] This is a condition that we cannot afford to tolerate if we value living in a just society.

Rather than ending this chapter on a pessimistic note, however, I would suggest that a more upbeat, alternative reading can also be gleaned from this record of post-conviction DNA testing. The experience shows that change is possible, that individuals can make a difference, and that persons of good will can cooperate even though they represent different constituencies with divergent views. Starting little more than ten years ago, a small group of dedicated lawyers, and in particular those connected with the Innocence Project, grasped the remedial power of DNA and began an effort that led to justice, albeit greatly delayed justice, for at least some of the wrongfully convicted. In doing so, they have alerted us to the danger of rigidly upholding finality as a prime value of our criminal justice system and have illuminated the many failings that infect criminal proceedings in the United States. The current legislative initiative with regard to postconviction DNA testing attests to the public's having become sensitized to these issues through accounts of DNA exonerations. We may now have a remarkable opportunity to make sorely needed changes in our system of criminal justice that could have significance long after the era of postconviction DNA testing has ended. We should make the most of this moment in time.

Notes

1. See www.innocenceproject.org (accessed December 31, 2003).

2. Peter Neufeld, "Preventing the Execution of the Innocent: Testimony before the House Judiciary Committee," *Hofstra Law Review* 29 (2001): 1155–1156 (in almost 75 percent of cases initially accepted by Innocence Project, files must be closed because crime scene biological evidence was not preserved). Barry C. Scheck has stated that needed biological material cannot be found in 75 percent of cases taken up by Innocence Project; Frank Green, "Lawyer Stresses Power of DNA; Tests Clear Even Some Who 'Confess,'" *Richmond Times-Dispatch*, July 17, 2001 (statement of Barry C. Scheck).

3. *Herrera v. Collins*, 506 U.S. 390, 408 (1993).

4. Ibid., 410.

5. Ibid., 411–412 ("Clemency is deeply rooted in our Anglo-American tradition of law, and is the historic remedy for preventing miscarriages of justice where judicial process has been exhausted").

6. Ibid., 402.

7. Ibid., 421–424 (O'Connor, J., concurring).

8. Cf. *Jaffee v. Redmond*, 518 U.S. 1, 2 (1996) (Court justified creating a new privilege for communications to a licensed social worker on the ground that "[t]he mental health of our citizenry, no less than its physical health, is a public good of transcendent importance").

9. Steve Mills, Maurice Possley, and Ken Armstrong, "3 Cases Weaken under Scrutiny: Series; Investigative Report. Executions in America," *Chicago Tribune*, December 17, 2000, A1. The release of prisoners on death row as a consequence of DNA testing has been linked to growing uneasiness about the death penalty. See, e.g., Jennifer L. Harry, "Death Penalty Disquiet Stirs Nation," *Corrections Today* 62 (2000): 122–128.

10. At least two persons who were not executed have been exonerated after their death: Frank Lee Smith, who died after fourteen years on Florida's death row (Frank Green, "DNA Tests Not Likely after an Execution; Va. Opposing Third Request of Its Kind," *Richmond Times-Dispatch*, March 26, 2001), A1; and a rape suspect who committed suicide in jail while his case was pending ("National Briefing Mid-Atlantic: Pennsylvania; Clearing Rape Charge for Man in Suicide," *New York Times*, January 9, 2003). Postexecution DNA testing was ordered by a Georgia court, but the results were inconclusive. Green, "DNA Tests Not Likely after an Execution." In November 2002, Virginia denied a request for postexecution testing brought by a group of newspapers in the case of Roger Keith Coleman. See Eric M. Weiss, "DNA Testing by Media Barred," *Washington Post*, November 2, 2002, B1. See also Sheryl McCarthy, "All Doubt Should Be Absent in Capital Cases," *New York Newsday*, November 11, 2002, A26. Virginia had also denied a postexecution request from the Richmond Catholic Diocese in 1997 to test DNA samples in the case of Joseph O'Dell and ordered the destruction of the evidence. In 2001, Virginia enacted a law authorizing the destruction of DNA samples immediately following an execution. Green, "DNA Tests Not Likely after an Execution."

11. See Edwin M. Borchard, *Convicting the Innocent* (New York: Garden City Publishing Co., 1932), passim.

12. See *United States v. Wade*, 388 U.S. 218 (1967) and *Gilbert v. California*, 388 U.S. 263 (1967) (holding that identifications made at lineups were inadmissible unless counsel for the suspect was present); *Stovall v. Denno*, 388 U.S. 293, 301–302 (1967) (due-process right recognized to exclude from evidence the results of an identification procedure that was "unnecessarily suggestive and conducive to irreparable mistaken identification").

13. In *Kirby v. Illinois*, 406 U.S. 682, 689 (1972), the Court greatly restricted the Wade-Gilbert right by making it applicable only to identification procedures taking place after formal adversary proceedings were initiated, and in *United States v. Ash*, 413 U.S. 300 (1973), the Court held that Wade-Gilbert did not apply to photographic show ups. The due-process right announced in *Stovall* has been found to rarely result in the exclusion of identification testimony. See Benjamin E. Rosenberg, "Rethinking the Right to Due Process in Connection with Pretrial Identification Procedures: An Analysis and Proposal," *Kentucky Law Journal* 79 (1990–1991): 259.

14. See, e.g., Elizabeth Loftus, *Eyewitness Testimony* (Cambridge, Mass.: Harvard University Press, 1996); Brian L. Cutler and Steven D. Penrod, *Mistaken Identification: The Eyewitness, Psychology, and the Law* (New York: Cambridge University Press, 1995); Gary L. Wells, *Eyewitness Testimony* (Toronto: Carswell Legal, 1988).

15. Gary L. Wells, "Applied Eyewitness Testimony Research: System Variables and Estimator Variables," *Journal of Personality and Social Psychology* 36 (1978): 1546, 1551–1555.

16. Edward Connors et al., *Convicted by Juries, Exonerated by Science: Case Studies in the Use of DNA Evidence to Establish Innocence after Trial* (Washington, D.C.: National Institute of Justice, 1996), 16–17 (exhibit 3 summarizes the evidence produced at trial in each of twenty-eight cases; all except for the homicides involved victim identification); see also Jim Dwyer, Peter Neufeld, and Barry Scheck, *Actual Innocence: Five Days to Execution and Other Dispatches from the Wrongly Convicted* (New York: Doubleday, 2000), 73 (84 percent of vacated wrongful convictions were dependent on mistaken identifications).

17. Ronald Cotton was imprisoned for eleven years when Jennifer Thompson, a college student with a 4.0 grade-point average, identified him as having raped her at knifepoint. Thompson has stated that she made a concerted effort to memorize her assailant's features: "I studied every single detail on the rapist's face. I looked at his hairline; I looked for scars, for tattoos, for anything that would help me identify him. When and if I survived the attack, I was going to make sure that he was put in prison and he was going to rot. When I went to the police department later that day, I worked on a composite sketch to the very best of my ability. I looked through hundreds of noses and eyes and eyebrows and hairlines and nostrils and lips. I identified my attacker. I knew this was the man. I was completely confident. I was sure." Several years later at a pretrial hearing after Cotton's conviction was overturned because exculpatory evidence had been excluded, Thompson was confronted with Bobby Poole, who had allegedly boasted of being Thompson's rapist. Thompson swore she had never seen him before. Cotton was convicted again and sentenced to two consecutive life sentences. When DNA testing was finally done, the results showed that Bobby Poole and not Ronald Cotton had raped Thompson. See Jennifer Thompson, "I Was Certain, but I Was Wrong," *New York Times*, June 18, 2000, sec. 4, p. 15.

18. Connors et al., *Convicted by Juries, Exonerated by Science*, 16–17; see also Jim Yardly, "Inquiry Focuses on Scientist Employed by Prosecutors," *New York Times*, May 2, 2001 (reporting on Barry Scheck's comments about the case of Robert Miller, who was sentenced for murder in 1988 after testimony that hairs found at the crime scene were consistent with his; another suspect, Ronnie Lott, had been excluded as a possible hair donor; DNA testing eventually exonerated Miller and inculpated Lott).

19. Max M. Houch and Bruce Budowle, "Correlation of Microscopic and Mitochondrial DNA Hair Comparison," *Journal of Forensic Science* 47 (2002): 964, 966 ("Of the 80 hairs that were microscopically associated, nine comparisons were excluded by mtDNA analysis"); Paul C. Giannelli, "Scientific Evidence in Civil and Criminal Cases," *Arizona State Law Journal* 33 (2001): 113–117 (discusses hair evidence and some of the cases in which DNA evidence ultimately exonerated the defendant).

20. See, e.g., Paul C. Giannelli, "The Abuse of Scientific Evidence in Criminal Cases: The Need for Independent Crime Laboratories," *Virginia Journal of Social Policy & the Law* 4 (1997): 439.

21. Committee on DNA Technology in Forensic Science: An Update, *The Evaluation of Forensic DNA Evidence* (Washington, D.C.: National Academies Press, 1996), chap. 3; Committee on DNA Technology in Forensic Science, *DNA Technology in Forensic Science* (Washington, D.C.: National Academies Press, 1992), 104–105.

22. David H. Kaye and George F. Sensabaugh, Jr., "Reference Guide on DNA Evidence," in *Reference Manual on Scientific Evidence* (Washington, D.C.: Federal Judicial Center, 2000), 509–515.

23. National Institute of Justice, *Forensic Sciences: Review of Status and Needs* (Washington, D.C.: U.S. Department of Justice, 1999), 43 ("During the past 5 years, quality-control and quality-assurance program improvements have been realized by forensic DNA laboratories. These improvements have not only enhanced the reliability of the methods employed, but laboratories have also increasingly found the criminal justice system receptive to admissibility issues"). As of 1998, just over half (56 percent) of the 120 DNA crime laboratories in the country were accredited by an official organization. As of 2001, 63 percent (of 110) were accredited. Bureau of Justice Statistics, *Survey of DNA Crime Laboratories, 2001* (Washington, D.C.: U.S. Department of Justice, 2002); Margaret Berger, "Raising the Bar: The Impact of DNA Testing on the Field of Forensics," in *Perspectives on Crime and Justice 2000–2001 Lecture Series* (Washington, D.C.: National Institute of Justice, U.S. Department of Justice, 2002).

24. Montana and Washington are currently reviewing cases handled by state forensic scientist Arnold Melnikoff, who had been the director of the Montana State Crime Laboratory and now works for the Washington state police, after DNA evidence cleared a Montana man who spent fifteen years in prison for the rape of a young girl. Adam Liptak, "2 States to Review Lab Work of Expert Who Erred on I.D.," *New York Times*, December 19, 2002, A24 (Melnikoff had testified that hair on victim matched defendant's—which FBI report found to be false—and made up probabilities about likelihood of match); Yardly, "Inquiry Focuses on Scientist Employed by Prosecutors" (Oklahoma's governor ordered investigation after FBI report found that an Oklahoma police forensic chemist had misidentified evidence or testified improperly in at least five of the eight cases the FBI reviewed; chemist had worked on approximately three thousand cases and had identified suspects on the basis of hair, blood, and fiber analysis; she testified in twenty-three cases resulting in death sentences, ten of which had already been carried out; in the case that prompted the FBI investigation, defendant was convicted of rape sixteen years earlier on the basis of chemist's testimony about hair matches; DNA testing and the FBI's review of the hair evidence excluded the defendant). See also note 55. The West Virginia Supreme Court stated that a state police crime lab analyst in that state may have lied or fabricated evidence in dozens of cases. Becky Bohrer, "Former Crime-Lab Chief's Cases under Review," *Philadelphia Inquirer*, December 22, 2002, A9; see also *Investigation of the West Virginia State Police Crime Laboratory, Serology Division*, 438 S.E.2d 501 (1993). In 2002, Las Vegas began reviewing hundreds of DNA tests after authorities discovered name labels on DNA profiles had been switched. Glenn Puit, "Police Forensics: DNA Mix-Up Prompts Audit at Lab," *Las Vegas Review-Journal*, April 19, 2002.

25. *Herrera*, 506 U.S. at 402.

26. See, e.g., Maria Sanminiatelli, "Virginia's DNA Database Averaging One Cold Hit a Day," Associated Press State & Local Wire, April 29, 2001. In April 2001, Virginia, the state that contributes the largest number of samples to the national database, averaged one cold hit per day and ultimately reached its thousandth cold hit in November 2002. See also Erin Hallissy, "Baffling Rapes, Slayings Solved; Federal 'Cold Hit' DNA Database Links Old Evidence to Felons," *San Francisco Chronicle*, December 9, 2002, A1. In 2000, Arizona had

153 cold hits from the database. Howard Fisher, "State Acts to Widen DNA Testing," *Arizona Daily Star*, April 12, 2002, A8.

27. National Commission on the Future of DNA Evidence, *The Future of Forensic DNA Testing: Predictions of the Research and Development Working Group* (Washington, D.C.: National Institute of Justice, U.S. Department of Justice, 2000), 15 ("DNA is remarkably stable, as is evidenced by its being identified long after death, for example, in Egyptian mummies or even extinct mammoths").

28. Ibid., 28 (mitochondrial DNA markers will make it easier to analyze degraded DNA and Y chromosome markers will make it possible to deal with sexual assault samples containing mixtures of DNA from a number of males).

29. Thompson, "I Was Certain, but I Was Wrong."

30. Barry C. Scheck, statement made during "Post Conviction Relief" session ("DNA and the Criminal Justice System" conference, John F. Kennedy School of Government, Harvard University (Cambridge, Mass., November 20, 2000) (estimating that between 50 and 60 percent of postconviction DNA tests incriminate the petitioner who sought testing).

31. In Arizona, Indiana, and Michigan, if the results of DNA testing are not favorable to an inmate who requests such testing, the court may request that the DNA sample be added to the federal or state DNA database. In Pennsylvania and Louisiana, inculpatory results may be entered in law enforcement databases. In Utah, the petitioner must waive all statutes of limitations in any jurisdictions as to any felony offense he has committed that is identified through DNA database comparison. Under the proposed federal Innocence Protection Act, inculpatory test results lead to submission of the inmate's DNA to the federal DNA database. See note 35 for citations to statutes.

32. Ibid.; see also Thompson, "I Was Certain, but I Was Wrong."

33. See N.Y. Crim. Proc. 440-30(1-a) (McKinney's 2001); 725 Ill. Comp. Stat. Ann. 5/116-3 (West 2001). These statutes contain no time limits on making such requests. Nevertheless, despite time bars in other states' general statutes regarding newly discovered evidence, some courts have on a variety of theories permitted inmates access to postconviction DNA testing even after the applicable period has run. See National Commission on the Future of DNA Evidence, *Postconviction DNA Testing: Recommendations for Handling Requests* (Washington, D.C.: National Institute of Justice, U.S. Department of Justice, 1999), chap. 2 (details the legal uncertainty that surrounds requests for postconviction DNA testing in states that do not have specific statutory authorization for such testing).

34. Numerous developments on a number of interrelated fronts have contributed to this demand for change. When, primarily through the efforts of the Innocence Project, inmates began to be released from prison on the basis of DNA testing, the National Institute of Justice commissioned a study that reported on twenty-eight cases in which DNA had exculpated inmates. See Connors et al., *Convicted by Juries, Exonerated by Science*. Attorney General Janet Reno then created, in 1998, the National Commission on the Future of DNA Evidence, whose first task, assigned to the Post-Conviction Issues Working Group, was to make recommendations for handling inmates' requests for DNA testing. The resulting report from the working group was published in September 1999 and was widely distributed. See National Commission on the Future of DNA Evidence, *Postconviction DNA Testing*. The working group also proposed a model statute for handling requests. All of these events received wide

media coverage, including a number of television specials. The media have continued to report in considerable depth on the rapidly accelerating number of convictions being vacated on the basis of postconviction DNA testing.

35. Ariz. Rev. Stat. § 13-4240 (2002); Ark. Code Ann. § 16-112-202 (Michie 2002); Cal. Penal Code § 1405 (West 2002); Col. Rev. Stat. § 18-1-413 (West 2003); Ct. Stat. § 54-102j (7) (2003); Del. Code Ann. tit. 11, § 4504 (2002); D.C. Code Ann. § 22-4133 (2002); Fla. Stat. Ann. 925.11 (West 2002); Ga. Code Ann. § 5-5-41 (West 2003); Idaho Code §§ 19-2719, 19-4902 (Michie 2002); 725 Ill. Comp. Stat. Ann. § 5/116-3 (West 2002); Ind. Code Ann. §§ 35-38-7-1 to 19 (West 2002); Kan. Stat. Ann. § 21–2512 (2001); Ky. Rev. Stat. Ch. 422.285 (2002); La. Code Crim. Proc. Ann. art. 926.1 (West 2002); Me. Rev. Stat. Ann. tit. 15, § 2137 (West 2001); Md. Code Ann., Crim. Proc. § 8-201 (2002); Mich. Comp. Laws Ann. § 770.16 (West 2002); Minn. Stat. Ann. § 590.01 (West 2002); Mo. Ann. Stat. § 547.035 (West 2002); Montana Code § 46-21-110 (2003); Neb. Rev. Stat. Ann. §§ 29-4117 to 4125 (Michie 2002); N.J. Stat. Ann. § 2A:84-32a (West 2002); N.M. Stat. Ann. § 31-1a-1 (Michie 2002); N.Y. Crim. Proc. Law § 440.30 (McKinney 2002); N.C. Gen. Stat. § 15a-269 (2002); Ohio Rev. Code §§ 2953.71–2953.83 (Baldwin 2003); Okla. Stat. tit. 22, §§ 1371, 1371.1, 1372 (2002); Ore. Rev. Stat. T. 14, ch. 138 Prec. 138.005 (West 2003); 42 Pa. C.S.A. § 9543.1 (2002); R.I. Gen. Laws 1956, § 10-9.1-11 (2002); Tenn. Code Ann. §§ 40-30-401 to 413 (2002); Tex. Code Crim. Proc. Ann. art. 64.03 (Vernon 2001); Utah Code Ann. §§ 78-35a-301 to 304 (2002); Va. Code Ann. § 19.2-327.1 (Michie 2002); Wash. Rev. Code § 10.73.170 (2002); Wisc. Stat. § 974.07 (2001). For a comprehensive discussion of the state statutes, see Kathy Swedlow, "Don't Believe Everything You Read: A Review of Modern 'Post-conviction' DNA Testing Statutes," *California Western Law Review* 38 (2002).

36. Legislation for postconviction DNA testing has also been proposed in Alabama, Hawaii, Iowa, Massachusetts. Mississippi, Nevada, South Dakota, and West Virginia. David Defoore, "Post-conviction DNA Testing: A Cry for Justice from the Wrongfully Convicted," *Texas Technology Law Review* 491 (2002).

37. The Innocence Protection Act of 2003 is at this writing pending before Congress. See H.R. 3214 (passed by the House of Representatives and referred to the Senate Judiciary Committee in December 2003).

38. See Craig Timberg, "Gilmore Signs Bill Permitting Felon DNA Tests; Death Row Inmates Eligible," *Washington Post*, May 3, 2001 (reporting that Virginia Governor Jim Gilmore had originally opposed bill and sought to amend it; his advisers explained that "he was reluctant to weaken the sense of finality that a conviction in Virginia now represents for victims and their families and that he also feared the law would unleash a torrent of new appeals").

39. Sangreem Hudson, "DNA Reality," *San Francisco Daily Journal*, April 10, 2001, 1.

40. Ibid., quoting Scheck. In 2001, the Brooklyn district attorney's office began reviewing cases to determine whether DNA evidence could exonerate incarcerated individuals. Of 703 cases reviewed, only two were examined in detail to determine whether DNA evidence could be recovered. The district attorney's office eliminated almost half of the cases because the defendant had confessed or acknowledged committing the crime of which he was eventually convicted. Daniel Wise, "Brooklyn Prosecutors Find Convictions Pass DNA Test," *New York Law Journal*, August 6, 2001, 1.

41. See N.Y. Crim. Proc. 440.30(1-a) (McKinney's 2001) (requires showing that had DNA results been introduced at trial, there is "reasonable probability that the verdict would have been more favorable to the defendant").

42. George Woody Clarke, statement made during "Regulating DNA Evidence" panel ("An International Conference on DNA and Human Rights," University of California at Berkeley, April 27, 2001). In May 2001, the California attorney-general's office announced that only thirty requests for testing had been received since the law went into effect on January 1 of that year and that none had been granted. "Few Inmates Use Law That Allows DNA Testing," *Los Angeles Times*, May 18, 2001, B9. In New Jersey, less than a dozen inmates took advantage of a free testing program, and of those who did, none was cleared. Richard Willing, "Few Inmates Seek Exonerations with Free DNA Tests," *USA Today*, July 30, 2002.

43. The recommendations of the Working Group on Post-Conviction Issues, in their framework for analysis, classified cases in which exclusionary results would exonerate the petitioner as category 1 cases. National Commission on the Future of DNA Evidence, *Postconviction DNA Testing*, 3–4. (Other examples are given of recurring fact patterns.) In *Cherrix v. Braxton*, 131 F.Supp.2d 756 (E.D. Va. 2000), a federal district judge held that the court had authority under the statute regarding funding assistance in capital cases to grant a state inmate's request for funds for DNA testing and to order testing; the court relied on the recommendations to determine that testing was warranted because the case fell into category 1.

44. For examples of when exclusionary results, although not exonerative, might be helpful, see ibid., 5–6.

45. Oklahoma Stat. Ann. § 1371.1 (West 2001) ("factual innocence requires the defendant to establish by clear and convincing evidence that no reasonable jury would have found the defendant guilty beyond a reasonable doubt").

46. New York Crim. Proc. Law 440.30(1-a) (McKinney's 2001).

47. See Scheck, statement made during "Post Conviction Relief" session ("DNA and the Criminal Justice System" conference). A full account of the Criner case can be found in the Houston Chronicle. See Harvey Rice, "Justice Deferred," *Houston Chronicle, Texas Magazine*, November 26, 2002.

48. *Campbell v. United States*, 365 U.S. 85, 96 (1961) ("the ordinary rule, based on considerations of fairness, does not place the burden upon a litigant of establishing facts peculiarly within the knowledge of his adversary").

49. Ind. Code Ann. § 35-38-7-15 (West 2002) (statute allows for elimination samples from third parties under "extraordinary circumstances"). For a discussion of court orders compelling consensual partners to provide DNA samples, see Cynthia Bryant, "When One Man's DNA Is Another's Exonerating Evidence: Compelling Consensual Sexual Partners of Rape Victims to Provide DNA Samples to Post-conviction Petitioners," *Columbia Journal of Law & Social Policy* 33 (2000): 113.

50. Utah Code Ann. § 78-35a-301 (enacted March 19, 2001) ("the evidence that is the subject of the request for testing has the potential to produce new, noncumulative evidence that will establish the person's actual innocence").

51. See Connecticut General Stat. Ann. § 52-582 (West 2001).

52. But see appellate court opinions that have interpreted state laws narrowly: *State v. Ghol-ston*, 697 N.E.2d 375 (Ill. App. Ct. 1998) (denying the defendant postconviction DNA testing on the ground that testing would not be "material" to the defendant's actual innocence claim). In *Gholston*, the court concluded that the absence of the defendant's DNA from the crime sample would not conclusively exclude him as the perpetrator, and that an exclusionary result would therefore be insufficient to override witness identifications and self-incriminating statements. See also *Coombs v. State*, 824 So.2d 958 (Fl. 2002) (denying defendant's motion for postconviction DNA testing on the ground that the motion was insufficient in explaining how testing would exonerate defendant, even though defendant argued that newer DNA testing could provide conclusive results where preconviction testing results in 1995 were inconclusive). The Texas Court of Appeals has interpreted Texas's statute as requiring the defendant to show "a reasonable probability exists that exculpatory DNA tests will prove [his] innocence." *Kutzner v. State*, 75 S.W.3d 427, 438 (Tex. Crim. App. 2002). Relying on *Kutzner*, a Texas appellate court denied defendant's motion for DNA testing, finding that exculpatory DNA tests of blood on the weapon used in the assault of which defendant had been convicted would not prove defendant's innocence. *Thompson v. State*, 95 S.W.3d 469 (Tex. Crim. App. 2002), at 2002 WL 31618806.

53. Tennessee Code Ann. § 40-26-106 (2000) (establishes presumption of no testing for convictions obtained after July 1, 1998); Kentucky Revised Statutes, Ch. 422.285 (2002).

54. West's Revised Code of Washington Ann. 10.73.170 (2000) (requests for testing on or before December 31, 2002) See note 69.

55. On May 7, 2001, an Oklahoma judge vacated the conviction of Jeffrey Pierce, the man whose case had triggered an investigation of a forensic chemist in Oklahoma. See Yardly, "Inquiry Focuses on Scientist Employed by Prosecutors." Pierce had served fifteen years of a sixty-five-year sentence. Jim Yardly, "Flaws in Chemist's Findings Free Man at Center of Inquiry," *New York Times*, May 8, 2001, A1.

56. Dwyer, Neufeld, and Scheck, *Actual Innocence*, 92 (convictions in 23 percent of DNA exonerations studied by the Innocence Project were based on false confessions or admissions). Similarly, a 1987 study of 350 exonerated capital defendants found that 14 percent of the convictions were a result of confessions that turned out to be false. Hugo Adam Bedau and Michael L. Radelet, "Miscarriages of Justice in Potentially Capital Cases," *Stanford Law Review* 40 (1987): 21.

57. Richard A. Leo and Richard J. Ofshe, "The Consequences of False Confessions: Deprivations of Liberty and Miscarriages of Justice in the Age of Psychological Interrogation," *Journal of Criminal Law and Criminology* 88 (1988): 429. ("As many investigators have recognized, the problems caused by police-induced false confessions are significant, recurrent, and deeply troubling"). In Florida, a forty-nine-year-old retarded man, Jerry Townsend, was released after spending almost twenty-two years in prison for a series of murders and a rape to which he had confessed; the review of his convictions was spurred when DNA testing exonerated another inmate on death row and identified the perpetrator of that crime as Eddie Mosley; Mosley, committed to a state mental hospital since 1988, was also identified through DNA testing in another murder-rape case in which Townsend had been a suspect, leading to a review of all cases in which Townsend or Mosley had been suspects. Ardy Friedberg and Jason T. Smith, "Townsend Gets His Freedom after Almost 22 Years," *South Florida Sun-Sentinel*, June 16, 2001 (attorneys say suspect was easily led to confess).

58. The confessions contained numerous inconsistencies about when, where, and how the rapes had occurred. These had been explored by defense counsel on cross-examination, as had the fact that none of the defendants' DNA matched the crime scene sample. See Jim Dwyer and Kevin Flynn, "New Light on Jogger's Rape Calls Evidence into Question," *New York Times*, December 1, 2002, 1; Saul Kassin, "False Confessions and the Jogger Case," *New York Times*, November 1, 2002.

59. National Commission on the Future of DNA Evidence, *Postconviction DNA Testing*, 44–46 (recommendations for defense counsel).

60. The statutes in the District of Columbia, Florida, Kansas, Nebraska, Tennessee, and Virginia give the court discretion to appoint counsel. In Michigan, if the DNA testing result are exculpatory, the statute authorizes appointment of counsel. See references to statutes in note 35.

61. But see Laura Maggi, "DNA Test for Inmates Elusive Despite Law: La. Fund Lacks Cash; Evidence Hard to Find," *The Times-Picayune* (New Orleans, La), December 16, 2002 (no money put in budget for DNA testing; although Louisiana governor said he would budget for testing the following year, his attorney said there was no need to pay for attorneys).

62. See John Winterdyk and Janne A. Holmgren, "DNA Evidence: Balancing the Scales of Justice," *Canadian Business & Current Affairs* 26 (2001): 11 (concluding after study that Canadian defense counsel have inadequate knowledge to adequately represent their clients).

63. See, e.g., a recent account that a federal program requiring HMOs and hospitals to report incompetent physicians is failing because these institutions refuse to furnish the required information. Robert Pear, "Inept Physicians Are Rarely Listed as Law Requires," *New York Times*, May 29, 2001, A1.

64. In Oklahoma, complaints had been voiced about the forensic laboratory's work long before the investigation of the laboratory ordered by the governor was begun. See Yardly, "Inquiry Focuses on Scientist Employed by Prosecutors."

65. After a scandal in its Rampart Division in which a group of officers was alleged "to have routinely robbed drug dealers, abused gang members and planted guns on suspects, the investigation of the Los Angeles Police Department languished for nearly two years with few if any real reforms being carried out." James Sterngold, "Police Monitor Struggles in Los Angeles," *New York Times*, June 6, 2001, A18. Eventually, over one hundred convictions were overturned. Kristina Sauerwein, "Shedding Light on Officers Who Help Prosecute with Cases Overturned in the Rampart Scandal in Mind," *Los Angeles Times*, December 20, 2002, B2.

66. On January 31, 2000, Governor George Ryan of Illinois imposed a moratorium on executions after the release of thirteen prisoners on death row. A 1999 investigation by the *Chicago Tribune* had pointed to numerous cases in which defendants were represented by lawyers who had at some time been disbarred or suspended and to the prosecutorial use of unreliable evidence furnished by jailhouse snitches, resulting from questionable forensic testing, or obtained through police torture. Steve Mills and Maurice Possley, "Death Penalty Debate Slowly Shifts; Executions Continue but Face More Scrutiny," *Chicago Tribune*, January 31, 2001, 1. Before he left office in January 2003, Ryan pardoned four men on death row and commuted the sentences of the remaining 167 on the ground that his extensive

review of case files and the three-year study of the Illinois system had convinced him of the innocence of people on death row and the unfairness of the system. Jodi Wilgoren, "Citing Issues of Fairness, Governor Clears Out Death Row in Illinois," *New York Times*, January 12, 2003, 1.

67. For a detailed exploration of the psychological and institutional factors that cause prosecutors to resist postconviction innocence claims, see Daniel S. Medwed, "The Zeal Deal: Prosecutorial Resistance to Post-Conviction Claims of Innocence," *B.U.L. Rev.* 84 (2004): 125.

68. After the exoneration of an Oklahoma inmate on the basis of DNA testing raised concerns about a police forensic chemist who had testified at his trial, the Oklahoma State Bureau of Investigation, at the recommendation of the FBI, began reviewing cases handled by the chemist and identified sixty cases that needed further review in which inmates were at that time serving sentences of life or life without parole; those inmates were mailed a formal DNA Forensic Testing Program application. "O.S.B.I Suspends Cases Review until Audit Completed," Associated Press State & Local Wire, June 5, 2001.

69. See, e.g., La. Code Crim. Proc. Ann. art. 926.1 (West 2002) (requests prohibited after August 2005); Tenn. Code Ann. § 40-26-106 (2000) (establishes presumption of no testing for convictions obtained after July 1, 1998); Wash. Rev. Code § 10.73.170 (2000) (requests for testing originally had to be made before December 31, 2002; deadline extended to December 31, 2004). Whether these deadlines will hold is unclear at this time. In a number of states in which deadlines expired, the legislatures extended the time for filing requests for DNA testing. See "Florida Lawyers Battle to Beat DNA Deadline," *USA Today*, September 25, 2003. In Florida, where the deadline expired on October 1, 2003, the Supreme Court held a hearing in November about what to do and how much time would be needed to screen all cases in which DNA testing might be able to clear an inmate. See "Court Hears Extension Arguments," *The Bar News* 30 (December 1, 2003).

70. James S. Liebman et al., *A Broken System, Part II: Why There Is So Much Error in Capital Cases, and What Can Be Done about It* (Washington, D.C.: U.S. Senate Committee on the Judiciary, 2002); James S. Liebman, "The Overproduction of Death," *Columbia Law Review* 100 (2000): 2030.

II

Balancing Privacy and Security

7

Genetic Privacy

George J. Annas

The Human Genome Project has brought with it many legal and ethical issues, but the most consistently contentious is genetic privacy. As DNA sequences become understood as information, and as this information becomes easier to use in digitized form, public concerns about Internet and e-commerce privacy are merging with concerns about medical-record privacy and genetic privacy. Privacy has returned to the center of American domestic public policy.

Privacy

Privacy is a complex concept involving several different but overlapping personal interests. It encompasses informational privacy (having control over highly personal information about ourselves), relational privacy (determining with whom we have personal, intimate relationships), privacy in decision making (freedom from the surveillance and influence of others when making personal decisions), and the right to exclude others from our personal things and places. In the United States, no single law protects all of these interests, and privacy law refers to the aggregate of privacy protections found in constitutions, statutes, regulations, and common law. Together these laws reflect the value U.S. citizens place on individual privacy, sometimes referred to as "the right to be left alone" and the right to be free of outside intrusion, not as an end in itself, but as a means of enhancing individual freedom in various aspects of our lives. This centrality of individual freedom in the health care context is evident in state laws that establish a patient's right to make informed choices about treatment, that place an obligation on physicians to maintain patient confidentiality, and that regulate the maintenance of medical records.[1]

Privacy laws in the United States are fragmented because of the multiple sources of law, including the federal government and all fifty states. Legislation is also often the result of negotiated agreements among segments of a diverse, pluralistic, and oftentimes polarized society, rather than of a real consensus. This is perhaps most readily seen in the rules that govern highly sensitive and personal data in the United States. Unlike the approach of the European Data Protection Directive, which establishes similar rights and duties relative to different kinds of personal data (health and finance), the approach in the United States involves different rights and duties for personal information depending on the kind of information involved.[2] There are even different rules for different types of information in medical records. For example, the United States has laws that govern medical-record information generally, as well as separate laws that govern specific types of medical information, such as HIV status, substance abuse treatment information, and mental health information. The new federal HIPAA regulations apply the same privacy rules to all medical information except psychotherapy notes.[3] Such exceptionalism has been criticized. The primary argument against specific laws designed to protect genetic information is that "genetic exceptionalism" would perpetuate the misconception that genetic information is uniquely private and sensitive.[4]

Genetic Privacy

Is DNA sequence information uniquely private, or is it just like other especially sensitive information contained in an individual's medical record? If it is not unique, existing medical-record confidentiality laws should be sufficient to protect genetic sequence information, and no new laws would be needed. Those who support genetic exceptionalism emphasize the unique distinguishing features of DNA sequence information. The DNA molecule itself can be viewed as a new form of medical record. It is a source of medical information, and like a personal medical record, it can be stored and accessed without the need to return to the person from whom the DNA was collected for authorization. But DNA sequence information contains information beyond an individual's medical history and current health status. DNA also contains information about the individual's future health risks and in this sense is analogous to a probabilistic, coded "future diary."[5] As the code is broken, DNA reveals information about an individual's probable risks of suffering from specific medical conditions in the future.

A number of commentators have noted how private and personal diaries are, and why they should be treated with unique respect. William Safire, for example, has argued that we keep our diaries "to reveal our youthful selves to our aging selves."[6]

The DNA molecule is the converse of that: The decoded DNA molecule reveals our aging selves to our younger selves. Of course it's probabilistic, not deterministic; and it's in a code that we are still only in the process of breaking. At some point, however, scientists are going to be better able to read our DNA and tell us something about the types of diseases that we are at risk of encountering as we age. There is nothing else quite like DNA sequence information.

Our current obsession with genetic-sequence information also means that it is likely to be taken more seriously than other information in a medical record that could also predict future risks, like high blood pressure or cholesterol levels. Information about the presence of proteins that specific genes may code for is also different from DNA sequence information because the presence of such proteins may change over time, and their levels, like cholesterol readings, can be determined over time only by retesting the patient. DNA sequence information is stable and remains the same. In contrast, proteomics (the search for all the proteins our genes code for) is more like cholesterol levels and will not require new privacy rules, but rather enforcement of existing medical records privacy rules. DNA sequence information may also contain information about behavioral traits, such as a propensity to violence, that are unrelated to health status, although significant skepticism is called for in this area.[7]

My use of the "future diary" metaphor has been criticized as potentially perpetuating a mistaken, deterministic view of genes.[8] I understand this criticism and also reject the idea that genes alone or even primarily determine our medical future. Nurture matters mightily. Nevertheless, I continue to believe the future diary metaphor best conveys the *private* nature of genetic information itself. Our future medical status is not determined solely by genetics, any more than our diaries are the only source of information about our past. The DNA information, like the diary, however, is a uniquely private part of our possible future. Moreover, an individual's DNA can also reveal information about risks and traits that are shared with genetic relatives and thus has been used to prove paternity and other relationships. DNA has the paradoxical quality of being unique to an individual, yet shared with others.[9]

Finally, even a conclusion that DNA sequence information (derived from analyzing the DNA molecule) is no more sensitive than other medical information tells us nothing about the need to protect the DNA molecule itself. In this regard, it is useful, for privacy purposes, to view the DNA molecule as a medical record in its own right. Possessing a DNA sample from an individual is analogous to having medical information about the individual stored on a computer disk, except with

DNA the information is stored in a blood or other tissue sample. Like the computer disk, the DNA sequence can be "read" by the application of technology. Thus, regardless of the rules developed to control the *use* of genetic information that is recorded in traditional paper and electronic medical records, separate rules are needed to regulate the *collection, analysis, storage,* and *release* of DNA samples themselves. Once a physician, researcher, or police investigator has a DNA sample, there is no practical need for further contact with the individual from whom the DNA was obtained, and additional DNA tests could be done on the stored sample (and thus on the individual) without notification or authorization. Some of these tests are, of course, not yet developed, but all will produce new genetic information about the individual.

DNA has also been culturally endowed with a power and significance exceeding that of other medical information.[10] Much of this significance is undoubtedly misplaced. Nonetheless, it can be justified insofar as genetic information can radically change the way people view themselves and their family members, as well as the way that others view them. The history of genetic testing, particularly in relation to rare monogenic diseases such as Huntington's disease, provides us with examples of this impact. Studies of individuals who have undergone testing in clinical settings demonstrate changes in self-perception caused by positive, as well as negative, test results.[11] Individuals who have been told, as a result of genetic testing, that they are at less risk of having a particular genetic disease than they had previously believed have reported difficulty in setting expectations for their personal and professional lives in view of a more open-ended future. Adjustments appear to have been particularly difficult for those who previously had made reproductive decisions on the presumption that they were at high risk for developing a particular disease. Consequently, it is good public policy to provide genetic counseling before and after testing. To protect the privacy of children and adolescents, some institutions have also adopted a policy of refusing parental requests to test children for late-onset diseases when no medical intervention is available to prevent or alleviate the disease.[12]

Only one U.S. court has squarely addressed whether constitutional rights to privacy are implicated by genetic testing. In *Norman-Bloodsaw v. Lawrence Berkeley Laboratory*, employees of a research facility owned and operated by state and federal agencies alleged that nonconsensual genetic testing by their employers violated their rights to privacy. Holding that the right to privacy protects against the collection of information by illicit means as well as unauthorized disclosures to third parties, the U.S. Court of Appeals for the Ninth Circuit stated: "One can think of few subject areas more personal and more likely to implicate privacy interests than that of one's health or genetic make-up."[13]

Ownership of DNA

In Ralph Nader's brief 2000 presidential candidacy for the Green Party, the line that he usually got the heaviest applause for was "Our genes are not for sale." That's another way to say that we own our bodies. And the consequence is that no one should be able to take or analyze our DNA without our permission, and no one should be able to sell it and commercialize it without our agreement.

The question of ownership of DNA is central, and in the United States we haven't really confronted it yet. The Genetic Privacy Act, which my colleagues Leonard Glantz and Winnie Roche drafted for the Ethical, Legal and Social Implications (ELSI) program of the federal Human Genome Project, provides that individuals own their own DNA, and that no one else can use an individual's DNA without the individual's authorization.[14] On the other hand, existing state statutes on genetic privacy do not so provide. Instead they implicitly follow the lead of the John Moore case, in which the California Supreme Court held that even though a physician had sold a cell line derived from John Moore's spleen to a private biotech company without his permission, John Moore could claim no property interest in his cells.[15] Nonetheless, the legal position that everybody but the individual from whom DNA is extracted can own DNA is not sustainable. Either no one should be permitted to own and sell DNA, or individuals should also have property rights to their own DNA.

Acknowledging property interests in DNA need not impede research any more than respect for individual privacy would. To the contrary, individuals are free to grant researchers property rights in their DNA and are much more likely to do so if their privacy can be guaranteed (as it can be if identifiers are not retained). The real issue is control over the private information contained in a person's DNA, and ownership is the traditional and most readily understandable way to describe and conceptualize control.

DNA Research and Privacy

Since the human genome was roughly sequenced, attention has shifted to research on genetic variation designed to located genes and gene sequences with disease-producing or -preventing properties. Some researchers have already taken steps to form partnerships and create large DNA banks that will furnish the material for this research. Others want to take advantage of the large number of stored tissue samples that already exist. In the United States, for example, the DNA of about twenty million people is amassed and stored each year in tissue collections ranging from fewer than two hundred to more than ninety-two million samples.[16] These collections include Guthrie cards, on which blood from newborns has been gathered for phenylketonuria screening since the 1960s; paraffin blocks used by pathologists to store specimens; blood bank samples; forensic specimens; and the U.S. military's bank of samples for use in identifying bodily remains. Perhaps the major reason that neither DNA sequence information nor DNA samples themselves have been afforded special privacy protection is the strongly held view of many genetic researchers and biotechnology companies that privacy protections would interfere with their work.

Several factors have contributed to the proliferation of DNA banking: the relative ease with which DNA can be collected, its coincidental presence in bodily specimens collected for other reasons, and its immutability. Regardless of the original purposes for storing specimens, however, as the ability to extract information from DNA increases and the focus of research shifts to genetic factors that contribute to human diseases and behaviors, repositories containing the DNA of sizable populations can be gold mines of genetic information. Thus it is not surprising that there is considerable interest on the part of biomedical researchers, companies that market genomic data, and the pharmaceutical industry to stake claims on these informational resources and to exploit them for their own purposes.

Commercial enterprises, as well as academic researchers, have equally strong interests in making its relatively easy to get access to DNA samples that can be linked to medical records for research purposes. Representatives of these constituencies have been vocal in arguing that requirements for informed consent and the right to withdraw data from ongoing research projects (two aspects of genetic privacy) would greatly hamper their research efforts.[17] When federal rules apply to such research—as is the case with federally funded projects and any projects related to obtaining Food and Drug Administration approval to market drugs or devices—a local Institutional Review Board (IRB), mandated by federal law and made up primarily of other researchers, must approve the research protocol and the informed consent process. I do not believe IRBs should waive basic federal research requirements on informed consent for DNA-based research (nor should they exempt researchers from them) except when they determine that the research in question will be conducted in such a way that the subjects *cannot* be personally identified. Only when identification of individuals is impossible is there no risk to their privacy.

The most internationally discussed DNA-based project has been deCODE in Iceland, a commercial project that has been opposed by the Iceland Medical Association, among others, for ethical shortcuts, including having "opt out" provisions instead of requiring informed consent of subjects.[18] The deCODE project, which has been endorsed by two acts of the Iceland parliament, involves the creation of two new databases, the first containing the medical records of all Iceland citizens, and the second, DNA samples from them (a third database, of genealogical records, already exists). deCODE intends to use these three databases in various combinations to seek out genetic variations that could be of pharmaceutical interest. The major ethical issues raised by this project are (1) the question of informed consent for inclusion of personal medical information in the database, which is currently included under the concept of presumed consent (which requires individuals to actively opt out of the research if they do not want their information in the database); (2) the question of informed consent for the inclusion of DNA in the DNA data bank in an identifiable manner (whether encrypted or not, and no matter which entity holds the encryption key); and (3) whether the right to withdraw from the research (including the right to withdraw both the DNA sample itself from the databank and all information generated about it) can be effectively exercised. Other issues include the security of the databases and the benefit to the community of the research project itself. Iceland thus provides a type of ethical laboratory that helps identify the major issues involved in population-based genetic research, as well as helping to inform us as to why international privacy rules are desirable.

Although Icelanders themselves do not seem overly concerned with the adequacy of deCODE's plans to protect their personal privacy, other countries have been less disposed to legislating away the autonomy and privacy of their citizens. Both Estonia and the United Kingdom, for example, have announced that their population-based DNA collections and research projects will contain strong consent and privacy protection provisions. The privacy problems inherent in large population-based projects could be avoided altogether by stripping DNA samples of their identifiers in a way that makes it impossible to link personal medical information with DNA samples (at least using standard identifying methods). Of course, most researchers want to retain these identifiers to do follow-up work or confirm diagnoses.[19] Such identification retention, however, puts individuals at risks for breach of confidentiality and invasion of privacy, and these risks are why both informed consent and strong privacy protection protocols are ethically necessary for genetic research. On the other hand, if strict privacy rules, which were enforced, are enacted, the necessity for IRB review and informed consent would be less compelling.

These considerations also apply to forensic DNA databases, since even convicted felons have privacy rights, including the right not to be used as research subjects without consent.[20] DNA is collected in the forensic setting to be used for identification purposes, much like a fingerprint, which is why DNA information is sometimes referred to as a "DNA fingerprint." This use is legitimate, but it does not give law enforcement officials unfettered dominion over the use of DNA. Even prisoners have a right not to have their DNA used for research purposed without specific, informed consent and IRB review of the research protocol.[21] I also believe it is virtually impossible to obtain voluntary consent for this type of research from prisoners, because they are in an inherently coercive environment and are thus not free to refuse. What type of DNA-based research might a prison system or the FBI want to conduct? The most potentially dangerous type of DNA research likely to be conducted on a convict population is the search for a criminal gene, a gene that predisposes people to violence. I don't think such a gene exists, but if it does, testing for it and identifying it opens the door to labeling people and then using the genetic label to viciously discriminate against them. And of course if a researcher studies just the DNA samples found in criminal banks, the researcher is likely to find some associations. Defense attorneys have argued that men with XYY chromosomal patterns (i.e., men with an extra Y chromosome) are more likely to engage in criminal behavior, based on the fact that there are more XYY men in jail than there are in the free-living population. They argued that the XYY syndrome should be a factor in excusing, or at least mitigating, criminal culpability, because the defendants could not control their behavioral characteristics. However, this defense has been almost uniformly unsuccessful because the fact that more XYY men are in jail does not show a causal relationship between XYY patterns and criminal behavior. An alternative hypothesis is simply that XYY men are taller than others, and so more likely to be seen or identified during or after a crime.[22]

Risks of disclosure of personal genetic information are so high that some prominent genetic researchers, including Francis Collins and Craig Venter, have suggested concentrating not on privacy rules, but instead on antidiscrimination legislation designed to protect individuals when their genetic information is disclosed and insurance companies, employers, or others want to use that information against them.

In June 2001, President George W. Bush indicated that he agreed and said he would support federal genetic antidiscrimination legislation.[23] No such legislation has passed both Houses of Congress. Although the Genetic Information Nondiscrimination Act of 2003 unanimously passed in the Senate in October 2003, it never came up for a vote in the House.[24] Antidiscrimination legislation is desirable, but it does not substitute for privacy rules that can prevent genetic information from being created in the first place without an individual's informed authorization.

A law recently enacted in Massachusetts, a state with a population more than twenty times larger than Iceland's, for example, mistakenly characterized in the press as "a sweeping set of genetic privacy protections," illustrates this point. Under this new law, written informed consent is a prerequisite to predictive (but not diagnostic) genetic testing and to disclosing the results of such tests by entities and practitioners that provide health care.[25] The law also limits the uses that insurers and employers can make of genetic information. However, it places no limitations on how researchers and biotech companies that engage in projects that require the use of identifiable samples and identifiable genetic information conduct their activities. Apparently those who drafted the statute were under the impression that they need not be concerned about protecting research subjects because research with human subjects is regulated by the federal government and failed to recognize that many activities of genomic companies do not fall under the jurisdiction of the federal regulations.

Policy Recommendations

My Boston University colleagues in the Department of Health Law, Bioethics, and Human Rights and I have argued in the past that a major step to achieving genetic privacy would be the passage of a comprehensive federal genetic-privacy act, such as the one my colleagues and I have proposed.[26] The primary purpose of such a law would be to give individuals control over their identifiable DNA samples and the genetic-sequence information extracted from them. The model act that we drafted explicitly provides that individuals have a property interest in their own DNA—and that this property interest gives them control over it. Control could also, however, be obtained by requiring explicit authorization from individuals for collection and use, including research and commercial use, of their DNA. In the absence of authorization, no one should know more about an individual's genetic makeup than that individual chooses to know, and the individual should also know who else knows (or will know) his private genetic information. Genetic privacy law should do the following:

- Recognize individuals' genetic rights, particularly
- the right to determine if and when their identifiable DNA samples are collected, stored, or analyzed
- the right to determine who has access to their identifiable DNA samples
- the right of access to their own genetic information
- the right to determine who has access to their genetic information
- the right to all information necessary for informed decision making in regard to the collection, storage, and analysis of their DNA samples and the disclosure of their private genetic information
- Limit parental rights to authorize the collection, storage, or analysis of a child's identifiable DNA sample so as to preserve the child's future autonomy and genetic privacy
- Prohibit uses of individually identifiable DNA samples that have not been authorized by the individual himself, except for some uses in solving crimes, determining paternity, or identifying bodily remains
- Prohibit disclosures of genetic information without the individual's explicit authorization
- Ensure strict enforcement of laws and institutional policies
- Provide accessible remedies for individuals whose rights are violated
- Institute sufficient penalties to deter and punish violations

Current U.S. state laws at best offer some economic protections and a patchwork of genetic privacy protections. But existing state laws have significant gaps and inconsistently regulate those who engage in DNA banking and genetic research. Nevertheless, existing privacy laws provide models and a foundation that can be built upon to protect genetic privacy and empower individuals in this genomic era. Until comprehensive federal legislation is passed, U.S. citizens will have to rely on those who create and maintain DNA banks to design, implement, and enforce self-imposed rules to protect individuals.[27]

DNA contains uniquely personal, powerful, and sensitive information about individuals and their families. Some individuals want to know as much of this information about themselves as possible and may be willing to share this information with their families and beyond. Others would rather remain ignorant about their own genetic makeup, and thus their risks for future illnesses, or at least want to keep others ignorant of their genetic makeup. Individual choices are best served by policies and laws that place primary control over individuals' DNA and genetic information in the hands of the individuals themselves.

Notes

Portions of this chapter are adapted from P. A. Roche and G. J. Annas, "Protecting Genetic Privacy," *Nature Reviews Genetics* 2 (2001).

1. See, e.g., Cal. Health & Saf. Code § 120980 (West 2000); Conn. Gen. Stat. § 19a-583 (West 1999); and Fla. Stat. § 394.4615 (West 2000).

2. See, e.g., Committee for a Study on Promoting Access to Scientific and Technical Data for the Public Interest, National Research Council, *A Question of Balance: Private Rights and Public Interest in Scientific and Technical Databases* (Washington, D.C.: National Academies Press, 1999).

3. Department of Health and Human Services, "Standards for Privacy of Individually Identifiable Health Information, Final Rule," *Federal Register* 65 (2000): 82461–82829. And see *Northwestern Memorial Hospital v. Ashcroft*, 2004 U.S. App. LEXIS 5724 (7th Cir. March 26, 2004).

4. Thomas Murray, "Genetic Exceptionalism and 'Future Diaries': Is Genetic Information Different from Other Medical Information?" in *Genetic Secrets: Protecting Privacy and Confidentiality in the Genetic Era*, ed. M. Rothstein (New Haven: Yale University Press, 1997), 60–76.

5. George J. Annas, "Privacy Rules for DNA Databanks: Protecting Coded 'Future Diaries,'" *Journal of the American Medical Association* 270 (1993): 2346–2350.

6. W. Safire, "Senate Inquiry," *New York Times*, October 23, 1993, A19.

7. Paul R. Billings, Jonathan Beckwith, and Joseph S. Alper, "The Genetic Analysis of Human Behavior: A New Era?" *Social Science & Medicine* 35 (1992): 227–238.

8. Murray, "Genetic Exceptionalism and 'Future Diaries,'" note 3.

9. E. Marshall, "Which Jefferson Was the Father?" *Science* 283 (1999): 153–154.

10. Dorothy M. Nelkin and Susan Lindee, *The DNA Mystique: The Gene as Cultural Icon* (New York: Freeman, 1995).

11. M. Huggins et al., "Predictive Testing for Huntington's Disease in Canada: Adverse Effects and Unexpected Results in Those Receiving a Decreased Risk," *American Journal of Medical Genetics* 42 (1992): 504–515; A. C. DudokdeWit et al., "Distress in Individuals Facing Predictive DNA Testing for Autosomal Dominant Late-Onset Disorders: Comparing Questionnaire Results with In-Depth Interviews," *American Journal of Medical Genetics* 75 (1998): 62–74.

12. American Society of Human Genetics and American College of Medical Genetics, "Ethical, Legal and Psychological Implications of Genetic Testing in Children and Adolescents: Points to Consider," *American Journal of Human Genetics* 57 (1995): 1233–1241.

13. *Norman-Bloodsaw v. Lawrence Berkeley Laboratory*, 135 F.3d 1260, 1269 (1998).

14. George J. Annas, Leonard H. Glantz, and Patricia A. Roche, *The Genetic Privacy Act and Commentary* (Boston: Health Law Department, Boston University School of Public Health, 1995) (available at www.bumc.bu.edu/sph/Lw); Patricia (Winnie) Roche, Leonard Glantz, and George J. Annas, "The Genetic Privacy Act: A Proposal for National Legislation," *Jurimetrics Journal* 37 (1996): 1–11.

15. *Moore v. Regents of University of California*, 793 P.2d 479, 271 Cal. Rptr. 146 (1990); see also George J. Annas, "Outrageous Fortune: Selling Other People's Cells," in *Standard of Care: The Law of American Bioethics*, ed. George J. Annas (New York: Oxford University Press, 1993): 167–177.

16. National Bioethics Advisory Commission, *Research Involving Human Biological Materials*, vol. 1, *Ethical Issues and Policy Guidance* (Rockville, Md.: National Bioethics Advisory Committee, 1999).

17. David Korn, "Genetic Privacy, Medical Information Privacy, and the Use of Human Tissue Specimens in Research," in *Genetic Testing and the Use of Information*, ed. Clarisa Long (Washington, D.C.: American Enterprise Press, 1999): 16–83.

18. H. T. Greely, "Iceland's Plan for Genomics Research: Facts and Implications," *Jurimetrics Journal* 40 (2000): 153–191; H. Jonantansson, "Iceland's Health Sector Database: A Significant Head Start in the Search for the Biological Holy Grail or an Irreversible Error?" *American Journal of Law and Medicine* 26 (2000): 31–67; George J. Annas, "Rules for Research on Human Genetic Variation—Lessons from Iceland," *New England Journal of Medicine* 342 (2000): 1830–1833.

19. E. W. Clayton et al., "Informed Consent for Genetic Research on Stored Tissue Samples," *Journal of the American Medical Association* 274 (1995): 1786–1792.

20. George J. Annas, Leonard H. Glantz, and B. F. Katz, *Informed Consent to Human Experimentation: The Subject's Dilemma* (Cambridge, Mass.: Ballinger, 1977).

21. 45 C.F.R. sec 46. 101 et seq. (1991 revision).

22. A. M. Dershowitz, "Karyotype, Predictability and Culpability," in *Genetics and the Law*, ed. A. Milunsky and George J. Annas (New York: Plenum, 1975): 63–72.

23. J. Cumings and G. R. Simpson, "Bush Readies Plan for Legislation to Prevent Genetic Discrimination," *Wall Street Journal*, June 25, 2001, B2.

24. Francis S. Collins and James D. Watson, "Genetic Discrimination: Time to Act," *Science* 302 (2003): 745.

25. 2000 Massachusetts Acts Chapter 254; R. Misha, "New Law Gives Genetic Privacy Protection," *Boston Globe*, August 23, 2000, B2.

26. See note 14.

27. George J. Annas, "The Limits of State Laws to Protect Genetic Information," *New England Journal of Medicine* 345 (2001): 385–388.

8

Ethical and Policy Guidance

R. Alta Charo

Biomedical researchers have long studied human biological materials—such as cells collected in research projects, biopsy specimens obtained for diagnostic purposes, and organs and tissues removed during surgery—to increase knowledge about human diseases and to develop better means of preventing, diagnosing, and treating these diseases. Today, new technologies and advances in biology provide even more effective tools for using such resources to improve medicine's diagnostic and therapeutic potential. Human biological materials also constitute an invaluable source of information for public-health planning and programming, through disease surveillance and studies of disease incidence and prevalence.

Yet the very power of these new technologies raises a number of important ethical issues. Is it appropriate to use stored biological materials in ways that originally were not contemplated either by the people from whom the materials were collected or by those who collected the materials? Does such use harm anyone's interest? Does it matter whether the material in question is identified, or identifiable, as to its source, or is linked, or linkable, to other medical or personal data regarding the source?[1]

Based on the many successes of past research that has used human biological materials, it seems highly likely that future studies involving such materials also will benefit millions of people. How should this prospect be weighed against the chance that the studies could harm or wrong the individuals whose material is being studied, their families, or other groups of which they are members? Under what circumstances should researchers seek informed consent from people whose biological materials (either existing or to be collected) they propose to study? How should consent requirements be adjusted if the sources of the existing biological materials would be difficult or impossible to locate, or if they have died? And should collections of such materials be made available for forensic uses, or will that undermine support for maintaining and expanding these collections for research purposes, a concern made even more significant in light of the proposal to permit law enforcement authorities to use medical information otherwise protected under the Health Insurance Portability and Accountability Act.[2]

The Research Value of Human Biological Materials

The medical and scientific practice of storing human biological materials is more than a hundred years old. Human biological collections, which include DNA banks, tissue banks, and repositories, vary considerably, ranging from large collections formally designated as repositories to blood or tissue informally stored in a researcher's laboratory freezer. Large collections include archived pathology materials and stored cards containing blood spots from newborn screening tests. Tissue specimens are stored at military facilities, in forensic DNA banks, in government laboratories, in diagnostic pathology and cytology laboratories, in university- and hospital-based research laboratories, in commercial enterprises, and in nonprofit organizations. Archives of human biological materials range in size from fewer than 200 specimens to more than 92 million. Conservatively estimated, at least 282 million specimens (from more than 176 million individual cases) are stored in the United States, and the collections are growing at a rate of over 20 million cases per year.

The most common sources of human biological materials are diagnostic or therapeutic interventions in which diseased tissue is removed or tissue or other material is obtained to determine the nature and extent of a disease. Even after the diagnosis or treatment is complete, a portion of the specimen routinely is retained for future clinical, research, or legal purposes. Specimens also are obtained during autopsies. In addition, volunteers donate organs, blood, or other tissue for transplantation or research, and some donate their bodies after death for transplantation of organs or anatomical studies. Each specimen may be stored in multiple forms, including slides, paraffin blocks, formalin-fixed tissue cultures, or extracted DNA. Repositories provide qualified commercial and noncommercial laboratories with access to specimens for both clinical and research purposes.

In addition to its future clinical use, a specimen of human biological material can be used to study basic biology or disease. It can be examined to determine its normal and abnormal attributes, or it can be manipulated to develop a research tool or a potentially marketable product. Just as a clinician chooses biological materials appropriate to the clinical situation at hand, a researcher's choice of such materials depends on the goals of the research project. The selected tissue can be used only once, or it can be used to generate a renewable source of material, such as by developing a cell line, a cloned gene, or a gene marker. In addition, proteins can be extracted, or DNA isolated, from particular specimens. There is substantial research value both in unidentified material (i.e., material that is not linked to an individual) and in material linked to an identifiable person and his or her continuing medical record. In the former, the value to the researcher of the human biological material is in the tissue itself and often in the associated clinical information about that individual, without the need to know the identity of the person from whom it came. For example, investigators may be interested in identifying a biological marker in a specific type of tissue, such as cells from individuals with Alzheimer's disease or specific tumors from a cancer patient. In such cases, beyond knowing the diagnosis of the individual from whom the specimen was obtained, researchers may not require more detailed medical records, either past or ongoing.

Sometimes, however, it is necessary to identify the source of the research sample, because the research value of the material depends on linking findings regarding the biology of the sample with updated information from medical or other records pertaining to its source. For example, in a longitudinal study to determine the validity of a genetic marker as a predictor of certain diseases, the researchers would need to be able to link each sample with the medical record of its source to ascertain whether those diseases developed. In one case, a recent study of late-onset Alzheimer disease linked the presence of the disease with the apolipoprotein E allele by studying the stored tissues of fifty-eight families with a history of Alzheimer disease and then examining autopsy records for evidence of the disease in those individuals whose tissue revealed the presence of that allele.[3]

Already, research using biological materials has produced tests to diagnose a predisposition to conditions such as cancer and heart disease and to a variety of genetic diseases that affect millions of individuals. In some cases, prevention or treatment is available once a diagnosis is made; in those cases, knowing the identity of the specimen source would permit communication of relevant medical information to the source that might be of importance to his or her health. In other cases, when medical interventions are unavailable, having one's specimen linked with a disease predictor is likely to be of less clinical value to the individual and might even be troubling.

Human biological materials also may be used for quality control in health care delivery, particularly in diagnostic and pathology laboratories. In addition, these materials are used to identify an individual, such as in paternity testing and in cases of abduction or soldiers missing in action, as well as in other forensic matters for which biological evidence is available for comparison. The advent of technologies that can extract a wide array of information from these materials generally has increased the potential uses in research and otherwise of human biological materials that are unrelated to individual patient care.

By using the power of new DNA technologies and other molecular techniques, scientists potentially can turn to millions of stored human biological materials as sources of valuable scientific, medical, anthropological, and sociological information. Indeed, these technologies are so powerful, even revolutionary, that they also hold the ability to uncover knowledge about individuals no longer alive. Three interesting cases, reported in recent years, serve as examples:

▪ In 1997, scientists at the University of Oxford announced that they had compared DNA extracted from the molar cavity of a nine-thousand-year-old skeleton (known as Cheddar Man) to DNA collected from twenty individuals currently residing in the village of Cheddar; this resulted in the establishment of a genetic tie between the skeleton and a schoolteacher who lived just half a mile from the cave where the bones were found.[4]

▪ Scientists used enzyme-linked assays to analyze tissues more than five thousand years old and to track the historic spread of diseases such as malaria and schistosomiasis, obtaining knowledge that can enlighten current efforts to control infectious disease.[5]

▪ In early 1999, a U.S. pathologist and a group of European molecular biologists announced that they had found DNA sequences in the Y chromosomes of the descendants of Thomas Jefferson that matched DNA from the descendants of Sally Hemings, a slave at Monticello. The data establish only that Thomas Jefferson was the most likely of several candidates who might be the father of Eston Hemings, Hemings' fifth child, but also have raised a storm of controversy.[6]

The demonstrated use of these technical capabilities suggests that human tissue and DNA specimens that have been sitting in storage banks for years, even a century, could be plumbed for new information to reveal something not only about the individual from whom the tissue was obtained, but possibly about entire groups of people who share genes, environmental exposures, and ethnic or even geographic characteristics. Clearly, the same is true for materials that may be collected in the future. DNA, whether already stored or yet to be collected, can be used to study genetic variation among people, to establish relationships between genes and characteristics (such as single-gene disorders), or more generally, to conduct basic studies of the cause and progression of disease, all with the long-term goal of improving human health. One of the many initiatives that is providing information that may help us achieve this goal is the federally funded Human Genome Project, which has completed most relevant sequencing of the human genome.

Is Genetic Information Different from Other Medical Information?

In the past few decades, concern about the misuse of genetic information often has spurred debate about the misapplication of medical information in general. Public discourse and concern about the potential availability of personal genetic information has been intense in recent years for a number of reasons, including (1) the lack of any protection from the misuse of this information outside the research context (e.g., employment discrimination), (2) the role of genetic information in early and often contentious public-policy debates about reproductive medicine and family planning, (3) a difficult history of and continuing concerns with relation to eugenics and genetic discrimination, and (4) the rapid pace of the Human Genome Project and other developments in human biology.[7]

Genetic information is one form of biological or medical information. Like certain other types of medical information, genetic analyses can reveal sensitive information about an individual. Some aspects of genetic information, however, seem to many to distinguish it from other types of medical information. For example, genetic information concerning an individual sometimes can reveal similar information regarding a person's relatives or entire groups of people.[8] In addition, the detailed information contained in a person's genes is largely unknown to that person. Moreover, because DNA is stable, stored specimens may become the source of increasing amounts of information as new genes are mapped. In the words of Francis Collins, director of the National Human Genome Research Institute, "We are hurtling towards a time where individual susceptibilities will be determinable on the basis of technologies that allow your DNA sequence to be sampled and statistical predictions to be made about your future risk of illness."[9] Some claim that the major distinguishing characteristics of genetic information are its predictive capabilities and its implications for individuals other than the person from whom the information was derived.[10] Larry Gostin, for example, has suggested that "genomic" data are qualitatively different from other health data because they are inherently linked to one person; in other words, one's DNA is unique (except in the case of identical twins). In addition, genetic information does not change over time. Although other pieces of medical information about an individual might change over the course of his or her lifetime, DNA, except in the case of mutations, does not.

Others argue, however, that genetic information is not inherently distinct from other types of medical information.[11] Other types of medical information may be strongly correlated with particular diseases. Moreover, infection with a virus has implications for people other than the person actually infected. Likewise, the health status of a person living in a toxic environment, such as near the Chernobyl nuclear accident site, has implications for others living in that same environment.

Clearly, many of the concerns that pertain to the misuse of personal genetic information apply equally to certain other types of personal medical information. In no other area, however, are so many of these concerns present at the same time with respect to a single piece of information.

Increasing Discussion about the Appropriate Research Use of Human Biological Materials

Increasing concerns about the use of medical information have fueled general debate about medical privacy and discrimination. Because medical research can reveal clinically relevant information about individuals, scientists must ensure that those who participate in research are protected adequately from unnecessary harms resulting from the inadvertent release of such information. Although protection of human subjects in research is of primary concern in the U.S. biomedical research system, research that uses biological materials, which are often distanced in time and space from the persons from whom they were obtained, raises unique challenges regarding the appropriate protection of research subjects.

Although medical research generally is considered a public good and is supported vigorously by the American public, the power of technology to find an extraordinary amount of detailed information in a single cell raises the specter that information about individuals will be discovered and used without their consent and possibly to their detriment. Although this type of information also might be obtained through a variety of other means, DNA analysis currently is the most powerful means for doing so and increasingly is the method of choice. In recent years, these varied concerns have resulted in consumer, scientific, and professional groups' beginning to address the issues surrounding the collection and use of human biological materials. In addition, media focus on highly contentious cases involving biological samples, such as the research use of stored neonatal blood spots for anonymous studies of HIV prevalence in a given population and the military's establishment of a DNA bank, has made the issue of research use of human biological materials a matter of increasing public concern.

In 1996, President Clinton appointed an advisory committee to make recommendations for federal policy on genetics and medical research. In the course of its deliberations, the National Bioethics Advisory Commission (NBAC) identified several trends that contribute to the need for a comprehensive public policy concerning the use of these biological materials for research purposes:

- increasing public perceptions that personal genetic and other medical information could be used to discriminate against individuals in employment or by denying them access to benefits such as health or life insurance, or could be stigmatizing in some way
- growing public concern about privacy of medical records
- disagreement among scientific and medical groups regarding conditions that need to be satisfied to ensure that appropriate ethical standards are incorporated into all research protocols using human biological materials, primarily as related to the requirements for review and to the nature of the required consent process

One particular area of concern centers on the question of whether the information that may be obtained from the research use of human biological materials places those who are the sources of the samples at unacceptable risk. For example, such data might reveal information about an individual's disease susceptibility (e.g., that the individual carries a gene that is associated with an increased risk of colon cancer or breast cancer). When an intervention exists that can be pursued to counteract the increased health risk, such as regular mammograms, dietary modification, or drug treatment, some might judge the information worth receiving and worth the psychological and financial risks associated with it. If, however, the analysis reveals information about a condition for which no intervention is currently available (e.g., susceptibility to Huntington disease or Alzheimer disease), many individuals might perceive the risks of uncovering such information as outweighing the benefits. In any case, concern may arise when analysis reveals information of this type, but the individual to whom the information pertains did not consent in advance to the analysis or show any interest in receiving the results. Some would argue that learning about an adverse health status should be undertaken intentionally by the individual concerned, since it can provoke anxiety and disrupt families, particularly if nothing can be done about it and the finding has implications for other family members.

Potential for Discrimination and Stigmatization

There is growing recognition that human biological materials can be analyzed to ascertain significant amounts of genetic and other medical information about the person from whom a specimen was obtained. In particular, there is increasing concern among some policymakers and patient groups that this information could be used to discriminate against individuals in insurance and employment or could be stigmatizing for individuals and families. In January 1998, the White House released a report, *Genetic Information and the Workplace*, prepared by the U.S. Department of Labor and Department of Health and Human Services (DHHS) and the Equal Employment Opportunity Commission. This report predicted that by the year 2000, 15 percent of employers would be making preparations to check the genetic status of prospective employees and cited a 1995 Harris poll that revealed that more than 85 percent of Americans are concerned that insurers and employers may have access to their genetic information.

Concern about insurers' and employers' having access to genetic information has a basis in fact. In the 1970s, several insurance companies and employers discriminated against sickle cell carriers, even though their carrier status did not and would not affect their health.[12] There is a history of concern that in the absence of universal access to health care or laws that prevent discrimination on the basis of health status, medical information may be used to deny individuals insurance or employment. In addition to these possible financial harms, research findings about one's future medical status can, in some cases, inflict psychological or social harms. It should be noted, however, that to date there is little empirical evidence documenting extensive employment or insurance discrimination based on genetic status.

Concerns About Privacy of Medical Records

Health care systems increasingly rely on information technology such as electronic records to manage and facilitate the flow of sensitive and clinically relevant health information. This increased reliance has had positive effects in clinical practice, but the trend also magnifies concerns about privacy of certain genetic and other medical information. Recent commentary about privacy of medical records and attempts to protect privacy through legislation are evidence of the growing public concern about these issues. Congress and DHHS have discussed legislative and regulatory approaches to protect patient privacy, resulting in the passage of HIPAA (the Health Insurance Profitability and Accountability Act (Public Law 104–191)), whose privacy provisions went into effect in 2003, and a final rule was issued that widely expands patient protections, while leaving some room for nonconsensual research on patient records. As research on biological materials is often accompanied by research on the corresponding medical record of the source of the materials, the two sets of rules, one concerning medical records and one concerning human tissue, combine to create a regime of partial protections for patient privacy while accommodating research needs.

An ongoing concern in medical care and in the protection of research subjects is the potential invasion of privacy or the compromise of confidentiality. Measures to govern the nature of consent obtained to participate in research protocols and the disclosure of results, and to provide appropriate protections, both of individual privacy and of the confidentiality of clinical and research data, are important if research using this information is to enjoy broad support. When research samples are identifiable (i.e., linked or linkable to the person who provided them), specific steps must be taken to ensure protections in the collection, storage, and use of the data that result from the testing and analysis of those samples. However, computerized medical records and databases raise concerns about who has access to data (i.e., the security of these databases) and about whether these data are linked to individual patient records. It is widely believed that current confidentiality practices are insufficient to safeguard medical information. In addition, different cultural and religious groups may have differing definitions of privacy or confidentiality.

Privacy concerns may also arise within the context of "secondary use" of specimens collected, that is, use or analysis of the specimens (and the use of information derived from such use or analysis) for purposes that extend beyond the purpose for which the specimens were originally collected. For example, when materials are collected during surgical procedures and are used solely for clinical purposes, the clinical use of these specimens raises few privacy concerns beyond those about the confidentiality of the medical record itself, because the materials are being used for the direct diagnostic or therapeutic benefit of an individual and because the custodian of the biological specimen does not allow others to have access to it. Only when the use of such materials extends beyond the original clinical use do privacy issues arise. For example, if the specimen collected in the scenario just described is subsequently used as part of a research study into familial linkage of a specific disease and the family pedigree is published as a result of the study, an individual might be easily identifiable even without any names attached.

Researchers note that information or material collected for one purpose may have tremendous value for secondary purposes, for example, for genetic analysis using previously unavailable technologies. But obtaining fresh informed consent for new research with previously collected materials has substantial costs, as the people from whom the tissue was taken may be difficult or impossible to locate.[13] It was in response to this dilemma that a 1999 NBAC report on the ethical issues surrounding research involving human biological materials recommended that tissue research be considered regulated human-subjects research whenever the original tissue source could be identified, but at the same time called for recognition that most tissue work is of minimal risk and ought to be eligible for a waiver of informed consent by the tissue source. Exceptions would include research in which there was any reason to believe the tissue source would refuse to participate and research in which particularly stigmatizing characteristics—such as propensity toward incurable or severe illness—might be investigated.[14] The report also called for new practices to be developed in clinics and laboratories, so that future tissue samples taken for clinical or research purposes would be collected in a manner that permitted tissue donors to decide whether their materials could be used for future research, and if so, whether any limits to the type of research should be noted (see Appendix).

Summary

Human tissue, and the DNA information it contains, is a national resource that can and should be used to advance medical research and improve public health. Nonetheless, such use should recognize that individuals have an interest in whether and how tissue samples taken from them are used in such research. Where the original donor of tissue to be used in such research can be identified, he or she should be consulted whenever research uses for the tissue will create a real risk of socio-economic harms. In addition, all uses should anticipate the need for and the consequences of contacting the donor with developing information; methods for communicating such information where helpful and yet avoiding harmful and pointless revelations must be developed before the tissue is used. Finally, the privacy interests of tissue sources must be respected, so that where there is reason to believe that someone would not want materials that originated from him or her to be used—regardless of the prospect of concrete harm in the form of employment or insurance discrimination—that preference should be respected.

Materials stored in forensic collections will frequently be different from those kept in medical collections, and the two types of repositories should be managed separately. Forensic banks need only a random sample and a standardized forensic analysis, after which the original tissue can be discarded. Medical collections, by contrast, often consist of specific tissue types—for example, tissue taken from a tumor—and often need long-term storage so that resampling can take place when and if new genetic markers are discovered that might be applicable to the tissue or the patient from whom it came. Collection and storage in a medical-research context, therefore, may fail to meet the standards required for management of tissue to be used in a criminal prosecution. When a blood specimen has been drawn from a party in a criminal case for purposes of scientific analysis (other than the determination of the blood's alcohol content), for example, the prosecution must authenticate the sample tested by proving a chain of custody, that is, by documenting the sample's handling from the time it was collected until the time it was analyzed. Without this documentation, the results may be inadmissible as evidence in a trial. In *Rabovsky v. Commonwealth*,[15] for example, blood samples were collected in a hospital from the victim of an alleged intentional insulin overdose, then transferred to a local laboratory, and finally transferred to a laboratory in another state for insulin level testing, but the results of the tests were ruled inadmissible, because no evidence was introduced to prove who collected the blood samples, how they were stored, how they were transported, or what method was used to test them. Forensic use of existing medical tissue banks would clearly be impossible under such a standard. Division of medical and forensic collections also simplifies policy issues concerning consent, as it keeps tissues taken voluntarily from patients and research subjects separate from those taken involuntarily from suspects and convicts.

The issue of consent in the context of criminal law has been extensively analyzed with respect to the collection of bodily tissue, both pursuant to custodial detention based on probable cause and with respect to noncustodial tissue collections, at least where the collection is consensual (for example, pursuant to a DNA dragnet while pursuing a serial rapist). The DNA collection methods employed by Chicago police in one recent case, for example, included informing donors of their right to refuse and that their samples would be used to create a DNA profile that might be used in future criminal investigations.[16] But even here, subsequent use of materials collected in one criminal investigation for a different criminal investigation raises questions concerning the rights of tissue providers to control the scope of the consent and thus the use of the tissue. Donors in the Chicago DNA dragnet signed a form consenting to use of the samples "for this investigation or any other investigation or any legitimate law enforcement purpose," and thus subsequent uses were clearly authorized. But in the absence of explicit consent, the question arises as to whether subsequent uses are permissible.

Of course, it may be argued that police use of previously donated tissue samples does not constitute a search at all, as there is no bodily invasion and the donor has already, by virtue of donating a sample, accepted that he or she has only a diminished expectation of privacy. But this would be inconsistent with Supreme Court cases that recognize an individual's right to limit a search and to determine the scope of his or her consent. It would also be completely at odds with the spirit of the rules developed for medical-research applications of tissue banks, all of which are premised on the individual's right to withhold consent to any use of the tissue that poses more than a minimal risk of economic or psychosocial harm to an identifiable tissue donor.

Concern about subsequent use of previously donated tissue is clearly related to a final reason for ensuring that tissues collected for medical research remain immune from forensic analysis, specifically, that separation will help to foster cooperation from patients and research subjects by limiting the risks associated with agreeing to long-term storage of their tissue. If researchers cannot promise confidentiality of test results, participation in tissue collection efforts is likely to drop precipitously, most especially if the risks go beyond social stigmatization or even health insurance complications to encompass the risk of criminal prosecution. Indeed, the recognition that a risk of criminal prosecution based on research results may deter participation has led to the development of a "certificate of confidentiality," a tool used in a variety of research contexts in which illegal behavior (e.g., illicit drug use) might be revealed.

Where data are being collected about sensitive issues (such as illegal behavior, alcohol or drug use, or sexual practices or preferences), protection of confidentiality consists of more than simply preventing accidental disclosures. There have been instances in which the identities of subjects or research data about particular subjects have been sought by law enforcement agencies, sometimes under subpoena, and with the threat of incarceration of the uncooperative researcher. Under federal law (and some state laws), researchers can obtain an advance grant of confidentiality that will provide protection even against a subpoena for research data (Public Health Service Act §301(d)). In May 1989, the Public Health Service (PHS) issued an interim policy statement (also called the "Interim Guidance") that sets forth PHS policy for exercising its authority to grant certificates of confidentiality. Section 301(d) extends to "biomedical, behavioral, clinical, or other research" an earlier authority (in §303 of the Public Health Service Act) that was previously available only for "research on mental health, including research on the use and effect of alcohol and other psychoactive drugs."

To take advantage of §301(d), the investigator must request a grant of confidentiality from the appropriate official. Protection for research on mental disorders or the use and effects of alcohol and other psychoactive drugs can be obtained from the National Institute on Alcohol Abuse and Alcoholism, the National Institute on Drug Abuse, or the National Institute of Mental Health, which, in 1991, became components of NIH. Certificates of confidentiality for biomedical, behavioral, clinical, or other research that does not fall into these categories are issued by the Assistant Secretary for Health. Protection is available for (1) direct federal activities (i.e., intramural research), (2) federally funded activities, and (3) research in the United States that has no federal funding. Under the interim policy, protection will be granted "sparingly," and only "when the research is of a sensitive nature where the protection is judged necessary to achieve the research objectives." The policy defines "sensitive" research as involving the collection of information falling into any of the following categories:

(a) information relating to sexual attitudes, preferences, or practices

(b) information relating to the use of alcohol, drugs, or other addictive products

(c) information pertaining to illegal conduct

(d) information that if released could reasonably be damaging to an individual's financial standing, employability, or reputation within the community

(e) information that would normally be recorded in a patient's medical record and that, if disclosed, could reasonably lead to social stigmatization or discrimination

(f) information pertaining to an individual's psychological well-being or mental health

Information in categories not listed here might also be considered sensitive if tissue banks were to become subject to use by law enforcement seeking to perform forensic DNA analysis on the samples, and protection might be granted in such cases upon appropriate justification and explanation.

The following appendix summarizes the NBAC's recommendations for realizing the twin goals of facilitating research and protecting research subjects, within the constraints of current law and regulation. Those recommendations have received a favorable review by large segments of the research and governmental community but have not yet been formally adopted by HHS. Further, the new HIPAA rules on medical-record research—a form of research often done in conjunction with tissue research—do not comport with the NBAC recommendations for situations in which when the underlying tissue donor (medical-record subject) is identifiable as to when such persons must be consulted before research proceeds. Similar rules for these two areas would be preferable, as both focus on the same balance between advancing research and preserving respect for the preferences and interests of the persons whose tissues and records are being studied.

Appendix: Recommendations of the National Bioethics Advisory Commission, Research Involving Human Biological Materials, vol. 1, Ethical Issues and Policy Guidance (1999)

Interpretation of the Existing Federal Regulations
NBAC offers the following recommendations to improve the interpretation and implementation of the existing federal regulations as they apply to research using human biological materials.

Recommendation 1   Federal regulations governing human subjects research (45 CFR 46) that apply to research involving human biological materials should be interpreted by the Office for Protection from Research Risks (OPRR), other federal agencies that are signatories to the Common Rule, IRBs, investigators, and others, in the following specific ways:

(a) Research conducted with unidentified samples is not human subjects research and is not regulated by the Common Rule.

(b) Research conducted with unlinked samples is research on human subjects and is regulated by the Common Rule, but is eligible for exemption from IRB review pursuant to 45 CFR 46.101(b)(4).

(c) Research conducted with coded or identified samples is research on human subjects and regulated by the Common Rule. It is not eligible for exemption unless the specimens or the samples are publicly available as defined by 45 CFR 46.101(b)(4).

Few collections of human biological materials are publicly available, although many are available to qualified researchers at reasonable cost. Therefore, OPRR should make clear in its guidance that in most cases this exemption does not apply to research using human biological materials.

The current federal regulations appear to make eligible for expedited review research on materials that will be collected for clinical purposes or those that will be collected in noninvasive or minimally invasive ways for research purposes. NBAC finds that there is no need to distinguish between collections originally created for clinical purposes and those created for research purposes. In both cases, research on the collected materials should be eligible for expedited review if the research presents no more than a minimal risk to the study subjects. (See the discussion of minimal risk below.)

Recommendation 2   OPRR should revise its guidance to make clear that all minimal-risk research involving human biological materials—regardless of how they were collected—should be eligible for expedited IRB review.

Special Concerns about the Use of Unlinked Samples

Given the importance of society's interest in treating disease and developing new therapies, a policy that severely restricts research access to unidentified and unlinked samples would severely hamper research and could waste a valuable research resource. As noted in Recommendation 1, research using unlinked samples may be exempt from review. However, if coded or identified samples are rendered unlinked by the investigator, special precautions are in order.

Recommendation 3   When an investigator proposes to create unlinked samples from coded or identified materials already under his or her control, an IRB (or other designated officials at the investigator's institution) may exempt the research from IRB review if it determines that (a) the process used to unlink the samples will be effective, and (b) the unlinking of the samples will not unnecessarily reduce the value of the research.

Requirements for Investigators Using Coded or Identified Samples
Repositories and IRBs share responsibility with investigators to ensure that research is designed and conducted in a manner that appropriately protects human subjects from unwarranted harms.

Recommendation 4   Before releasing coded and/or identified samples from its collection, a repository should require that the investigator requesting the samples either provide documentation from the investigator's IRB that the research will be conducted in compliance with applicable federal regulations or explain in writing why the research is not subject to those regulations.

Recommendation 5   When reviewing and approving a protocol for research on human biological materials, IRBs should require the investigator to set forth

(a) a thorough justification of the research design, including a description of procedures used to minimize risk to subjects,

(b) a full description of the process by which samples will be obtained,

(c) any plans to obtain access to the medical records of the subjects, and

(d) a full description of the mechanisms that will be used to maximize the protection against inadvertent release of confidential information.

When an investigator obtains access to a patient's medical records, either to identify sample sources or to gather additional medical information, human subjects research is being conducted.

IRBs should adopt policies to govern such research, consistent with existing OPRR guidance related to medical records research.

Obtaining Informed Consent
Research using coded or identified samples requires the consent of the source, unless the criteria for a consent waiver have been satisfied. Unfortunately, the consent obtained at the time the specimen was obtained may not always be adequate to satisfy this requirement. When research is contemplated using existing samples, the expressed wishes of the individuals who provided the materials must be respected. Where informed consent documents exist, they may indicate whether individuals wanted their sample to be used in future research and in some instances may specify the type of research.

When human biological materials are collected, whether in a research or clinical setting, it is appropriate to ask subjects for their consent to future use of their samples, even in cases where such uses are at the time unknown. In this latter case, however, particular considerations are needed to determine whether to honor prospective wishes.

Whether obtaining consent to the research use of human biological materials in a research or clinical setting, and whether the consent is new or renewed, efforts should be made to be as explicit as possible about the uses to which the material might be put and whether it is possible that the research might be conducted in such a way that the individual could be identified.

Obviously, different conditions will exist for different research protocols, in different settings, and among individuals. NBAC notes that the current debate about the appropriate use of millions of stored specimens endures because of the uncertain nature of past consents. Investigators and others who collected and stored human biological materials now have the opportunity to correct past inadequacies by obtaining more specific and clearly understood informed consent.

Recommendation 6   When informed consent to the research use of human biological materials is required, it should be obtained separately from informed consent to clinical procedures.

Recommendation 7   The person who obtains informed consent in clinical settings should make clear to potential subjects that their refusal to consent to the research use of biological materials will in no way affect the quality of their clinical care.

Recommendation 8   When an investigator is conducting research on coded or identified samples obtained prior to the implementation of NBAC's recommendations, general releases for research given in conjunction with a clinical or surgical procedure must not be presumed to cover all types of research over an indefinite period of time. Investigators and IRBs should review existing consent documents to determine whether the subjects anticipated and agreed to participate in the type of research proposed. If the existing documents are inadequate and consent cannot be waived, the investigator must obtain informed consent from the subjects for the current research or in appropriate circumstances have the identifiers stripped so that samples are unlinked.

Recommendation 9   To facilitate collection, storage, and appropriate use of human biological materials in the future, consent forms should be developed to provide potential subjects with a sufficient number of options to help them understand clearly the nature of the decision they are about to make. Such options might include, for example:

(a) refusing use of their biological materials in research,

(b) permitting only unidentified or unlinked use of their biological materials in research,

(c) permitting coded or identified use of their biological materials for one particular study only, with no further contact permitted to ask for permission to do further studies,

(d) permitting coded or identified use of their biological materials for one particular study only, with further contact permitted to ask for permission to do further studies,

(e) permitting coded or identified use of their biological materials for any study relating to the condition for which the sample was originally collected, with further contact allowed to seek permission for other types of studies, or

(f) permitting coded use of their biological materials for any kind of future study.*

Criteria for Waiver of Consent

When an investigator proposes to conduct research with coded or identified samples, it is considered research with human subjects. Ordinarily the potential research subject is asked whether he or she agrees to participate. Seeking this consent demonstrates respect for the person's right to choose whether to cooperate with the scientific enterprise, and it permits individuals to protect themselves against unwanted or risky invasions of privacy. But informed consent is merely one aspect of human subjects protection. It is an adjunct to—rather than a substitute for—IRB review to determine if the risks of a study are minimized and acceptable in relation to its benefits.

When a study is of minimal risk, informed consent is no longer needed by a subject as a form of self-protection against research harms. However, it is still appropriate to seek consent in order to show respect for the subject, unless it is impracticable to locate him or her in order to obtain it.

---

* Commissioners Capron, Miike, and Shapiro wrote statements regarding their concerns about various aspects of this recommendation (see page 65 of the full report).

Thus, when important research poses little or no risk to subjects whose consent would be difficult or impossible to obtain, it is appropriate to waive the consent requirement.

Recommendation 10 IRBs should operate on the presumption that research on coded samples is of minimal risk to the human subject if

(a) the study adequately protects the confidentiality of personally identifiable information obtained in the course of research,

(b) the study does not involve the inappropriate release of information to third parties, and

(c) the study design incorporates an appropriate plan for whether and how to reveal findings to the sources or their physicians should the findings merit such disclosure.

Failure to obtain informed consent may adversely affect the rights and welfare of subjects in two basic ways. First, the subject may be improperly denied the opportunity to choose whether to assume the risks that the research presents, and second, the subject may be harmed or wronged as a result of his or her involvement in research to which he or she has not consented.

Further, when state or federal law, or customary practice, gives subjects a right to refuse to have their biological materials used in research, then a consent waiver would affect their rights adversely. Medical records privacy statutes currently in place or under consideration generally allow for unconsented research use and could be interpreted to suggest a similar standard for research using human biological materials. But as new statutes are enacted, it is possible that subjects will be given explicit rights to limit access to their biological materials.

Recommendation 11 In determining whether a waiver of consent would adversely affect subjects' rights and welfare, IRBs should be certain to consider

(a) whether the waiver would violate any state or federal statute or customary practice regarding entitlement to privacy or confidentiality,

(b) whether the study will examine traits commonly considered to have political, cultural, or economic significance to the study subjects, and

(c) whether the study's results might adversely affect the welfare of the subject's community.

Even when research poses no more than minimal risk and a consent waiver would not affect the rights and welfare of subjects, respect for subjects requires that their consent be sought.

However, on some occasions, demonstrating this respect through consent requirements could completely halt important research. An investigator who requests a waiver of the informed consent requirement for research use of human biological materials under the current federal regulations must provide to the IRB evidence that it is not practicable to obtain consent.

Unfortunately, neither the regulations nor OPRR offers any guidance on what defines practicability.

Recommendation 12   If research using existing coded or identified human biological materials is determined to present minimal risk, IRBs may presume that it would be impracticable to meet the consent requirement (45 CFR 46.116(d)(3)). This interpretation of the regulations applies only to the use of human biological materials collected before the adoption of the recommendations contained in this report (specifically Recommendations 6 through 9 regarding informed consent). Materials collected after that point must be obtained according to the recommended informed consent process and, therefore, IRBs should apply their usual standards for the practicability requirement.

NBAC recognizes that if its recommendation that coded samples be treated as though they are identifiable is adopted, there may be an increase in the number of research protocols that will require IRB review. If, however, such protocols are then determined by an IRB to present minimal risk to a subject's rights and welfare, the requirement for consent may be waived if the practicability requirement is revised for this category of research. However, it must be noted that by dropping the requirement that consent must be obtained if practicable, NBAC does so with the expectation that the process and content of informed consent for the collection of new specimens will be explicit regarding the intentions of the subjects and the research use of their materials. (See Recommendations 6 through 9 concerning informed consent.)

According to current regulations, the fourth condition for the waiver of consent stipulates that "whenever appropriate, the subjects will be provided with additional pertinent information after participation" (45 CFR 46.116(d)(4)). Thus, according to the regulations, an IRB, while waiving consent (by finding and documenting the first three required conditions), could require that subjects be informed that they were subjects of research and that they be provided details of the study—a so-called debriefing requirement. In general, NBAC concludes that this fourth criterion for waiver of consent is not relevant to research using human biological materials and, in fact, might be harmful if it forced investigators to recontact individuals who might not have been aware that their materials were being used in research.

Recommendation 13   OPRR should make clear to investigators and IRBs that the fourth criterion for waiver, that "whenever appropriate, the subjects will be provided with additional pertinent information after participation" (45 CFR 46.116(d)(4)), usually does not apply to research using human biological materials.

Reporting Research Results to Subjects
Experts disagree about whether findings from research should be communicated to subjects. However, most do believe that such findings should not be conveyed to subjects unless they are confirmed and reliable and constitute clinically significant or scientifically relevant information.

Recommendation 14   IRBs should develop general guidelines for the disclosure of the results of research to subjects and require investigators to address these issues explicitly in their research plans.

In general, these guidelines should reflect the presumption that the disclosure of research results to subjects represents an exceptional circumstance. Such disclosure should occur only when all of the following apply:

(a) the findings are scientifically valid and confirmed,

(b) the findings have significant implications for the subject's health concerns, and

(c) a course of action to ameliorate or treat these concerns is readily available.

Recommendation 15   The investigator in his or her research protocol should describe anticipated research findings and circumstances that might lead to a decision to disclose the findings to a subject, as well as a plan for how to manage such a disclosure.

Recommendation 16   When research results are disclosed to a subject, appropriate medical advice or referral should be provided.

Considerations of Potential Harms to Others

The federal regulations governing the protection of research subjects extend only to individuals who can be identified as the sources of the biological samples. The exclusive focus of the regulations on the individual research subject is arbitrary from an ethical standpoint, because persons other than the subject can benefit or be harmed as a consequence of the research.

Recommendation 17 Research using stored human biological materials, even when not potentially harmful to individuals from whom the samples are taken, may be potentially harmful to groups associated with the individual. To the extent such potential harms can be anticipated, investigators should to the extent possible plan their research so as to minimize such harm and should consult, when appropriate, representatives of the relevant groups regarding study design. In addition, when research on unlinked samples that poses a significant risk of group harms is otherwise eligible for exemption from IRB review, the exemption should not be granted if IRB review might help the investigator to design the study in such a way as to avoid those harms.

Recommendation 18 If it is anticipated that a specific research protocol poses a risk to a specific group, this risk should be disclosed during any required informed consent process.

Publication and Dissemination of Research Results

Publishing research results with identifiable information in scientific or medical journals and elsewhere may pose a risk to the privacy and confidentiality of research subjects. Public disclosure of such information through written descriptions or pedigrees may cause subjects to experience adverse psychosocial effects. In addition, without the informed consent of the individual, such disclosure infringes on the rights of the subject or patient. Because of the familial nature of information in pedigrees, their publication poses particularly difficult questions regarding consent. Investigators and journal editors should be aware that the ways in which research results are publicized or disseminated could affect the privacy of human subjects.

NBAC believes that the source of funding, i.e., public or private, should not be an important consideration in determining the ethical acceptability of the research.

Recommendation 19   Investigators' plans for disseminating results of research on human biological materials should include, when appropriate, provisions to minimize the potential harms to individuals or associated groups.

Recommendation 20   Journals should adopt the policy that the published results of research studies involving human subjects must specify whether the research was conducted in compliance with the requirements of the Common Rule. This policy should extend to all human subjects research, including studies that are privately funded or are otherwise exempt from these requirements.

Professional Education and Responsibilities

Public and professional education plays an essential role in developing and implementing effective public policy regarding use of human biological materials for research. By education, NBAC is referring not simply to the provision of information with the aim of adding to the net store of knowledge by any one person or group; rather, education refers to the ongoing effort to inform, challenge, and engage. Widespread and continuing deliberation on the subject of this report must occur to inform and educate the public about developments in the field of genetics and other areas in the biomedical sciences, especially when they affect important cultural practices, values, and beliefs.

Recommendation 21   The National Institutes of Health, professional societies, and health care organizations should continue and expand their efforts to train investigators about the ethical issues and regulations regarding research on human biological materials and to develop exemplary practices for resolving such issues.

Recommendation 22   Compliance with the recommendations set forth in this report will require additional resources. All research sponsors (government, private sector enterprises, and academic institutions) should work together to make these resources available.

Use of Medical Records in Research on Human Biological Materials

In recent years, attention increasingly has been paid by policymakers to the need to protect the health information of the individual. Extensive efforts at the state and federal levels to enact such protections have resulted in the setting of a variety of limitations on access to patient medical records. NBAC notes that debates about medical privacy are relevant to researchers using human biological materials in two ways. First, these researchers often need access to patient medical records, either to identify research sample sources or to gather accompanying clinical information. Such activities constitute human subjects research and should be treated accordingly. Second, the development of statutes and regulations to protect patient medical records could have the unintended consequence of creating a dual system of protections, one for the medical record and one for human biological materials. Moreover, restrictions on access to the medical record could impede legitimate and appropriate access on the part of investigators whose protocols have undergone proper review.

Recommendation 23   Because many of the same issues arise in the context of research on both medical records and human biological materials, when drafting medical records privacy laws, state and federal legislators should seek to harmonize rules governing both types of research. Such legislation, while seeking to protect patient confidentiality and autonomy, should also ensure that appropriate access for legitimate research purposes is maintained.

Notes

1. E. W. Clayton et al., "Informed Consent for Genetic Research on Stored Tissue Samples," *Journal of the American Medical Association* 274 (1995): 1786–1792.

2. *Health Insurance Portability and Accountability Act of 1996*, Pub. L. No. 104191, 110 Stat. 1936 (codified as amended in scattered sections of 29 U.S.C.A. and 42 U.S.C.A.); see also 65 FR 82462, *Federal Register* Vol. 65, No. 250, Rules and Regulations Department of Health and Human Services (HHS), Office of the Secretary, Office of the Assistant Secretary for Planning and Evaluation, 45 CFR Parts 160 and 164, Rin: 0991-AB08, Standards for Privacy of Individually Identifiable Health Information, Part II, 65 FR 82462, Date: Thursday, December 28, 2000.

3. H. Payami et al., "Gender Differences in Apolipoprotein E–Associated Risk for Familial Alzheimer Disease: A Possible Clue to the Higher Incidence of Alzheimer Disease in Women," *American Journal of Human Genetics* 58, no. 4 (1996): 803–811.

4. M. DiChristina, "Stone Age Kin: A Briton's Relationship with a 9,000-Year-Old Skeleton Is Established through Mitochondrial DNA," *Popular Science* 250, no. 6 (1997): 90.

5. See Egyptian Mummy Tissue bank information at www.mcc.ac.uk/Museum/General/mummy.htm.

6. E. A. Foster et al., "Jefferson Fathered Slave's Last Child," *Nature* 396 (1998): 27–28.

7. Lori B. Andrews et al., *Assessing Genetic Risks: Implications for Health and Social Policy* (Washington, D.C.: National Academies Press, 1994).

8. Ad Hoc Committee on DNA Technology, American Society of Human Genetics, "DNA Banking and DNA Analysis: Points to Consider," *American Journal of Human Genetics* 42 (1988): 781–783.

9. Francis S. Collins et al., "New Goals for the U.S. Human Genome Project: 1998–2003," *Science* 282 (1998): 283, 682–689.

10. Institute of Medicine, *Assessing Genetic Risks* (Washington, D.C.: National Academies Press, 1994).

11. Thomas Murray, "Genetic Exceptionalism and 'Future Diaries': Is Genetic Information Different from Other Medical Information?" in *Genetic Secrets*, ed. M. Rothstein (New Haven: Yale University Press, 1997), 60–73.

12. Joanne Seltzer, "The Cassandra Complex: An Employer's Dilemma in the Genetic Workplace," *Hofstra Law Review* 27: 411–470.

13. Executive Council, American Association of Medical Colleges, *Medical Records and Genetic Privacy, Health Data Security, Patient Privacy, and the Use of Archival Patient Materials in Research* (Washington, D.C.: American Medical Association/American College of Medical Genetics, 1997); Storage of Genetics Materials Committee, American Society of Human Genetics, "Statement on Storage and Use of Genetic Materials," *American Journal of Human Genetics* 57 (1995): 1499–1500; American Society of Human Genetics, "DNA Banking and DNA Analysis," 781–783; Ad Hoc Committee on Genetic Testing/Insurance, American Society of Human Genetics, "Genetic Testing and Insurance," *American Journal of Human Genetics* 56 (1995): 327–331; Rapid Action Task Force on Informed Consent for Genetic Research, American Society of Human Genetics, "Statement on Informed Consent for Genetic Research," *American Journal of Human Genetics* 59 (1996): 471–474; Social Issues Subcommittee on Familial Disclosure, American Society of Human Genetics, "Professional Disclosure of Familial Genetic Information," *American Journal of Human Genetics* 62 (1998): 474–483.

14. National Bioethics Advisory Commission, *Research Involving Human Biological Materials*, vol. 1, *Ethical Issues and Policy Guidance* (Rockville, Md.: National Bioethics Advisory Commission, 1999).

15. 973 S.W.2d 6, 77 A.L.R.5th 711 (Ky. 1998).

16. See Jonathan Eig, "Code of a Killer," *Chicago Magazine*, December 1999; Sabrina L. Miller and Terry Wilson, "Suspect Glad He's Caught, Cops Say; Taped Confessions, DNA Help Make Case," *Chicago Tribune*, February 1, 2000; Frank Main and Fran Spielman, "Englewood Suspect Attended Community Policing Meetings," *Chicago Sun-Times*, February 5, 2000; Frank Main and Fran Spielman, "Alleged Killer Volunteered as Kid Escort," *Chicago Sun-Times*, February 5, 2000; Lorraine Forte, "Police Charge Man in 10 Deaths; Suspected Killer Stalked Englewood," *Chicago Sun-Times*, January 31, 2000.

9

Privacy and Forensic DNA Data Banks

Barry Steinhardt

DNA Is Different

Let me start with a point that I hope we can all agree on. Drawing a DNA sample is simply not the same as taking a fingerprint. Fingerprints are two-dimensional representations of the physical attributes of our fingertips. They are useful only as a form of identification. DNA profiling may be used for identification purposes, but the DNA itself represents far more than a fingerprint. Indeed, it trivializes DNA data banking to call it a genetic fingerprint.[1]

I am certainly aware that the primary purpose of forensic DNA databases like CODIS is identification and that the profiles are of thirteen loci that currently provide no other information. However, I reject the term "junk DNA," because as the Human Genome Project and other studies continue, those loci may well turn out to contain other useful genetic information.[2]

More significantly, the amount of personal and private data contained in a DNA specimen from which the profile is drawn makes its seizure extraordinary in both its nature and scope. The DNA samples that are being held by federal, state, and local governments can provide insights into the most personal family relationships and the most intimate workings of the human body, including the likelihood of the occurrence of thousands of genetic conditions and diseases. DNA may reveal private information such as legitimacy at birth, and there are many who will claim that there are genetic markers for aggression, substance addiction, criminal tendencies, and sexual orientation.

And because genetic information pertains not only to the individual whose DNA is sampled, but to everyone who shares in that person's bloodline, potential threats to genetic privacy posed by their collection extend well beyond the millions of people whose samples are currently on file.

In short, the rapid expansion of DNA data banking raises the specter of a brave new world where genetic information is routinely collected and its use results in abuse and discrimination. I would love to be proven wrong, but I am skeptical that we can hold the line and ward off the brave new world of genetic determinism.

Why am I skeptical? First, I am skeptical because there is a long history of function creep in databases. Despite the initial promises of their creators, databases created for a discrete purpose eventually take on new functions and purposes. Second, I am skeptical because there is a long and sad history of eugenics and genetic discrimination in this nation. Third, I am skeptical because the state laws that authorize DNA data banking offer scant protection against abuse, and many lawmakers hold expansive notions about their uses. Finally, I am skeptical because as long as we continue to hold on to millions of biological samples, the temptation to use them for purposes that go beyond law enforcement identification will simply be too great.

Function Creep

Function creep seems to be a matter of human nature. In the 1930s promises were made that social security numbers would be used only as an aid for the new retirement program that was being implemented at the time, but over the past 60 years or more, they have gradually become the universal identifier that their creators claimed they would not be.[3] Similarly, census records created for general statistical purposes were used during World War II to round up innocent Japanese Americans and to place them in internment camps.[4]

We are already beginning to see function creep in DNA databases. In a very short time, we have witnessed the ever-widening scope of the target groups from whom law enforcement collects DNA and rapid-fire proposals to expand genetic databases to include new categories and ever-greater numbers of persons.

In less than a decade, we have gone from collecting DNA from convicted sex offenders—on the theory that they are likely to be recidivists and that they frequently leave biological evidence—to collecting it from all violent offenders; to collecting it from all persons convicted of a crime; to collecting it from juvenile offenders in twenty-nine states; and now to proposals, and laws in Louisiana and California, to collect it from mere arrestees.[5] (Further discussion of the issue of arrestee testing appears below.)

There have even been proposals from sources such as the Michigan Commission on Genetic Privacy[6] and New York City Mayor Rudolph Giuliani[7] to permanently preserve blood samples of newborns that have been obtained to detect rare congenital diseases and to store them for law enforcement and research purposes. These and other proposals beg the question: Where will we draw the line? Must we collect DNA samples from each and every citizen, guilty or innocent? Are we willing to live in a society in which even the most personal details (as contained within our genes) are collected and made available to the public without our individual consent? Moreover, as described later in the chapter, current laws provide little protection against potential abuses of DNA data—a disturbing possibility given the tremendous power of genetic information.

One particularly insidious form of function creep is likely to be generated by those proponents of DNA data banking who continue to cling to notions of a genetic cause of crime. In 1996, the year before the legislature's enactment of the law authorizing the Massachusetts DNA database, the legislature commissioned a study to research the biological origins of crime that focused on the genetic causes. As will be explained later in this chapter, the study specifically focused on genes as the basis for criminal behavior. The report foresaw a future in which "genetics begin . . . to play a role in the effort to evaluate the causes of crime" and even cited two articles regarding the now-debunked "XYY syndrome."[8]

In addition, those who hold DNA data refuse to destroy or return that data even after the stated purpose has been satisfied. This phenomenon is not limited to criminal forensic databases. The Department of Defense (DOD), for example, has three million biological samples collected from service personnel for the stated purpose of identifying remains or body parts of a soldier killed on duty. But it keeps those samples for information for *fifty years*—long after the subjects have left the military.[9] And the DOD refuses to promulgate regulations to ensure that no third parties will have access to the records. Isn't it likely that once the genetic information is collected and banked, pressures will mount to use it for purposes, such as the identification of criminal suspects or medical research, other than the one for which it was gathered?

Current State Laws Provide Little Privacy Protection

What complicates this situation still further is that most of the state laws that govern forensic DNA testing provide little or no protection against unrelated use of DNA obtained for investigative purposes. This paucity of privacy protection raises not only public-policy issues, but also constitutional issues that have not yet been addressed by the courts.

Table 9.1
States with statutes that allow access to DNA for non–law enforcement purposes

---

Arizona (Ariz. Rev. Stat. § 31-281 (1999))
Colorado (Colo. Rev. Stat. Ann. § 17-2-201 (West (1999))
Hawaii (Haw. Rev. Stat. §§ 706-603, 846-7 (1999))
Idaho (Idaho Code §§ 19-5513, -5514 (1999))
Illinois (725 Ill. Comp. Stat. 207/45 (West 1999); 730 Ill. Comp. Stat. 5/5-4-3(5)(f) (West 1999))
Iowa (Iowa Code Ann. § 13.10 (West 1999))
Kansas (Kan. Stat. Ann. § 21-2511 (West 1998))
Louisiana (La. Rev. Stat. Ann. §§ 15:609, :611, :614(A)(1), :617, :618 (West 1999))
Maine (Me. Rev. Stat. Ann. tit. 25 § 1577 (West 1999))
Maryland (Md. Ann. Code art. 88B, § 12A) (1999)
Massachusetts (Mass. Gen. Laws Ann. ch. 22E, §§ 10, 15 (West 1999))
Michigan (Mich. Comp. Laws. Ann. § 28.176 (West 1999))
Mississippi (Miss. Code Ann. § 45-33-15(2)(a) (1999))
Missouri (Mo. Ann. Stat. §§ 650.057(3); .502 (West 1999))
Montana (Mont. Code Ann. §§ 44-6-102, -106, -107 (1999))
Nevada (Nev. Rev. Stat. § 176.0913 (1998))
New Hampshire (N.H. Rev. Stat. Ann.s §§ 632-A:21, -A:22, -A:24 (1999))
New Jersey (N.J. Stat. Ann. §§ 53:1-20:21, -20:25 (West 1999))
North Carolina (N.C. Gen. Stat. §§ 15A-226.10, -266.5 (1999))
Pennsylvania (35 Pa. Cons. Stat. Ann. §§ 7651.308, .309, .311 (West 2000))
Rhode Island (R.I. Gen. Laws §§12-1.5-10, -11, -13 (West 1999))
South Carolina (S.C. Code Ann. §§ 23-3-640, -650, -660 (Law Co-op. 1999))
Utah (Utah Code Ann. §§ 53-10-406, 63-2-202, -302 (1999))
Wyoming (Wyo. Stat. Ann. §§ 7-19-402, -404, -405 (Michie 1999))

These problems can be best understood by grouping the different statutes governing DNA sampling into broad categories with regard to the use that can be made of DNA information—both the forensic DNA profiled and the raw biological sample that contains DNA. Twenty-four states allow DNA samples that have been collected only for law enforcement identification to be used for a variety of other non–law enforcement purposes (see table 9.1). Massachusetts's law, for example, contains an open-ended authorization for any disclosure that is, or may be, required as a condition of federal funding and allows the disclosure of information, including personally identifiable information, for "advancing other humanitarian purposes." Several other states have similar language in their DNA laws, including Louisiana and North Carolina.

Table 9.2
States with statutes that allow access to DNA information to public officials other than law enforcement

---

Hawaii (Haw. Rev. Stat. §§ 706-603, 846-7 (1999))
Illinois (725 Ill. Comp. Stat. 207/45 (West 1999); 730 Ill. Comp. Stat. 5/5-4-3(5)(f) (West 1999))
Iowa (Iowa Code Ann. § 13.10 (West 1999))
Louisiana (La. Rev. Stat. Ann. §§ 15:609, :611, :614(A)(1), :617, :618 (West 1999))
Massachusetts (Mass. Gen. Laws Ann. ch. 22E, §§ 10, 15 (West 1999))
Michigan (Mich. Comp. Laws. Ann. § 28.176 (West 1999))
Mississippi (Miss. Code Ann. § 45-33-15(2)(a) (1999))
Missouri (Mo. Ann. Stat. §§ 650.057(3); .502 (West 1999))
Nevada (Nev. Rev. Stat. § 176.0913 (1998))
North Carolina (N.C. Gen. Stat. §§ 15A-226.10, -266.5 (1999))
Pennsylvania (35 Pa. Cons. Stat. Ann. §§ 7651.308, .309, .311 (West 2000))
Rhode Island (R.I. Gen. Laws §§12-1.5-10, -11, -13 (West 1999))
South Carolina (S.C. Code Ann. §§ 23-3-640, -650, -660 (Law Co-op. 1999))
Utah (Utah Code Ann. §§ 53-10-406, 63-2-202. -302 (1999))
Wyoming (Wyo. Stat. Ann. §§ 7-19-402, -404, -405 (Michie 1999))

Nevada's law simply provides "that samples be used for an analysis to determine the genetic markers of the blood." There is no definition of the term *genetic markers*, which on its face could include any information that could be derived from DNA. Furthermore, there are no restrictions on the use or availability of the DNA sample or test results.

New Jersey law states that DNA test results may be used "for purposes as required for federal funding." Since so many social programs are dependent on federal funding, this vague language creates the possibility of genetic screening and possible discrimination in many aspects of modern life, not just the criminal justice context.

Mississippi has no statutory restrictions on the use of forensic DNA and leaves it to the Mississippi Crime Laboratory (MCL) to determine any restrictions. Utah's DNA disclosure requirements provide only minimal protection regarding access, use, and dissemination. For example, Utah's laws allow insurance companies, psychologists, and other third parties to access state-collected DNA information. Fifteen states allow access to public officials other than law enforcement (see table 9.2).

All but two states permit access to DNA records for vaguely defined law enforcement purposes that go well beyond limited use for the purposes of identification, thus implicitly allowing genetic tests for physical and mental traits or for predisposition to disease or "criminality" (see table 9.3). North Dakota's statute, for example, requires DNA records, including biological samples, to be made available to "any public official who requires that information in connection with discharge of the official's official duties." Similarly loose standards can be found in many DNA database laws in the other forty-seven states.

In addition, seventeen states have no rules that require the expungement of DNA records upon reversals of convictions. These states include Illinois, Iowa, Kansas, Nevada, Mississippi, and South Dakota (see table 9.4).

Finally, not one state statute requires that biological samples collected for identification purposes be destroyed after identification testing is completed.[10]

Table 9.3
States with statutes that allow law enforcement to use DNA evidence for purposes other than identification

Alabama (Ala. Code §§ 36-18-26-29, -31 (1998))
Alaska (Alaska Stat. § 44.41.035 (Michie 1999))
Arizona (Ariz. Rev. Stat. § 31-281 (1999))
Arkansas (Ark. Code Ann. §§ 12-12-1105, -1112 (Michie 1999))
California (Cal. Code. Penal § 299 (Deering 1999))
Colorado (Colo. Rev. Stat. Ann. § 17-2-201 (West (1999))
Connecticut (Conn. Gen. Stat. Ann. §§ 54-102j, -102k, -102l (West 1999))
Delaware (Del. Code Ann. tit. 29, § 4713 (1999))
Florida (Fla. Stat. Ann. § 943.325 (West 1999))
Georgia (Ga. Code Ann. §§24-4-60, -63, -65 (1999))
Hawaii (Haw. Rev. Stat. §§ 706-603, 846-7 (1999))
Idaho (Idaho Code §§ 19-5513, -5514 (1999))
Illinois (725 Ill. Comp. Stat. 207/45 (West 1999); 730 Ill. Comp. Stat. 5/5-4-3(5)(f) (West 1999))
Indiana (Ind. Code Ann. §§ 10-1-9-8, -17, -18, -20 (West 1999))
Iowa (Iowa Code Ann. § 13.10 (West 1999))
Kansas (Kan. Stat. Ann. § 21-2511 (West 1998))
Kentucky (Ky. Rev. Stat. Ann. § 17.175 (Banks-Baldwin 1998))
Louisiana (La. Rev. Stat. Ann. §§ 15:609, :611, :614(A)(1), :617, :618 (West 1999))
Maryland (Md. Ann. Code art. 88B, § 12(A) (1999))
Massachusetts (Mass. Gen. Laws Ann. ch. 22E, §§ 10, 15 (West 1999))

Table 9.3
(continued)

Michigan (Mich. Comp. Laws. Ann. § 28.176 (West 1999))

Minnesota (Minn. Stat. Ann. §§ 299c. 155, 609A.03(7) (West 1999))

Mississippi (Miss. Code Ann. § 45-33-15(2)(a) (1999))

Missouri (Mo. Ann. Stat. §§ 650.057(3), .502 (West 1999))

Montana (Mont. Code Ann. §§ 44-6-102, -106, -107 (1999))

Nebraska (Neb. Rev. Stat. §§ 29-4108, -4109 (1999))

Nevada (Nev. Rev. Stat. § 176.0913 (1998))

New Hampshire (N.H. Rev. Stat. Ann. §§ 632-A:21, -A:22, -A:24 (1999))

New Jersey (N.J. Stat. Ann. §§ 53:1-20:21, -20:25 (West 1999))

New Mexico (N.M. Stat. Ann. §§ 29-16-8, -10 (Michie 1999)))

New York (N.Y. Exec. Law § 995-c (McKinney 1999))

North Carolina (N.C. Gen. Stat. §§ 15A-226.10, -266.5 (1999))

North Dakota (N.D. Cent. Code §§ 31-13-05, -06, -07 (1999))

Oklahoma (Okla. State. Ann. tit. 74, §§ 150.27a (A), (C), (D) (West 1999))

Oregon (Or. Rev. Stat. §§ 181.010, .085 (1998))

Pennsylvania (35 Pa. Cons. Stat. Ann. §§ 7651.308, .309, .311 (West 2000))

Rhode Island (R.I. Gen. Laws §§12-1.5-10, -11, -13 (West 1999))

South Carolina (S.C. Code Ann. §§ 23-3-640, -650, -660 (Law Co-op. 1999))

South Dakota (S.D. Codified Laws §§ 23-5-7, -17 (Michie 1999))

Tennessee (Tenn. Code Ann. § 38-6-113 (1999))

Texas (Tex. Gov't Code Ann. §§ 411.143, .147, .151 (West 1999))

Utah (Utah Code Ann. §§ 53-10-406, 63-2-202, -302 (1999))

Vermont (Vt. Stat. Ann. tit. 20, §§ 1937, 1940, 1941 (West 1999))

Virginia (Va. Code Ann. §§ 19.2-310.5, -310.7 (Michie 1999))

Washington (Wash. Rev. Code Ann. § 43.43.756 (West 1999))

West Virginia (W.Va. Code §§ 15-2B-10, -11 (1999))

Wisconsin (Wis. Stat. Ann. § 165.77 (West 1999))

Wyoming (Wyo. Stat. Ann. §§ 7-19-402, -404, -405 (Michie 1999))

Table 9.4
States that do not require expungement of DNA records upon reversal of conviction

---

Arizona (Ariz. Rev. Stat. § 31-281 (1999))

Colorado (Colo. Rev. Stat. Ann. § 17-2-201 (West (1999))

Florida (Fla. Stat. Ann. § 943.325 (West 1999))

Hawaii (Haw. Rev. Stat. §§ 706-603, 846-7 (1999))

Illinois (725 Ill. Comp. Stat. 207/45 (West 1999); 730 Ill. Comp. Stat. 5/5-4-3(5)(f) (West 1999))

Iowa (Iowa Code Ann. § 13.10 (West 1999))

Kansas (Kan. Stat. Ann. § 21-2511 (West 1998))

Minnesota (Minn. Stat. Ann. § 299c.155 (West 1999); Minn. Stat. Ann.§s 609A.03(7) (West 1999))

Mississippi (Miss. Code Ann. § 45-33-15(2)(a) (1999))

Missouri (Mo. Ann. Stat. §§ 650.057(3), .502 (West 1999))

Nevada (Nev. Rev. Stat. § 176.0913 (1998))

Ohio (Ohio Rev. Code Ann. § 109.573 (Banks-Baldwin 1999))

Oklahoma (Okla. State. Ann. tit. 74, §§ 150.27a (A), (C), (D) (West 1999))

South Dakota (S.D. Codified Laws §§ 23-5-7, -17 (Michie 1999))

Tennessee (Tenn. Code Ann. § 38-6-113 (1999))

Washington (Wash. Rev. Code Ann. § 43.43.756 (West 1999))

Wyoming (Wyo. Stat. Ann. §§ 7-19-402, -404, -405 (Michie 1999))

Government Disclosure of Nonprofile Information Raises Constitutional Concerns

These statutes raise privacy issues of constitutional dimensions. The Supreme Court has noted in several cases "the threat to privacy implicit in the accumulation of vast amounts of personal information in computerized data banks or other massive government files."[11] Specifically, in *Whalen v. Roe*, the High Court recognized that "[t]he right to collect and use such data for public purposes is typically accompanied by a concomitant statutory or regulatory duty to avoid unwarranted disclosures."[12] In its opinion, the Court noted that this duty may have particularly strong constitutional repercussions depending on the circumstances.[13] Furthermore, under this constitutionally based right to data privacy, the government must implement procedures that exhibit "a proper concern with, and protection of, the individual's interest in privacy."[14] Given the fact that DNA is so sensitive and provides such a wealth of personalized information, the collection of DNA brings a concomitant constitutional government duty to protect the privacy of the data compiled through DNA analysis. DNA data cannot and should not be disclosed beyond the limited purpose of identification, and tough privacy standards must be implemented to conform to the Constitution's requirements.

Indeed, the Court has held "as a categorical matter that a third party's request for law enforcement records or information about a private citizen can reasonably be expected to invade that citizen's privacy, and that when the request seeks no 'official information' about a Government agency, but merely records that the Government happens to be storing, the invasion of privacy is 'unwarranted.' "[15] The High Court has struck down other database schemes for a variety of reasons, particularly when such schemes failed to provide sufficient privacy protections or violated other fundamental rights guaranteed under the Constitution.[16]

Statutes that permit uses of compelled DNA beyond the original forensic identification purpose may very well run afoul of the Constitution. Since it is not practical to expect reform in the fifty states, Congress should step in and should prohibit access to CODIS and deny federal funding for DNA testing to those states that permit access to DNA for any purpose other than law enforcement identification.

Eugenics and Discrimination

It is worth bearing in mind, too, that there is a long, unfortunate history of despicable behavior by governments toward people whose genetic composition has been considered "abnormal" under the prevailing societal standards of the day. In recounting that history and documenting its privacy concerns, a report of the National Research Council's Panel on DNA Technology in Forensic Science said:

These privacy concerns are far from abstract. The eugenics movement in this country, which resulted in thousands of involuntary sterilizations, the suggested screening of violent men for extra Y chromosomes, the sickle cell screening tests employed to prohibit marriages, and the current privacy concerns over HIV screening, underlie the Panel's following recommendation: Use of a data bank for other than law enforcement suspect identification purposes should be expressly prohibited and subject the abuse to criminal penalties.[17]

The advent of DNA data banking carries another disturbing prospect: the resurgence of social Darwinism and eugenics. As one author pointed out:

Despite the great advances in recent years, controversy over applications of genetic screening is not new. A century ago, indeed well into the mid-twentieth century, eugenics was a major public policy issue, with people being sterilized, imprisoned, deported, or killed because they carried traits that a particular society wanted to minimize. By today's standards the screening tests were crude. They were often applied with an inadequate scientific basis and a lack of regard for the individuals. One may recognize the same criticisms aimed at genetic screening for susceptibility biomarkers today.[18]

For example, for many years it was commonplace to forcibly sterilize "mental defectives" who were held in state institutions.[19] Indeed, this tactic was so popular that thirty-five states had laws on the subject, and an estimated sixty to one hundred thousand people were subjected to this procedure.[20] In Indiana, a special Committee on Mental Defectives was created to stockpile medical information from health care workers and government officials, then identify "feebleminded" people and other potential targets for surgery. One can only hope that those individuals who were sterilized because of the Supreme Court's affirmation of these procedures in *Buck v. Bell* would not be subjected to the same treatment today.[21]

Genetic discrimination by the government is not merely an artifact of the distant past. During the 1970s, the Air Force refused to allow healthy individuals who carried one copy of the sickle cell gene to engage in flight training, even though two copies of the gene are needed for symptoms of sickle cell disease to develop. This restriction was based upon the then untested (and now known to be incorrect) belief that people with a single such gene could display symptoms of sickle cell disease under low-oxygen conditions, even though they would not actually have sickle cell disease.[22]

Because the vast majority of sickle cell carriers are individuals of African descent, this Air Force policy had the insidious effect of reducing the number of African Americans who became pilots. The policy was ultimately discontinued, but only after an Air Force trainee sued to have it changed in 1979.[23]

Genetic discrimination by private industry is becoming increasingly commonplace as well. The Council for Responsible Genetics, a nonprofit advocacy group based in Cambridge, Massachusetts, has documented hundreds of cases in which healthy people have been denied insurance or a job based on genetic "predictions."[24] As reported in *Scientific American*, a 1999 survey conducted by the American Management Association found that 30 percent of large and midsized companies collected some form of genetic information about their workers.[25] The *Scientific American* article also noted that "[a]s the cost of DNA testing goes down, the number of businesses testing their workers is expected to skyrocket."[26]

In February 2001, the Equal Employment Opportunity Commission (EEOC) sued Burlington Northern Santa Fe Railroad, claiming that the transportation giant had conducted genetic tests related to carpal tunnel syndrome among its workers.[27] Burlington Northern had previously required such genetic-factors tests, along with physical examinations, to evaluate employee injury claims.[28] Eventually, the company settled the EEOC action (as well as a similar union lawsuit), halted the testing program, and agreed to destroy the DNA samples it had collected and all records pertaining to them.[29]

Even as the predictive validity of genetic information (such as the single sickle cell gene) is being challenged and reevaluated, such information is being used to make important life decisions about such matters as employment and essential insurance and is still used to discriminate against the "asymptomatically ill": individuals who are not sick, but whose genetic makeup leads insurers or employers to fear that they may develop certain illnesses in the future (and that the insurer or employer might have to bear the costs of those illnesses).[30]

The widespread screening and warehousing of genetic information raises the disturbing probability that history will repeat itself. As the Commission on Behavioral and Social Sciences and Education of the National Research Council has warned in a similar context:

The potential for social damage . . . is as great today as it was in the 1920s, because the United States remains a country of many identifiable ethnic and racial subpopulations, some of which are relatively disadvantaged economically and educationally. . . . [B]lacks, Hispanics, and Native Americans, all groups of people . . . who are economically and socially disadvantaged, are vulnerable to being stereotyped as of inferior intelligence.[31]

Meanwhile, genes have been linked to many specific disorders and diseases, including common forms of cancer and heart disease.[32] Some scientists are now convinced that every disease has a genetic component.[33] A number of researchers also have suggested more controversial genetic links to homosexuality, aggression and criminality, obesity, mental illness, and alcoholism.[34] Even the suspicion of such controversial links could cause grave injury to a person's reputation.[35]

Genetics and Crime

An obvious use for all of the genetic information being stored by the criminal justice system is a search for genetic links to crime. Regardless of how quixotic such a search may seem, it remains tantalizing to the very people, particularly legislators, who will decide whether government should pursue it.

One early suspect in the search for a "crime gene" was the so-called XYY syndrome, which refers to a chromosomal abnormality in some men who have not one, but two, Y chromosomes.[36] Some early studies in the field of human genetics claimed that XYY men were more violent and aggressive and more likely to commit crimes than other men. However, the idea that XYY syndrome is related to crime or antisocial personality disorder has now been discredited.[37] Instead, the majority of modern studies have concluded that the exact effect of the XYY chromosomal pattern is difficult to define,[38] for "although increased height, behavior difficulties, and infertility are common, the extra Y is sometimes found in otherwise normal men."[39]

Even if it were found that XYY men were jailed more frequently than the majority XY male population, linking XYY status to criminal behavior would still be a dangerous leap. For example, one study of XYY men concluded that XYY men actually commit fewer crimes than XY men, but that they may be incarcerated at a higher rate than XY men because of the possible negative impact XYY syndrome has on intelligence.[40]

In 1996, the year before Massachusetts enacted a law authorizing its own DNA database, the state's legislature commissioned a study to research the biological origins of crime. The authorizing legislation for that study described it as follows:

[T]he department of correction, in conjunction with the department of public health and the department of education, shall conduct a study into the biological cause of crime based on the premise that scientists have been studying biological risk factors which they believe predispose individuals to criminal behavior; provided further, that said study should incorporate these findings to work toward a more effective approach toward criminology.[41]

The research that the legislature commissioned resulted in a report, entitled, *Questions Concerning Biological Risk Factors for Criminal Behavior*, issued June 30, 1996.[42] That report specifically points out its focus on genes as the basis for criminal behavior, stating that it "concentrates on research that seeks to make a direct link between genetics or biology and crime."

The study foresaw a future in which "genetics begins to play a role in the effort to evaluate the causes of crime" and even cited two articles regarding the debunked XYY syndrome. The report also acknowledged several concerns regarding genetic privacy:

- Efforts to find a biological cause for crime or violence has [sic] proved controversial.

- Sensitivity about the issue of eugenics has heightened concerns about genetic research of this topic.

- [T]here has been substantial discussion among researchers in this field about the need for careful and thoughtful analysis of issues invoking consideration of minority community issues.

- The ethical implications of genetics research in this area must be carefully weighed as a part of any such investigation.[43]

Despite these warnings, the law the Massachusetts legislature passed allows virtually unlimited use of DNA.[44]

The existence of large pools of DNA from persons in the criminal justice system, the broad leeway to use the DNA that exists in states like Massachusetts, and the continuing belief that there is a genetic "cause" of crime creates the very real potential for abuse.

Postconviction Testing: The Current Reality

Postconviction testing for a variety of crimes has become a fait accompli in the United States. All fifty states now authorize such testing—although the crimes they cover vary widely—and all states are moving to participate in CODIS. Although the courts have generally held that taking a DNA sample constitutes a search, the authorizing statutes have been challenged and upheld, primarily on the grounds that convicted persons have a lessened expectation of privacy.[45]

The Future

Although the legal issues surrounding postconviction testing have largely been resolved, there are a variety of other significant legal and public-policy issues that remain to be settled.

Arrestee Testing

There is a growing movement to expand DNA testing to include people who have merely been arrested for a crime. Louisiana has already authorized, but apparently not yet implemented, DNA testing for persons who have been arrested for certain crimes but have not yet had their day in court.[46] Similarly, California authorizes DNA testing of "suspects" and allows long-term retention of the genetic data that result from the testing, while Virginia requires DNA samples to be collected from anyone arrested for a violent felony.[47] Many government officials from around the country are calling for similar measures.[48]

While it is one thing to test convicted criminals, it is a far different enterprise to test people who have not even been convicted of a crime. Even if one accepts the court rulings that DNA data banking for convicted felons is permissible, either because a special need is present where persons have been convicted of crimes with high recidivism rates and the presence of biological evidence, like sexual assaults, or because convicted felons have a diminished expectation of privacy, neither of those circumstances applies to persons who have simply been arrested. Forensic databases should not house the genetic profiles of persons who have never been convicted of a crime. To allow them to do so is to equate arrest with guilt and to empower police officers, rather than judges and juries, to force persons to provide the state with evidence that harbors many of their most intimate secrets and those of their blood relatives.

The Supreme Court has held that for Fourth Amendment purposes, tests that penetrate beneath the skin, whether they are blood tests, breathalyzers or otherwise, are searches.[49] Indeed, because DNA is so sensitive and can provide so much information about the individual from whom it is taken, its collection should be compared to the drawing of blood samples (even when other methods of collection besides a blood sample are used), which the Supreme Court has held generally requires a warrant.[50] The Court has noted that "[s]earch warrants are ordinarily required for searches of dwellings, and, absent an emergency, no less could be required where intrusions into the human body are concerned."[51]

It is true that courts have allowed certain types of bodily inspections of arrestees, such as the taking of fingerprints, but DNA is very different.[52] DNA samples contain far more information than fingerprints; whereas fingerprints are useful only as a form of identification, DNA is a powerful biological catalog of information. The legal standards for taking DNA evidence must therefore be distinguished from the standards that govern the taking of fingerprints. The real (if not exact) comparison is to the drawing of blood samples, which the Supreme Court has held generally requires a warrant when arrestees are involved.[53]

The courts have generally permitted DNA testing of convicts on the basis of their "diminished expectations" of privacy. To be specific, the rights of these individuals are "diminished" to the extent that their rights are "fundamentally inconsistent" with the "needs and exigencies" of "the regime to which they have been lawfully committed."[54] However, as a federal appeals court ruled in a recent case, "while parolees enjoy lesser Fourth Amendment rights than other citizens, their rights are not *extinguished*. Even parolees maintain a reasonable expectation of privacy in their own bodies."[55] That same appeals panel also held that the "special needs" exception to the Fourth Amendment did not apply to DNA testing of parolees and that individualized suspicion was required before the government could perform such testing, citing several U.S. Supreme Court decisions as support for limiting the exception to "programs or activities 'not designed to serve the ordinary needs of law enforcement.'"[56]

Even if one accepts this questionable notion that the "special needs" exception of the Fourth Amendment applies to convicted criminals, that argument does not apply to arrestees. While DNA evidence can be used to identify incarcerated individuals, there are far less intrusive ways to identify people in custody. It cannot be argued that forcing arrestees to provide blood serves any legitimate security purpose, even if they are in pretrial detention. Nor, by definition, can DNA be used to ensure compliance with any specified term of postconviction supervised release. Put simply, these persons have not been convicted of any crime and may never be.

Many arrests obviously do not result in a conviction. For example, a national survey of the adjudication outcomes for felony defendants in the seventy-five largest counties in the country in 1990 revealed that in felony assault cases, half the charges were dismissed outright, and in 14 percent of cases, the charges were reduced to a misdemeanor.[57]

Additionally, there is a disturbing element of racial disparity in arrests that runs throughout our criminal justice system that will only be compounded by the creation of databases of persons arrested but not convicted of crimes. A study released by the California State Assembly's Commission on the Status of African American Males in the early 1990s revealed that 64 percent of the drug arrests of whites and 81 percent of those of Latinos were not sustainable, and that an astonishing 92 percent of the black men arrested by police on drug charges were subsequently released for lack of evidence or inadmissible evidence.[58]

Racial profiling and stereotyping is a reality of our criminal justice system. For example, New Jersey has now conceded that its state police engaged in racial profiling over a period of at least ten years in incidents that included the recent shooting of four unarmed black teenagers and were documented by nearly one hundred thousand pages of state police memoranda, reports, and other papers.[59] The problem was determined to be so serious that the state entered into a consent decree with the Department of Justice that, among other things, barred police officers from relying "to any degree on the race or national or ethnic origin of motorists in selecting vehicles for traffic stops and in deciding upon the scope and substance of post-stop actions, except where state troopers are on the look-out for a specific suspect who has been identified in part by his or her race or national or ethnic origin."[60] In a telling moment, the head of the New Jersey state police was fired for remarks suggesting that minorities could be targeted because they were more likely to use drugs—an assertion that is not factually correct.[61] Minorities are more likely to be arrested, but no more likely than whites to use drugs.[62]

Similar findings have been made in other jurisdictions. A study of police stops on a strip of interstate in Maryland over several months in 1995 found that 73 percent of the cars stopped and searched were driven by African Americans, even though they comprised only 14 percent of the people driving along the interstate. Although the arrest rates were about the same for whites and persons of color (approximately 28 percent), the disproportionate number of stops of minorities resulted in a disproportionate number of persons of color being arrested.[63]

These concerns have taken on an added dimension since September 11, 2001, as many people of Arabic, Middle Eastern, or South Asian descent have been detained, arrested, or harassed by government authorities. In numerous incidences, such individuals have been handcuffed, detained, or searched essentially because of their background, or as law enforcement officers explained in one of these confrontations, because the officers simply didn't like the way the person looked.[64] Meanwhile, the FBI has seen fit to begin counting mosques and Islamic followers in neighborhoods, the results of which allegedly may be used to set numeric investigation and wiretap goals.[65] These developments are further evidence that racism continues to plague our criminal justice system—a problem that will be exacerbated by DNA testing of arrestees.

Then there is the most practical of considerations—indeed, the only consideration that gives reason to hope that we will not move further down the path of DNA surveillance by instituting arrestee testing. There were about 13.7 million arrests made in the United States in 2001.[66] From a law enforcement perspective, does it really make sense to invest dollars in collecting and processing samples for persons who have never been convicted of a crime, let alone a crime of the sort in which DNA evidence is most likely to be probative? Wouldn't it make more sense to put scarce resources into processing the samples that law enforcement agencies already have and will generate in the future under existing programs? Indeed, these considerations led the National Commission on the Future of DNA Evidence to recommend that the Department of Justice hold off on collecting DNA samples from arrestees.[67]

Usual-Suspect Databases

The number of "suspect databases," sometimes called "suspect elimination databases," seems to be growing. Indeed, this disturbing phenomenon was the subject of a 2000 hearing by the National Commission on the Future of DNA Evidence. Testimony during the hearing suggested that police officers in a number of cities were doing DNA collection sweeps.[68] This practice results in usual-suspect databases created without any probable cause, without any privacy protections for the subjects, and without any oversight.[69]

The problems with these types of database and the means used to compile them were illustrated in a 1994 Ann Arbor, Michigan case in which as part of an investigation of sexual assaults, DNA samples were taken from 160 men merely because they were black. Even after the samples were tested, police were still not able to identify a suspect, despite this widespread collection of genetic information; a suspect was eventually arrested later, as he tried to commit another felony. However, after the arrest was made, one of the innocent men who had provided a DNA sample, Blair Shelton, asked to have it returned. When police officials refused to release the sample, Shelton sued the state and won, but only after two years of protracted court battles.[70]

Nor are these problems confined to Michigan. A recent article in the *Los Angeles Times* documented several cases in which law enforcement officials have conducted wide-scale collections of DNA data. For example, in one case, law enforcement agents in Costa Mesa, California, took samples from 188 people for four years without getting a match. In that particular investigation, police officers dropped any pretense of individualized suspicion and took samples from random people on the street in the neighborhood where the crime took place. Police officials launched a similar sweep in another case that netted 113 samples and said they planned to collect such information on a regular basis.[71] The article also notes that

some police departments . . . are now using DNA as the starting point, testing hundreds of people in search of a break. Over the last few years, detectives in Los Angeles, Huntington Beach, Miami, Louisiana, and elsewhere have experimented with such DNA dragnets in cases ranging from the hunt for a serial rapist in New York's Bronx to the unsolved 1985 murder of a Los Angeles County sheriff's deputy. The operations are expensive and have so far solved few crimes.[72]

The number of people tested in these sweeps can be surprisingly high; in one Miami case, law enforcement officials took samples from more than 2,300 individuals; another 600 men were tested as part of an unrelated investigation in Louisiana.[73]

Police officials usually describe these searches as "consensual" and "voluntary." Frequently persons being searched are presented with a "consent form." The consent given on such forms may allow DNA sampling for use only in connection with the investigation of a particular crime, or it may allow for more open-ended use. The consent forms generally do not promise to destroy the sample or test result after the "suspect" has been eliminated.

In most cases, it is illusory to call these searches "voluntary." The circumstances are inherently coercive. An innocent person is presented with a choice by an armed police officer: submit to a DNA search or be subject to further investigation that may include a trip to the station house. The circumstances are especially coercive to young men of color, who are the frequent target of these DNA dragnets. These men have learned from hard experience that actual innocence does not guarantee that one will not be subject to harassment if one does not "cooperate" with police.

The absence of real consent under such circumstances makes these searches constitutionally suspect. Certainly the retention of samples and test results raises grave constitutional questions.

To the extent that these essentially random searches continue—I do not believe that they should—they should be conducted only pursuant to a consent form that limits the use of the samples obtained to the particular crime being investigated and guarantees destruction of the samples and the test results for those who are eliminated as a suspect in the matter under investigation.

Destruction of DNA Samples

State and federal laws authorizing DNA testing make no provisions for destroying biological samples once they have served their purpose (producing a DNA identification code). Whereas the proponents of forensic DNA testing would like us to believe that samples taken for DNA testing will never be used for anything besides catching criminals, the sad truth is that if those samples are retained, at some point, they will be used improperly.

Compounding this problem is the paucity of laws—none, certainly, at the federal level—that comprehensively prohibit genetic discrimination by employers, insurers, or medical care providers. More and more DNA is being collected, and with the advances in genetic research that make that DNA more and more valuable, instances of discrimination and misuse will increase as well.

Although placing statutory restrictions on forensic DNA samples would be a good start, statutes can be repealed or amended. A more permanent way to protect privacy is to destroy the samples themselves.

The retention of biological samples gathered in connection with forensic DNA testing can no longer be justified now that the scientific community has settled on a uniform set of DNA locations to be tested and a common testing methodology. This scientific consensus has been incorporated into requirements for CODIS, and there is simply no longer a legitimate rationale for retaining the biological samples after they have been tested and the results have been entered into CODIS.[74]

Conclusion

Forensic DNA databases contain private and highly sensitive information belonging to potentially millions of suspects, inmates, parolees, and probationers. As currently operated, these databases pose a grave threat to the federal and state constitutional rights of all those who are compelled to provide DNA specimens. This threat is not grounded in a hypothetical; this fear is a rational one, based on a logical analysis of the form and substance of the DNA databases in existence.

At a bare minimum, DNA databases should be subject to the following restrictions, which should be included in federal laws:

1. The biological samples (blood, saliva, etc.) upon which DNA identification testing is performed should be destroyed within a reasonable period after testing is completed and pending criminal matters are resolved.

2. The genetic profiles entered into criminal databases should be limited to those from persons convicted of serious violent felonies, where biological evidence is relevant.

3. There should be a ban on nonconsensual genetic testing of accused persons who have not been tried and convicted, except where a court has granted an order requiring such testing.

4. States should make DNA testing available to criminal defendants who claim they are innocent and remove postconviction bars to consideration of evidence obtained through such testing.

5. DNA samples should not be taken from arrestees.

6. If a person consents to DNA testing, that consent must be voluntary, informed, and in writing. Such consent should explicitly provide that the sample and test results will be destroyed if the subject ceases to be a suspect in the investigation of the specific crime for which the sample was collected.

7. All existing suspect databases and samples involving persons who have been eliminated from suspicion should be destroyed.

Notes

1. See Committee on DNA Technology in Forensic Science, *DNA Technology in Forensic Science* (Washington, D.C.: National Academies Press, 1992), which notes that "DNA typing raises considerably greater issues of privacy than does ordinary fingerprinting" (113).

2. See, e.g., Maggie Fox, "Junk DNA May Not Be Such Junk, Genomic Studies Find," Reuters, February 12, 2001.

3. See, e.g., 42 U.S.C. § 405 (c)(2)(C)(i),(vi) (2000) (permitting welfare offices and motor vehicle service administrations to utilize social security numbers); 26 U.S.C. § 6109 (d) (allowing social security numbers to be used for taxpayer identification purposes).

4. Commission on Wartime Relocation and Internment of Civilians, *Personal Justice Denied* (Washington, D.C.: U.S. Government Printing Office, 1982), 104–105.

5. See, e.g., La. Rev. Stat. Ann. § 15:609 (2000); Ca. Penal Code § 297(b)(West 2000); Va. Code Ann. § 19.2–310.2:1 (2004).

6. Michigan Commission on Genetic Privacy and Progress, *Final Report and Recommendations"* (1999), available at www.michigan.gov/documents/GeneticsReport_11649_7.pdf. See also Dee-Ann Durbin, "Genetic Privacy Commission Issues State Report," Associated Press, February 6, 1999.

7. Declan McCullagh, "What to Do with DNA Data?" *Wired News*, February 6, 1999, available at www.wired.com.

8. Massachusetts Department of Correction and Massachusetts Department of Public Health, *Questions Concerning Biological Risk Factors for Criminal Behavior* (Massachusetts Department of Correction, Milford, MA, and Massachusetts Department of Public Health, Boston, MA, 1996).

9. See U.S. Coast Guard, "DNA Samples Information Sheet" (1999), available at www.uscg.mil/hq/mcpocg/1medical/rcdna01.htm; Assistant Secretary of Defense (Health Affairs), "Policy Refinements for the Armed Forces Repository of Specimen Samples for the Identification of Remains" (memorandum, Department of Defense, 1996); Washington, D.C., *Mayfield v. Dalton*, 901 F. Supp. 300 (D. Hawaii 1995), *vacated* 109 F. 3d 1423 (9th Cir. 1997).

10. Some states do *allow* (but do not *require*) the eventual destruction or return of the samples upon reversals of convictions. See, e.g., R.I. Gen Laws §§ 12-1.5–13; N.Y. Exec. Code § 995-c(9).

11. *Whalen v. Roe*, 429 U.S. 589, 605 (1977).

12. Ibid.

13. Ibid.

14. Ibid.

15. *U.S. Department of Justice v. Reporters Committee*, 489 U.S. 749, 780 (1989).

16. See *Thornburgh v. American College of Obstetricians and Gynecologists*, 476 U.S. 747 (1986); *United States Department of Defense v. FLRA*, 510 U.S. 487 (1994).

17. National Research Council, *DNA Technology in Forensic Science* (Washington, D.C.: National Academy Press, 1992).

18. Michael Gochfeld, "Susceptibility Biomarkers in the Workplace: Historical Perspective," in *Biomarkers: Medical and Workplace Applications*, ed. Mortimer L. Mendelsohn, Lawrence C. Mohr, and John P. Peeters (Washington, D.C.: Joseph Henry Press, 1998), 5–6.

19. See *Buck v. Bell*, 274 U.S. 200, 207 (1927) (Holmes, J.) (affirming a Virginia law allowing forced sterilizations of mentally retarded persons who were in state institutions and

stating, "It is better for all the world, if instead of waiting to execute degenerate offspring for crime . . . society can prevent those who are manifestly unfit from continuing their kind. . . . Three generations of imbeciles are enough").

20. "Breeding Better Citizens," *20/20* (ABC television broadcast, March 22, 2000).

21. Stephen Jay Gould, *The Mismeasure of Man* (New York: Norton, 1981), 336. See also *Skinner v. Oklahoma*, 316 U.S. 535, 541 (1942) (discussing the harm that can come from "evil or reckless hands" in regard to "races or types which are inimical to the dominant group").

22. See Council for Responsible Genetics, "Genetic Privacy: A Discussion Paper on DNA Databanking," (Cambridge, Mass., 1995). See also Donald E. Shapiro and Michelle L. Weinberg, "DNA Data Banking: The Dangerous Erosion of Privacy," *Cleveland State Law Review* 38 (1990): 455.

23. See Council for Responsible Genetics, "Genetic Privacy," 6 n.4. See also Shapiro and Weinberg, "DNA Data Banking," 480 n.132.

24. Council for Responsible Genetics, "Genetic Discrimination" (Cambridge, Mass., 2001).

25. Diane Martindale, "Pink Slip in Your Genes: Evidence Builds That Employers Hire and Fire Based on Genetic Tests; Meanwhile Protective Legislation Languishes," *Scientific American* (January 2001): 19–20.

26. Ibid.

27. U.S. Equal Employment Opportunity Commission, "E.E.O.C. Petitions Court to Ban Genetic Testing of Railroad Workers in First E.E.O.C. Case Challenging Genetic Testing under Americans with Disabilities Act" (press release, February 9, 2001); see also Kristen Philipkoski, "The Debate over Tell-Tale Genes," *Wired News*, February 14, 2001.

28. Burlington Northern Santa Fe Railway Company, "B.N.S.F. Ends DNA Testing for Carpal Tunnel Syndrome" (press release, February 12, 2001).

29. Ibid. See also Rip Watson, "Burlington Northern Settles Suit over Genetic Tests," *Bloomberg News*, April 11, 2001.

30. Paul R. Billings et al., "Discrimination as a Consequence of Genetic Testing," *American Journal of Human Genetics* 50 (1992): 476; Joseph S. Alper et al., "Genetic Discrimination and Screening for Hemochromatosis," *Journal of Public Health Policy* 15, no. 3 (1994): 345, 349–350 (discussing examples of denials of employment and insurance to asymptomatic carriers of hemochromatosis, a relatively common but significant genetic disorder that is symptomless and amenable to treatment at low cost).

31. John A. Hartigan and Alexandra K. Wigdor, eds., *Fairness in Employment Testing: Validity Generalization, Minority Issues, and the General Aptitude Test Battery* (Washington, D.C.: National Academies Press, 1989), 27.

32. See, e.g., Melissa Schorr, "DNA Detector? A New Method of Detecting Colon Cancer Inspects Stool Samples for DNA Mutations," ABCNews.com, October 24 2001, available at www.canoer.umn.edu/page/newmeccnews2.html; see also Melissa Schorr, "Opening a Path to Gene Therapy," *WIRED News*, Nov. 15, 2000, available at www.wired.com/news/technology/0,1282,40186,00.html.

33. David Whitehouse, "Life's 'First Chapter' Ready for Publication," BBC News, December 1, 1999, available at news.bbc.co.uk/hi/english/sci/tech/newsid_533000/533614.stm; see also Randolph M. Neese and George C. Williams, "Evolution and the Origins of Disease," *Scientific American*, November 1998.

34. Natalie Angier, "Matter over Mind? The Curse of Living within One's Genes," *New York Times*, December 18, 1994, D1.

35. See Billings et al., "Discrimination as a Consequence of Genetic Testing," 481; see also Kathy L. Hudson et al., "Genetic Discrimination and Health Insurance: An Urgent Need for Reform," *Science* 270 (1995); Lawrence O. Gostin, "Health Information Privacy," *Cornell Law Review* 80 (1995): 451, 490 (citing impact of disclosure of information, including economic, social, and psychological harms).

36. A human chromosome is a structure found in the nucleus of each cell that contains a linear thread of DNA and transmits genetic information. W. A. Newman Dorland, ed., *Dorland's Illustrated Medical Dictionary*, 26th ed. (Philadelphia: Saunders, 1994), 267. About "1 in 350 newborn males has the complement 47,XXY or 47,XYY." Jean D. Wilson et al., eds., *Harrison's Principles of Internal Medicine*, 12th ed., vol. 2 (New York: McGraw-Hill, 1991), 50.

37. Wilson et al., *Harrison's Principles of Internal Medicine*, 12th ed., vol. 2, 2137.

38. Ibid., 53.

39. M. Linden, B. Bender, and A. Robinson, "Sex Chromosome Tetrasomy and Pentasomy," *Pediatrics* 96, no. 4 (1995): 672 ("Within each polysomy X and/or Y group, substantial variability exists, such that a generalized prognosis is not possible").

40. D. R. Owen, "The 47,XYY Male: A Review," *Psychological Bulletin* 78 (1972): 209–233.

41. 1996 Mass. Acts ch. 12, § 2 at 13.

42. Massachusetts Department of Correction and Massachusetts Department of Public Health, *Questions Concerning Biological Risk Factors for Criminal Behavior*.

43. Ibid. (bullets added).

44. See generally Mass. Gen. L. ch. 22E, § 1–15; 515.

45. See, e.g., *Boling v. Romer*, 101 F. 3d 1336 (10th Cir. 1996); *Rise v. State of Oregon*, 59 F.3d 1556 (9th Cir. 1995); *Jones v. Murray*, 962 F.2d 302 (4th Cir. 1992).

46. La. Rev. Stat. Ann. § 15:609.

47. Ca. Penal Code § 297(2)–(3); Va. Code Ann. § 19.2-310.2:1.

48. See, e.g., Rudolph W. Giuliani, mayor, New York City, 1999 State of the City Address (January 14, 1999); Ayana Mathis, "Stop, Drop, and Swab: New York Police Ponder Portable DNA Labs," *Village Voice*, May 31–June 6, 2000.

49. See, e.g., *Skinner v. Railway Labor Executives' Association*, 489 U.S. 602, 616 (1989).

50. *Schmerber v. California*, 384 U.S. 757 (1966).

51. Ibid., at 770.

52. See, e.g., *United States v. Sechrist*, 640 F.2d 81 (7th Cir. 1981); *United States v. Laub Baking Co.*, 283 F. Supp. 217 (N.D. Ohio 1968).

53. *Schmerber*, 384 U.S. at 770.

54. *Hudson v. Palmer*, 468 U.S. 517, 523 (1984); *Wolff v. McDonnell*, 418 U.S. 539, 555–556 (1974).

55. *United States v. Kincade*, No. 02-50380, slipop. at 14616 (9th Cir. Dec. 2, 2003).

56. Ibid., at 14621–14627 (citing *City of Indianapolis v. Edmond*, 531 U.S. 32 (2000); *Ferguson v. City of Charleston*, 532 U.S. 67 (2001)).

57. Pheny Z. Smith, *Felony Defendants in Large Urban Counties, 1990: National Pretrial Reporting Program* (Washington, D.C.: U.S. Department of Justice, Office of Justice Programs, Bureau of Justice Statistics, 1993), 13.

58. See Jerome G. Miller, "From Social Safety Net to Drag Net: African American Males in the Criminal Justice System," *Washington & Lee Law Review* 51 (1994): 479–490; Sonia Nazano, "Odds Grim for Black Men in California," *Washington Post*, December 12, 1993, A23.

59. See John McAlpin, "Documents Reveal Profiling," Associated Press, November 27, 2000; "Turnpike Shooting Settlement," Associated Press, February 2, 2001; Michael Jennings, "Verniero Impeachment Decision Due by Collins," *Trenton Times*, April 25, 2001.

60. Joint Application for Entry of Consent Decree, *United States v. New Jersey* (Civil No. 99-5970 (MLC)) (D.N.J. 1999), available at www.usdoj.gov/crt/split/documents/jerseysa.htm.

61. Angie Cannon, "D.W.B.: Driving While Black—Motorists Are Fighting Back against Unfair Stops and Searches," *U.S. News & World Report*, March 19, 1999; Kathy Barret Carter and Ron Marsico, "Whitman Fires Chief of State Police," (Newark) *New Jersey Star Ledger*, March 1, 1999.

62. See, e.g., Miller, "From Social Safety Net to Dragnet," 55.

63. See Michael Higgins, "Looking the Part: With Criminal Profiles Being Used More Widely to Spot Possible Terrorists and Drug Couriers, Claims of Bias Are Also on the Rise," *American Bar Association Journal* 83 (1997).

64. See, e.g., Thomas Ginsberg, "Profiling Charged on 'Nightmare' Flight," *Philadelphia Inquirer*, September 19, 2002, available at www.philly.com/mld/philly/news/4102992.htm; see also Carol Eisenberg, "A Troubling Year for Muslims in America," *Newsday*, September 2, 2002; Marisa Taylor, "'Operation Game Day' Tied to Super Bowl Preparations," *San Diego Union-Tribune*, January 22, 2003.

65. Eric Lichtblau, "F.B.I.' Counting of Muslims Draws Fire," *New York Times*, January 29, 2002.

66. Federal Bureau of Investigation, *Crime in the United States: 2001* (Washington, D.C.: U.S. Department of Justice, 2002), 232–233.

67. National Commission on the Future of DNA Evidence, "Recommendation of the National Commission on the Future of DNA Evidence to the Attorney General Regarding Arrestee DNA Sample Collection" (National Institute of Justice, U.S. Department of Justice, 2001, available at www.ojp.usdoj.gov/nij/dna/arrestrc.html).

68. National Commission on the Future of DNA Evidence, Suspect-Elimination Sample DNA Databases: Hearings before the National Commission on the Future of DNA Evidence,

September 24–25, 2000. In a number of cases, law enforcement agents have issued arrest warrants with only DNA evidence as the identifier. See, e.g., David Kravets, "DNA-Based Arrest Warrant Stands," Associated Press, February 24, 2001. For egregious examples from overseas, see "Mass DNA Screening Used in Rape Case," Associated Press, April 8, 2000.

69. See Barbara Ross, "Cop Talks of DNA Trickery against Serial Kill Suspect," *New York Daily News*, April 15, 2000.

70. See Jack Leonard, "Using DNA to Trawl for Killers," *Los Angeles Times*, March 10, 2001.

71. Ibid.

72. Ibid.

73. Ibid. See also Ryan Goudelocke and Melissa Moore, "B.R. Police Say Hundreds DNA-Tested," *Baton Rouge Advocate*, November 19, 2002.

74. See generally Federal Bureau of Investigation *Handbook of Forensic Services* (Washington, DC: Federal Bureau of Investigation, 1999); see also Dwight E. Adams, Deputy Assistant Director, Forensic Analysis Branch, Federal Bureau of Investigation, statement to the House Committee on the Judiciary, Subcommittee on Crime, *Hearings on H.R. 2810, H.R. 3087, and H.R. 3375*, 106th Cong., 2nd sess., March 23, 2000, available at www.house.gov/judiciary/adam0323.htm.

10

DNA Tests and Databases in Criminal Justice: Individual Rights and the Common Good

Amitai Etzioni

This chapter examines several issues raised by the extensive use of DNA tests and databases in advancing public safety. The examination draws on a communitarian perspective that balances the common good with individual rights rather than presuming that rights routinely trump the common good.

Specifically, the chapter examines major arguments made by critics who oppose extensive usages of DNA tests and especially the retention of results (or the samples from which the results were drawn) in databases for law enforcement purposes. (To save breath I shall refer to "DNA usages" from here on.) Most of the criticisms come from civil libertarians. Although none seem to completely oppose DNA usages, all demand that the state be greatly limited in conducting DNA testing, in storing the results, and in drawing on them. The critics' basic approach is to combine a general distrust of the government with a strong commitment to the value of being let alone.

The chapter opens with a response to the challenge that DNA usages will usher in eugenics, because this claim is so detrimental that until it is set aside, there is little point to dealing with other criticisms. The chapter then turns to assessing the extent to which DNA usages serve the common good and to evaluating claims that numerous DNA usages violate the Fourth Amendment, violate privacy, and contribute to the development of a surveillance state. In the last section, the chapter analyzes the question of what kinds of DNA material (if any) should be kept in DNA banks and whether inmates should be granted a new right: to be tested.

The Threat of Eugenics

The most severe criticism hurled at DNA usages is that they will lead to Nazi-like policies whereby people will be killed or discriminated against based on their genes.

For instance, Barry Steinhardt, associate director of the American Civil Liberties Union, stated before the House Judiciary Committee's Subcommittee on Crime, "It is worth recalling that there is a long unfortunate history of despicable behavior by governments toward people whose genetic composition has been considered 'abnormal' under the prevailing societal standards of the day."[1] And the National Research Council's report *DNA Technology in Forensic Sciences* raised the same issue in reference to an earlier America: "The eugenics movement in this country . . . resulted in thousands of involuntary sterilizations."[2] (Steinhardt makes a similar argument chapter 9.)

In response, one notes first that the availability of DNA tests and banks did not cause the rise of totalitarian regimes or their introduction of eugenics, as is evident from the fact that the Nazis implemented such policies on a very large scale before DNA tests existed. The same holds for whatever eugenics policies have been introduced by other governments, including that of the United States. Nor are there any signs that totalitarian tendencies or interest in eugenics has increased in those democratic societies that have introduced DNA testing. To put it more sharply but not less accurately, to date, government policies rooted in eugenics have existed only before the development of scientific DNA testing—and not since.

True, as new biotech procedures and databases are further developed, they will make it easier for a future government to abuse these tools. But the same holds for many new scientific and technological developments, including most, if not all, modes of communication and transportation. It makes little sense to forgo or severely limit the use of a new device that yields major benefits out of a fear that someday some government may abuse it. To suppress DNA usages because they might become instead abuses is akin to arguing that we should not allow the building of rapid trains because they might be used to transport victims to concentration camps or should refrain from developing computers because Big Brother might benefit from them. This last analogy is particularly apt, because such objections were raised in the early days of computers by some of the same groups that now object to DNA usages, using rather similar arguments. (One may say that critics do not oppose all DNA usages, and hence the analogies do not apply. Fair enough. Let's just say that critics advocate so many limits on DNA usages that it is akin to limiting the trains' speed to ten miles per hour.)

Second, a government that would introduce policies founded in eugenics is likely to inflict numerous other abuses on its people. This is what has invariably happened in the past. In the United States, laws discriminating against women, racial and ethnic minorities, and gay people have roots in eugenics, and the society has been at least a bit authoritarian in implementing them. The best protection against the abuse of DNA tests and other basically beneficial products and devices is to work to ensure that the institutions and values that undergird free societies are strong and to defend them vigorously.

In addition, civil libertarians ignore the fact that DNA tests can help ward off totalitarianism. Totalitarian governments arise in response to breakdowns in the social order, when basic human needs, especially public safety, are grossly neglected. When a society does not take steps to prevent major social ills and to strengthen social order, an increasing number of citizens demand strong-armed authorities to restore law and order. By greatly helping to sustain law and order, DNA tests and banks play a significant role in curbing the type of breakdown in social order that can lead to totalitarianism.

Individual Rights and the Common Good: Libertarian versus Communitarian

Civil libertarians often take the position in reference to DNA databases, as they do in reference to most other law enforcement techniques, that individual rights must be vigorously protected. They state that they do not in principle oppose considerations of the common good, especially public safety, but given their great distrust of the government, they demand that all such considerations be carefully scrutinized. Public-safety procedures are presumed to be guilty (of abuse by government) until proven otherwise, and the standard of proof is set very high.[3]

The approach followed in this chapter, which relies on responsive communitarian thinking,[4] treats individual rights and the common good as two profound, legitimate moral claims and seeks to work out a carefully crafted balance between the two. When possible, as it is to some extent in the case of DNA, as I will show shortly, both claims should be satisfied. And when the two claims conflict, we should determine whether a *limited* and carefully *circumscribed* reduction of one yields a *substantial* gain for the other. This should be allowed only if strong "notches" are developed to prevent sliding down a slippery slope.[5]

Accordingly, the examination turns next to assessing the scope of benefits to the common good that DNA usages provide, followed by a discussion of DNA's contribution to the *protection* of individual rights, and then to an assessment of claims that DNA usages violate such rights.

Benefits for the Common Good

In its few years of operation, the British National DNA Database, which was the first national DNA database in the world, has provided over sixteen thousand links between suspects and DNA left at crime scenes. At this point, according to Britain's Forensic Science Service, the database matches between seven and eight hundred crimes to suspects or to other crimes each week.[6] Some would argue that this figure exaggerates the effectiveness of the database.[7]

In the United States, where DNA databases are newer and much less developed than in Britain, the FBI's multitiered DNA database system, CODIS, had "assisted in over 1,100 investigations in 24 states" by March 2000.[8] Many of the benefits of the databases have yet to be realized, because large numbers of DNA samples that have been collected have not yet been analyzed and coded and hence are not included in the databases.[9] And DNA has yet to be collected from many convicted criminals.

Nevertheless, in the United States, as one source put it, "For a decade, DNA tests have been the most powerful tool available to police and prosecutors investigating new crimes, helping to pinpoint suspects in rape and murder cases, while alerting authorities when they were on the wrong track."[10] Paul Ferrara, the director of Virginia's DNA database program, said DNA testing "is revolutionizing the way police do their work."[11]

In the short period in which DNA databases have been in use for forensic purposes, they have played a significant role in taking large numbers of criminals off the street. Numerous old, "cold" crimes that had long occupied the time and resources of law enforcement have now been solved. Serial killers and rapists have been much more readily identified. As tests and data banks—which currently encompass but a small number of criminals—are expanded, the benefits of DNA usages will be greatly increased.

Indeed, this has already begun to occur in those states with less stringent database inclusion criteria that have committed themselves to reducing backlogs. Virginia, which with 28 percent of the national database is the largest state contributor of samples to CODIS, has averaged one cold hit per day since April 2001[12] and was, as of July 2002, averaging two and one-half hits per day.[13] The state's cold-hit success rate is likely to continue to increase as a result of the January 1, 2003, expansion of its database to include all those charged with, but not yet convicted of, violent felonies; state officials predict that 1,000 to 1,500 samples will be taken each month from arrested suspects.[14]

There seem to be no data on the deterrent effect that DNA usages have. However, it would be very surprising if, as it becomes increasingly evident to potential criminals that even one hair or drop of sweat can link them to a crime or a crime scene, this will have no deterrent effect. It is hence likely that DNA usages will lead not only to more convictions, but also to fewer crimes' being committed in the first place, which is the best of all worlds. In short, the benefits to public safety of DNA usages are very substantial.

One might argue that almost no one opposes all forensic DNA usages. However, the vastly overblown rhetoric used to associate DNA testing with eugenics policies does not discriminate among various law enforcement (or even other public) usages. In any case, a full review of the merit of such usages requires assessing the merits of proceeding with those usages. Hence the discussion up to this point.

Advancing Individual Rights

DNA tests and databases serve not merely to dramatically increase public safety, but also to protect individual rights. One of the strongest and indeed noblest claims of free societies is that it is better to let a thousand guilty people go free than to imprison one innocent person. This is a very powerful commitment that attests to how abhorrent a free society holds incarceration of the innocent. Extensive and accessible DNA testing and databases can be strongly justified on this ground alone: they already have freed from prison—even death row!—a substantial number of innocent people who had been falsely convicted and incarcerated. Even though it took several years for DNA testing to become admissible in U.S. courts, and even though DNA data banks are only now being set up on a large scale in the United States, a significant number of wrongly convicted people have already been freed. As of mid-2003, the Innocence Project had helped exonerate 127 convicts.[15]

Moreover, Barry Scheck reported in a statement before the Senate Judiciary Committee on June 13, 2000, that "[i]n 16 of [the first] 73 post-conviction exonerations [in North America], DNA testing has not only remedied a terrible miscarriage of justice, but led to the identification of the real perpetrator."[16] He correctly added that "[w]ith the expanded use of DNA databanks and the continued technological advances in DNA testing, not only will post-conviction DNA exonerations increase, but the rate at which the real perpetrators are apprehended will grow as well."[17]

Not only have DNA usages resulted in numerous exonerations, but these exonerations in turn have shed light on systemic problems within the criminal justice system—problems that have themselves contributed to individual-rights violations.

In a report sponsored by the U.S. Department of Justice documenting twenty-eight cases of wrongful conviction, Edward J. Imwinkelried, professor of law at the University of California, Davis, notes that "[i]n all 28 cases, without the benefit of DNA evidence, triers of fact had to rely on eyewitness testimony, which turned out to be inaccurate."[18] Similarly, some sixty of the first eighty-two people exonerated by the Innocence Project were convicted on the basis of eyewitness identification; more than half the cases involved police or prosecutorial misconduct, including manipulation of confessions and the withholding of key evidence from the defense. Other common problems included incompetent court-appointed defense lawyers, fraudulent scientific evidence, and false testimony from bribed inmates.[19] DNA tests are many times more reliable than police procedures heretofore very often relied upon to make people into suspects (and convicts). If one compares using DNA tests to identify a perpetrator to using eyewitnesses and police lineups, which are notoriously unreliable,[20] one immediately sees the double virtue of DNA testing: It vastly enhances the probability that those who are guilty will be convicted and that those who are innocent will be rapidly cleared, despite the early indications that made them into suspects. Imwinkelried thus pointedly asks, "if we impose a unique restriction on scientific testimony, on balance are the courts more likely to reach just results—or are we condemning the courts to reliance on suspect types of testimony that call into question the caliber of justice dispensed in our courts?"[21]

Moreover, by making it possible to identify quickly the guilty person from among a group of suspects (a process to be much further accelerated as handheld, quick-response DNA tests become available),[22] DNA usages greatly reduce the humiliation and costs entailed in being a suspect in a police investigation. (Paul Ferrara, director of the Virginia Division of Forensic Science, reports, "We typically and routinely eliminate approximately 25 percent to 30 percent of the suspects who the police have centered on in their investigation using our DNA analysis.")[23] Picture the following situation, which is based on a real case. A rape has occurred in a hospital. Eleven people had ready access to the room in which the rape occurred over the night in question. Before DNA tests were available, the police would have quite legitimately questioned all eleven people, asking them to provide alibis, checking their records for past offenses, and interviewing their supervisors, friends, and family members. If the rapist was not identified, the case might linger for years; none of the eleven potential suspects would be cleared, and a cloud would hang over them at work and in the community despite the presumption of innocence that is guaranteed in trial court but not in the court of public opinion. In the new world of rapid DNA testing, the police would ask each of the eleven to provide a sample of saliva, or a hair, and all suspects (or all but one) would be completely cleared almost on the spot, without any other measures having to be taken, and without the undesirable effects of people being long suspected.

Granted, this hypothetical case makes several assumptions. It assumes that some semen (or hair or saliva) was found at the crime scene; that it belonged to the rapist;[24] that the eleven people voluntarily provide the samples or that the police would be granted the right to collect them involuntarily; and that the police sweep would be limited to "true" suspects. (More about all these points later.) However, none of these assumptions is unrealistic.

There are other ways in which DNA tests and databases greatly help to better protect individual rights (as well as public safety). DNA databases are also helping to exonerate not only wrongfully convicted inmates, but wrongfully dismissed victims of crime. In Madison, Wisconsin, a legally blind woman whom investigators had originally accused of falsifying her story of rape and assault was vindicated four years later when the semen sample from the victim matched the DNA of a state convict who had a history of criminal sexual conduct.[25] A Georgia woman endured similar disbelief of her story of rape by knifepoint when police found no fingerprints at the scene of the rape, no significant bruising on her body, and no signs of forced entry into her home; a female detective who arrived at the scene told her that falsifying a rape report is a felony. Six years later, when the Georgia Bureau of Investigation entered DNA samples from state prisoners into its database and cross-referenced them against the state crime scenes evidence database, the woman's rape was linked to Athens serial rapist John Scieszka, serving a life sentence for raping five University of Georgia women.[26] Interestingly, these stories of "victim exonerations" reveal similar problems in the criminal justice system as do stories of convict exonerations. The Wisconsin rape victim, for instance, claims she recanted her story when police pressured her to do so during intense questioning, and her federal lawsuit against Madison police detectives for mistreatment was dismissed. In fact, the district attorney filed a charge against her of obstructing officers (later dropped) when she recanted her original story.[27]

In short, one should first note that DNA usages often can enhance both public safety and individual rights. If one truly places a great deal of importance on the release of innocent people from jail, what is considered righting the ultimate wrong, and on limiting the exposure of innocent suspects to police interrogation, one should welcome the extensive use of DNA testing on this ground alone.

Threats to Individual Rights

Having established the very considerable extent to which the common good is served by DNA tests and databases and their contributions to the protection of individual rights, the discussion turns to claims that DNA usages impinge on these rights. The question of balance hinges on whether rights are greatly harmed or, alternatively, barely affected by DNA usages.

Critics of DNA usages raise numerous objections that are intertwined and shade into each other. Although they differ regarding the specifics, critics employ the same arguments: that DNA usages violate basic rights such as the constitutional protection against unreasonable search and seizure, that they constitute a particularly gross violation of privacy, and that by adding to the rapid development of a surveillance society, they undermine the right to be left alone. Given that no critic seems to favor banning *all* DNA usages (for criminal justice purposes), although they often sound as if they do,[28] the contested issues are what kind of evidence may be collected, from whom, what is to be done with the DNA material and analyses once available, and who may have access to these materials and analyses. In short, how can DNA testing and databases be effectively utilized without significantly offending individual rights?

The reliability of DNA tests, which was contested in court when they were less developed, is now considered so high that, as a rule, it is no longer disputed. (There have been only a handful of mismatches worldwide, and most of these resulted from mishandling of samples or laboratory errors. In Britain, there was one well-known mismatch that did not result from laboratory error. This case was readily corrected through further testing, and significantly, Britain's tests use only six loci, whereas the United States uses thirteen loci in its testing, which makes mismatching in the United States even less likely, that is, extremely unlikely.)[29]

Fourth Amendment Concerns

The Fourth Amendment is not a barrier per se to DNA usages. The Fourth Amendment establishes the most communitarian of all the rights enumerated in the Constitution, because on the face of it, it recognizes the public interest. By banning unreasonable searches and seizures, it recognizes that there are reasonable ones: those in the public interest. (Compare its text to the First Amendment, which reads, in part, "Congress shall make no law," and hence is widely recognized as more absolute than the Fourth Amendment.) However, this still leaves much room for differences of opinion about where the point of balance between liberty and other public concerns lies, and about what makes a search reasonable or unreasonable in general, specifically in the area at hand. Civil libertarians almost invariably argue in regard to any new law enforcement technique and procedure (and about many old ones) that it constitutes an unreasonable search.

Most DNA usages raise the same objection among civil libertarians. For instance, the New York Civil Liberties Union opposes most DNA usages on the ground that they violate the Fourth Amendment.[30] And Dorothy Nelkin and Lori Andrews recount claims by Virginia inmates whose DNA was collected for a database that "in the absence of individualised suspicion, mandatory extraction of DNA samples violated their Fourth Amendment right against search and seizure."[31]

Opponents of DNA collections for databases, both from convicts and from other groups, point to the lack of "individualized suspicion" because this is the courts' general standard for probable cause. (It is said to draw the line between reasonable and unreasonable searches.) However, searches lacking individualized suspicion have repeatedly been upheld by the courts if there are other good reasons for them, whether these reasons are said to fall under a "special-needs exception" or a "public-safety exception" to the Fourth Amendment. Sobriety checkpoints that stop all or randomly chosen drivers, rather than only those whose driving shows signs of their being intoxicated, have been held to be justified (and hence legal), as has the use of metal detectors in airports, public buildings, and many other places that search the belongings and persons of millions of people each day.

Moreover, the Constitution is a living document that has always been reinterpreted to take into account the changing social and historical situation. Without such recalibration, there would be no constitutional right to privacy (articulated only in the mid-1960s); the right to free speech would have a rather more limited meaning than attributed to it today; and African Americans would not count as full persons. Similarly, searches of whole categories of people, when they are not based on ascribed status such as race and gender, are permitted by a modern interpretation of the Fourth Amendment, reflecting the modern need to deal with large numbers of people and new kinds of threats to their safety.

Whatever legal argument one relies upon to justify them, the fact is that the courts have found such searches legitimate. This is in line with the communitarian conception of individual rights and the common good articulated earlier. DNA usages are, in principle, justified on the same grounds as other suspicionless searches, but the question remains: Who may legitimately be subject to them? Just as mandatory drug testing of one and all is not justified because there is no compelling public interest, DNA testing of all people is not justified. The question becomes, When *is* there a compelling public interest in conducting DNA testing of an individual, and in these cases, which, if any, of that individual's rights are violated?

Rights issues differ in their relation to three categories of people: convicted criminals (violent and nonviolent), suspects, and innocent people. There is relatively little disagreement that given the high propensity of *criminals* to commit additional crimes once released from prison,[32] given that their DNA may help to solve crimes they committed before they were caught and convicted of the crime for which they were sentenced, and given that there is a well-established legal tradition of greatly scaling back the rights of felons even when there is much less public interest (for instance, they are not allowed to vote), collecting DNA material from them and keeping the evidence is very much in line with the American constitutional tradition. People who commit crimes surrender many of their rights, from their liberty to their privacy.

Which criminals should be included in DNA data banks? Only violent ones? Or also those who commit *nonviolent* crimes such as burglary and car theft? Since the early 1990s, Virginia and Florida have compared the DNA of convicted offenders, including burglars, to the DNA found at the scenes of unsolved crimes. According to one newspaper article, in state investigations, "more than half the DNA investigations of unsolved violent crimes led to burglars."[33] At that time Ferrara said, "People think of burglars as these . . . 'gentlemen bandit' types, but that is often not the case."[34] In Virginia, 60 percent of the crimes solved through DNA matching have been linked to convicted burglars, and about 50 percent of such crimes in Florida have been matched to burglars.[35] Ferrara specifically credits his state's all-felon DNA testing law for its cold-hit success. "If our databank didn't include property crimes," he noted, "then only 15 percent of the hits we made would have been made."[36]

According to an editorial in *USA Today*, "Research in England and the United States in recent years has shown that violent criminals such as rapists frequently commit felonies such as burglary before they turn to violence. Limiting the routine collection of DNA blood samples robs police of data that have proved to be effective in solving serious crimes."[37] Similarly, in the debate in Florida over a proposed law that would include burglars in Florida's DNA database, "[t]he FDLE [Florida Department of Law Enforcement] cites statistics showing a correlation between burglars and rapists. It says more than half of the state's rapists started out as burglars.

Collecting the DNA of burglars could lead them to current or future rapists."[38] On the other hand, the editors of the *St. Petersburg Times* continue, "that justification applies just as easily to a host of other types of crimes. If a large percentage of rapists received speeding tickets, would that justify expanding the DNA database to include those with moving violations?"[39]

When the communitarian principle is applied, it may, at first, seem that if a high percentage of nonviolent offenders go on to commit violent crimes, then their DNA should be collected and banked, and if the percentage is a lower number, then their DNA should not be collected and banked. If the correlation is low between nonviolent offenders and past or future violent crime, then collecting their DNA serves the public interest relatively little, whereas if it is high, the service to the public interest is considerable. But there are other considerations. Even if there is only a low correlation between a particular type of nonviolent crime and violent crime, collecting the DNA of convicted nonviolent felons may still be justified, because they have significantly lowered rights. It must therefore be determined how high a correlation is necessary to justify testing in reference to any particular kind of nonviolent crime at issue. For instance, society might deem that failing to pay child support offends its values more (or less) than embezzling and thereby decide that one category of offenders is entitled to fewer rights than another. It may then take such a ranking of nonviolent crimes into account when judging whether DNA should be collected from any particular category of offenders, which is a separate consideration from the question of how likely it is that those who committed one of these crimes will also commit a violent one.

Regarding the issue of relatives that may be pulled up during a search because they match on, say, eleven out of thirteen loci; DNA should always be used in conjunction with other types of evidence, such as eyewitness and circumstantial. Granted this means that at least for a brief moment a relative of an actual perpetrator of a particular crime will be treated de facto as a suspect in that crime merely as a result of his or her blood relationship to the actual perpetrator. But the same holds even for nonrelatives in searches based on other "evidence," such as eyewitnesses. We can hardly stop reviewing people's whereabouts or other personal information just because we are not yet sure that they are the criminal wanted in a particular crime.[40]

Although civil libertarians strongly oppose the testing of nonviolent offenders, they are even more vehement in their opposition to testing *suspects* (including arrestees) and above all *innocent* people, even if people consent.

There is a tendency to lump together all people who have not been convicted of a crime because of a very widely held belief that our justice system presumes people to be innocent until proven guilty. Although this is of course true, the fact is that *suspects in free societies are treated rather differently from both innocent people and convicted criminals.* If one prefers, one can talk about innocent-innocent (or fully innocent) people and innocent-suspects (out of respect for the norm that no one is guilty until he or she is convicted). But such wording is not only awkward but also conceals the fact that, whatever suspects are called, they are treated neither as innocent people nor as convicted criminals.

To lay out my position in regard to DNA testing of arrestees and others not (yet) convicted of a crime, it is necessary to define the term *suspect*. When the term is used loosely, practically anyone can be considered a suspect in any crime, as in the phrase "I think he did it." This broad sense of *suspect* is the one used when, for instance, people suggest, as Troy Duster did during the "DNA and the Criminal Justice System" conference, that we must be wary of the danger that police might treat whole populations as suspects, as is the case for African Americans when the police engage in racial profiling.[41]

As I use the term here, however, it is much more narrowly defined. A *suspect* for the purposes of this discussion is a person who has undergone some kind of legal process that makes it clear that he or she is suspected of having committed a crime. The best-known mechanism for making innocent (and guilty) people into suspects, and the one that is relatively less contested than others, is seeking a warrant from a judge to search a person's home or body. (Others include arresting a person and stopping and detaining someone who is running from a crime scene.) These mechanisms make people legally suspect, even if the search yields no relevant evidence or they are eventually released from custody or acquitted at trial, as long as there is sufficient evidence to detain or search them. (As I discuss briefly later in the chapter, there are mechanisms that should protect people from being arrested or detained without such evidence.)

Once a person is defined as a suspect through a legal process, his or her rights are diminished in comparison to those of innocent people, although not as much as are the rights of convicted felons. Suspects' homes, cars, and persons may be legally searched; suspects may be brought to a police station for questioning and even arrested and held in prison for defined periods of time; and their passports may be suspended.[42] Above all, they may be fingerprinted, whether or not they consent, which is of special importance given that there are certain similarities between fingerprinting and DNA testing and databases, as both serve to identify a person and tie him or her to a crime. None of these measures can be legally taken against innocent people who are not under suspicion in a crime investigation.

Given that suspects have diminished rights, including much lower rights to privacy, than innocent people, and given (as I shall show) that DNA tests can be made to be minimally intrusive, there is, on the face of it, no obvious reason why suspects should not be tested and their DNA included in databases. Indeed, in several states DNA profiles that are coded for suspects from one case are run against the DNA profiles from unsolved cases to see if the suspect from the one case might have committed a different crime.

Unfortunately, in accordance with the DNA Identification Act of 1994, CODIS cannot run broad searches in which DNA profiles from suspects are compared to the bank of DNA from unresolved cases. The states that do this kind of searching can draw only on data in their own DNA data banks. (CODIS is legally allowed to conduct such broad searches only after suspects have been convicted.)

A subsidiary question is whether the results of DNA tests conducted on suspects should be kept (presuming that the suspect in question is not convicted of the crime for which he is under investigation). If a suspect is not convicted, his DNA, like other evidence in the case, should be kept in a searchable DNA data bank for a certain period of time and then expunged or sequestered (kept in a nonsearchable location) if the suspect has not had any other problems with the law. If sequestered, the evidence would no longer be available to police in their searches regarding unsolved crimes but would be available if the person were to be convicted of a new crime—for sentencing purposes, for instance.[43] (Reference to evidence here includes samples and not merely profiles.)

I have already shown that DNA testing of suspects seems very much in the public interest. In short, public authorities cannot indiscriminately declare as suspects anyone they wish to test. There are relatively clear markers that protect the innocent from suspicion in criminal investigations and mechanisms to protect these markers. If these mechanisms are too weak and allow innocent people to be turned into suspects too readily, then these mechanisms should be strengthened—whether or not DNA tests are performed on suspects. But if they work properly, then there is no obvious reason to refrain from collecting DNA from suspects and storing it, at least temporarily, in data banks.

Civil libertarians are especially aghast at the thought of DNA being collected from innocent people. They not only are worried that DNA may be mandatorily collected from all people but also hold that if people are asked by the authorities to consent to DNA testing, their consent is likely not to be truly voluntary.[44] Mandatory collection of DNA from innocent people for law enforcement purposes, as Kaye and Smith advocate in chapter 12, is indeed abhorrent, whether coerced or not. If DNA is collected for a particular purpose, such as for identification of infants or military personnel, penalties should be imposed if it is used in any other way, and the material should be carefully safeguarded. (These matters are discussed further later in the chapter.) To collect DNA from all people in a free society would be to treat all members of that society as if they were suspects, if not criminals. And there would be minimal public benefit from such a measure (which would decrease even further as more and more criminals and suspects were included in databases). In short, the situation of nonsuspect citizens is the opposite of the situation of criminals: full rights and little public benefit from DNA testing versus diminished rights and high public benefit from DNA testing. However, the police must be allowed to ask for DNA samples from people not considered suspects, even though the submission of DNA should not be mandatory for all citizens.

At the same time, if there is evidence that undue pressure has been applied in obtaining it, DNA evidence—like all other evidence obtained under coercion—should be dismissed. However, the mere fact that the police requested a DNA sample should not be construed as undue pressure. Such requests can be essential in a whole set of situations for effective law enforcement (including speedy clearing of suspects), and if consent is freely given, they entail no diminution of rights.

Privacy Violation

DNA testing is said to be particularly intrusive for two reasons. First, critics argue that blood testing is especially intrusive because it involves entering the body.[45] It is not simply an invasion of privacy, but an intrusion into our self-possession of our bodies.[46] Second, DNA testing is said to be particularly intrusive because it reveals much more information about the person tested than does, for instance, fingerprinting. The question, then, arises, as Eric Juengst puts it, "What should society be allowed to learn about its citizens in the course of attempting to identify them?"[47]

The first concern is less weighty than the second one, even if one does not agree with the ruling in *People v. Wealer*, in which the Illinois Court of Appeals upheld the constitutionality of an Illinois DNA data bank statute on the grounds that blood testing is minimally intrusive[48] (or with the *Jones* court, which cited *Skinner* to establish that blood testing is a "not significant" intrusion).

DNA tests can be performed with a lower degree of bodily intrusion even than blood tests require. New York City, for instance, plans to base its bank on saliva taken from people at the same time they are fingerprinted. In fact, DNA can be collected not only from blood, but also from skin cells and dandruff, as well as from the cells contained in saliva, sweat, or urine or attached to strands of hair.[49] Thus, samples other than blood can reliably be used for DNA testing, and collecting them is much less intrusive than collecting blood (or even urine, which often must be provided under supervised conditions).

The second concern, that DNA testing poses a threat to informational privacy, is less easily dealt with.[50] In considering it, we ought to keep in mind several factors, all of which suggest that the threat to privacy is much lower than some have suggested. First, unless one simply views the government as some kind of ruthless enemy, there is no reason to believe that it will use DNA that is collected for criminal-identification purposes to find out about people's family history, illnesses, and so on. In addition, bans on such research and disclosure of such personal information have been introduced. So far there has not been a single reported violation of these restrictions. And even if a few did occur, this might lead to tightening security and raising penalties but still would not justify preventing the storage of the proper information. After all, we do not shut down other basically beneficial systems, from airline traffic to courts, because some mistakes occur. Making policy based on horror stories is a horrible idea.

Second, DNA tests that are done on blood stains, semen, saliva, and biological tissue found at crime scenes are not a violation of privacy. Courts have ruled (relying on *Katz v. United States*) that there is no privacy violation involved in investigative activities in places a reasonable person would have no expectation of privacy and society does not presume one exists. This makes sense. If a man walks down Main Street wearing only his birthday suit, he has little reason to complain if people see his private parts. It seems reasonable to assume that criminals who leave behind the DNA samples taken from crime scenes have no more expectation of privacy than if they leave behind fingerprints. (This holds not only for crime scenes, but for all other public places. If one leaves a document in a park confessing to one's crime, one can hardly expect that it will not be used as evidence.)

If a DNA sample is taken from a criminal or suspect under court orders, this does constitute a diminution of his privacy. But as already indicated, this intrusion can be minimized by collecting hair or saliva rather than blood and by limiting access to the test results. And to reiterate, criminals and suspects have diminished privacy rights in general. Even for innocent people privacy has never been considered an absolute right.

Slippery Slope and Racial Discrimination

Critics employ two other arguments against DNA usages: the slippery-slope argument, and the argument that such usages pose a danger of racial and other forms of discrimination. The first argument is exemplified by a remark from a Boston public defender who, in reference to the collection of DNA from inmates, probationers, and parolees, asked rhetorically, "Why not round up poor people?"[51] Paul E. Tracy and Vincent Morgan write:

These various scenarios follow a clear-cut progression. A sex-offender-only database seems virtually unobjectionable. The conviction-based databases seem a little more expansive, but still they do not seem particularly troubling. After all, a judge or a jury found the accused guilty. That should be enough. The arrest-based systems are the current thresholds, but here, we have no assurance of guilt, only suspicion. With the total population database, even if one takes cost out of the equation, it still seems a little too futuristic. Something about it just seems contrary to our notions of individual autonomy, and our sense of personal privacy.[52]

Others argue that DNA tests do or will lead to racial and other forms of discrimination. Steinhardt and Duster (see chapters 9 and 14, respectively) and Peter Neufeld are among those who fear that DNA databases would lead to discrimination because studies might show that people who commit more crimes than others share some DNA markers, and hence all those with these attributes would be discriminated against.[53]

Both arguments deserve attention, but the main question is where they take us. If the conclusion is that DNA tests and banks should not be used, these arguments must be set aside for reasons already discussed: Rather than abandoning generally useful systems when mistakes occur, we ought to work to correct them. Thus the above arguments are meant to suggest that we must carefully notch the slippery slope, set clear markers for what is allowed and not allowed, and establish penalties for the abuse of genetic information; if policies governing DNA usages include adequate protections of this type, they deserve our full support.[54] Just as no responsible person would argue that we should stop enforcing traffic laws and conducting sobriety tests merely because, in some places, racial profiling has been used, civil libertarians should not assert that DNA banks should be closed simply because they fear that one day those banks may be used to discriminate against some people.

DNA Adds to the Surveillance Society

Another major source of the opposition to DNA usages is derived from the concern that DNA databases would significantly add to the capacity of the government to track its citizens. DNA fingerprinting is said to add to information-gathering technologies that "are rendering individuals more and more transparent, and relentlessly reducing the private spaces into which people have traditionally been able to retreat for refuge and self-definition."[55] Such surveillance technologies raise two kinds of issues. One is how to limit which investigative tools the government may use, even concerning convicted criminals. This question is the focus of my book *The Limits of Privacy*[56] and cannot be reexamined here in a few lines. Suffice it to say that government intrusion can be justified only when there is a serious public interest, no other approaches to solve that particular public concern are possible (e.g., mobilizing the community's norms and voice), and the intrusion is kept as minimal as possible.

The second issue regarding surveillance technologies is how to regulate their use by the private sector. It turns out that the problem with intrusive surveillance in the United States currently is not the government, the Big Brother on which civil libertarians have historically focused their attention. Instead, over the last ten years or so, almost all of the new surveillance techniques and databases, including genetic tests, have been developed by the private sector, by Big Bucks.[57]

Although the feared abuse of these new capabilities by the government is almost completely hypothetical—"one day, a future government might . . ."—abuses of surveillance technologies by the private sector are well documented. These include the violation of commitments not to collect information about children aged thirteen or younger without the consent of their parents[58] and violations of corporations' posted privacy policies in regard to those who frequent their Web sites.[59]

DNA tests and databases may at first seem to be an exception to the previously stated rule that the private sector is responsible for introducing new surveillance technologies. DNA usages, after all, have been largely introduced by the government. However, the largest force driving the use of DNA tests and databases for purposes other than criminal justice is private biotechnology firms. Here, too, whereas fears of government abuse have concerned hypothetical futuristic scenarios, this is not the case for DNA use in the private sector. So far, the main abuses of DNA information have been by employers, who have used the results of genetic tests to eliminate job applicants from contention or to ease genetically undesirable people out of jobs. As early as 1996 a study documented 206 cases of genetic discrimination against asymptomatic individuals.[60] Richard Sobel and Harold J. Bursztain report that "a recent survey of employers by the American Management Association finds that 30 percent ask for genetic information about employees and 7 percent admit to using the information for hiring and promotion decisions."[61] And there must be additional, unreported cases of the abuse of genetic information, as people often are not told why they have not been hired, have not been promoted, or have been let go or are given vague or inaccurate explanations. Private-sector abuse of genetic information is not limited to employers. There are already reports of funeral parlor directors who have collected DNA for private purposes.[62] Hospitals often retain blood samples taken from patients and use these samples in ways unrelated to the patients' own care.

Confronted with the reality of the surveillance society, we can move in one of two basic directions. We can accept that new technologies, especially biometric ones (DNA tests and banks included), make a very high level of surveillance a fact of life that cannot be avoided. Indeed, several recent books have suggested that "privacy is dead."[63] (The head of Sun Microsystems has stated, "You already have zero privacy; get over it.")[64]

The other response to the expanding surveillance society is to greatly restrict surveillance capabilities, as many civil liberations demand. In this case, though, civil libertarians must recognize that the main source of this new protection must be the government they so mistrust. New laws will have to be enacted, and the main actors that will need to be restrained will be private ones. Merely limiting the databases the government may maintain would be like curbing gun violence by prohibiting police departments from selling handguns they have confiscated—a good idea, but one that deals with a tiny fraction of the market. And merely limiting the government's ability to use privately maintained databases would mean that these databases could be used for de facto discrimination regarding employment, credit, and housing but could not be used for law enforcement and other common-good purposes.

Currently, laws governing information gathering mainly reflect an earlier view of the surveillance society: They greatly limit what the government can legally do with the information it collects and impose penalties for government abuses. In effect, as of the summer of 2003, the only two encompassing nationwide (federal) privacy protection laws, which banned the collection of numerous kinds of information and severely limited the use of the information that has already been collected, are the privacy regulations that, in 2000, were incorporated into the Health Insurance

Portability and Accountability Act of 1996 and the Privacy Act of 1974,[65] which applies to the federal government but not to the private sector. Some new federal regulations were introduced in 1998 concerning the protection of the privacy of children and in 2000 concerning the protection of financial records; large-scale regulation of medical privacy, including genetic privacy, is expected. But still, as of the time this book went to press, there are next to no limitations on what private companies, including labs and hospitals, can do with blood and other samples that contain DNA or what they can do with the results of DNA tests they have already conducted. And of course, anything that is so freely available in the private sector is at least potentially available to the government.

To argue that the government should be the main protector against DNA abuses is not to suggest that the government itself is not to be limited by law and scrutinized. It is like hiring guards who need to be supervised and whose scope of duties needs to be circumscribed. The government still needs to be monitored to ensure that public usages of DNA will be proper. This observation leads to the questions, What usages are proper? What should be included in databases, and who should have access to them?

What to Bank and Who Should Have Access

Civil libertarians argue that the data collected and stored in DNA databases should be greatly limited in content and that the samples themselves should be destroyed and only limited profiles (electronic records of the information needed to identify and match a person) kept.[66] The FBI already limits the extent of the informational-privacy invasion involved in DNA profiling. The DNA markers used in CODIS "were specifically selected as law enforcement identification markers because they were not directly linked to any genetic code for a medical condition."[67]

First, keeping samples taken from materials found at crime scenes and those taken from arrestees and criminals is justified for now on the ground that DNA tests are still rapidly developing. If the samples are destroyed, any new information they may yield as better technology is developed will not be available if future criminals and suspects need it to prove their innocence, nor will it be available to the government for solving crimes. We need only recall samples that were destroyed but a few years back, when DNA tests were less accurate, and how much damage was consequently done to both individual rights and the common good. One can also readily agree with Scheck, who has proposed a duty to preserve biological evidence while an inmate is incarcerated,[68] noting that "[i]n 75 percent of our Innocence Project cases, where we have already determined that a DNA test would demonstrate innocence if it were favorable to the inmate, the evidence is lost or destroyed."[69]

Someone might argue that, at this point, DNA tests are so reliable that no additional gains in information yields can be expected. However, improvements do occur, such as decreases in the amount of material one needs to extract DNA.[70] In Arizona in 2000, Larry Youngblood was exonerated for the sodomization of a young boy, a crime for which he had been convicted almost two decades earlier. Whereas the small amount of semen that was found was insufficient for reliable testing at the time of Young blood's trial, new testing procedures showed conclusively that the police had the wrong man.[71] Surely additional improvements that cannot now be envisioned can be expected. Existing DNA samples should be kept for at least five more years after the trial, to see whether or not they are needed for retesting as a result of test improvements.

Second, the use of criminal justice DNA databases for nonforensic purposes (particularly an issue for physical samples, but also for digital files) should be banned, and the use of non-criminal-justice databases (e.g., medical-research databases) for forensic purposes should also be prohibited. The reasons for this position range from principled to prudential. In principle, whereas the government can justify (for the categories of persons discussed, under the conditions discussed) collecting DNA samples without consent for criminal justice purposes, it cannot justify collecting DNA for other purposes, such as producing income (hence the legitimate criticisms of certain state governments when they sold driver's license information).[72] More difficult are those cases in which the government might make the data from forensic DNA databases available for other public purposes such as medical research and the determination of paternity (as Ohio allows). Such cases require a whole separate discussion. Such additional discussion is not, however, needed in regard to information collected for medical purposes, which should not be used for forensic purposes for many obvious reasons.

New Inmate Right

A growing number of inmates have asked to have their DNA tested to prove their innocence, sometimes repeatedly, as improved technology has become available. From their viewpoint, there is nothing to be lost. Although as of November 2002, twenty-six states permitted inmate access to postconviction testing, up from two states in 1999, many states continue to resist these requests in accordance with finality doctrines that set time limits for the introduction of new evidence after sentencing. They argue that there must be some limit, lest cases be strung along endlessly by frivolous appeals.[73] However, given the high regard in which we as a society hold protecting innocent people, and given the considerable number of cases in which such tests have exonerated people, such a right should be provided, at least for one test per inmate. Another suggestion along the same lines is that DNA testing should be done within seven to fourteen days of a crime to help ensure that innocent suspects are not even tried, much less incarcerated.

At the same time, we should not allow inmates to turn DNA tests into a new tactic for delaying their sentences from being carried out and for imposing costs on the government by demanding test after test, arguing that the previous one has not been carried out quite properly, that it may have been misinterpreted, and so on. Under normal circumstances, one test per inmate should be the limit. Otherwise, this new right will unduly limit the ability of the criminal justice system to carry out its duties.[74] This is far from a minor concession to inmates' interests. District attorneys have repeatedly argued that, given the limited testing facilities and resources, tests for inmates delay inputting crime scene DNA into databases and allow killers and rapists to continue to roam free.

In Conclusion

The fear that DNA tests and databases will usher in eugenics-based government policymaking is unfounded. Governments that introduce laws and policies rooted in eugenics generally violate a wide range of human rights and abolish democracy, and hence such governments must be fought whether or not there are DNA tests. In fact, such tests contribute significantly to the maintenance of conditions under which such governments are unlikely to arise.

The starting point of a communitarian approach to the issue at hand is that both rights and the common good place major moral claims on us (as the Fourth Amendment suggests), rather than that ours is a rights-centered society and that if rights are to be limited in any way the burden of proof is on the advocates of the common good.

In this context, one should note that often DNA usages serve both to protect the rights of innocent people and to enhance public safety. However, when the two do conflict, one should take into consideration the very high value of DNA for public safety. Moreover, as we have seen, our right not to be subject to unreasonable search and seizure, our right to privacy, and our right to be generally left alone are not infringed upon (or only minimally so) by DNA tests and databases that encompass criminals and suspects. Innocent people, though, should not be tested for criminal justice purposes, unless they truly volunteer to do so. Other parties should not have access to criminal justice databases, and public authorities should not have access to DNA tests and databases produced for private purposes (such as medical and military ones), although the relationship among such databases is beyond the purview of this study.

Most important, the traditional distrust of the government by civil libertarians is misplaced in the case of DNA testing and databases, because in the contemporary United States, the main violation of rights in this area is by private corporations. In fact, the government will have to play a major role in protecting citizens from such abuses.

Notes

I am indebted to Andrew Volmert for extensive research assistance for this chapter. In revising this chapter, I benefited from extensive discussions of the issues at hand at the "DNA and the Criminal Justice System" conference, John F. Kennedy School of Government, Harvard University, Cambridge, Mass., November 19–21, 2000 (proceedings of the conference are available at www.dnapolicy.net).

1. Barry Steinhardt, statement to the House Committee on the Judiciary, Subcommittee on Crime, *Hearings on H.R. 2810, H.R. 3087, and H.R. 3375,* 106th Cong., 2nd sess., March 23, 2000; available at www.house.gov/judiciary/stei0323.htm.

2. Quoted in ibid.

3. For more discussion see Amitai Etzioni, *The Limits of Privacy* (New York: Basic Books, 1999).

4. See *The Responsive Communitarian Platform: Rights and Responsibilities* (Washington, D.C.: Communitarian Network, 1991); see also Amitai Etzioni, *The New Golden Rule: Community and Morality in a Democractic Society* (New York: Basic Books, 1996), chaps. 1 and 2.

5. For further discussion of notching principles, see Amitai Etzioni, *The Spirit of Community: The Reinvention of American Society* (New York: Touchstone, 1993), 177–190.

6. Forensic Science Service, "Frequently Asked Questions," available on the Forensic Science Service home page at www.forensic.gov.uk/forensic/entry.htm.

7. For example, it is unclear how many convictions result that otherwise would not have.

8. Dwight E. Adams, deputy assistant director, Forensic Analysis Branch, Federal Bureau of Investigation, statement to the House Committee on the Judiciary, Subcommittee on Crime,

Hearings on H.R. 2810, H.R. 3087, and H.R. 3375, 106th Cong., 2nd sess., March 23, 2000, available at www.house.gov/judiciary/adam0323.htm.

9. About five hundred thousand convicted offender samples to be inputted into the CODIS database had yet to be analyzed as of this writing, compared to the roughly four hundred and fifty thousand that were to be analyzed for STRs by the end of 2003. National Institute of Justice, Recommendation of the National Commission on the Future of DNA Evidence; available at www.ojp.usdoj.gov/nij/dna/codisic.html. Accessed 1/5/03.

10. Brooke A. Masters, "DNA Testing in Old Cases Is Disputed; Lack of National Policy Raises Fairness Issue," *Washington Post*, September 10, 2000, A1.

11. Quoted in Manuel Roig-Franzia, "DNA Tests Help Find Moving Suspects," *Washington Post*, November 26, 2000.

12. Maria Sanminiatelli, "Virginia's DNA Database Averaging One Cold Hit a Day," Associated Press State & Local Wire, April 29, 2001.

13. John Branton, "Inmates' DNA Taken for Crime Database," *The Columbian* (Clark County, Wash.), July 22, 2002, C8.

14. Maria Glod, "Va. to Begin Taking DNA after Arrests for Felonies; Prosecutors, Rights Activists Split on Database Expansion," *Washington Post*, January 1, 2003.

15. www.innocenceproject.org.

16. Barry Scheck, statement to the Senate Committee on the Judiciary, *Post-conviction DNA Testing: When Is Justice Served?* 106th Cong., 2nd sess., June 13, 2000, available at www.senate.gov/~judiciary/wl6132000.htm.

17. Ibid.

18. "Commentary by Edward J. Imwinkelried," in Edward Connors et al., *Convicted by Juries, Exonerated by Science: Case Studies in the Use of DNA Evidence* to Establish Innocence after Trial (Washington, D.C.: National Institute of Justice (1996), xiv.

19. "A Pandora's Box," *Economist*, December 14, 2002.

20. As Supreme Court Justice William J. Brennan wrote in his opinion in *United States v. Wade*, "The vagaries of eyewitness identification are well known; the annals of criminal law are rife with instances of mistaken identification." *United States v. Wade*, 388 U.S. 218, 87 S. Ct. 1926, 1933 (1967). It has been widely documented that eyewitness accounts are unreliable. Gary L. Wells and Eric P. Seelau summarize findings regarding eyewitness identification: "Although there is no way to estimate the frequency of mistaken identification in actual cases, numerous analyses over several decades have consistently shown that mistaken eyewitness identification is the single largest source of wrongful convictions." Gary L. Wells and Eric P. Seelau, "Eyewitness Identification: Psychological Research and Legal Policy on Lineups," *Psychology, Public Policy, and Law* 1 (1995): 765. See also "Commentary by Edward J. Imwinkelried," xiii.

21. "Commentary by Edward J. Imwinkelried," xiv.

22. Kevin Flynn, "Fighting Crime with Ingenuity, 007 Style; Gee-Whiz Police Gadgets Get a Trial Run in New York," *New York Times*, March 7, 2000, B1.

23. "Interview: Dr. Paul Ferrara, Director of Virginia Division of Forensic Science, Discusses Gathering of DNA Evidence," *All Things Considered* (National Public Radio, July 27, 2000).

24. An article in *USA Today* reported numerous cases in which criminals have become DNA savvy. Some criminals have begun wearing condoms during rapes, and some have tried to fool law enforcement by planting other people's DNA at crime scenes. Richard Willing, "Criminals Try to Outwit DNA," *USA Today*, August 28, 2000. Great Britain also reports a rise in rapes in which the rapist attempts to establish a relationship with his future victims at bars or clubs so that any DNA evidence he leaves behind can be explained. Clare Dyer, "Rapists Target Pubs and Clubs," *Guardian* (London), January 7, 2003.

25. Steven Elbow, "Rape Case Resurfaces; DNA Database Points to Suspect," *Capital Times* (Madison, Wis.), June 29, 2001.

26. Craig Schneider, "Georgia's DNA Files Extend Long Arm of the Law," *Atlanta Journal and Constitution*, February 3, 2002.

27. Elbow, "Rape Case Resurfaces."

28. See, for instance, Philip L. Bereano, "The Impact of DNA-Based Identification Systems on Civil Liberties," in *DNA on Trial: Genetic Identification and Criminal Justice*, ed. Paul R. Billings (New York: Cold Spring Harbor Laboratory Press, 1992). A similar position was expressed by Peter Neufeld and Barry Steinhardt in their presentation "Privacy/Ethics Principles in the Creation and Use of DNA Databases" during "DNA and the Criminal Justice System," November 21, 2000.

29. On the mismatch occurred in Britain, see Richard Willing, "Mismatch Calls DNA Tests into Question; Case in Britain Was 'to Be Expected' as Databases Include More Samples," *USA Today*, February 8, 2000. A mismatch occurred as a result of accidental sample contamination in New Zealand. "Reports Show DNA Crime Errors," *Evening Post* (Wellington, New Zealand), March 10, 2000.

30. John Kifner, "Police Propose DNA Testing for Every Person Arrested," *New York Times*, December 13, 1998.

31. Dorothy Nelkin and Lori Andrews, "DNA Identification and Surveillance Creep," *Sociology of Health and Illness* 21, no. 5 (1999): 695.

32. See Allen J. Beck and Bernard E. Shipley, *Recidivism of Prisoners Released in 1983* (Washington, D.C.: Bureau of Justice Statistics, U.S. Department of Justice, 1989). For discussion of recidivism generally and sex offenders specifically, see Amitai Etzioni, "Sex Offenders' Privacy versus Children's Safety: Megan's Laws and the Alternatives," in *The Limits of Privacy* (New York: Basic Books, 1999), chap. 2.

33. Richard Willing, "DNA Links Burglars to Harder Crime," *USA Today*, December 7, 1998.

34. Ibid.

35. See ibid. David Coffman of the Florida Department of Law Enforcement reported in his presentation "Developing DNA Databases" during "DNA and the Criminal Justice System," November 20, 2000, that "52 percent of the offenders linked to sexual assaults and homicides by DNA database matches have had prior burglaries." Transcript available at www.ksg.harvard.edu/dna/transcribe_table_page.htm.

36. Sanminiatelli, "Virginia's DNA Database Averaging One Cold Hit a Day." For more on all-felon laws, see chapter 16 of this volume.

37. "DNA Key to Fighting Crime: Privacy Fears About This Law-Enforcement Tool Are Overblown," editorial, *USA Today*, August 21, 2000, 16A.

38. "Balancing DNA Use," *St. Petersburg Times*, March 29, 2000, 14A; see also Coffman's presentation "Developing DNA Databases" at "DNA and the Criminal Justice System."

39. "Balancing DNA Use."

40. For more on low-stringency searches, see chapter 16 of this volume.

41. "Privacy/Ethics Principles in the Creation and Use of DNA Databases."

42. Note that some of these matters are covered by state laws, and hence there are some differences in these matters among states.

43. See Amitai Etzioni, "Civic Repentance: Just and Effective," in *Repentance: A Comparative Perspective*, ed. Amitai Etzioni and David Carney (Lanham, Md: Rowman and Littlefield, 1997), 1–20.

44. See, for example, Fred Drobner, "DNA Dragnets: Constitutional Aspects of Mass DNA Identification Testing," *Capital University Law Review* 28 (2000): 505–507.

45. Eric T. Juengst, "I-DNA-Fication, Personal Privacy and Social Justice," *Chicago-Kent Law Review* 75 (1999): 62.

46. Nelkin and Andrews, "DNA Identification and Surveillance Creep," 696.

47. Juengst, "I-DNA-Fication, Personal Privacy and Social Justice," 63.

48. See Michael J. Markett, "Genetic Diaries: An Analysis of Privacy Protection in DNA Data Banks," *Suffolk University Law Review* 30 (1996): 203–204.

49. See National Commission on the Future of DNA Evidence, *What Every Law Enforcement Officer Should Know About DNA Evidence* (Washington, D.C.: National Institute of Justice, U.S. Department of Justice, 1999), available at www.ojp.usdoj.gov/nij/pubs-sum/000614.htm.

50. Juengst, "I-DNA-Fication, Personal Privacy and Social Justice," 64.

51. Carey Goldberg, "DNA Databanks Giving Police a Powerful Weapon, and Critics," *New York Times*, February 19, 1998, quoted in Nelkin and Andrews, "DNA Identification and Surveillance Creep," 698.

52. Paul E. Tracy and Vincent Morgan, "Criminology: Big Brother and His Science Kit; DNA Databases for 21st Century Crime Control?" *Journal of Criminal Law and Criminology* 90 (2000): 672. See also Timothy Lynch, "Databases Ripe for Abuse: Further Expansion a Mistake; Soon They'll Want All Citizens' DNA," *USA Today*, August 21, 2000, A16.

53. Presentations by Peter Neufeld, Barry Steinhardt, and Troy Duster, "Privacy/Ethic Principles in the Creation and Use of DNA Databases" during "DNA and the Criminal Justice System."

54. On notching, see Etzioni, *The Spirit of Community*, 177–191.

55. Reg Whitaker, *The End of Privacy: How Total Surveillance Is Becoming a Reality* (New York: New Press, 1999), 4.

56. Etzioni, *The Limits of Privacy*.

57. Ibid., especially chaps. 4 and 5.

58. "Personal Information Collection from Children," in Federal Trade Commission, *Privacy Online: A Report to Congress* (Washington, D.C.: Federal Trade Commission, 1998), available at www.ftc.gov/reports/privacy3/toc.htm.

59. Ibid.

60. Suzanne E. Stripe, "Genetic Testing Battle Pits Insurers against Consumers," *Best's Review—Life/Health Insurance Edition*, August 1996, 37. See also National Academy of Sciences, *For the Record: Protecting Electronic Health Information* (Washington, D.C.: National Academies Press, 1997), 77.

61. Richard Sobel and Harold Bursztain, "Ban Genetic Discrimination," *Boston Globe*, August 7, 2000, A15.

62. See Dorothy Nelkin and Lori Andrews, "Whose Genes Are They, Anyway?" *Chronicle of Higher Education*, May 21, 1999, B6.

63. Simson Garfinkel, *Database Nation: The Death of Privacy in the 21st Century* (Beijing: O'Reilly, 2000); Jeffrey Rosen, *The Unwanted Gaze: The Destruction of Privacy in America* (New York: Random House, 2000); Whitaker, *The End of Privacy*; Charles Jonscher, *The Evolution of Wired Life: From the Alphabet to the Soul-Catcher Chip—How Information Technologies Change Our World* (New York: Wiley, 1999).

64. Quoted in Dominique Jackson, The World According to . . . Malcolm Crompton," *The Australian* (Sydney), July 18, 2000, 56.

65. See Amitai Etzioni, "Medical Records: Big Brother versus Big Bucks," in *The Limits of Privacy* (New York: Basic Books, 1999), chap. 5.

66. See the presentation by Steinhardt, "Privacy/Ethics Principles in the Creation and Use of DNA Databases"; see also Juengst, "I-DNA-Fication, Personal Privacy and Social Justice," 64–67.

67. Adams, statement to the House Committee on the Judiciary, Subcommittee on Crime, *Hearings on H.R. 2810, H.R. 3087, and H.R. 3375.*

68. Scheck, statement to the Senate Committee on the Judiciary, *Post-conviction DNA Testing.*

69. Ibid.

70. In recent years, for example, STRs have increasingly replaced VNTRs in testing because they allow more accurate analysis of smaller samples. CODIS uses thirteen core STR loci in its analysis. National Commission on the Future of DNA Evidence, *The Future of Forensic DNA Testing: Predictions of the Research and Development Working Group"* (Washington, D.C.: National Insitute of Justice, U.S. Department of Justice, 2000), 1–2. Another new process being developed at the University of Denver allows DNA analysis of smaller and older samples by focusing on mitochondrial DNA. John Ingold, "Team Takes DNA to New Level; Du Process Could Transform Forensics," *Denver Post*, November 12, 2002.

71. Tim O'Brien, "DNA Tests Are Worth Doing If Innocence Can Be Proved," *Milwaukee Journal Sentinel*, September 11, 2000; see also Youngblood's profile at www.innocenceproject.org.

72. Linda Greenhouse, "Justices Uphold Ban on States' Sales of Drivers' License Information," *New York Times*, January 13, 2000, A29.

73. See Jim Dwyer, Peter Neufeld, and Barry Scheck, *Actual Innocence: Five Days to Execution and Other Dispatches from the Wrongly Convicted* (New York: Doubleday, 2000), 247. See also Brooke A. Masters, "Virginia May Drop Deadline for Death Row Retrials; High Court Has Questioned Several Cases," *Washington Post*, October 14, 2000, A1.

74. For fine additional discussion and recommendations, see National Commission on the Future of DNA Evidence, *Postconviction DNA Testing: Recommendations for Handling Requests* (Washington, D.C.: National Institute of Justice, U.S. Department of Justice, 1999).

11

Strands of Privacy: DNA Databases, Informational Privacy, and the OECD Guidelines

Viktor Mayer-Schönberger

The need for some protection of personal privacy when setting up and using DNA databases is fairly uncontroversial.[1] However, striking the right balance between too little protection for privacy to be preserved and too much protection for law enforcement to effectively function is more than merely complex; experts also disagree on exactly how that balance can be found.

Positioning the Right to Privacy

Before delving into concrete policy debates, it is important to remind ourselves that privacy is only one of a number of individual rights that are at stake when DNA databases are set up and used. For example, Radhika Rao has eloquently made the case for property claims when it comes to the use of genetic material.[2] Others have looked at the problem through the lens of a Fourth Amendment right.[3] Autonomy and self-identity have been suggested,[4] as have group rights and group identities.[5] Hence, the balancing implicit in any regulatory framework must take all of these individual and group rights into consideration, not just the privacy claim.

Furthermore, privacy in itself is not a homogenous right,[6] but a bundle of very different underlying values. Jerry Kang has identified three such values: physical privacy, decisional privacy, and informational privacy.[7] Physical privacy is concerned with the protection of one's home and one's bodily integrity. Decisional privacy entails the right to render personal decisions without undue external pressure, and informational privacy is the right to control one's personal information.[8]

Taking Kang's definition and mapping it onto the debate concerning privacy and DNA databases, it is striking that the physical privacy strand has received substantially more attention than the other two. This is surprising, because the real threat of DNA databases is surely not government's intrusion into one's bodily integrity.

As Eric Juengst[9] contends, taking a DNA sample through a mouth swab is relatively less invasive than other things done today in various contexts: taking blood or urine samples. Indeed, DNA databases pose a privacy threat not because of the way samples are taken, but because of the information inherent in these samples. Yet article after article looks at the constitutionality of DNA testing under the rubric of the Fourth Amendment's prohibition of unwarranted government searches and seizures—a prohibition much closer linked to physical privacy.[10]

The reason for this unbalanced preference of one strand of privacy when it comes to DNA databases has, I think less to do with an inaccurate assessment of the potential threats involved and much more to do with the peculiar legal history of privacy protection in the United States. Privacy protection entered the legal debate with the famous 1890 Brandeis/Warren article advocating a tort action to protect privacy.[11] As a constitutional right, privacy surfaced prominently in the Supreme Court decision in *Griswold v. Connecticut*.[12] In *Griswold*, which held unconstitutional a law prohibiting the use of contraceptives, the court could not agree on where, exactly, in the Constitution the right to privacy can be found—a plurality said it was somewhere in the Constitution's penumbras. Moreover, the Court conceived the right narrowly in terms of physical and, to a lesser extent, decisional privacy, but not in terms of informational privacy. Later, *Roe v. Wade*[13] and similar cases[14] solidified this conception. Commentators have tried to discern some hints of informational privacy protection from these decisions, albeit with limited success.[15]

Thus according to current Supreme Court jurisprudence, the extent to which the constitutionally protected right to privacy explicitly protects informational privacy is questionable. As a result, most commentators have focused on ensuring some protection of informational privacy through the use of accepted physical and decisional privacy protection or through the use of other rights claims.

Unfortunately, this perceived need to anchor a privacy analysis in a constitutional provision may prevent us from envisioning a more balanced picture of the privacy strands at stake. In a way it is like the old joke of the man who has lost his keys at night in a dark alley but keeps looking for them under a street lamp because this is where it easier to search.

Furthermore, employing such a restrictive view of privacy indirectly causes a shift of regulatory locus, which too artificially constrains our analysis of the fundamental privacy problem of DNA databases. As I have mentioned, the potential danger is the information distilled from the DNA sequences and, even more precisely, the individual's lack of control over such information. But because control over information is connected with informational privacy, a value not explicitly protected by present constitutional privacy jurisprudence, commentators have refocused their scrutiny toward the activity afforded some constitutional protection: the collection of the DNA samples. Sample collection may have little direct connection with the actual privacy threat, but it can be seen through the jurisprudentially accepted lenses of physical and decisional privacy. Hence, this unintuitive, albeit understandable, shift of analytical scrutiny from the *use* of DNA *information* to the *collection* of DNA *samples*.

Assessing the privacy impact of existing DNA database regulations may require such constitutional analysis. However, suggesting a solid basis for future DNA database regulation does not necessarily need to rely solely on present constitutional jurisprudence. To be sure, in the end, regulation cannot afford less protection than the constitution guarantees. It may, however, strike a balance between the needs of law enforcement and the protection of individual values by providing more or different kinds of informational-privacy protection.

What we need to keep in mind is that there are two strands of privacy claim analysis. One is ex post, looking at existing (or envisioned) regulation and whether such regulation would pass constitutional muster. This is what has mostly been written about. The other is the ex ante envisioning of a regulatory framework in which an informational privacy claim beyond the minimal protection afforded by the Constitution is balanced against the needs of law enforcement. The difficulty surfaces when we use the bounding conditions of the former strand of analysis to envision the latter. This leads us both to devalue the importance of informational privacy and to wrongly shift the focus from the use of personal information to its collection techniques.

Instead of confusing and confounding these two distinct discourses, we ought to clearly separate them and look at the issue of what kind of regulatory regime can safeguard informational privacy while maintaining enforcement effectiveness. Such an approach would not be novel, not even in the field of informational privacy.

The OECD Privacy Guidelines

Back in the 1970s, the United States embarked on crafting legislative guidelines for the protection of informational privacy in medical and health services settings.[16] These guidelines were solidly grounded in the constitutional framework, but they were forward looking. They were designed to inform legislative and regulatory processes. And they reacted to a different kind of privacy threat, that of loss of control over sensitive personal information.

The guidelines were originally designed to address informational privacy issues in health care in the United States. They have since been used to form the foundation of much more general guidelines for the use of personal data. Conscious of the ever-increasing flow of personal information across borders and through global data networks, the United States transferred this broadening process formulating forward-looking guidelines to an international body, the Organization for Economic Cooperation and Development (OECD), one of the elements of the U.S.-sponsored post–World War II international framework, of which the United States is a member. The other member states of the OECD, themselves faced with the problem of protecting informational privacy, quickly grasped the importance and usefulness of such a process. After years of intense analysis, deliberation and drafting, the OECD "Guidelines on the Protection of Privacy and Transborder Flow of Personal Data"[17] were formally adopted in 1980.

Domestic regulators are not bound by these guidelines as they are by constitutional rights. The power of the guidelines lies in the substance of what they suggest and the expertise of their drafters, not in their formal acceptance as a higher law. As such, these guidelines have offered legislatures around the world a choice when creating laws affecting informational privacy. Dozens of nations have taken the guidelines to heart and followed their spirit, if not their letter, in their informational privacy and data protection statutes.[18]

The guidelines do not stipulate an absolute right to privacy, contrary to the rhetoric of some commentators. Indeed, even their title suggests that they are designed to aid in the creation of an appropriate balance between the necessity of processing, storing, and disseminating personal information and the individual's need for informational privacy. The guidelines specify eight principles of privacy-sensitive processing of personal data:

- The *collection limitation principle* stipulates that the collection of personal information must not be limitless, and that personal information should be lawfully and fairly obtained and, where appropriate, with the consent of the individual concerned.[19]

- The *data quality principle* focuses on the need of information to be relevant to the purpose for which it is collected and used, and for it to be kept up to date.[20]

- The *purpose specification principle* sets out the requirement that personal information collected for one purpose cannot subsequently be used for a different, incompatible purpose.[21]
- The *use limitation principle* specifies that personal information may not be disclosed or used for other than the original purposes except with the individual's consent or "by the authority of law."[22]
- The *security safeguard principle* requires security measures to prevent loss or unauthorized access, modification, or disclosure of personal information.[23]
- The *openness principle* demands that the use of personal information be transparent to the user.
- The *individual-participation principle* permits the individual to have access to the personal information stored about him or her and also gives him or her the right to have inaccurate information modified.[24]
- Finally, the *accountability principle* stipulates that the processor of personal information must be held liable for violations of his or her duties.[25]

There is nothing radical in these eight principles. They appear sound, balanced, and reasonable. They are based on informational privacy and, as such, are legislative aspirations, not constitutional mandates. They exemplify *informational* privacy, though they are not limited to it. Indeed, interwoven in these principles are strands of *decisional* privacy. This is most obvious in the emphasis on consent. But the purpose specification and use limitation principles also include an important corollary to decisional privacy: Only if the decisions of individuals are followed and circumvention of those decisions is prohibited is true decisional privacy possible. The same applies to the individual participation and accountability principles: Only if the individual knows that personal information about him or her is available can he or she make an informed decision, and only if the processor is liable for his or her conduct can individuals have their decisions about personal information enforced. Even traces of protecting *physical* privacy can be found in the guidelines. For example, the security safeguard principle mandates that unauthorized others be prevented from accessing personal information about an individual, and thus from unlawfully intruding into the individual's personal sphere.

As I have shown, a substantial part of the academic debate on DNA databases and privacy focuses on physical and decisional, but not informational, privacy strands. This may be useful for an ex post analysis of the constitutionality of DNA database regulations. However, it clouds our understanding of, and consequently constrains our options when thinking about, the appropriate design of future DNA database regulations. One way of overcoming this deficiency is by including informational privacy in the assessment of potential DNA database regulations. Although *informational privacy* is a broad and fairly opaque term, the OECD guidelines provide solid, applicable, and tried principles that can assist regulators in striking such a privacy-sensitive balance.

Hence, we may use the OECD guidelines to aid us in designing privacy-enhancing DNA database regulations. The assistance provided by the OECD guidelines is multilayered. Quite obviously, the guidelines may help us answer vexing policy questions in a way that does not compromise individual informational privacy. Thus the application of the principles embedded in the guidelines may result in the making of concrete policy choices. The guidelines may also perform a second function. On a number of policy issues regarding DNA databases, experts like bioethicists have eloquently argued for a specific option based on ethical considerations.[26] In such cases, applying the guidelines may provide not new answers, but rather an additional reason why a specific option is most suitable. To be sure, the principles expressed in the guidelines are not more normative than ethics considerations. But they do provide a sort of "second opinion" based less on ethical values than on abstract yet pragmatic analysis and balancing. In short, then, the guidelines may assist us not only in *how* to choose, but also *why* to choose.

When applying the guidelines it is important to keep two of their design fundamentals in mind. First, the eight principles contained in the guidelines are not pure privacy principles that need to be balanced against some other legislative need, like effective law enforcement. Instead, these eight principles are already the result of an abstract balancing act. Countervailing values are already factored in. Hence, for example, balancing them again with another countervailing principle would not create a balance, as intended, but rather would tip the scale in favor of the non-privacy value. Consequently, these eight principles need "simply" be applied to concrete policy issues. This "application," of course, entails a concrete balancing, but no additional abstract balancing act is necessary.

Second, the guidelines are to be understood as minimum standards of information privacy, capable of being supplemented by further protection of privacy.[27] Consequently, when applying the guidelines to a regulatory issue concerning the use of DNA databases, regulators may decide to protect the individual's informational privacy to a greater extent than what the eight principles would stipulate. After all, this is not a legal but a policy question. Indeed, when the Council of Europe and later the

European Union drafted and adopted binding international privacy covenants based on the guidelines, they substantially extended informational privacy protection.[28]

The remainder of this chapter describes and analyzes, using the guidelines' eight principles, seven "hard" policy options that legislatures may face when regulating the use of DNA databases.

Who Should be Included in the DNA Database?

Any storage and use of personal information is an invasion of that individual's privacy. This is certainly true for DNA information. The question is whether the privacy invasion is outweighed by a stronger societal interest in using the information. Hence, any regulatory framework enabling a DNA database to be set up has to address the privacy issue and make a compelling case for having and using such a database.

Some commentators argue for the creation of a comprehensive DNA database containing the DNA information of all citizens (see chapter 12). For their arguments to succeed in the context of the guidelines, they would have to show that the benefits of adding everyone's DNA information to the database clearly outweigh the privacy concerns at stake, with the added difficulty that the suggested societal benefits necessarily have to remain in the abstract. Whether such a strong abstract claim can be made remains an open question. But one rule of thumb can be offered here: The more stringently the proposed framework for regulating a comprehensive DNA database protects privacy, the easier it will be to tip the balance in favor of creating, maintaining, and using such a database.

The more common existing DNA database statutes call for including only certain groups of individuals in it. In general, this invades fewer individuals' privacy and may thus be seen as preferable to those that provide for broader inclusion. However, selecting a particular individual and mandating that his or her DNA information, but not that of others, be stored in a DNA database, though less invasive in the abstract, is inherently problematic. For the individual affected, it is not only a simple invasion of privacy. It is an *unequal* invasion of privacy—singling out him or her for the invasion but not others. Consequently, such proposals must also be scrutinized in light of equality considerations (see chapter 14).

The guidelines' principles place an emphasis on the purpose of the use of personal information and the need to narrowly tailor the means of collection to the purpose the collection of the information is intended to advance. This is where the collection limitation principle, the data quality principle, the purpose specification principle, and the use limitation principle come together. The more invasive the means of collection, the better the fit with the purpose has to be.

Hence mandating that any suspect submit a DNA sample to be included in a DNA database may further the general goal of law enforcement and criminal justice, and thus fulfill the abstract requirement of the means fitting the ends that is implicit in the guidelines' principles. But singling out certain individuals and not others for inclusion requires more than such an abstract justification. Arguably, a more concrete justification may be the propensity of some individuals to commit crime after crime. To be sure, the available data suggesting a correlation between prior and future criminal activity is not without its problems. But even if one accepts such a linkage, the correlation provides no foundation for including in the database information from (or even for taking samples from) mere suspects, whose propensity to commit even one crime has not yet been proven.[29] Only through a conviction are the foundations for a strong enough purpose created to make possible the tip of the balance and permit the intrusion into one's informational privacy in accordance with the guidelines' principles.

Limiting DNA databases to convicts, however, is only a necessary precondition and does not itself constitute sufficient balancing. Not all convicts are alike. Nor are all DNA database searches. Balancing the government's purpose against privacy invasion is not an utterly abstract test of the fit between the means and the ends. Balancing entails taking into account the specifics of each such invasion, even if only in some generalizable way.

For example, committing a severe crime permits the state to intrude further into one's privacy than committing a lesser crime. This sliding scale facilitates assessing the "weight" of the privacy right of the individual in question. Crimes against persons, like murder or rape, are particularly unacceptable in our society. This is why individuals committing such crimes face the strongest forms of punishment and may have to accept a reduced right to privacy. Similarly, the weight of the government benefit is related to why the government wants to solve a particular crime. Here, too, searching for (and finding) a murderer provides a greater benefit than searching for the proverbial "chicken thief." The required balancing combines these two factors. The government's case is strongest when searching for a murderer among convicted murderers and much weaker when trying to find a chicken thief among convicted chicken thieves. The regulatory challenge is to create a DNA database statute that takes this kind of balancing into account.

This is particularly difficult when these two opposite, but determinative, factors are found to be correlated. Unfortunately, some studies suggest that they are: that individuals convicted of burglary and similar property crimes have a high propensity to commit crimes against other human beings as well. In a world of black and white, of exclusion or inclusion in the DNA database, does this statistical correlation carry enough weight to tip the balance in favor of DNA database inclusion, even if the individual is just a chicken thief?

The question implies a binary choice—black or white, yes or no—whereas in reality there may be many shades of gray. The key to overcoming this problem is understanding, as the guidelines suggest, that the intrusive action involved in DNA databases is not just taking a DNA sample and storing it in a database. The privacy intrusion happens *every time* an individual's record is accessed as part of a search. Every time this happens the balancing has to take place and the benefits have to outweigh the intrusion. This broadens our conceptual framework. DNA information may allowably be stored from some convicts but not searched every time, thus permitting a more gradated approach.

Specific balancing of this type may sound complex, time consuming and costly—and thus impractical. But the guidelines help us solve this problem, too. As I have mentioned, they incorporate balancing through how they emphasize purpose analysis. Looking at the purpose of the intrusive action, they create a more manageable means-ends test. To use the previous example, the murderer's record may be accessed every time, the chicken thief's only if the search is for an unresolved murder case. Only certain types of (serious) crimes provide a strong enough justification—and thus a strong enough purpose—to justify the privacy intrusion inherent in the database search.

The emphasis on purpose in the guidelines forces one to take a hard look at just how important the purpose of a particular search of a DNA database is. They help us understand that every usage of DNA information—every search run against a DNA record—is an intrusive act. The purpose of finding a murderer may justify that intrusive search; the purpose of finding a chicken thief may not.

What Information Should Be Included in the DNA Record?

There has been substantial debate regarding whether DNA records should contain information only on so-called noncoding regions of DNA or should also include information about functional genes that may result not just in identifiable, but also in biologically informative, DNA. This debate has somewhat ended in the United States since the FBI established standardized forensic markers in noncoding regions.[30]

Is restriction of the information stored in the database to noncoding regions in line with the guidelines' principles? The collection limitation principle clearly states that there should be limits on the collection of personal information, and the data quality principle further stipulates that such information should be collected only insofar as it is relevant to the purpose at hand. The purpose of DNA databases is the identification of individuals. For such an identification purpose, the inclusion of biologically informative regions is not necessary. Hence, the guidelines mandate that only noncoding regions of DNA be used. The current FBI policy is thus in line with the guidelines' principles.

In this case, applying the guidelines to a specific situation has not resulted in an alternative answer, it has confirmed what is already practiced. But applying the guidelines has provided us with an additional reason—"data ecology"—that restricting the use of DNA information to noncoding regions is the appropriate policy choice.

Should DNA Samples Remain Stored or Be Destroyed?

A related policy issue is whether DNA samples should remain in storage or be destroyed after the relevant identification information has been extracted and entered into the database. Supporters of destroying the samples argue that DNA records are supposed to provide the ability to identify an individual based on genetic information. Once this identification information is taken from the sample, there is no need to keep the sample as a backup. Opponents of such a restrictive policy point out that one should not throw away information that may be potentially important. Future advancements in DNA-matching techniques may provide a better means of identification through discovery of additional noncoding regions. To this argument, the supporters of sample destruction retort that better identification can only mean identification with a lower probability of a false identification. Should matching of DNA information identify a person and implicate him or her in a crime and techniques be available that make misidentification less likely, one can always draw a fresh sample from the suspected individual and test it.

Such critics have a point. There is no absolute reason to keep samples. By the same token, governments may find it more convenient or cheaper to use different

DNA-typing technology in the future. With the samples gone, governments may effectively lock themselves into a particular (and perhaps soon outdated) technology. The policy question then is one of individual rights versus governmental efficiency. Keeping DNA samples "just in case" technology advances has to be balanced against the fact that storing samples would, at least theoretically, enable the keepers of these samples to look at coding regions of DNA, which I have shown violates the guidelines. Consequently, storing DNA samples would automatically violate the guidelines unless the regulatory framework for DNA databases explicitly prohibits the use of information from coding regions.

But it is questionable whether even such a statutory prohibition is enough to square the storing of samples with the guidelines' principles. The reason is once again the principle of collection limitation, combined with the data quality and use limitation principles. Recall that the reason for taking DNA samples is the creation of a DNA database for identification purposes. If this is the only reason given when collecting the samples, one cannot—according to the use limitation principle—later use these samples for a different purpose, such as looking at biologically informative parts of the sample. The data quality and collection limitation principles together mandate that information be stored only to the extent that it is relevant for the purpose for which the collection was made. But what exactly is that purpose?

If the purpose of storage is identification, regardless of efficiency, keeping the samples is unnecessary. All DNA identification information is already in the database once the sample has been tested and the results entered. But what if the purpose is modified to include *efficient* identification during the next ten or twenty years by future technical means? Arguably, this would require keeping the samples. With the purpose so modified, keeping the samples would not in itself violate the data quality principle. But the guidelines' principles not only stress the tailoring of the means to the ends in order to limit resulting privacy intrusions; they also require that the end, or purpose, be compelling. The issue then is shifted from the specifics of the data quality principle to purpose analysis. As has been discussed earlier, purpose analysis looks at the specific intrusive action. A carte blanche approach in which all samples are kept is likely too broad to pass this test. If samples are to be kept, there has to be a specific justification for this additional privacy intrusion. Very abstract notions of potential technical breakthroughs that may provide governments with efficiency gains in the future do not provide enough of a justification. Hence, although keeping DNA samples after analysis would not necessarily violate the guidelines, the onus would be on the government to provide a specific and narrowly tailored combination of means and ends that would justify this action.

How Long Should DNA Records Be Stored?

In addition to the issue of whether and when to destroy *samples*, a regulatory framework for DNA databases also has to consider the conditions under which an individual *record*—genetic information that has already been extracted from a sample—should no longer be used. The first such condition is the most important one: In cases of postconviction relief, the individual's DNA information would have already been stored in the database based on his or her conviction. If that conviction is overturned, the reason for that individual's entry in the database is lost. With no legitimate purpose to fulfill, the record needs to be deleted.

A tougher question is whether DNA records should be deleted, or access to them limited, at some time after an individual has been released from prison. This is an interesting question because it brings us face to face with another intricate issue: the issue of meta-information. If only individuals convicted of certain types of crimes are registered in the DNA database, then the mere fact that somebody's record can be found in the database represents a sensitive piece of personal information.

In our society we maintain registries of convicted criminals—and with good reason. We use such registries to identify suspects in future or previous (unsolved) crimes based on the assumption that criminals may have a propensity to break the law. By the same token, breaking the law once, especially when the crime involved is comparatively minor, should not stigmatize an individual forever. To complicate matters, we must not forget that a privacy intrusion takes place not just when the sample is taken and the information is stored in the database. An intrusion happens whenever the stored record is accessed. Each time that happens the benefits of each of these intrusive actions must outweigh the costs of violating the right to privacy of the individual from whom the sample was taken. Once a person has been released from prison, all of his or her rights have been restored, and time has passed, the person's privacy claim becomes comparatively stronger and weightier and ultimately may tip the balance against the intrusive action. Moreover, purposes for database searches differ. Searching the database to solve a murder case may be a strong enough purpose to access even older DNA records from people released from prison. Searching for the proverbial chicken thief may not.

Many federal and state laws preclude the use of prior convictions in criminal and civil cases after a certain time.[31] By deciding to afford certain individuals a second chance by restricting the use of their criminal record, we as a society have concluded that after a certain time there is little or no legitimate purpose in using this information. Records in the DNA database are another way of identifying an individual as a former convict. Accordingly, the regulatory framework for DNA databases has to mandate that storage of DNA information in the database not be indefinite, but that it instead be synchronized with existing legal restrictions and societal values.

Should Individuals Have Access to Their DNA Records?

Even though DNA records may be deleted from a database under certain circumstances, in most cases they will be stored in the database for a long period of time. During this time, should individuals have a right to access the information that is stored about them? This may sound like a fairly unimportant issue. Why would an individual desire to access his or her own DNA information?

The individual participation principle enshrined in the guidelines serves two distinct purposes. The first is related to the quality of information stored in the database. Each DNA record contains a number of genetic identifiers, but it also includes the name and possibly other personal data about the individual. As with any other sensitive data collection, sound procedures must be in place in the collection of DNA information to prevent false information from being stored. Yet the storage of erroneous information in DNA records, although improbable, is at least theoretically possible.

The experts drafting the OECD guidelines found that permitting individuals to access their records is an effective way to identify erroneous information and correct it. The right to access thus improves the quality of the data collection over time. To be sure, it is unlikely that individuals will be able to spot an error in their DNA information; but errors may also be contained in associated bits of information, which they would be able to identify. The real benefit, however, is in a related second purpose of the individual participation principle: the implicit general transparency it brings to DNA databases. Nongovernmental organizations concerned about the accuracy of DNA testing and DNA databases, quality control, and government oversight could assist individuals in accessing their records and verifying the information. With independent, trustworthy third parties able to verify data in DNA databases, the database itself becomes better understood and loses its threatening mystique. Third-party access and verification also guarantees transparency and citizen-based oversight over a very potent source of information.

The guidelines suggest a general right of access to information stored about one. Applying the guidelines to DNA databases would require a right of access to be included in the provisions regulating the database. The actual costs involved in fulfilling an access request can be passed on to the individual, especially when the individual makes repeated access requests in a short period of time.

Should DNA Records Be Used for Creating a Reference Group?

Matching identifiers in a DNA sample with those in somebody's DNA data already stored in the database establishes a link between the individual and the sample. However, it is theoretically possible that somebody else not in the database might have the same genetic identifiers and thus be linked to the sample as well. Full DNA identification entails a second step, the assessment of the probability of somebody else's having the same genetic information as the sample being matched. This probability is calculated against a reference pool of genetic information. In other words, all DNA identification is always relative.

Setting up a DNA identification system requires not only the creation of a DNA database of genetic information on identifiable individuals. It also requires the creation of a genetic reference pool against which probabilities are calculated, large enough so that the probability of false positives is sufficiently small. Often, DNA information to be stored in the database is automatically added to the reference pool as well. This creates a reference pool in which individuals stored in the database—current and former convicts—are substantially overrepresented. This may lead to a bias in the reference pool, which may make probability calculations less accurate and reliable. The possibility of such a bias has troubled a number of experts, who have called for a broadening of the reference pool. Can we gain any additional insight into the debate on how the reference pool for a DNA database should be created from applying the guidelines' principles?

The reference pool is basically an anonymous source of comparative information. As such, it is not linked to specific individuals. The guidelines apply only to personal information, which is defined as information "relating to an identified or identifiable individual."[32] If the reference pool for a DNA database is assembled in such a way that no back tracing to an individual is possible—and there is no reason that it cannot be so constructed—then the guidelines would not apply.

But even if the reference pool for a database were traceable, and thus the guidelines did apply, adding an individual's DNA information to the reference database as well as to the criminal database would not necessarily violate any of the guidelines' principles. Arguably, it would just extend the existing purpose of use, yet not beyond what is acceptable to further the overall purpose for which the DNA samples were collected in the first place.

Should DNA Records Be Shared with Other Nations?

Manuel Castells has eloquently described the increase in cross-border crime in recent years.[33] As crime globalizes, so, some would say, must law enforcement. Accessing other countries' DNA information, or even sharing one's national database with them, would allow law enforcement to counterbalance the trend toward globalization on the criminal side. At the same time, sharing DNA information with other governments would permit this information to leave a nation's regulatory framework for DNA information and thus would increase the risks to individuals that their personal information might be misused.

The problem of personal information's "escaping" from a national regulatory regime is not unique to DNA databases. In fact, one of the OECD privacy guidelines' central aims was to strike an appropriate balance between the need to access or transfer personal information across borders and the need to maintain the privacy rights of individuals. To this end, the guidelines require, at a minimum, that personal information be moved[34] across borders only if the nation receiving the information "substantially observes" the guidelines as well, and if the export does not take place in order to circumvent domestic privacy regulations.[35] This is a sensible requirement. What good would privacy regulations do on a national level if such regulations could easily be circumvented by transmitting information abroad?

However, the guidelines restrict the transborder flow of personal information further. If, based on the sensitivity of the information, additional domestic privacy regulations have been imposed, such personal information can be transferred abroad and thus shared only with nations that have an equivalent level of additional privacy protection in place.[36] Thus for sensitive information the guidelines permit a higher level of privacy to be enforced when sharing such information with other nations. Applied to the transborder sharing of DNA database information, the guidelines mandate that such sharing take place only if the country receiving the information has privacy regulations in place for the use of DNA information that are both compatible with the guidelines and not less stringent than domestic privacy regulations governing DNA database information.

Given this structure for information sharing among countries, two very different regimes for international access to DNA databases are imaginable. The first is based on a model of national but interdependent regulatory frameworks. Each nation chooses its own level of privacy regulation for DNA information. When a nation wants to exchange information with another nation, or even just to access DNA information in another nation's database, it may have to comply not only with its own but also with the other nation's regulatory framework. Whether or not a nation then decides to set up access arrangements with another nation may depend on how badly it wants the access versus how costly, in terms of accepting another regulatory framework, it thinks such access is. A nation whose data many others want to access can in effect substantially influence the regulatory frameworks of other nations. If, for example, the United States wants very much to access the Canadian DNA database, Canada may be able to influence the U.S. regulatory framework for DNA information. If Canada provides more privacy protection for DNA records, the United States may be prompted to adhere to these higher standards, either when accessing Canadian records or more generally.

When we add the voluntary OECD guidelines to this picture, various forms of regulatory dynamics may ensue, depending on which nation has the greatest pull, that is, has the highest number of others who want to enter into access agreements with it. If that nation is strong on privacy, overall privacy protection across nations may increase. The opposite scenario, in which a nation with no or limited privacy protection forces others to lower their standards, is in principle precluded by the guidelines, which set a minimum standard.[37]

Given the power, size, and importance of the United States, many nations will want to share DNA information with it. This may help to create a U.S.-led de facto international privacy consensus. One has to keep in mind, however, that the European Union has enacted very stringent privacy regulations, essentially harmonizing national privacy laws of its members at a high level. Moreover, the E.U. privacy regime incorporates the guidelines' basic principle of sharing information across borders only when adequate privacy protection in the recipient state is ensured. In contrast to the voluntary guidelines discussed here, the E.U. privacy regime is based on an E.U. directive,[38] a binding and enforceable legal document. Overall, this may create a considerable international pull toward a European level of protection as all E.U. member states, taken together, may carry a weight equal to or even greater than the that of United States, thus potentially forcing the United States to strengthen its privacy protection in regard to DNA information.[39]

A second international access regime that could arise is based on a cooperative model of international coordination. Under such a model, a multilateral regime would be set up for the sharing of DNA information and the protection of privacy, thus preventing inefficiencies arising from national regulatory frameworks. Instead of national frameworks, there would be an internationally accepted consensus on the appropriate level of protection for DNA information. Such an approach would ensure free access to DNA database information for all members of this multilateral regime.

Given past difficulties in the transborder flow of personal information between the United States and the European Union,[40] and keeping in mind the sensitivity of privacy concerns in countries that are important (to the United States) like Canada, the United States may want to actively pursue the creation of such a coordinated multilateral regime. As an active proponent of such a regime, the United States would be able to substantially influence the outcome, in addition to creating a more efficient system than one based on numerous, differing bilateral agreements. Even so, in developing such a regime, the United States would have to negotiate with nations with privacy statutes based on the OECD guidelines. As these nations are bound by the minimum-standard requirement for transborder flows of personal information, their negotiating flexibility would be constrained. This would likely lead to a multilateral regime in which the minimum standard of the guidelines was in fact the common denominator.

Whichever international access regime is chosen, the guidelines will have a substantial impact on the substantive policy options available. For this reason, it makes eminent sense for the United States to keep the guidelines in mind when drafting its DNA database statutes. Doing so may make expanding the international DNA database network easier and faster and provide a necessary tool to combat international crime. This weaves the thread back from applying international guidelines (which stem from privacy rules originally crafted in the United States) to domestic policy matters to the international level, exemplifying the interconnectedness not only of present information networks, but also of policymaking in a globalized world.

Conclusion

Envisioning the appropriate level of privacy protection for the use of DNA databases is a complex endeavor. In this chapter I have suggested broadening the analytic base by weaving a stronger informational privacy strand into the regulatory fabric. Envisioning how to do so is made easier by the existence of tried and proven privacy guidelines, formulated by the OECD. The eight principles imbedded in those guidelines provide a pragmatic framework through which to address, reason about, and answer a number of vexing policy questions on the privacy regulation of DNA databases. These principles neither constitute formal legal guidelines nor provide answers to all the questions involved, but they may aid policymakers in envisioning an appropriate legal framework, and in the end they help us understand that these, like many other policy issues in a globalized world, can hardly be dealt with from a purely domestic perspective.

Notes

I would like to thank Benjamin Dorr, who, by thinking hard about privacy, made me think hard about it, too.

1. This assumption, though uncontroversial, is not universally held. For a discussion see Anita L. Allen, "Privacy–as–Data Control: Conceptual, Practical and Moral Limits of the Paradigm," *Connecticut Law Review* 32 (2000): 861.

2. Radhika Rao, "Property, Privacy, and the Human Body," *Boston University Law Review* 80 (2000): 359.

3. See, e.g., Robert Craig Scherer, "Mandatory Genetic Dogtags and the Fourth Amendment: The Need for a New Post-Skinner Test," *Georgia Law Review* 85 (1997): 2007; Deborah F. Barfield, "DNA—Fingerprinting—Justifying the Special Need for Fourth Amendment's Intrusion into the Zone of Privacy," *Richmond Journal of Law and Technology*, no. 6 (2000): 27; J. Clay Smith, "The Precarious Implications of DNA Profiling," *University of Pittsburgh Law Review* 55 (1994): 865.

4. Jonathan Kahn, "Biotechnology and the Legal Constitution of the Self: Managing Identity in Science, the Market, and Society," *Hastings Law Review* 51 (2000).

5. Jonathan Kimmelman, "Risking Ethical Insolvency: A Survey of Trends in Criminal DNA Databanking," *Journal of Law, Medicine and Ethics* 28 (2000): 209; Erika L. Johnson, "'A Menace to Society': The Use of Criminal Profiles and Its Effects on Black Males," *Howard Law Journal* 38 (1995): 629.

6. It is a subject of substantial academic debate whether privacy is a right or a claim of right. See Ruth Gavison, "Privacy and the Limits of Law," in *Philosophical Dimensions of Privacy: An Anthology*, ed. Ferdinand David Schoeman (Cambridge: Cambridge University Press, 1984), 346, 348.

7. Jerry Kang, "Informational Privacy in Cyberspace Transactions," *Stanford Law Review* 59 (1998): 1193. Scoglio has added a fourth category that he terms "formational privacy" and envisions it to provide a common foundation for the other three. Stefano Scoglio, *Transforming Privacy: A Transpersonal Philosophy of Rights* (Westport, Ct.: Praeger, 1998).

8. See chapter 9 of this volume, especially the section on privacy.

9. Eric T. Juengst, "I-DNA-Fictation, Personal Privacy and Social Justice," *Chicago-Kent Law Review* 75 (1999): 63.

10. See note 3.

11. Samuel Warren and Louis Brandeis, "The Right to Privacy," *Harvard Law Review* 4 (1890): 193.

12. *Griswold v. Connecticut*, 381 U.S. 479 (1965).

13. *Roe v. Wade*, 410 U.S. 113 (1973).

14. For example, *Planned Parenthood of Central Missouri v. Danforth*, 428 U.S. 52 (1976); *Thornburgh v. American College of Obstetricians & Gynecologists*, 476 U.S. 747 (1986).

15. For an excellent and eloquent argument along these lines, see Paul Schwartz, "Internet Privacy and the State," *Connecticut Law Review* 32 (2000): 815.

16. See Secretary's Advisory Committee on Automated Personal Data Systems, *Records, Computers and the Rights of Citizens* (Washington, D.C.: Department of Health, Education, and Welfare, 1973), available online at http://aspe.hhs.gov/datacncl/1973privacy/tocprefacemembers.htm.

17. Organization for Economic Cooperation and Development, "Guidelines on the Protection of Privacy and Transborder Flow of Personal Data," available at www.oecd.org/dsti/sti/it/secur/prod/PRIV-EN.HTM.

18. For example, the U.S.-E.U. Safe Harbor agreement on privacy is based on the OECD guideline principles; the Center for Democracy and Technology calls the guidelines "the baseline for evaluating privacy and data protection initiatives" (www.cdt.org/privacy/guide/basic/oecdguidelines.html) and notes that 183 U.S. companies claim to adhere to the them; New Zealand's privacy commissioner refers to the OECD guidelines as an "international standard" (www.privacy.org.nz/media/pia.html); and Cowles advises global businesses to follow the guidelines if they want to play it safe with regard to privacy laws in many nations (see Maria Green Cowles, The U.S. On-line Data Privacy Debate: When Domestic Politics Becomes a Global Game, www.aicgs.org/at-issue/ai-cowles.shtml; see also James Michel, *Privacy and Human Rights: An International and Comparative Study, with Special Reference to Developments in Information Technology* [Paris: UNESCO, 1994]).

19. "7. There should be limits to the collection of personal data and any such data should be obtained by lawful and fair means and, where appropriate, with the knowledge or consent of the data subject."

20. "8. Personal data should be relevant to the purposes for which they are to be used, and, to the extent necessary for those purposes, should be accurate, complete and kept up-to-date."

21. "9. The purposes for which personal data are collected should be specified not later than at the time of data collection and the subsequent use limited to the fulfillment of those purposes or such others as are not incompatible with those purposes and as are specified on each occasion of change of purpose."

22. "10. Personal data should not be disclosed, made available or otherwise used for purposes other than those specified in accordance with Paragraph 9 except: a) with the consent of the data subject; or b) by the authority of law."

23. "11. Personal data should be protected by reasonable security safeguards against such risks as loss or unauthorised access, destruction, use, modification or disclosure of data."

24. "13. An individual should have the right: (a) to obtain from a data controller, or otherwise, confirmation of whether or not the data controller has data relating to him; (b) to have communicated to him, data relating to him within a reasonable time; at a charge, if any, that is not excessive; in a reasonable manner; and in a form that is readily intelligible to him; (c) to be given reasons if a request made under subparagraphs (a) and (b) is denied, and to be able to challenge such denial; and (d) to challenge data relating to him and, if the challenge is successful to have the data erased, rectified, completed or amended."

25. "14. A data controller should be accountable for complying with measures which give effect to the principles stated above."

26. Juengst, "I-DNA-Fictation, Personal Privacy and Social Justice," 63.

27. "6. These guidelines should be regarded as minimum standards which are capable of being supplemented by additional measures for the protection of privacy and individual liberties."

28. See "Council of Europe Convention for the Protection of Individuals with Regard to Automatic Processing of Personal Data" (European Treaty Series No. 108, Strasbourg, 1981). See also Directive 95/46/EC of the European Parliament and of the Council of 24 October 1995 on the protection of individuals with regard to the processing of personal data and on the free movement of such data, 1995 Official Journal L 281, 31.

29. Some state legislatures seem to think otherwise, perhaps especially in the wake of September 11; see, e.g., Stephen Braun, "Virginia Aggressively Uses DNA to Solve Other Cases," *Los Angeles Times*, January 13, 2003, available at www.latimes.com/la-na_dna13jan13001446,0,5525121.story. Similarly, Britain has started to permit police to retain the genetic profiles of those suspected or interviewed about a crime, even if they are never charged or convicted or are later exonerated. Employing eerily Orwellian rhetoric the British Court of Appeals upheld this practice, arguing that it is in order because it "is obvious that the larger the databank of fingerprints and DNA samples available to the police, the greater the value of the databank will be in preventing crime and detecting those responsible for crime" (Stephen Robinson, "A Free Country," *Daily Telegraph* (City), September 13, 2002, 29). The need to balance such an intrusion against a right to privacy has all but vanished. Efficiency in criminal investigation seems to be the only justification needed.

30. The debate may be revived by the discovery that noncoding regions contain relevant information as well; see "Junk DNA Proves Business Boon for Aust's Genetic Technologies," AAP Newsfeed, December 12, 2002.

31. See, e.g., Federal Rule of Evidence 609(a)(1), or on the state level, Mississippi Rule of Evidence 609 (stipulating a time frame of ten-years after conviction) or Texas Rule of Evidence 609 (ten year rule); for an example from employment discrimination law, see NY CLS Correc 752 (2001) (prohibiting unfair discrimination against persons previously convicted).

32. OECD, "Guidelines," article 1(b).

33. Manuel Castells, *End of Millennium* (Malden, Mass.: Blackwell, 1998), 166.

34. This covers any movement of personal data across borders, including arguably justly retrieved information transferred across borders when accessing other nations' databases.

35. "A Member country should refrain from restricting transborder flows of personal data between itself and another Member country except where the latter does not yet substantially observe these Guidelines or where the re-export of such data would circumvent its domestic privacy legislation." OECD, "Guidelines," article 17.

36. "A Member country may also impose restrictions in respect of certain categories of personal data for which its domestic privacy legislation includes specific regulations in view of the nature of those data and for which the other Member country provides no equivalent protection." OECD, "Guidelines," article 17.

37. Of course, compliance with the guidelines is itself voluntary.

38. The directive is a legal document enacted by the European Union and addressed to its member states; see Treaty Establishing the European Community, October 11, 1997, O.J. (C 340) 145, art. 249 ("A directive shall be binding, as the result to be achieved, upon each Member State to which it is addressed, but shall leave to the national authorities the choice of forms and methods").

39. See also Viktor Mayer-Schönberger, "The EU Directive on Data Protection in Telecommunications," in *Competition, Regulation, and Convergence*, ed. Sharon Eisner Gillett and Ingo Vogelsang (Mahwah, N.J.: Erlbaum, 1999), 121.

40. For an excellent analysis of the E.U. stance on transborder data flows, see Paul M. Schwartz, "European Data Protection Law and Restrictions on International Data Flow," *Iowa Law Review* 80 (1995).

12

DNA Databases for Law Enforcement: The Coverage Question and the Case for a Population-Wide Database

D. H. Kaye and Michael E. Smith

The most controversial issue in the design of DNA databases for law enforcement's use in criminal investigation is the question of coverage: Whose DNA profiles should be stored in these databases? The range of possible coverage extends from convicted violent sex offenders, to all convicted felons, to everyone arrested, to the entire population (see chapter 16). This chapter questions the rationales for drawing the line at all convicted offenders (which is fast becoming standard practice) or at all arrestees (which may be where we are headed). It suggests that such coverage results in sampling DNA disproportionately from racial minorities, which exacerbates racial tensions and undermines the rule of law while reducing the preventative and investigative value of the databases. It argues that a population-wide database with strict privacy protections may supply a better answer to the coverage question—and to the privacy concerns raised by any government program to take and analyze individuals' DNA.

The first part of the chapter discusses two theories that might dictate which offenders should be included in these databases. The first theory holds that by virtue of a conviction, offenders forfeit the Fourth Amendment right to be free from unreasonable searches and seizures. This forfeiture-of-rights theory would confine the databases to convicted offenders, but it cannot be squared with settled constitutional principles. The second theory holds that because convicted offenders are more likely to reoffend than are other groups, they pose a special risk that justifies the incursion on their Fourth Amendment rights that might be necessary to acquire their DNA. Although this recidivism theory may seem more protective of individual liberties, it is not: It fails to constrict coverage to convicted offenders or even to arrestees.

The second part of the chapter considers extensions of coverage to various groups of people not convicted of crimes. It suggests that the Constitution may permit DNA to be collected from persons who have only been arrested and even from many who have been neither convicted nor arrested.

The third part of the chapter questions the desirability of limiting database coverage to convicted offenders or to convicted offenders and arrestees (or "suspects"). It notes that by restricting coverage to these groups, we are fast producing a racially distorted system in which, however lawfully the DNA samples are taken, they are taken disproportionately from members of racial minorities. We conclude that a population-wide database would be more effective and fairer than any system in which conviction or arrest is the threshold for database inclusion, and we indicate how such a system can be structured to protect personal privacy.

If Only Offender Profiles Are Included, Which Offenses Should Trigger Inclusion?

DNA profiles of convicted sex offenders are obvious candidates for inclusion in DNA databases. Indeed, most states began by authorizing databases limited to sex-offender profiles as part of their general effort to better protect women and children from sexual assault. Given the general abhorrence of sex offenders, together with the popular image of rapists as sexual predators who strike again and again and the ubiquity of potentially incriminating biological evidence in most rape cases, databases of convicted sex-offender records were not especially controversial.[1]

However, it soon became difficult to confine to this group the statutory authority to take DNA samples. First, the data never supported the view that recidivism is dramatically higher for sex offenders in general than for other categories of offenders. To the contrary, recidivism rates are similar or even higher for other offender groupings.[2] Second, potentially incriminating DNA evidence is hardly peculiar to sex crimes. Traces of blood, saliva, hair, and other DNA-bearing material are left at the scene of many types of crimes.[3] Finally, although sexual assault is among the most detested of crimes, the public does not have high regard for murderers, burglars, and petty thieves either.

The result is pressure to extend the coverage of the databases to all violent felons—and then to all felons and many misdemeanants (see chapter 16). Defining the point at which the collection of DNA profiles should stop requires a theory for including profiles in the database in the first place. Two such theories can be found in case law on the constitutionality of offender databases. One we call the *forfeiture-of-rights theory*. It holds that upon criminal conviction, individuals forfeit any right they might otherwise enjoy to be free from having their DNA typed and the resulting profile placed on file.[4] But this notion of "forfeiture" is a conclusion in search of an argument. To be sure, a conviction at a trial in which the defendant is afforded due process of law may trigger the most serious of punishments—from deprivation of life, to loss of liberty, to loss of property. The Constitution explicitly countenances these punishments.[5] But there are limits to what other deprivations of liberty or property are constitutionally permissible. As the Supreme Court explained in *Hudson v. Palmer*,[6] "prisoners [must] be accorded those rights not fundamentally inconsistent with imprisonment itself or incompatible with the objectives of incarceration." The state could hardly provide that a citizen convicted of even the most heinous crime thereby forfeits the right to free speech,[7] the privilege against self-incrimination,[8] or the plethora of other rights secured by the Constitution.[9]

How, then, could the bare fact of conviction bring a forfeiture of the right to be free from unreasonable searches and seizures? It is true that in *Hudson*, a narrow majority of the Court, in upholding random "shakedown" searches of prison cells, wrote that "the Fourth Amendment proscription against unreasonable searches does not apply within the confines of the prison cell."[10] The reason, however, was not that those convicted of a crime lose their Fourth Amendment rights. It was that "privacy rights for prisoners in their individual cells simply cannot be reconciled with the concept of incarceration and the needs and objectives of penal institutions."[11]

This is not to say that individuals who have been convicted of crimes must be treated as if they had not been. For example, unless there is some right to be free from surveillance in public places, the police could decide to engage in more-intense public surveillance of ex-convicts on the theory that they pose greater risks to public safety—just as they could decide to keep a close watch on teenagers hanging out in groups. A prior conviction also can be a factor in determining whether there is probable cause to arrest an ex-convict suspected of another crime, and at trial, prior convictions often are admitted into evidence. Nevertheless, in itself, a conviction does not strip a person of the Fourth Amendment's protection against unreasonable searches, and there is no reason to view every postconviction search as reasonable.[12] In sum, if convicts forfeit their Fourth Amendment rights, it must be for some reason beyond the mere fact of conviction or imprisonment.

Thus, a second justification for convicted-offender DNA databases is woven through the court opinions that find them permissible in the face of Fourth Amendment challenges. This is a *predictivist* theory: If persons convicted at least once are more likely to commit future crimes for which DNA evidence might be found than are those with no such criminal histories, then including DNA profiles of samples taken when these offenders are convicted would be expected to help—perhaps substantially—to deter and solve crimes. This theory thus distinguishes criminals on the ground that they pose greater risks.[13] It requires us to look at the connection between "collection crimes" (those that trigger the collection of DNA upon conviction) and "target" or "traceable offenses" (those for which biological trace evidence might be found). For a crime to qualify as a collection crime, the probability that a person guilty of the collection crime (C) will commit (or has committed) any target crime (T) must exceed the probability that a person who has not committed any instance of C will commit (or has committed) T. In other words, C must be a risk factor for one or more target crimes, meaning that individuals who are convicted for a collection offense C are a greater risk for committing a target offense T than people who are not guilty of the collection offense C.

The logic of the predictivist theory for limiting DNA databases to some subset of convicted offenders can be stated neatly, but it is difficult to apply. The justification turns on (1) the likelihood of future crime, by category of current conviction, as well as (2) the likelihood that the scenes of future crimes committed by offenders of any given type will present investigators with incriminating DNA evidence. Currently available data on these probabilities are sketchy, and it proves difficult to limit the sweep of the predictivist argument to convicted offenders. A later arrest, upon probable cause to believe the arrestee has committed a crime, is more likely among those who have been arrested at some point in the past, and prior arrest generally has some predictive value, whether or not a conviction follows. But there are many predictors of who will engage in future crimes, some of them more powerful than prior arrest or prior conviction. Dysfunctional family or neighborhood, disengagement from labor market or school, past antisocial acts, age, gender, and a host of other personal and environmental factors are, particularly in combination, statistical predictors of future criminal conduct.[14] Thus, the predictivist theory offers no satisfactory basis for separating people who have been convicted of crimes (or who have been arrested) from other people who carry comparable or even greater probabilities of leaving incriminating traces of DNA behind in the commission of a future crime.

If the simple forfeiture-of-rights theory is untenable because a convict does not lose all civil rights as a result of the verdict against him, and if the predictivist theory tends to justify much more inclusive databases, what principle remains to confine the databases to convicted offenders? If inclusion were to hinge on conviction, not arrest, then perhaps the fact of a conviction could properly be used as a side constraint on predictivism. That is, one might acknowledge that there is some reason to include an individual's profile in the database whenever there is an elevated probability of that person's subsequently committing a crime of a type for which incriminating DNA evidence is sometimes found by investigators, but that it would be unfair to do so unless the individual at least once before has been found guilty of some crime.

This side-constraint argument sounds promising, but it too fails. Criminal punishment is a social practice of blaming and imposing significant burdens on individuals in response to their doing what a legislature has declared sufficiently wrong to deserve official censure and punishment.[15] It is appropriate to insist that these harms not be imposed on an individual in the absence of a fair adjudication establishing that the individual committed the crime with which he is charged.[16] But acquiring DNA profiles and storing them in a searchable database looks very little like punishment, for which conviction is a prerequisite. The bodily intrusion required to extract the information can be kept to a minimum by using saliva, buccal swabs (from the inside of the cheek), or a laser-based device that samples blood without leaving a mark. As we explain later, the loci used to type the DNA can be limited to those that are no more socially meaningful or potentially stigmatizing than a simple fingerprint. Rather than constituting a criminal sanction, collecting and storing DNA identification profiles in a database is a form of discovering and remembering information about someone. It neither communicates condemnation nor burdens individual autonomy as do punishments authorized by the criminal law.

This is not to say that burdens could not flow from one's inclusion in a DNA identification database. Human error will inevitably cause a database sample to be mistyped or mislabeled in a way that raises suspicion about or produces an accusation against an innocent person whose profile is erroneously matched to a crime scene sample, but the already established practice of extracting fresh samples from suspects identified by database searches greatly reduces the chance of accusation, conviction, and punishment of innocent persons. Of course, an initial false accusation entails some burden on a suspect even if it is quickly dispelled, but pursuing leads that turn out to be unproductive is not forbidden by the important principle that the state may not punish the innocent.[17] Indeed, that principle supports thorough investigations, and any thorough investigation creates burdens for individuals about whom investigators have initial suspicions. As we explain later in the chapter, innocent persons are far more likely to be burdened by suspicion and false accusation if we lack a comprehensive DNA identification database than if we use one.

In short, inclusion of an individual's DNA profile in a forensic database simply is not punishment and need not carry any stigma of criminality unless we make it so by continuing to restrict coverage to persons arrested for or convicted of crimes. There is not a persuasive argument that under constitutional or other principles, a felony or other conviction is essential to inclusion. It therefore is prudent to consider in what ways the databases might become more inclusive, and what advantages and disadvantages extended DNA databases might bring.

Which Other Groups Might Be Included?

Police Suspects and Volunteers

Some suspects give samples "voluntarily" when asked to do so by the police. For example, on July 4, 1992, someone killed Sean Googin next to Cazenovia Lake in upstate New York, took his body out into the water in an aluminum canoe, weighted his fatigue jacket with rocks from shore, then left him in a grave of lake grass. State police combed the area and quizzed local residents. They took blood from about fifty citizens, some of them possible suspects, others hometown kids who wanted to help solve the killing of one of their neighbors. "No one, not one, ever refused us in Cazenovia," said the senior investigator. "They couldn't roll up their sleeves fast enough."[18]

Of course, not all suspects are so cooperative. But DNA often can be acquired through a court order based on probable cause or the lesser standard of reasonable suspicion.[19] Inasmuch as any invasion of bodily integrity and informational privacy is complete once the sample is collected and analyzed, a strong argument can be made that the state has the constitutional power to add such lawfully acquired profiles to a DNA database for use in unrelated investigations, even when the typing of a suspect's or volunteer's DNA excludes him from further suspicion in the case for which it is collected.[20] In essence, the argument is that there is no search when a lawfully acquired profile is entered in a DNA database or is compared to profiles from unsolved crimes.[21]

Even elimination samples could end up in databases.[22] For example, many of the men tested in the Cazenovia Lake case were not considered suspects. Could the police create a database of such local residents for possible use in future investigations? Or consider a rape case in which a semen stain is found on the bed where the rape occurred. The prosecution may need to eliminate the victim's boyfriend or husband as the possible source of that stain so that it can be attributed to the defendant without equivocation. If the victim's partner consents, as is typical, and there is no discussion of what will be done with the information afterward, does the Fourth Amendment allow the state to add it to a database?

The answer would be in the affirmative if an "initial-voluntariness" standard applies. Under an approach based on this standard, the pivotal question is whether the individual voluntarily supplied the sample when it was taken. If so, there was constitutionally sufficient consent to the initial search, and the police may make subsequent use of the resulting information without seeking a magistrate's approval. In contrast, an approach based on a "limited-scope-of-consent" standard asks not merely whether the initial consent was the product of illegitimate coercion, but also whether there was consent, explicit or implicit, to the subsequent use of the sample. Cases can be found that seem to support both approaches.

The Initial-Voluntariness Standard In the context of the search of a car in which stolen checks were found under the rear seat, the Supreme Court held in *Schneckloth v. Bustamonte*[23] that consent is effective as long as it is not coerced.[24] Unlike a waiver of rights at trial, which must be "knowing" and "intelligent," consent to a search need not be based on complete information. Indeed, in *Washington v. State* the Supreme Court of Florida held that police may trick suspects into giving DNA samples for one investigation by asking them to provide them for unrelated investigations. Alice Berdat, a ninety-three-year-old woman, was murdered in her bedroom. She had been badly beaten and vaginally and anally raped. Anthony Washington was imprisoned at a work release center two miles from the woman's home. He did not show up at his job during the time of the rape, and he sold Berdat's gold watch to a coworker. The detective investigating the murder did not tell Washington that he suspected him of this murder. Instead, he asked Washington for blood and hair samples to use in an unrelated sexual-battery case. Washington provided these samples. When the state sought to use the samples in the murder case, Washington moved to suppress them. The trial court denied the motion, and Washington was convicted of the murder, burglary, and sexual battery. The Supreme Court of Florida affirmed the conviction, reasoning as follows: "Washington stated that he understood his rights, orally waived them, and freely and voluntarily provided [the detective] with hair and blood samples. . . . [O]nce the samples were validly obtained, albeit in an unrelated case, the police were not restrained from using the samples as evidence in the murder case."[25]

This result is consistent with decisions of the U.S. Supreme Court in Fifth Amendment cases in which police obtain information while interrogating suspects without informing them of the true purpose of the interrogation[26] or by feeding them false information.[27] Thus the legality of using undercover agents and sting operations without prior judicial approval based on probable cause rests on the premise that the government can secure information by trickery, or at the very least, without disclosing all the facts that a citizen might wish to know.[28]

The Limited-Scope-of-Consent Standard   However, the issue in *Schneckloth* was not the scope of consent. It was whether the consent to the search of the car then and there—a search of well-defined scope and duration—was valid notwithstanding the lack of a *Miranda*-like warning that would have revealed that the police had no right to search without consent. *Schneckloth* merely holds that the validity of such consent is measured by a totality-of-the-circumstances test for voluntariness.[29] There was no ambiguity about the extent of the search to which consent was given; indeed, the occupant of the car opened the glove compartment and trunk for the police. *Washington* involves the separate question of whether, having consented to give up the samples for one use (the sexual-battery case), the suspect runs the risk that the state will make a second use of them (in the murder cases).

It is tempting to suggest that the second use is permissible under the general principle that once the state acquires physical evidence legitimately, the Fourth Amendment does not bar it from subsequent uses of the same evidence. This principle rests on the theory that the invasion of privacy or liberty lies in the initial intrusion or seizure. The additional use may have adverse consequences to the defendant, but it is not itself a further invasion of privacy or liberty. It is, for example, reasonable to hold that information legitimately discovered in the search of an apartment pursuant to a warrant based on probable cause with respect to one crime also may be used in the investigation of a subsequent crime. After all, the entry into the apartment is complete and fully justified by the warrant.

Arguably, this subsequent-use theory breaks down when applied to consent-based searches. The invasion of privacy may be complete when the consenting individual allows the police access to property or gives them a bodily sample, but the justification is that the individual has elected not to invoke the right to be free from unreasonable searches and seizures. This justification may not be apposite when the consent is limited to a particular use. In that situation, the argument goes, the search cannot extend beyond the initial scope of consent (without subsequent consent or a court order).

The problem with this somewhat formal analysis is that the consent exception to the general requirement of a warrant based on probable cause flows from the reasonableness clause of the Fourth Amendment rather than from the doctrine of waiver. The basic teaching of *Schneckloth* remains: Voluntariness, not informed consent, establishes that a warrantless search is constitutionally reasonable, at least in most contexts. To be sure, there may be unusual situations in which an individual must know of the contemplated secondary uses of a DNA sample for putative consent to be valid, but the use of the sample in *Washington* in the murder case as well as in the sexual-battery case does not seem to be one of them. It seems fair to say that unless a suspect is explicit about the limited scope of his consent in providing a sample, he runs the risk that the police will use the sample in more than one investigation. But law enforcement's legitimacy might be compromised if, without explicit consent, the state were routinely to add profiles from "voluntary" samples to DNA identification databases—even if the Constitution permits it, and even though doing so would benefit public safety. Should the police do so? The objection has its greatest force with regard to pure elimination samples: samples taken from individuals who were never suspected of wrongdoing and may have provided the samples to fulfill what they perceived to be their civic duty who could find themselves entangled in unrelated investigations. And if it is decided that law enforcement officials may retain profiles from such samples for use in future investigations, a further question arises: Should police seeking an elimination sample be clear that the DNA profile resulting from the sample will be available for use in future investigations? Should a form be required (much like a *Miranda* warning) that states, in effect, "I consent to having my DNA profile included in a database that will be used in future criminal investigations"? Or would such consent be an empty formality, not voluntary at all, since many people who are approached by the police reasonably assume that if they do not consent, they will continue to be suspects in the cases then under investigation?[30] In our view, whenever police seek consent for DNA sampling, a clear record of the scope of consent at the outset is desirable, and the fear that refusal to cooperate will heighten or create suspicions does not rise to the level of coercion that would vitiate consent under the normal voluntariness standard.

Arrestees

Some states authorize sampling and typing DNA even without consent or a court order whenever an individual is arrested for one of the offenses specified in the authorizing statute.[31] Various arguments have been advanced to show the constitutionality of this practice.[32] For instance, lower courts have long recognized a "true identity" exception to the warrant and probable-cause requirements of the Fourth Amendment. They have always held that the state may create and store photographic and fingerprint records that establish a permanent record of the identity of all arrested individuals. Although the DNA molecule itself differs from a fingerprint in that it could reveal significant hereditary conditions or propensities to contract certain diseases, a DNA type need be no more informative than an ordinary fingerprint. For example, the thirteen core STR loci used in current criminal-offender databases are noncoding, nonregulatory loci that are not linked to any genes in a way that would permit one to discern from them any socially stigmatizing conditions.[33] The profile of an individual's DNA molecule that is stored in a properly constructed DNA identification database (like CODIS) is a series of numbers. The numbers have no meaning except as a representation of molecular sequences at DNA loci that are not indicative of an individual's personal traits or propensities.[34] In this sense, the CODIS thirteen-STR profile is very much like a social security number, though it is longer and is assigned by chance, not by the federal government. In itself, the series of numbers can tell nothing about a person.[35] But because the sequence of numbers is so likely to be unique (with the exception of those of identical twins), it can be linked to identifiers (such as name, date of birth, social security number) and used to determine the source of DNA found in the course of criminal investigations or to identify human remains or persons who are lost or missing.

If the Constitution allows the police to keep a fingerprint or a photograph as a biometric identifier, as many courts have held, it is hard to see why they cannot keep a DNA profile properly limited to vacuous loci. Once the state legitimately possesses the DNA record of an arrestee, it requires no further information from the individual to examine a database of DNA types found in the crime scene evidence from unsolved crimes to ascertain whether any match the profile. Thus, using the arrestee's profile to query the database for a matching type would not be a new search or seizure within the meaning of the Fourth Amendment. Neither would it be a new search or seizure to add that profile, for use in future criminal investigations, to others taken from arrestees or convicted offenders.

Two recent Supreme Court cases cloud this simple analysis, however. Under *City of Indianapolis v. Edmond*[36] and *Ferguson v. City of Charleston*,[37] the fact that a warrantless search could have been conducted for an administrative purpose and its fruits used to prove a criminal charge is not necessarily sufficient to dispense with the need for a warrant and probable cause. In *Edmond*, the Court struck down a program in which police used dogs to sniff for drugs in vehicles pulled over in groups at fixed roadblocks. Distinguishing sharply between "highway safety interests and the general interest in crime control," the majority reasoned that "[b]ecause the primary purpose of the Indianapolis narcotics checkpoint program is to uncover evidence of ordinary criminal wrongdoing, the program contravenes the Fourth Amendment."[38] In *Ferguson*, the Court invalidated a program in which a state university hospital tested urine samples from pregnant women for cocaine and reported positive results to the police so that those women, fearing prosecution, would be induced to participate in substance abuse counseling offered as an alternative to criminal prosecution. Again, the majority of the Court emphasized "the relevant primary purpose," which was said to be " 'the arrest and prosecution of drug-abusing mothers.' "[39]

Edmond and *Ferguson* do not repeal the principle that police may make an additional use of lawfully acquired information, but they do reveal that the additional-use doctrine does not insulate from the warrant requirement a multipurpose program whose primary purpose is the enforcement of the criminal law. Certainly, the Indianapolis police could have employed roadblocks to check for intoxicated drivers if those roadblocks conformed to established Supreme Court requirements for roadblocks having this purpose.[40] While conducting this check, they could have brought a drug-sniffing dog near the driver's vehicle; after all, the use of a dog to detect the odor of narcotics is not a search.[41] Therefore, the dissent argued, "[t]he State's use of a drug-sniffing dog, according to the Court's holding, annuls what is otherwise plainly constitutional."[42] To which the majority responded: "the constitutional defect of the program is that its primary purpose is to advance the general interest in crime control."[43] Likewise, the *Ferguson* Court focused on "programmatic purpose"[44] and emphasized that "the direct and primary purpose of [the] policy was to generate evidence for law enforcement purposes."[45] In bold, *Edmond* and *Ferguson* indicate that where the *primary purpose* of a *program* involving searches or seizures is to generate evidence for criminal prosecutions, the Fourth Amendment ordinarily requires a warrant supported by probable cause.

Ordinary law enforcement would appear to be the primary purpose of a program requiring arrestees to provide DNA samples, typing those samples at standard forensic loci, and including the profiles in an identification database that can be searched for a profile matching DNA recovered in connection with unsolved past (or future) crimes.[46] By itself, the fact that an additional purpose of such a database would be administrative maintenance of unalterable biometric identifiers of those who have been arrested would not automatically make the program permissible. Under *Edmond* and *Ferguson*, if the primary purpose is still law enforcement, the program would need to be justified on another theory.[47]

Such a theory is readily available. Stopping drivers and searching automobiles for narcotics and testing women for cocaine use represent substantially greater intrusions on privacy than sampling individuals' DNA and typing it at the normal forensic loci. A DNA identification database can be structured to respect most individual privacy interests, and it can be administered fairly. Because there are powerful crime-control reasons for a state to establish arrestee DNA databases, it is neither heretical nor misguided to ask whether the Supreme Court will in due course recognize an exception to the warrant requirement for biometric identifiers like fingerprints and DNA profiles.

The answer turns on the Court's balancing of competing interests. The pivotal factors are the gravity of the privacy invasion, the practicality and value of requiring advance judicial approval and individual suspicion, and the importance of the government interests advanced by the database system. Although the point is surely debatable, a case can be made that this balance tips in favor of allowing arrestee DNA profiles to be retained in DNA databases even if no conviction results from the arrests.[48]

Of course, such a judgment does not imply that it would be desirable to collect and retain DNA profiles of arrestees. It simply means that the Constitution does not necessarily preclude it. As we point out in the next part of the chapter, there are significant drawbacks to using arrest as the threshold for acquiring database profiles.

Indirect Acquisition by the State

Shed DNA   Thus far, we have discussed classes of people whose DNA the police may acquire directly from them. But without giving it a thought, we all leave trails of DNA behind as we move through the world. New York police have taken a DNA sample from a suspect's abandoned coffee cup[49] and from saliva that a homeless man spit on the street.[50] In New Zealand, police extracted DNA from a drinking straw in a milkshake that a man was seen enjoying in a shopping mall just before he committed an armed robbery. (Checking the unsolved case database of samples led to his being charged with twenty-eight other offenses.)[51] In Chicago, police pocketed the butt of a cigarette they supplied to a suspect during an interrogation.[52]

If DNA or "genetic information" is the "property" of the individual in whose cells it is found, as a few state statutes declare, is collecting and analyzing the DNA found on the cup, the sidewalk, the straw, and the cigarette in the cases just mentioned an interference with this ownership interest?[53] The meaning of "ownership" in this context is opaque.[54] If I am struck by an automobile on a public street and bleed on the crosswalk, does that mean that I can prevent everyone else from taking a few drops or demand that the blood be returned by the street sweeper who wipes it up?

Even if one accepts the proposition that a DNA sample left in a public place, or its profile, is in some sense the property of the individual from whom it originated, the Fourth Amendment does not bar the state from acquiring it.[55] If a robber being pursued by the police drops the keys to his apartment but outruns the police, they may pick up the keys, and the state may use them to show that a person who later is apprehended is indeed the robber who eluded capture. Similarly, shed DNA constitutionally can be taken to the laboratory and analyzed, and the profile placed in a database.[56]

Relinquished DNA Nearly three hundred million DNA samples sit in tissue repositories in the United States.[57] Police agencies under public and political pressure to remove a serial killer from the streets will, in time, seek access to these samples, not just for specific investigations, but also to include profiles of them in law enforcement data banks. Here, too, a respectable argument can be made that, for better or worse, the Constitution poses no serious barrier. In *United States v. Miller*,[58] the Supreme Court held that when a person voluntarily relinquishes checks and deposit slips to a bank, subpoenas requiring the bank to produce these materials do not intrude "into any area in which [the defendant] had a protected Fourth Amendment interest." Are medical records any different? Lower courts have reached conflicting results,[59] but *Miller* is not easily distinguished.[60]

In sum, under existing doctrine, the Fourth Amendment is quite porous to determined efforts by police to acquire the DNA of specific individuals and of large classes of individuals. If police are thought likely to abuse this power, legislation to limit such investigative efforts is called for. However, the true privacy interest in one's DNA identification profile is thin. With our whole DNA (not just the identification profile) so accessible to law enforcement, in law and in fact, it is prudent to ask whether our privacy interest in that DNA would be better protected by deliberate, careful creation of a population-wide database of DNA identification profiles, unrelated to medical or other records of our affairs, specifically and exclusively for the state's investigation of crime, natural disasters, and missing-persons cases.

The Prospect of Universality

One Possible Path to a Population-Wide Database

Creating a national identification database all at once would be prohibitively expensive today, even if we had the laboratory capacity to do it. But DNA-typing technology is advancing at a pace reminiscent of Moore's law for microprocessor capacity, which has made the personal computer a fixture on every desk.[61] Soon it will be feasible to create a DNA identification record for everyone, at least prospectively. For example, it would be easy to extract identification profiles as an adjunct to public health service programs that for many years have screened blood samples from almost all newborns to identify infants with treatable genetic diseases.[62] The identification profiles could be transmitted to a single, secure national database. To the extent that additional sampling would be necessary—to include immigrants or citizens born abroad, for example—these samples could be destroyed as soon as the typing is complete. In fact, an instrument could be built that would extract an identifying profile and destroy the sample at the same time. Proper procedures for sampling the DNA, extracting the identifying profile, and immediately destroying the sample would protect everyone's genetic privacy.

The loci used for such identification profiles would be limited to sequences that have no relationship to health or other physical or mental traits and propensities. As discussed earlier in the chapter, each profile would be a set of digits devoid of any special meaning, comparable to a social security or passport number. Access to the database would be limited to law enforcement personnel investigating specific crimes in which DNA trace evidence already has been found. Law enforcement agencies would not need—and should not be permitted—to handle, much less retain, the samples.

A system of this sort would resemble, to the greatest extent possible, a digitized collection of identifying features very much like ordinary fingerprints. However, it would be far more useful in deterring potential offenses, in generating investigative leads, and in exonerating the innocent.[63] There would be no need to resort to inefficient DNA dragnets of entire neighborhoods, as have been conducted in California, Florida, Louisiana, Michigan, New York, and elsewhere,[64] nor would there be need for investigators to infer probable racial or ethnic status from crime scene DNA samples, as some observers fear. Not only would a comprehensive database be valuable for public-safety purposes, but it could also be useful in identifying bodily remains in mass disasters or other tragedies and in returning missing persons to their families.[65]

Yet almost all the authors represented in this volume oppose, implicitly or explicitly, a population-wide database. Opinions range from hostility toward all DNA databases (see chapter 9)[66] to a recognition that universal coverage has some advantages that make a comprehensive database a serious policy option (see chapter 4). We believe that a properly designed and administered national database might well be the best solution to the coverage question with which this chapter began. It would entail but a limited intrusion on individual freedom and privacy while advancing both public safety and racial evenhandedness in the criminal justice system and serving as a firewall against far greater intrusions on privacy by law enforcement authorities pawing through medical and other records looking for a match to DNA found at the scenes of notorious crimes. We began with no enthusiasm for the idea, but the more we considered the drawbacks of the likely alternatives and the plausibility of procedures for database creation that would limit government's access to sensitive genetic information, the more we found it to be a viable policy choice.[67] To explain our conclusion, we survey the arguments that have been made against a national database, then consider in more detail the advantages such a database offers over the current system.

Opposition to a Population-Wide Database

Public Acceptance   Opponents of broad DNA databases sometimes suggest that it is pointless to consider a population-wide database because the public opposes it.[68] They note that in the 1940s, Congress did not adopt proposed legislation providing for universal fingerprinting and identity cards.[69] Since the American public today regards DNA with a mixture of suspicion, horror, and awe, it is said, a population-wide DNA database is too far from popular acceptance to be worth considering.[70] However, a database constructed in the manner we have described offers pronounced advantages over the present system of incremental expansions of law enforcement databases. The prospect should not be dismissed on the basis of surmises about public opinion, for public opinion is a fickle master and an unreliable determinant of future policy.[71] Certainly, public opinion has undergone sea changes on issues such as sexual mores, narcotics and the use of alcohol and tobacco, capital punishment, and gun control. The public has heard almost no serious debate about the desirability or noxiousness of a population-wide DNA identification database. Until such a debate takes place, we should not shy away from examining the merits and demerits of even the most expansive database.

Constitutionality   A second argument against pursuit of a population-wide database is that even if it were popular, it would be unconstitutional. The most powerful constitutional challenge flows from the Fourth Amendment requirement, discussed in the chapter's first section, that government searches be reasonable, which the Supreme Court has interpreted to require a judicial warrant based on probable cause, unless the search lies within one of the "specifically established and well-delineated exceptions" to the warrant requirement.[72] Yet in some respects, a population-wide database of the type we have described would be easier to defend under Supreme Court precedent than are conventional convicted-offender databases.

For both types of database, a threshold question is whether the acquisition of DNA would even amount to a "search" within the meaning of the Fourth Amendment. There is no doubt that blood samples taken from infants by governmental edict would "constitute searches of 'persons,' and depend antecedently upon seizures of 'persons.'"[73] But what if the DNA were acquired by applying a sticky pad to the infant's skin to acquire some exfoliating epidermal cells without even a scratch? Would the reduced level of bodily invasion and the fact that these cells are constantly exposed to the public and being shed from the surface of the body lead a court to hold that no search is involved? In *Palmer v. State*,[74] the Indiana Supreme Court reasoned that the warrantless acquisition of the defendant's fingerprints during his trial did not constitute a seizure forbidden by the Fourth Amendment because "fingerprints are an identifying factor readily available to the world at large." Other courts have held that shining an ultraviolet lamp on a suspect's skin to expose chemicals transferred from stolen money is not a search.[75]

One might hope that the Supreme Court's latest encounter with defining a search in *Kyllo v. United States* [76] would clarify the viability of such a "public exposure" theory. In *Kyllo*, a federal agent used an infrared detector to find that "the roof over the garage and a side wall of petitioner's home were relatively hot compared to the rest of the home and substantially warmer than neighboring homes in the triplex. . . . Based on tips from informants, utility bills, and the thermal imaging, a federal magistrate judge issued a warrant authorizing a search of [Kyllo's] home, and the agents found an indoor growing operation involving more than 100 plants." Before trial, Kyllo moved to suppress the evidence on the ground that the thermal imaging required a warrant. When the motion was denied, he entered a conditional guilty plea and appealed. The Ninth Circuit Court of Appeals ultimately affirmed the denial of Kyllo's motion to suppress, reasoning that defendant had neither a subjective nor an objectively reasonable expectation that "amorphous 'hot spots' on the roof and exterior wall" would go unobserved. In other words, according to the court of appeals, there was no search.

A sharply divided Supreme Court reversed the appeals court's decision. At first blush, this reversal seems to undermine the view that inspecting materials on the surface of the body is not a search. After all, if the use of an instrument to capture infrared rays coming from the surface of a house is a search, it might seem that the use of an instrument to capture and analyze DNA on the surface of the body is as well. However, the rationale of *Kyllo* is quite limited. Justice Antonin Scalia's opinion for a majority of five Justices looks to the historically recognized zone of privacy in which government surveillance is prohibited. Apparently assuming that eighteenth-century constables would have had to enter the house to detect heat sources—a trespass that is the very paradigm of a search—the majority announced that the infrared scan also was a search. As the Court put it, "obtaining by sense-enhancing technology any information regarding the interior of the home that could not otherwise have been obtained without physical 'intrusion into a constitutionally protected area,' constitutes a search—at least where (as here) the technology in question is not in general public use." In other words, *Kyllo* establishes no more than that the use of technology that is functionally equivalent to trespassing into a home to acquire information is a search. This result, the Court suggested, is necessary for "the preservation of that degree of privacy against government that existed when the Fourth Amendment was adopted." To hold otherwise, the majority insisted, would "permit police technology to erode the privacy [originally] guaranteed by the Fourth Amendment."

In contrast, the Fourth Amendment's protections against searches (as opposed to seizures) of the person lack "roots deep in the common law."[77] As the *Schmerber* Court observed, in "dealing with intrusions into the human body rather than with state interferences with property relationships or private papers—'houses, papers, and effects'—we write on a clean slate."[78] Therefore, *Kyllo*'s functional-equivalence test does not dictate the conclusion that it is a search to take cells from the surface of a person's skin that are constantly being shed and to analyze the DNA they contain. Unlike infrared scanning that, in effect, places the police in the interior of a house, DNA sampling and analysis are not functionally equivalent to any eighteenth-century practice proscribed by the Fourth Amendment.

Even so, the sensitive nature of some of the information locked in the helices of the DNA molecule leads us to believe that DNA sampling is a Fourth Amendment search, even if the sample is obtained noninvasively.[79] Indeed, we find this argument persuasive. Our point here, however, is simply that the question is far from settled. Certainly, *Kyllo* does not dictate the outcome.

The same can be said of the next question in any Fourth Amendment analysis: If sampling DNA is a search, is it constitutionally reasonable? The reasonableness standard might well permit construction of a system of the type we have described. Taking DNA from newborns who are already in the hospital where their blood is routinely sampled does not detain them and would involve no additional search. With analysis restricted to suitable loci, the extracted profile could be used only for identification.[80] The Court's opinions in *Edmond* and *Ferguson* are less of a barrier here than they are to arrestee DNA databases. The primary purpose of acquiring DNA samples from newborns always has been, and would remain, screening for treatable genetic conditions such as phenylketonuria. And even if the primary purpose of the sampling were taken to be ordinary law enforcement, the argument advanced earlier in the chapter for a new exception to the warrant requirement would apply.[81] A "biometric exception" would be less problematic than other exceptions (such as the "automobile exception") that have become fixtures of Fourth Amendment jurisprudence.

How these questions ultimately will be resolved is exceedingly difficult to predict. Perhaps the Constitution forbids government typing for identification purposes of the DNA of anyone not convicted of a crime, or of anyone not arrested. Perhaps not. At this time, we simply cannot be sure that the Fourth Amendment guarantees that the line will be drawn at conviction, or even at arrest. Those who fear law enforcement control of a DNA identification database unless it is predicated on conviction or arrest may need to seek more predictable protection than the Fourth Amendment. If the general public comes to a clear and stable view that it is worth sacrificing the public-safety and racial-justice advantages of a comprehensive DNA identification database to limit possible state intrusions on our privacy and autonomy, then a comprehensive database will not come into existence. If the general public is ambivalent, if it remains uninformed about the likely consequences of pursuing or repudiating a comprehensive database, if the questions are not taken up in public and political discourse, or if false confidence is placed in a prediction about the future course of Fourth Amendment jurisprudence, then it is as likely as not that the nation will find itself, in time, with a near-universal DNA database that is *more* threatening to privacy than the one described here.[82]

A Nation of Suspects   A third objection to a universal database is that such a database would constitute a "step toward an Orwellian society"[83] that will make "us [into] a 'nation of suspects' and radically alter[] the relationship between the citizen and [the] government."[84] "Storing information on otherwise unsuspected individuals," it is said, "expresses an ethos of suspicion."[85] As rhetoric, this is powerful stuff, but its substance is fluffier. Privacy is an important value, but the privacy threat from digital records of DNA types that reveal nothing about a person's nature or status is not self-evident. Certainly, it bears no resemblance to George Orwell's dystopia in which the state monitored every conversation and action and responded to mere thoughts of disloyalty with profound "re-education." Establishing a system that has the ability to link individuals to crime scenes to the greatest possible extent without probing their minds or invading their homes or possessions does not make everyone a suspect in any meaningful or problematic sense. Indeed, a population-wide database should quickly limit the number of suspects—typically to a single person—in many crimes, and by promptly eliminating everyone else as viable suspects, reduce the burden on many individuals who would have been primary suspects without the database.

Loss of Anonymity   As Viktor Mayer-Schönberger observes in chapter 11, "privacy in itself is not a homogenous right, but a bundle of very different underlying values" (225). It is not privacy in general that is put at risk when the state has an ability to match found DNA with a profile retained in an identification database. It is not even autonomy. Rather, DNA databases threaten three forms of anonymity.

Temporal Anonymity   There is a largely unspoken assumption, deeply rooted in American history and culture, that if we are moved to do so, it is possible for us to leave the past behind and to reinvent ourselves in another place. But this seems a romantic, unrealistic prospect today. The lives we lead leave a trail in medical records, in credit card records, in school records, in employment files—in any records that link to our social security numbers, driver's license numbers, and the like. We can be found if the state, or anyone with means, really cares to find us. No doubt biometric identifiers, from fingerprints to facial-recognition systems, to iris scans, to DNA profiles, make it harder still to transform one's identity. But anonymity in the sense of re-creating one's identity—of riding into town, as it were, to start a new life without carrying the weight of the past—is a quixotism.

Conduct Anonymity   There is a second form of anonymity often worth protecting: the anonymity of those engaged in certain desirable conduct, such as making charitable donations, expressing unpopular opinions, or informing authorities of wrongdoing or dangerous situations. We sometimes protect such anonymity as a right guaranteed by the Constitution[86] or as a privilege codified by statute or established by common law.[87] But a population-wide DNA identification database maintained for law enforcement purposes would not interfere with those types of protections.

In other situations, conduct anonymity is an enemy of public safety. It is a rare offender who expects to be identified and apprehended when he or she commits a crime. If witnesses to offenses do not recognize the offenders, the offenders will likely elude apprehension. Knowing this, a person bent on crime who is anonymous in a place where the opportunity presents itself is undeterred. Conversely, there is no special trick to apprehending a burglar, a robber, or a hit-and-run driver (or deterring an otherwise motivated offender) whose name can be given to police by a passerby. To the extent that a comprehensive DNA identification database merely reduces anonymity for criminal conduct, it infringes no interest worthy of protection.

Spatial Anonymity   There is a particular form of conduct anonymity that is valued by nearly everyone in our culture and is likely to remain so: spatial anonymity— the ability to keep one's movements and location confidential. Spatial anonymity is not threatened by all biometric identification systems, but it is threatened by systems that can link individuals to particular locations. The shadowy figure disappearing into the London fog and the nondescript face lost among many in the crowd are anonymous. The ability to be at a particular place and time without revealing one's identity is vital to criminal enterprises, but ordinary individuals want to be free to visit a friend, enter a store, or take a drive into the country without being tracked by the government. Pervasive government surveillance that tracks one's locations at all times of the day and night would strip us of the "breathing room" in which our liberty takes shape: We require a private sphere of action in which to be ourselves, free from observation.

Nevertheless, a population-wide DNA identification database would not destroy all spatial anonymity—the confidentiality of one's movements could be preserved—since it is not feasible to reconstruct a person's travels by looking at DNA molecules. A comprehensive DNA identification database would not present the potential "abuse" of "twenty-four-hour surveillance of any citizen" that gave the Supreme Court momentary pause in the course of holding that the use of a radio beeper to track a car to a defendant's house did not even rise to the level of a search within the meaning of the Fourth Amendment.[88]

Still, the fact remains that it is technologically possible for a determined search for remnants of hair, saliva, or other DNA-bearing material to uncover traces of many peoples' DNA at crime scenes or other locations. For instance, there will be a loss of anonymity if and when police are able to deduce, from these biological traces, all the people who frequented the bedroom of a murder victim. This power to reconstruct past events, however partially, will be a invaluable to criminal investigators, but it must be recognized that it will diminish our spatial anonymity—the privacy of our movements—by reducing our ability to enter bedrooms (or other locations that might prove embarrassing) without risk of our presence there later being discovered.

Expense   A final objection to a population-wide database is that it would not be worth the cost, which might be thought to be immense. This cost would include the capital investment in biochemical and electronic devices for collecting, analyzing, storing, and accessing the data, as well as the labor cost of police and other personnel who would be needed to build and operate the system. However, these costs could be kept to a minimum with technology that types the identification loci at the same time that neonatal disease screening is performed and uploads the resulting biometric identification data to the national DNA identification database without law enforcement personnel's ever possessing or even handling the DNA itself. The marginal cost of creating records in such a system would not be zero, but it would be small. Suppose that the cost of the additional DNA testing of neonatal samples for law enforcement were one dollar per sample and that the marginal cost of operating the larger database were twenty-five cents per sample. At present, some four million babies are born every year in the United States. Even assuming (unrealistically) that population growth were to as much as double the annual number of births by the time a decision to implement a comprehensive database were made, the cost would be on the order of $10 million per year. Admittedly, marginal-cost projections of this sort are speculative, and ours could be quite optimistic. But if the actual costs were, say, even twenty times as great,[89] the annual marginal cost of the system would be $200 million, a cost that would be offset by savings as (1) the need to collect and analyze samples from convicted offenders diminishes; (2) expensive, area-wide, consent-based searches in notorious cases become unnecessary; and (3) more cases are resolved by database searches that cut the time of labor-intensive detective work. Considering that Congress has authorized hundreds of millions of dollars to help states process DNA evidence, the incremental cost of assembling a population-wide database prospectively is not obviously excessive. However, the cost-benefit judgment in this case requires some attention to the hard-to-monetize benefits in crime reduction and to the increased legitimacy in law enforcement that a comprehensive national database would bring. We turn, then, to the advantages associated with a population-wide DNA database.

Advantages of a Population-Wide Database

The current approach to creating law enforcement databases focuses exclusively on individuals' contacts with the criminal justice system. When a criminal conviction, an arrest, or a stop by traffic or foot patrol is the trigger for sampling a person's DNA, profiling it, and retaining that profile in a database for use in future criminal investigations, the database will be racially skewed and will fall far short of the full potential of DNA technology to exonerate innocent suspects, to identify the guilty, to protect victims of crime, and to assist in the identification of missing persons.[90]

Efficacy   Those who insist that it is sufficient for law enforcement purposes to record the DNA profiles only of those convicted of felonies are, perhaps without realizing it, proposing to sacrifice most of the preventative and investigative force of the technology. As explained in the first part of the chapter, the justification put forward for making felony conviction the threshold for inclusion in the DNA identification database is that the likelihood of further felony offenses is especially elevated among those previously convicted of a felony. However, 62 percent of those arrested and prosecuted for a felony have no prior felony conviction.[91] Furthermore, among those arrested and prosecuted for serious felonies, those arrested and prosecuted for rape are the least likely to have a prior felony conviction of any kind: Only about 30 percent have such a prior record, as compared to almost 50 percent for burglary.[92] A DNA database cannot deter a possible offender or lead to his apprehension before his profile is included in the database. Therefore, a convicted-felon database is of no help in deterring or investigating felonies committed by persons not previously convicted of a felony—and they are a majority of those arrested on felony charges.

Moving the criterion for database inclusion to felony arrests or to arrests of any type still excludes those responsible for a major proportion of all felony offenses. Of those arrested and prosecuted for serious felonies, 44 percent have never before been arrested on a felony charge, and about a third carry no arrest record at all.[93]

Thus substantial public-safety benefits would likely flow from investment in a population-wide database. We know that many offenders commit a number of crimes—sometimes a very large number—before they are convicted for the first time. We also know that from 1993 through 1998, when Virginia's convicted-offender database had under 30,000 samples, it generated between zero and thirteen hits per year. In 2002, with nearly 190,000 samples, it averaged over one hit every day.[94] In Great Britain, where the database reached 1.5 million profiles in February 2002, British criminal investigators were averaging 1,600 hits per week.[95] Many more hits would result from a truly comprehensive national system combined with more thorough collection and prompt analysis of crime scene DNA. When one considers the personal and social costs of the crimes that might be prevented, the balance might well favor the most inclusive database.[96]

Database Inclusiveness, Racial Justice, and the Legitimacy of Law   There can be no doubt that any database of DNA profiles will be dramatically skewed by race if the sampling and typing of DNA becomes a routine consequence of criminal conviction.[97] Without seismic changes in Americans' behavior or in the criminal justice system, nearly 30 percent of black males, but less than 5 percent of white males, will be imprisoned on a felony conviction at some point in their lives.[98] Arrest, prosecution, and conviction are so pervasive in black communities that, on any given day, a black American is five times more likely to be in jail than is a white,[99] and an adult black male is four times more likely to be under some form of correctional supervision,[100] six-and-a-half times more likely to be incarcerated somewhere,[101] and eight times more likely to be in prison[102] than his white counterpart.

Racial skewing of the existing DNA databases will be reduced somewhat if the legal authority to sample and type offenders' DNA continues to expand and comes to include the multitudes convicted of lesser (but more numerous) felonies and misdemeanors. Racial imbalance in the databases would be further reduced if, as leading law enforcement leaders have urged,[103] arrest rather than conviction becomes the occasion for sampling DNA and including profiles in the database. But the decrease in racial disparity would come not come from racial parity in arrest rates, for the annual arrest rate among blacks is more than two and a half times the white rate,[104] and a black man's lifetime chances of being arrested are more than double a white man's.[105] Rather, expanding the DNA databases to include arrestees would diminish the racial disparity by bringing many more whites into the databases, for about half of all males experience at least one misdemeanor or felony arrest in their lifetimes.[106]

Thus although a black man's relative chance of being included would be reduced from at least four times a white man's in a convicted-offender database to roughly twice a white man's in an arrestee database, about 90 percent of urban black males would be included if DNA were routinely sampled on arrest. Such an "arrest-only" database would have the look and feel of a universal DNA database for black males, whose already jaundiced view of law enforcement's legitimacy[107] is itself a threat to public safety.[108] White men would not likely be pleased either. Some would surely be offended by the racial imbalance in their favor, particularly one so redolent of past genetic discrimination, and many would be distressed to learn that absent dramatic change in their behavior or in police practices, at least half of them would have their DNA profiles entered into the database after being arrested for a felony or misdemeanor. If legislation gave arresting officers the authority to conduct DNA sampling when making arrests for traffic offenses, then a majority of the entire population might eventually find its way into the database.[109]

If legislation authorizing DNA sampling on arrest gave arresting officers discretion to sample DNA or not, the identification database coverage might well be reduced somewhat, but there is little comfort in the prospect of individual officers on the highways sampling DNA from those who strike them as likely perpetrators of other crimes while sending the rest on their way. Under those conditions, racial conflict in police encounters with civilians and racial disparities in the database would be likely to grow considerably worse. Neither would state legislatures be likely to make parsimonious decisions about which arrests permitted and which required DNA sampling. As is happening with convictions, if arrest becomes the threshold for inclusion in the databases, the pressure for comprehensive coverage (i.e., sampling of *all* those arrested) is likely to be nearly irresistible.[110]

The likely reach of an arrest-based database should give pause to anyone hoping to limit database coverage to a small fraction of the population. Inclusion in a DNA identification database of half or more of the male population and nearly all African American men is an odd result for a policy intended to limit government's control of samples and profiles of our DNA—and it is one that would further damage the legitimacy of the criminal law and of law enforcement agencies in areas in which public safety is most in disrepair.[111] Finally, the data on prevalence of arrest in the population should provoke skepticism about two propositions often advanced in opposition to a comprehensive identification database: (1) that it is financially and logistically feasible to sample DNA on arrest, but not feasible to sample everyone, and (2) that privacy interests will be substantially protected if DNA is taken and typed only from those who have been arrested.

In contrast, a population-wide DNA database could serve as at least a partial, much-needed antidote for the racial distortions that plague the criminal justice system. DNA evidence does not care about race. A database profile either does or does not match a particular crime scene sample. With a population-wide database, the identity of any individual whose DNA matches DNA found at a crime scene would be known—no matter what the race. Routine production of a short list of people whose DNA matches samples found at a crime scene thus could help counteract the presence or perception of racism in the investigation of crime. When a person is arrested and incriminating crime scene DNA evidence points to the guilt of another person whose DNA profile is in the database, prompt exoneration and release of the innocent person is likely to follow, regardless of the initial suspect's race or status. If an innocent defendant does go to trial in such a case, the crime scene DNA evidence and the results of the database search would be available, regardless of the defendant's race, to raise reasonable doubt about guilt.

This is not to say that a population-wide database would eliminate all racial inequities in law enforcement. Obviously it would not. For instance, Troy Duster argues in chapter 14 that even the most inclusive database will not cure the racial distortions that result from selectively enforcing drug laws against African Americans or from enforcing evenhandedly drug laws that have a disparate impact on them. He is, of course, correct. But to concede that a comprehensive DNA identification-only database is no panacea for the racial ills that plague the criminal justice system is not to deny its power to mitigate what has become a crippling problem. It is simply much fairer and more useful to include DNA identification profiles from all whites, and from all other groups, than it is to amass databases predominantly consisting of the profiles of African Americans and other minorities.

Conclusion

The current debate over the scope of DNA databases for law enforcement is myopic in its focus on which crimes should be collection offenses and at which stage in the criminal process DNA samples should be taken. In principle, it is not at all clear why the obligation to provide personally identifying DNA data should be restricted to those individuals who are swept into or punished by the criminal justice system. In practice, settling for a DNA identification database restricted to convicts, or to convicts and arrestees, is sure to aggravate racial polarization in society, undermine the legitimacy of law and law enforcement, and further compromise public safety by halting far short of the deterrent and investigative capability that a population-wide database would afford. Like the double helix of the DNA molecule, privacy and equality are intertwined in complex ways. When they are untangled and evaluated, the case for a population-wide DNA database is strong.

Notes

D. H. Kaye is Regents' Professor at the Arizona State University College of Law and a Fellow of the Center for the Study of Law, Science, and Technology. Michael E. Smith is professor of law at the University of Wisconsin. They served as reporter and chair, respectively, of the Legal Issues Working Group of the National Commission on the Future of DNA Evidence. The views expressed here are not those of the commission, the working group, or, as far as they know, anyone else. They thank Pat Langan and Stuart Sheingold for information on the prevalence of arrests and Burt Binenfeld for research assistance.

1. But see Paul R. Billings, ed., *DNA on Trial: Genetic Identification and Criminal Justice* (Woodbury, N.Y.: Cold Spring Harbor Laboratory Press, 1992).

2. For example, the Bureau of Justice Statistics examined the arrest and conviction records of a representative sample of all prisoners released in 1983 from prisons in eleven states. See Lawrence A. Greenfeld, *Sex Offenses and Offenders: An Analysis of Data on Rape and Sexual Assault* (Washington, D.C.: Bureau of Justice Statistics, U.S. Department of Justice, 1997), 26. For rapists, the rate of rearrest over the three-year period after release was 60 percent; their reconviction rate was 36 percent. For all violent offenders, the rates were still higher: 60 percent and 42 percent, respectively (Greenfeld, *Sex Offenses and Offenders*, 27; Katherine K. Baker, "Once a Rapist? Motivational Evidence and Relevancy in Rape Law," *Harvard Law Review* 110 [1997]: 578–580; Thomas J. Reed, "Reading Gaol Revisited: Admission of Uncharged Misconduct Evidence in Sex Offender Cases," *American Journal of Criminal Law* 21 [1993]: 149, 154–155; Paul R. Rice, "The Evidence Project: Proposed Revisions to the Federal Rules of Evidence with Supporting Commentary, Introduction," *Federal Rules Decisions* 171 [1997]: 479). However, these data are not sufficient to exclude the possibility that even if sex offenders are not more often recidivists, they commit a relatively larger number of offenses per recidivist in the follow-up period.

3. By 1999, the United Kingdom's Forensic Science Service was able to develop a DNA profile in 5 percent of all property crime samples, and most of the hits in the database for England and Wales now come from burglary and vehicle theft cases rather than from rapes or murders. "Forensics Help Trap 1,000 Car Thieves," *Bristol Evening Post*, June 27, 2001, 7; David Werrett, "The Strategic Use of DNA Profiling" available at 2001 WL 22486231. Early critics of DNA databases seemed unaware of the potential value of DNA analysis in such cases. See, e.g., Philip L. Bereano, "The Impact of DNA-Based Identification Systems on Civil Liberties," in *DNA on Trial: Genetic Identification and Criminal Justice*, ed. Paul R. Billings (Woodbury, N.Y.: Cold Spring Harbor Laboratory Press, 1992), 119, 121 ("[M]uch crime leaves no identifying tissue behind (e.g., burglary)").

4. Cf. *Jones v. Murray*, 962 F.2d 302, 306 (1992) ("With the person's loss of liberty upon arrest comes the loss of at least some, if not all, rights to personal privacy otherwise protected by the Fourth Amendment"); *Rise v. Oregon*, 59 F.3d 1556, 1560 (1995) ("[C]onvicted felons . . . do not have the same expectations of privacy in their identifying genetic information that 'free persons' have").

5. See U.S. Constitution, Amendments V and XIV.

6. *Hudson v. Palmer*, 468 U.S. 517, 523 (1984).

7. See, e.g., *Prison Legal News v. Cook*, 238 F.3d 1145 (2001) (holding unconstitutional a state policy prohibiting the receipt by inmates of standard-rate mail, as applied to subscription nonprofit organization mail); *Shaw v. Murphy*, 532 U.S. 223, 231 (2001) (recognizing that prisoners retain some First Amendment rights, but refusing to accord "special protection to . . . speech that includes legal advice").

8. See, e.g., *Lile v. McKune*, 224 F.3d 1175 (2000).

9. See *Hudson v. Palmer*, 468 U.S. 517, 523–524 (1984) (citations omitted):

Like others, prisoners have the constitutional right to petition the Government for redress of their grievances, which includes a reasonable right of access to the courts. . . . Prisoners must also be provided with "reasonable opportunities" to exercise their religious freedom guaranteed under the First Amendment. Similarly, they retain those First Amendment rights of speech "not inconsistent with [their] status as . . . prisoner[s] or with the legitimate penological objectives of the corrections system." They enjoy the protection of due process. And the Eighth Amendment ensures that they will not be subject to "cruel and unusual punishments." The continuing guarantee of these substantial rights to prison inmates is testimony to a belief that the way a society treats those who have transgressed against it is evidence of the essential character of that society.

See also *Turner v. Safley*, 482 U.S. 78 (1987).

10. *Hudson v. Palmer*, 526.

11. Ibid.

12. In *United States v. Knights*, 534 U.S. 112 (2001), the Supreme Court unanimously upheld a warrantless search of a probationer's apartment for explosives. The Court determined that the search satisfied the Fourth Amendment's "touchstone" of "reasonableness" because (1) the court granting probation imposed the condition that the convict submit to any search "by any . . . law enforcement officer," and (2) the officer here had "reasonable suspicion that a probationer subject to a search condition [was] engaged in criminal activity" involving

explosives. The condition of probation, the Court reasoned, produced "significantly diminished privacy interests," rendering reasonable suspicion rather than probable cause sufficient "to make the intrusion on the individual's privacy interest reasonable." Rather than rely on a pure forfeiture theory, the Court demanded individualized suspicion, and it explicitly avoided deciding "whether the probation condition so diminished, or completely eliminated Knights's reasonable expectation of privacy . . . that a search by a law enforcement officer without any individualized suspicion would have satisfied the reasonableness requirement of the Fourth Amendment." Ibid., n.6.

13. See *Jones v. Murray*, 962 F. 2d 302, 304 (1992).

14. See generally, e.g., David Farrington and Roger Tarling, eds., *Prediction in Criminology* (Albany: State University of New York Press, 1985); D. Gottfredson and M. Tonry, eds., *Prediction and Classification: Criminal Justice Decision Making* (Chicago: University of Chicago Press, 1987); Daniel S. Goodman, "Demographic Evidence in Capital Sentencing," *Stanford Law Review* 39 (1987); Jack F. Williams, "Process and Prediction: Return to a Fuzzy Model of Pretrial Detention," *Minnesota Law Review* 79 (1994).

15. See generally, e.g., Dan M. Kahan, "Social Influence, Social Meaning, and Deterrence," *Virginia Law Review* 83 (1997): 349.

16. See generally, e.g., Paul H. Robinson, "Punishing Dangerousness: Cloaking Preventive Detention as Criminal Justice," *Harvard Law Review* 114 (2001): 1429.

17. The risk of false accusations from database searches is a prudential consideration in designing and operating a law enforcement database. It is a reason to have strict quality control and assurance measures and to educate police and the public that a database hit is not the end of a criminal investigation. This makes it probable that a population-wide database will be administered more carefully than one restricted to the convicted or the arrested. See chapter 4 of this volume.

18. See Dick Case, "Trail of Blood in Worried Town," *Syracuse Post-Standard*, April 3, 2001, A7, available at 2001 WL 5563620. Even so, the case went unsolved until 2001, when the DNA profile of a man arrested in 1999 and convicted of sodomy was added to New York's statewide database.

19. See, e.g., *Bousman v. Iowa District Court for Clinton County*, 630 N.W.2d 789, 801 (explaining that although an "order [for oral swabs] must be supported by reasonable grounds to suspect that the subject of the order committed the crime under investigation[,] [p]robable cause to believe that the subject of the order actually committed the crime is not necessary."); *In Re Non-Testimonial Identification Order Directed to R. H.*, 762 A.2d 1239 (2000); *Doe v. Senechal*, 725 N.E.2d 225 (2000).

20. Cases reaching this conclusion include *Bickley v. State*, 489 S.E.2d 167 (1997); *People v. King*, 663 N.Y.S.2d 610, 614 (1997); *Smith v. State*, 734 N.E.2d 706, 709 (2000); *Wilson v. State*, 1268–1272.

21. Cf. *United States v. Calandra*, 414 U.S. 338, 354 (1974) (explaining that grand jury "[q]uestions based on illegally obtained evidence are only a derivative use of the product of a past unlawful search and seizure. They work no new Fourth Amendment wrong").

22. See Cecelia Crouse and David H. Kaye, "The Retention and Subsequent Use of Suspect, Elimination, and Victim DNA Samples or Records" (paper presented to the National Commission on the Future of DNA Evidence, Cambridge, Mass., November 3, 2000).

23. 412 U.S. 218 (1973).

24. However, the issue in *Schneckloth* was not the scope of consent. It was whether the consent to a search of well-defined scope and duration was valid notwithstanding the lack of a *Miranda*-like warning that would have informed the driver that the police had no right to search without his consent. Consequently, it can be argued that *Schneckloth* does not necessarily imply that a suspect assumes the risk that police will use a sample in unrelated investigations.

25. *Washington v. State*, 653 So.2d 362, 364 (Fla. 1994).

26. *Colorado v. Spring*, 479 U.S. 564 (1987).

27. E.g., *Oregon v. Mathiason*, 429 U.S. 492, 495–496 (1977) (per curiam) (officer's falsely telling suspect that suspect's fingerprints had been found at crime scene).

28. See, e.g., *Illinois v. Perkins*, 496 U.S. 292 (1990) ("*Miranda* forbids coercion, not mere strategic deception by taking advantage of a suspect's misplaced trust in one the suspect supposes to be a fellow prisoner. . . . Ploys to mislead a suspect or lull him into a false sense of security that do not rise to the level of compulsion or coercion to speak are not within *Miranda*'s concerns").

29. As Supreme Court Justice Potter Stewart explained:

We hold only that when the subject of a search is not in custody and the State attempts to justify a search on the basis of his consent, the Fourth and Fourteenth Amendments require that it demonstrate that the consent was in fact voluntarily given, and not the result of duress or coercion, express or implied. Voluntariness is a question of fact to be determined from all the circumstances, and while the subject's knowledge of a right to refuse is a factor to be taken into account, the prosecution is not required to demonstrate such knowledge as a prerequisite to establishing a voluntary consent. (*Schneckloth*, 412 U.S., 248–249)

30. See, e.g., Jack Leonard, "Using DNA to Trawl for Killers," *Los Angeles Times*, March 10, 2001, A1 (describing views of "privacy advocates").

31. See 15 La. Rev. Stat. § 609(a) (West 2000); S.D. Codified Laws § 23-5-14 (Michie 2001); Maria Gold, "Va. to Begin Taking DNA after Arrests for Felonies: Prosecutors, Rights Activists Split on Database Expansion," *Washington Post*, January 1, 2003, at B1; Stephen Braun, "Virginia Aggressively Uses DNA to Solve Other Cases: A Law Allows Police to Compel Suspects in Violent Offenses to Give Samples for Study in Unsolved Crimes," *Los Angeles Times*, January 13, 2003.

32. See David H. Kaye, "The Constitutionality of DNA Sampling on Arrest," *Cornell Journal of Law and Public Policy* 10 (2001): 455.

33. See Mark Benecke, "Coding or Non-coding, That Is the Question," *3 EMB Reports* 498, 500–501 (2002); David H. Kaye, "Bioethics, Bench and Bar: Selected Arguments in *Landry v. Attorney General*," *Jurimetrics Journal* 40 (2000), 193; Randall S. Murch and Bruce Budowle, "Are Developments in Forensic Applications of DNA Technology Consistent with Privacy Protections?" in *Genetic Secrets: Protecting Privacy and Confidentiality in the Genetic Era*, ed. Mark A. Rothstein (New Haven: Yale University Press, 1997), 212, 224.

34. Biologists often use the phrase *DNA genotype* to refer to DNA sequences, even when the sequences have nothing to do with genes. See, e.g., David H. Kaye and George F.

Sensabaugh, Jr., "Reference Guide on DNA Evidence," in *Reference Manual on Scientific Evidence*, 485 (Washington, D.C.: Federal Judicial Center, 2000). This is because all DNA sequences are inherited like genes, but the phrase can be terribly misleading if it invites people to think that all DNA loci contain significant, intensely personal information. The vast majority do not.

35. In chapter 14 of this volume, Troy Duster makes the important point that even some noncoding sequences can be statistically associated with the socially constructed categories of race or ethnicity. But he does not explain why inferences of race based on crime scene DNA evidence are any more problematic, when they serve to focus a criminal investigation, than eyewitness accounts of race, which often serve that purpose now.

36. *City of Indianapolis v. Edmond*, 531 U.S. 32 (2000).

37. *Ferguson v. City of Charleston*, 532 U.S. 67 (2001).

38. *Edmond*, 41–42. Justice O'Connor wrote the majority opinion; six justices subscribed to this view.

39. *Ferguson*, 532 U.S. at 81–82.

40. See *Michigan Department of State Police v. Sitz*, 496 U.S. 444 (1990).

41. Every justice accepted this proposition. See *Edmond*, 532 U.S., 42.

42. Ibid., 48 (Rehnquist, C. J., dissenting).

43. Ibid., 44 n.1.

44. *Ferguson*, 532 U.S., 81.

45. Ibid., 83–84.

46. *United States v. Miles*, 228 F.Supp.2d 1130 (E.D. Cal. 2002). Several courts have reached a contrary conclusion, reasoning that gathering intelligence information before any specific individual is suspected of a crime is not "ordinary law enforcement." E.g., *United States v. Sczubelek*, 2003 WL 1818109 (D.Del. 2003); *Nicholas v. Goord*, 2003 WL 256774 (S.D.N.Y. 2003); *United States v. Reynard*, 220 F.Supp.2d 1142 (S.D.Cal. 2002). A few courts have upheld database laws by blithely ignoring *Edmond* and *Ferguson*. *Groceman v. Department of Justice*, 2002 WL 1398559 (N.D.Tex. 2002); *State v. Maass*, 64 P.3d 382 (Kan. 2003).

47. Having recognized that the government's "special-needs" argument for compelling a probationer to submit a DNA sample for inclusion in the federal DNA data bank was undercut by *Edmond* and *Ferguson*, the district court in *Miles*, 228 F.Supp.2d 1130, immediately concluded that the federal statute was unconstitutional as applied to probationers. This conclusion is suspect, because it overlooks the possibility that an exception other than the special-needs exception might provide the necessary justification for the program of searches or seizures. A divided panel of the Ninth Circuit Court of Appeals used essentially the same problematic reasoning in *United States v. Kincade*, 345 F.3d 1095 (9th Cir. 2003), rev. en banc granted, 353F.3d 1000 (9th Cir. 2004).

48. Kaye, "The Constitutionality of DNA Sampling on Arrest."

49. "The Crier Report: Mandatory DNA Testing" (Fox television broadcast, March 11, 1999), available at 1999 WL 18330169; Richard Willing, "As Police Rely More on DNA, States Take a Closer Look," *USA Today*, June 6, 2000.

50. See Christopher Francescani, "Sex Fiend Admits He Killed 5 in Brooklyn," *New York Post*, March 10, 2001; William K. Rashbaum, "Man Cleared by DNA Tests Led Police to Murder Suspect," *New York Times*, August 6, 2000.

51. See S. A. Harbison, J. F. Hamilton, and S. J. Walsh, "The New Zealand DNA Databank: Its Development and Significance as a Crime Solving Tool," *Science and Justice* 41 (2001): 36.

52. Tony Gordon, "DNA Sample Links Man to Burglary," *Chicago Daily Herald*, July 3, 2001.

53. See, e.g., Colo. Rev. Stat. Ann. § 10-3-1104.7 (1) (a) (West 2000) ("Genetic information is the unique property of the individual to whom the information pertains"). The language is patterned after a model Genetic Privacy Act prepared and promoted by a group at Boston University. See, e.g., Patricia (Winnie) Roche, Leonard Glantz, and George J. Annas, "The Genetic Privacy Act: A Proposal for National Legislation," *Jurimetrics Journal* 37 (1996).

54. The discussion in chapter 7 of this volume only heightens the mystery. George Annas writes in that chapter that "the legal position that everybody but the individual from whom DNA is extracted can own DNA is not sustainable. Either no one should be permitted to own and sell DNA, or individuals should have property rights to their own DNA" (139). Passages such as this one fail to clarify the "property" in question. Is it the molecules from human cells? Physical copies of those molecules, or copies of useful parts of them? Abstract representations of the molecules (in the form of sequence data)? Patents on human genes, which require an understanding of their functions? Which of these putative forms of property is an individual not allowed to own when everyone else is? If the concern is privacy of information about the individual, why change the common law as it applies to all body parts? See, e.g., Bartha Maria Knoppers, Claude M. Laberge, and Marie Hirtle, eds., *Human DNA: Law and Policy, International and Comparative Perspectives* (New York: Kluwer Academic, 1997).

55. *See* Edward J. Imwinkelried and D. H. Kaye, "DNA Typing: Emerging or Neglected Issues," *Washington Law Review* 76 (2001): 413, 438–440.

56. It could be argued, however, that analysis at loci that relate to socially significant characteristics rather than the loci that have only biometric significance should be treated as a search that requires a warrant and probable cause. Cf. *Patterson v. State*, 742 N.E.2d 4, 10 n. 3 (Ind. Ct. App. 2000) (noting privacy concerns associated with such loci).

57. National Bioethics Advisory Commission, *Research Involving Human Biological Materials*, vol. 1, *Ethical Issues and Policy Guidance* (Rockville, Md.: National Bioethics Advisory Commission, 1999), 13.

58. *United States v. Miller*, 425 U.S. 435, 440 (1976).

59. See Imwinkelried and Kaye, "DNA Typing," 431–434.

60. Ibid.

61. In 1965, Graham Moore observed that each new microprocessor chip contains roughly twice as much capacity as its predecessor, and each chip was released within 18–24 months of the previous chip. To date, "Moore's law" has remained surprisingly accurate. See "What Is Moore's Law?" available at www.welchco.com/02/06/01/05/BK/00101.htm.

62. See Phil Reilly, "Legal and Public Policy Issues in DNA Forensics," *Nature Reviews Genetics* 2 (2001): 315. Public health service programs for newborn screening reach practically all children born in the United States. See, e.g., "Newborn Screening," (fact sheet, Centers for Disease Control and Prevention, National Center for Environmental Health, Division of Laboratory Sciences, March 7, 2001), available at www.cdc.gov/nceh/dls/newborn_screening.htm.

63. On the last point, see Akhil Reed Amar, "A Safe Intrusion," *American Lawyer*, June 11, 2001; Akhil Reed Amar, "Foreword: The Document and the Doctrine," *Harvard Law Review* 114 (2000): 126.

64. See Philip P. Pan, "Pr. George's Chief Has Used Serial Testing Before; Farrell Oversaw DNA Sampling of 2,300 in Fla.," *Washington Post*, January 31, 1998.

65. Of course, one can attempt to obtain DNA samples from a missing person's belongings or relatives, but these ad hoc efforts can be agonizing and expensive, especially in cases of mass destruction. See David W. Chen, "Searching Again for Traces of Those Gone Forever," *New York Times*, February 9, 2002 (reporting that "[a]fter Sept. 11, thousands of items were collected from families who lost relatives in the World Trade Center attack, in a hurried and often scattershot effort to help identify remains," but "the New York City medical examiner's office says that more than half of the possible DNA samples it has received are inadequate to make such matches" and "[a]s a result, hundreds of families must repeat an ordeal they never thought they would have to endure again: another round of the cruelly intimate search for traces of those gone forever").

66. See also Peter Neufeld ("Who Should Be Included in a Databank/Database?" panel discussion, "DNA and the Criminal Justice System" conference, John F. Kennedy School of Government, Harvard University, Cambridge, Mass., November 21, 2000). Harvard University, Cambridge, Mass., November 21, 2000; transcript of the panel discussion is available at http://conference2000.dnapolicy.net/).

67. We find it impossible to be anything but appalled at the prospect of the government's (or others'—perhaps others', more than the government's) possessing everyone's genomes and being able to peer into and analyze at leisure the genetic code that can give up secrets we do not even know we have. This is the prospect that turns debate from the *method* of DNA sample collection to the *uses* made of the samples. We could not favor authorizing law enforcement of sample DNA for a more inclusive forensic DNA database, much less a comprehensive one, unless the creation of such a comprehensive database were coupled with transparent procedures to assure destruction of whatever tissue samples are used, once the nonphenotypic loci used for identification only have been typed and the their profile has been recorded. But we foresee technology soon being available that would permit destruction of a sample almost simultaneously with its profile's being recorded, and we can specify procedures that would keep whole DNA out of law enforcement control by requiring a hospital or other agency that routinely analyzes samples for health or other non–law enforcement purposes to transmit only an identification profile to an identification database. Similarly, we could not favor secondary analysis for the identification loci of DNA sampled for other purposes (by health authorities, for example) unless transparent procedures ensured that the samples themselves would be kept out of law enforcement's control.

68. See, e.g., Peter Neufeld ("the argument frankly is that most people in the country are not in favor of the universal databank").

69. The fingerprint and identity card bills were the following: *Citizen Identification Act of 1943*, H.R. 601, 79th Cong. (1st Sess. 1945) (would have required every citizen more than eleven years of age to appear, be fingerprinted, give information under oath, and carry an identity card); *Citizen Identification Act of 1943*, S. 1191, 78th Cong. (1st Sess. 1943) (same); *Citizen Identification Act of 1942*, H.R. 6256, 77th Cong. (1st Sess. 1941) (would have required every citizen more than fifteen years of age to appear, be fingerprinted, give information under oath, and carry an identity card); *Universal Fingerprinting Act of 1941*, H.R. 3157, 77th Cong. (1st Sess. 1941) (would have required every person in or entering the United States to be fingerprinted); cf. *Alien Identification Act of 1942*, H.R. 6258, 77th Cong. (1st Sess. 1941) (would have required every alien in the United States to appear, be fingerprinted, give information under oath, and carry an identity card).

70. Neufeld, "Who Should Be Included in a Databank/Database?" ("a majority of the population in this country would oppose a universal database even if in the universal database they only looked at the thirteen STR markers and then destroyed the sample"); cf. Peter Neufeld, "Who's in Your Genes?" (paper presented at the Electronic Freedom Frontier Conference, March 19, 1992; transcript available at www.eff.org/pub/Privacy/Medical/cfp2_gene_panel.transcript) (suggesting that few people "would be in favor of a law that would require each of you to donate a sample of your DNA, your children's DNA, and your loved ones' DNA into a national data bank controlled by police, which ... might mean access to employers, insurers, or other social scientists or research scientists"). These impressions of the popular view may be right, but what people would and would not favor depends greatly on how the proposal is framed and what information they have before them.

71. Even today, the true state of public opinion is unclear. Already, there is advocacy of a population-wide databases in the United States and other liberal democracies. See Akhil Reed Amar, "A Search for Justice in Our Genes," *New York Times*, May 7, 2002; Martin Evison, "DNA Database Could End Problem of Identity Fraud," *Nature* 420 (2002): 359; Robert Williamson and Rony Duncan, "DNA Testing for All," *Nature* 418 (2002): 585; "The Government Should Require a DNA Sample, but Keep it Private," editorial, *Fulton County Daily Report*, June 21, 2001.

72. See, e.g., *Mincey v. Arizona*, 437 U.S. 385, 390 (1978) (asserting that "[t]he Fourth Amendment proscribes all unreasonable searches and seizures, and it is a cardinal principle that 'searches conducted outside the judicial process, without prior approval by judge or magistrate, are per se unreasonable under the Fourth Amendment—subject only to a few specifically established and well-delineated exceptions,'" quoting *Katz v. United States*, 389 U.S. 347, 357 (1967) (footnotes omitted), and citing *South Dakota v. Opperman*, 428 U.S. 364, 381 (1976) (Powell, J., concurring); *Coolidge v. New Hampshire*, 403 U.S. 443, 481 (1971); *Vale v. Louisiana*, 399 U.S. 30, 34 (1970); *Terry v. Ohio*, 392 U.S. 1, 20 (1968); *Trupiano v. United States*, 334 U.S. 699, 705 (1948)).

The foundation for the general rule is less than clear. The first clause of the Fourth Amendment bars unreasonable searches and seizures, and the second clause requires that warrants be based on probable cause and meet certain other requirements. But the amendment is silent

280 D. H. Kaye and Michael E. Smith

on how the reasonableness clause and the warrant clause interact, and the historical record does not suggest that the former encompasses the latter. See Akhil Reed Amar, *The Constitution and Criminal Procedure: First Principles* (New Haven: Yale University Press, 1997).

73. *Schmerber v. California*, 384 U.S. 757, 767 (1966) (referring to blood samples taken from a driver being treated in a hospital for injuries received in an automobile accident).

74. *Palmer v. State*, 679 N.E.2d 887, 891 (Ind. 1997).

75. E.g., *United States v. Richardson*, 388 F.2d 842, 845 (6th Cir. 1968). However, this is probably the minority view. See *People v. Santistevan*, 715 P.2d 792 (Colo. 1986); *State v. Hardaway*, 36 P.3d 900 (Mont. 2001).

76. *Kyllo v. United States*, 533 U.S. 27, 30 (2001).

77. Ibid., 34.

78. *Schmerber v. California*, 767–768.

79. See Kaye, "The Constitutionality of DNA Sampling on Arrest," 482.

80. An important qualification must be noted. Even loci that are noncoding and unlinked to genes that are related to diseases or behaviors are inherited as Mendelian traits. Consequently, records in a database that includes parents and their children could be examined to test parentage. Unwanted discovery of illegitimacy would constitute an obvious and real invasion of personal and familial privacy.

81. Cf. Amar, "Foreword," 126 (suggesting that a universal DNA database would be permissible under a reasonableness inquiry "as defined by the values of the rest of the Constitution" but that "it is far from clear that current doctrine would allow this scheme, because it contemplates intrusions for criminal law-enforcement purposes in the absence of . . . individualized suspicion . . . a category of search that doctrine strongly disfavors").

82. The likely database in these circumstances would be more threatening because the vast collection of DNA samples and analyses held by hospitals, HMOs, and their corporate relatives, and the increasing digitization of those records, is generating a comprehensive DNA database that, though not ideally constructed for forensic use, is not really off-limits to law enforcement. If law enforcement authorities are not authorized to create a comprehensive database of DNA identification profiles, investigators will look to other databases when the offender-only database yields no match to DNA found at the scene of particularly notorious crimes—serial sexual assaults and homicides in particular. There they will find identified whole DNA and DNA profiles of various kinds, linked to complete medical files containing a wealth of intensely private information. See Lawrence O. Gostin, "Health Information Privacy," *Cornell Law Review* 80 (1995): 451, 463–470, 491–492.

83. Jean E. McEwen, "Sherlock Holmes Meets Genetic Fingerprinting," *Boston College Law School Magazine* (Spring 1994): 40.

84. George J. Annas, "Privacy Rules for DNA Databanks: Protecting Coded 'Future Diaries,'" *Journal of the American Medical Association* 270 (1993): 2347; Jean E. McEwen, "DNA Databanks," in *Genetic Secrets: Protecting Privacy and Confidentiality in the Genetic Age*, ed. Mark A. Rothstein (New Haven: Yale University Press, 1997), 236 ("[A] population-wide DNA data bank could fundamentally alter the relationship between individuals and the state, essentially turning us into a nation of suspects").

85. Jonathan Kimmelman, "The Promise and Perils of Criminal DNA Databanking," *Nature Biotechnology* 18 (2000): 696; cf. Kimmelman, "Risking Ethical Insolvency: A Survey of Trends in Criminal DNA Databanking," *Journal of Law, Medicine and Ethics* 28 (2000): 209 (complaining that "[a]n overly expansive and mandatory DNA databanking scheme injures the trust relationship between a government and its subjects").

86. *Watchtower Bible and Tract Society of N.Y., Inc. v. Village of Stratton*, 636 U.S. 150, 153 (2002); *Talley v. California*, 362 U.S. 60, 63–65 (1960); *NAACP v. Alabama*, 357 U.W. 449, 460–466 (1958); but see *United States v. Harriss*, 347 U.S. 612, 623–626 (1954).

87. See, e.g., *Senear v. Daily Journal-American*, 641 P. 2d 1180, 1181–1183 (1982) (common-law reporter's shield privilege); Edward J. Imwinkelried, *The New Wigmore: Evidentiary Privileges* § 7.3 (New York: Aspen Law & Business, 2002) (government's privilege to keep the identity of an informant confidential).

88. *United States v. Knotts*, 460 U.S. 276, 283 (1983).

89. Cf. Jamie Downs, Director and Chief Medical Examiner, Alabama Department of Forensic Science, Statement to the Subcommittee on Government Efficiency, Financial Management and Intergovernmental Relations, *Oversight Hearing: How Effectively Are State and Federal Agencies Working Together to Implement the Use of New DNA Technologies?* 107th Cong., 1st Sess., June 12, 2001, noting that the *average* current cost of processing a CODIS sample is twenty-five dollars).

90. At least one state already encourages parents to obtain and store samples of their children's blood (at their own expense) in case the child is murdered or mutilated beyond recognition. See "Florida Tries DNA Sampling to Protect Children," *New York Times*, January 27, 1999.

91. This is usually stated the other way: "more than half" of felony defendants have prior "felony records" and "two-thirds have prior arrests." See, e.g., Brian A. Reaves, "Executive Summary," *Felony Defendants in Large Urban Counties, 1994* (Washington, D.C.: Bureau of Justice Statistics, U.S. Department of Justice, 1998), 2 (reporting that "[a]bout two-thirds of all defendants had been arrested previously," "Fifty-six percent of defendants had a felony arrest record," and an "estimated 38 percent of defendants had at least one prior conviction for a felony").

92. See table, "Felony Arrest and Conviction Record of Felony Defendants in the 75 Largest Counties 1994," ibid., 1. Not surprisingly, in light of those data, half of those imprisoned after felony conviction are going to prison for the first time. Ibid.

93. Ibid., 2.

94. See Virginia Division of Forensic Science, "DNA Databank Hits & Samples Collected as of 12/31/2002," available at http://www.dfs.state.va.us/information/whatsnew.cfm (reporting 445 hits in 2002, when the database had grown to 188,940 profiles).

95. See "Major Tool for Crime Detection Receives Boost," M2 Presswire, February 21, 2002, available at 2002 WL 4160490. The Home Secretary took the occasion of this milestone to announce that "[t]here is currently more than a 70 per cent chance of a stain found at a crime scene being matched to a name" in the U.K. national database. Ibid.

96. Of course, it is nearly impossible to document and quantify the net benefits, as we cannot know how many crimes would be prevented or solved by any given expansion of the national DNA identification database. We cannot even predict the extent to which those who are bent on crime will try to outsmart the technology by taking care not to leave any DNA at the scenes of their crimes or to obscure the evidence they do leave. See Richard Willing, "Criminals Try to Outwit DNA," *USA Today*, August 28, 2000.

97. States have been moving steadily in this direction. See chapter 16, this volume.

98. See Thomas P. Bonczar and Allen J. Beck, *Lifetime Likelihood of Going to State or Federal Prison* (Washington, D.C.: Bureau of Justice Statistics, U.S. Department of Justice, 1997). Similar data are not available to project the lifetime likelihood of *conviction* by race, but every group's lifetime likelihood of conviction will be higher than its lifetime likelihood of imprisonment.

99. Allen J. Beck and Jennifer C. Karberg, *Prison and Jail Inmates at Midyear 2000* (Washington, D.C.: Bureau of Justice Statistics, U.S. Department of Justice, 2001) (132 whites per 100,000 whites in the population were in local jails at midyear 2000, compared to 736 blacks per 100,000 blacks).

100. See Allen J. Beck, "Trends in U.S. Correctional Populations," in *The Dilemmas of Corrections: Contemporary Readings*, ed. Kenneth C. Haas and Geoffrey P. Alpert (Waveland, Ill.: Waveland Press, 1999).

101. See Beck and Karberg, *Prison and Jail Inmates at Midyear 2000*, table 13 ("Number of Inmates in State or Federal Prisons and Local Jails per 100,000 Residents, by Gender, Race, Hispanic Origin and Age, June 30, 2000").

102. See ibid., table 14, reporting 417 white males in state or federal prison per 100,000 white males in the population, compared to 3,408 black male prisoners per 100,000 black males.

103. See Kaye, "The Constitutionality of DNA Sampling on Arrest," 458 n.12; testimony of New York City Police Commissioner Howard Safir before the National Commission on the Future of DNA Evidence, Dallas, Tex., March 1, 1999, available at www.ojp.usdoj.gov/nij/dnamtgtrans4/trans-n.html (calling for legislation to "give us the authority to take samples from all those arrested for fingerprintable offenses, which includes all misdemeanors in our penal law"); Laylan Copelin, "Allow DNA Samples at Arrests, Officials Urge: Police Chief, DA Seek Database to Streamline Crime Fighting; Critics Warn of Data Overload," *Austin American-Statesman*, June 9, 2000, at A1; Rose Marie Arce, "Surveillance and DNA Testing Are Among the Police Weapons; *Newsday*, January 11, 2000, at A17 (reporting that "Police Commissioner Howard Safir wants to expand [DNA] testing exponentially to include taking DNA samples from everyone arrested for 'fingerprintable' offenses. . . . [S]amples taken either by swabbing the mouth for saliva or through fingerprint oil [would be analyzed for] only the genetic data that identifies people [which would be retained in a database of] something like bar codes").

104. Federal Bureau of Investigation, *Crime in the United States: 1999* (Washington, D.C.: U.S. Department of Justice, 2000), 230 (table 43, reporting 6,283,294 arrests of whites and 2,600,510 of blacks in 1999); U. S. Census Bureau, *Statistical Abstract of the United States: 2000* (Washington, D.C.: U.S. Department of Commerce, 2001), 12 (table 10, reporting 224,611,000 whites and 34,863,000 blacks in the 1999 U.S. population).

105. The lifetime likelihood of arrest cannot be drawn directly from routinely collected data, but it can be projected from annual arrest statistics and from cohort studies (in which a jurisdiction's police records are combed for contacts with anyone born in that jurisdiction in a given year). See Alfred Blumstein and Elizabeth Graddy, "Prevalence and Recidivism Index Arrests: A Feedback Model," *Law and Society Review* 16 (1981–1982): 279–280 (using various national data sets and the *Uniform Crime Reports* for 1968 through 1977 to estimate the lifetime chances of *felony* arrest at 51 percent for black males in the nation's fifty-six largest cities, more than triple the 14 percent chance of felony arrest for white males in those cities).

The lifetime likelihood of arrest is greater when account is taken of juvenile arrests and misdemeanor arrests—and higher again if arrests for moving violations are included. See Paul E. Tracy, Marvin E. Wolfgang, and Robert M. Figlio, *Delinquency Careers in Two Birth Cohorts*, The Plenum Series in Crime and Justice (New York: Kluwer Academic/Plenum, 1990) (among males born in Philadelphia in 1958 who grew up there, 42 percent of the nonwhites had felony or misdemeanor police contacts before their eighteenth birthdays, in contrast to 23 percent of the whites); Robert Tillman, "The Size of the 'Criminal Population': The Prevalence and Incidence of Adult Arrest," 25 *Criminology* 561 (1987) (finding that 65 percent of nonwhite males born in California in 1956 were arrested there at least once in the twelve years between their eighteenth and thirtieth birthdays, compared to 40 percent of white men, and that 30 percent of black women were arrested during that period, compared to 10 percent of white women); David van Alstyne and Vincent Manti, *The Prevalence and Incidence of Arrests among Adult Males in New York State*, vol. 2 (Albany, N.Y.: New York State Division of Criminal Justice Services, 1987) (finding that overall, 46 percent of males born in New York in 1956 were arrested at least once for a felony or misdemeanor in New York between ages sixteen and twenty-nine, and that 71 percent of nonwhite males were arrested, in contrast to 41 percent of white males); see also Lyle W. Shannon, *Assessing the Relationship of Adult Criminal Careers to Juvenile Careers* (Office of Juvenile Justice and Delinquency Prevention, U.S. Department of Justice, 1980) (finding that 29.9 percent of males born in Racine, Wisconsin, in 1942 had a police contact for a felony or misdemeanor before reaching age eighteen, as did 35.7 percent of a 1949 cohort and 31 percent of a 1955 cohort, and that if moving violations are included, 60 percent eventually found their way into police records; Jerome G. Miller, "From Social Safety Net to Dragnet: African American Males in the Criminal Justice System," *Washington and Lee Law Review* 51 (1994): 479, 485 (on review of these studies and others, estimating that "the percentage of nonwhite males [in cities] who could expect to be arrested and at least briefly jailed would [be] 90%").

106. See also Joan Petersilia, "Criminal Career Research: A Review of Recent Evidence," in *Crime and Justice: An Annual Review of Research*, ed. Norval Morris and Michael Tonry (Chicago: University of Chicago Press, 1980), 321, 344 (showing, on reanalysis of data covering the adult years of Shannon's cohorts in Racine, Wisconsin, that 46.5 percent of the 1942 cohort, 59.9 percent of the 1949 cohort, and 43.7 percent of the 1955 cohort had had at least one recorded police contact for a felony or misdemeanor by age twenty-nine); Tillman, "The Size of the 'Criminal Population,'" at 567 (concluding that "[t]aken together, the results of previous [studies of the prevalence of arrest] indicate that among urban males 60 percent will have been arrested (or have a recorded 'police contact') for a nontraffic offense and 25 percent will be arrested for an index offense at some point during their lifetimes").

107. See Michael Tonry, *Malign Neglect: Race, Crime and Punishment in America* (New York: Oxford University Press, 1995); Randall Kennedy, *Race, Crime, and the Law* (New York: Pantheon, 1997), 24–26.

108. See Tom Tyler, *Why People Obey the Law* (New Haven: Yale University Press, 1991) (finding that compliance with the criminal law is secured not so much by the threat of punishment as by perceptions that the laws are congruent with moral obligations [or at least enacted properly by legitimate authority] and that they are executed fairly).

109. Most automobile stops would seem to be seizures for Fourth Amendment purposes (see *INS v. Delgado*, 466 U.S. 210, 216 [1984]), but whether they would be arrests within the meaning of a statute authorizing the taking of a DNA sample "upon arrest" would depend on the specific legislation in the individual states. (And even if an automobile stop for a traffic violation starts out as something less than an arrest, probable cause usually exists, and if the jurisdiction permits arrest for the violation, it lies within the officer's discretion whether to escalate the stop [which has already occurred] to an arrest, whether to search incident to that arrest, and whether to transport the driver to a facility for booking and detention pending first appearance in court. When a motorist is stopped by police for an offense for which arrest is permissible, there is no constitutional bar to the police's consummating the arrest and conducting a full search incident to it. *United States v. Robinson*, 414 U.S. 218 [1973]; cf. *Atwater v. City of Lago Vista*, 531 U.S. 990 [2000].)

110. See, e.g., "Testing Suspects to Prevent Tragedies," *New York Post*, August 18, 2000. ("If cops were allowed to take DNA samples from all the suspects they arrest, Laura Nusser and Patricia Sullivan might be alive today.")

111. Furthermore, making arrest the legal threshold for DNA profiling requires only the existence, at some point in time, of probable cause to believe the person is committing or has committed a crime. As most young black males know all too well, police officers are not constitutionally prohibited from making pretextual arrests when probable cause exists, nor are they barred from focusing arrest activity in any particular area or on any particular subgroup of the population—so long as a rational basis for the selection can be offered in justification. Indeed, probable cause to arrest is spread thick and wide through the populace, attaching to the innocent-in-fact as well as to those guilty of the crime for which probable cause exists. It is a low threshold for sampling DNA and a poor shield against the government's storing our DNA profiles in law enforcement databases—and against abuse of that power.

III

The Coming Storm: Crime and Behavioral Genetics

13

DNA and Human-Behavior Genetics: Implications for the Criminal Justice System

Garland Allen

Introduction

For the past fifteen years, the scientific community and the general public have been subjected to a blitz of information about "the gene" or "the genes" for every conceivable trait in the human repertoire: physical, molecular, biochemical, and behavioral (figure 13.1). This interest reflects both (1) the excitement engendered by legitimate advances in molecular genetics—in the identifying and sequencing of a number of genes affecting human health (Huntington disease, cystic fibrosis) arising from the Human Genome Project; and (2) a considerable amount of research, by psychiatrists and psychologists in particular, into the hereditary basis of human personality and behavior, giving rise to a relatively new field known as human-behavior genetics.

From the scientific point of view these two avenues of research have had quite different levels of achievement. As evidenced by such sober projects as Victor McKusick's catalog of human genetic traits, several thousand traits (mostly diseases) have been mapped, a significant percentage of those sequenced, and their clinical effects well-documented. On the other hand, virtually all of the research in human-behavior genetics has produced conclusions that have been highly controversial, often unreplicable, and in several cases, eventually retracted. It is thus surprising to find that behavior genetics has received such voluminous attention in the scientific and especially the popular media. Part of the reason for the publicity, of course, is that both research efforts have included in their public image optimistic promises to cure all sorts of personal and social ills through genetic engineering (replacing dysfunctional genes with functional genes) and through pharmacotherapy (using drugs to compensate for the altered products of defective genes). Whether these promises are realistic or not is a much-debated subject, but it is not the central issue

Figure 13.1
Life cover

I want to address in this chapter. What I do want to address is the validity and practicality of claims about a genetic basis for human social, behavioral, and personality traits relevant to the criminal justice system. This will involve raising several types of questions and, in the short space available, suggesting how these questions might be dealt with in the judicial context.

The first group of questions focuses on the genetic claims themselves:

1. What do genetic claims about human-behavior entail?

2. How valid are these claims given the methods, and therefore the data, available for establishing them?

3. Can genetic data predict human-behavioral outcomes?

The second group of questions focuses on the use to which such claims, even if shown to be scientifically valid, could feasibly be put in issues of criminal justice:

1. Can genetic claims be used to identify potential offenders and thus serve a preventive role?

2. Can genetic claims be used in defense arguments to overturn convictions or lighten sentences for offenders in much the same way insanity arguments are currently used?

To help answer some of these questions I will start with a very small amount of biology. My first contention is that claims of a major genetic component to most human social behaviors are based on a very simplistic and naive notion of how biological—especially genetic—systems work. To aid in understanding the various aspects of the biological argument, a short glossary of technical terms is included in table 13.1.

Biology and Genetic Determinism

Textbook after textbook and numerous popular articles today treat us to phrases like "the gene/the genes for..." or "The genes that cause X condition." Such phrases suggest that genes are some sort of invariant blueprint from which fixed adult traits spring full blown. Although phrases such as "the gene for X..." may indeed be regarded as shorthand expressions by geneticists, they tend to take on a life of their own in everyday discourse and thus convey certain meanings about the nature of genes and how they function. Especially in the context of the application of current genetic knowledge to the criminal justice system, the popular conception

Table 13.1
Some biological definitions

Genotype	The genes, or segments of DNA, that are related to a particular characteristic, such as eye color or the production of sickle cell hemoglobin. The genotype of an organism represents not only the particular sequence of DNA an individual inherits from his or her parents, but also what the individual can pass on to his or her offspring.
Phenotype	The particular form of a trait that the individual displays, such as blue or brown eyes or the clinical symptoms of sickle cell anemia.
Embryogenesis	The process by which the individual grows and differentiates from a fertilized egg to an adult. During this process the genes are transcribed and translated into proteins that interact with other molecular components of the cells, and cells with other cells, to produce the embryo and eventually the adult. Genes altered by mutation (see below) or environmental factors can operate during development to change the phenotypic outcome.
Mutation	A hereditary change in the DNA of a gene that can alter a protein and thus the phenotype of the individual. Not all mutations lead to a significant change in phenotype; most that do are deleterious, though some may be favorable changes—and these are, indeed, part of the raw material of evolution.
Norm of Reaction	The range of phenotypes that can be expressed by a particular gene under a range of environment conditions. Thus, a gene for height in a plant would have a certain norm of reaction as measured by the average height attained under different temperature or moisture conditions. Norm of reaction expresses the plasticity of genes under various environmental inputs.

of genes and genetics conveyed by "the gene for . . ." can be highly problematic, even legally and morally dangerous. The view that genes directly determine—in a *significant way*—a large number of human social and behavioral traits is sometimes referred to as *genetic determinism*. Determinist views on this sort have had a long and unfortunate history. They held sway in the early decades of the twentieth century as the centerpiece of the eugenics movement, resurfaced again in the 1960s and 1970s in the race-IQ issue, and are with us again today in much of the human-behavior genetics literature.

Let me say at the outset that there is a genuine biological discipline, animal-behavior genetics, in which rigorous and controlled experimentation can be applied to a variety of behaviors such as courtship rituals, parental behavior, bird or cricket songs, spider web construction, and primate sociality, to name just a few. Studies of this kind have demonstrated that (1) rather complex behaviors can be genetically programmed to a highly specific degree, and thus there is no inherent reason to suppose, from a biological point of view, that behavior cannot be to some extent genetically controlled; (2) virtually all behaviors involve some cue or input from the environment for full development to occur (for example, many bird songs are genetically controlled, but individual birds must hear the song once or twice before executing it perfectly themselves); and (3) every specific type of behavior has to be studied on its own to understand how heredity and environment interact to produce the behavior in the adult. It is not possible to make predictions about behaviors in one species from analogies to a similar behavior in other species (for example, the similarity in facial expression between dogs, apes, and humans may not necessarily reflect similarity in feeling or intended behavior).

As professionals, most animal-behavior geneticists have recognized the vast difference that separates their work from that of those who attempt to make speculative claims for humans. In 1995, when the president of the Behavior Genetics Association at the time, Glayde Whitney, said in his presidential address that it was time behavior geneticists admitted that the study of racial differences in such human traits as IQ or other complex behaviors was a legitimate area of research, a number of members, including the president-elect, were so shocked that they walked out.[1] Many felt that the association's hard-earned reputation of supporting only research that could be carried out rigorously, and its previous decision to refrain from drawing speculative conclusions about humans, was publicly compromised by Whitney's statements. The fallout resulted in a split in the association, with those interested in the behavior of nonhuman species breaking away to form a new society.

From a biological point of view, what are the problems with genetic-determinist claims and with their application to human-behavioral traits? The most basic flaw in genetic-determinist thinking is that it is developmentally blind, that is, it fails to take seriously the embryological mechanisms by which a fertilized egg becomes an adult organism. Genes—the segments of DNA that we inherit from our parents—are an absolutely essential part of that process, but only a part. Genes function to produce a generally predictable process of embryonic development in each species (fertilized hens' eggs produce chickens, fertilized dogs' eggs produce dogs, and fertilized human eggs produce humans): "like begets like," in the old-fashioned sense of that adage. No amount of altered environmental inputs can make a chicken egg develop into a dog or even a crow. In this general sense genes are correctly understood as *determiners*. Even here, however, it is important to recognize that genes do nothing by themselves. They require both a genetic environment (other genes, sometimes referred to as the *genetic background*) and an external environment (other tissues and components of the developing embryo, as well as the environment external to the organism itself, the "outside environment"). Both environments must be rather specific for development to occur normally, or at all. For example, lower the incubation temperature of a chicken egg from its normal 37 degrees to 20 degrees Celsius (i.e., from about 96 degrees to about 68 degrees Fahrenheit) or raise it to 45 degrees Celsius) (113 degrees Fahrenheit) and development will be greatly altered, if it occurs at all. Genes are powerless without the proper genetic background and external environment in which to function (figure 13.2).

When development does occur under altered genetic or environmental conditions, the form of individual adult traits can be quite variable. Because we know relatively little about the exact mechanics of development for any specific trait—that is, what combination of genetic and environmental conditions turns certain genes on and others off at particular times during embryogenesis—development has been, for the past century or more, and remains today, the mystery of mysteries in modern biology. Although new genetic techniques have begun to provide tools for investi-

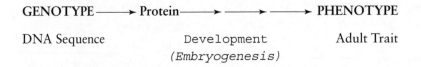

GENOTYPE ⟶ Protein ⟶ ⟶ ⟶ PHENOTYPE

DNA Sequence   Development   Adult Trait
                           (Embryogenesis)

Factors Leading to Phenotypic Variability

Genetic Background:
Epistasis (gene-gene interactions)
Control of gene activity (transcription factors)
Control of processing of gene products

Environmental Background:
Physiological (nutrition, ions, drugs)
Cellular (cell-cell interactions)
Physical (temperature, light)

Figure 13.2
Development process

gating this process on the cellular and molecular levels, we still know relatively little about how it occurs. Most important, we know as yet even less about how any given gene of interest (for example, the cystic fibrosis gene that will be discussed later in the chapter) interacts with other genes in the embryo's genome or how it interacts with environmental factors, both before and after birth (development in animals does not stop with hatching of the egg or birth of the child) to produce the corresponding adult trait or, most especially, its variants.

What has become clear through recent findings is that in most cases it is impossible to predict, from the fact that an embryo has a particular gene or genes, exactly what its adult phenotype will be like. Developmental biologists have carried out carefully controlled laboratory experiments on organisms such as the roundworm *Caenorhabditis elegans* (*C. elegans*, for short), the fruit fly *Drosophila*, amphibians, chicks, and a large variety of organisms whose whole genomes are now known. These experiments have emphasized one important lesson: Genes act differently under different conditions. Genes display what is called a *norm of reaction*, meaning that their expression varies according to the environments in which they develop. We are all familiar with examples in which phenotype is altered by the environment—most particularly in plants, in which the height, shape, flowering capacity, and so on are strongly influenced by external factors such as amount of water, quality of soil, humidity, altitude, and sunlight. There is a counterpart to this norm of reaction in animals as well, though in some cases the developmental process is less plastic than that routinely observed in plants. The standard examples of genetic traits used in textbooks (seed coat color or texture as in Mendel's peas, black or white coat color in guinea pigs, and human eye color) are chosen because they are the most discrete and least variable, giving the general impression that such patterns are the rule. In fact, they are the exception.

The recent revelation that the human genome, instead of containing 140,000 or more genes as originally estimated, is made up of as few as 30,000 genes, underscores the complex interactions that must occur during development. As geneticist Richard Strohman stressed in a recent paper,[2] the surprise expressed by Human Genome Project geneticists at the small number of genes was based on a kind of general determinist thinking—that is, that there needed to be a single gene for each of our hundreds of thousands of adult "traits." In fact, we (and all organisms) apparently do a lot in our development through gene-gene and gene-environment interactions. A process known as "alternative splicing" (in which the messenger RNA transcribed directly from the cell's DNA can be cut and spliced to yield dozens or even hundreds of different proteins), discovered over twenty years ago, has revealed one mechanism by which different outcomes can result from the same genes. Like a contractor who has a certain number of modular plans that can be combined and recombined to produce a number of quite different structures, the organism—especially the human organism, with all its complexity—develops using a relatively small number of components that interact with one another (e.g., via their chemical products, the proteins) to produce the many variants of our inherited traits. Development, the interaction that leads to traits, is the crucial ingredient often left out of the genetic determinists' equation. Although most human-behavior geneticists pay lip service to the environment (for example, those who claim that there is a genetic basis for criminal or violent behavior acknowledge that upbringing and socioeconomic conditions also play a role), in reality both researchers and popularizers focus the vast majority of their attention only on the gene.

If gene-gene and gene-environment interactions are crucial in understanding the origins of physical and biochemical traits, they are even more important in understanding complex traits like human-behavior, mental function, and personality. Here, the human-behavior geneticist encounters an even more difficult problem than that faced by the animal-behavior geneticist. For ethical reasons we are limited in the experimentation we can carry out on human beings, whether adults, children, or fetuses. We cannot control environmental conditions rigorously in raising children, something that would be necessary to ascertain whatever interaction might be operative in determining, for example, a tendency toward violent or criminal behavior. As a result, human-behavior geneticists have been forced to adopt more indirect methods, such as reliance on twin and adoption studies, in which behavioral traits in adults are correlated with the degree of biological relatedness between parent and child or between collateral relatives (siblings, first cousins, etc.). These methods provide circumstantial evidence at best, primarily because they are unable to correct for, or even identify, the myriad factors involved in the development of a child from conception to maturity. I do not fault human-behavior geneticists for the complexity of the problem they wish to investigate; I do fault them for all too frequently failing to recognize that complexity and therefore the difficulty of drawing rigorous conclusions from their investigations. My assessment is that human-behavior genetics at present can contribute little or nothing of use in determining the causes of certain human social behaviors—like criminality—and that to proceed under any other assumption will certainly lead to a legal and ethical quagmire equivalent to that encountered by the eugenics movement of 1910–1940 and its push toward massive sterilization, and eventually euthanasia, of the so-called unfit.

Before continuing, let me emphasize that all human-behavior has an underlying genetic basis in the sense that for us to carry out behavioral actions, we need a nervous system, sense organs, and muscles, all of which develop from information contained in the genotype. Humans are capable of kinds of behavior different from that of other primates (language, use of a high degree of technology, for example) or gall wasps because of the underlying genetic structure of our nervous system. But those behavioral capabilities are experienced species wide and are not generally the issues of interest to human-behavior geneticists. What behavior geneticists seem to be far more interested in are *individual differences* among members of the species or of subgroups (e.g., racial or geographical populations within the species): in other words, why person *A* commits criminal acts and person *B* does not, or why one particular group (e.g., African Americans) has a higher rate of criminal conviction than another (e.g., Caucasians).

A second point I wish to emphasize is that *all individual differences in human-behavior are biological* at some level. We are material, biological beings in every aspect of our existence. Learned and environmentally induced effects on the phenotype of organisms are also biologically based, but they are not genetic in origin, nor do they become incorporated into the genotype of the individual that acquired them. For example, if person A memorizes poem *A* and person B memorizes poem *B*, and if molecular methods were refined enough, it would be possible to detect different molecular configurations and synaptic connections in the two individuals that reflected the two different sets of stored information. Although we know very little at present about how such fine-level changes associated with environmental inputs in human beings actually are expressed on a cellular level, some exciting research on the neurobiology of learning is being carried out on simpler organisms such as sea slugs (*Aplysia*) and the fruit fly *Drosophila*. Hopefully this research will provide us with a more detailed picture of how different environmental inputs become encoded in the inter- and intracellular make-up of the organism. The question is not whether genetics or environment is involved in producing a phenotype, but instead how genes and enviroment interact to produce given behaviors and personalities.

At the moment, there is no easy or practical way to sort out these two components of most human phenotypes, especially behavioral ones, so it is impossible to claim that there is no genetic component to a complex social trait, for example, criminality. However the difficulty in replicating claims of genetic causality in the past, coupled with our knowledge, however rudimentary, about human development, makes the prospect dim of ever working out in a rigorous way how much genes affect complex behaviors. Some of the methodological problems involved in human-behavior genetics research are discussed in the next section.

Methodological Pitfalls in Behavior Genetics Research

There are a number of methodological problems encountered in human-behavior genetics research that seriously undermine the strong claims made by many researchers and publicized by the media and other popularizers. Because space is limited, I will list only some of the more common of these problems. All have been discussed in greater detail by various authors.[3]

1. *Definition of phenotype.* Human social behaviors and personality traits are highly complex entities and involve many components. To make genetic claims about a particular trait, it is necessary to be able to define the trait clearly and unambiguously. In most studies in the past there has been a tendency to employ essentialist and reified definitions of such behaviors as criminality, alcoholism, or homosexuality. Essentialist thinking derives from Plato's notion of universal categories and involves treating complex and variable entities as if they had a single underlying *essence* or nature. Reification involves treating abstract categories, such as criminality or "intelligence," as if they were concrete entities like height or eye color. For example, to treat the theft of a loaf of bread, a car, and company funds as if they all had the same core characteristics or cause would be essentialist thinking. And further, to treat them as if they were a "thing" that had material reality and could, for example, be quantified like physical traits would be reification. Essentialist thinking and reification err by lumping together a wide variety of often quite different phenomena, ascribing to them a unity and sense of physical reality they may not possess.

2. *Subjectivity of definitions.* A related problem in attempting to define phenotypes is that categorization of social behaviors is a highly subjective process. What is an alcoholic, a homosexual, a criminal? Are manic depression (bipolar disorder) and schizophrenia two separate kinds of mental problem, as was once thought, or are they, perhaps, different manifestations of the same basic problem, as more and more psychiatrists now think? There may be some practical utility among clinicians to giving a single, shorthand name to a complex of behavioral traits, but that does not

mean the behavior is a single thing or has the same underlying causes in different cases. People may commit a criminal act, or many criminal acts, for a wide variety of reasons, so that labeling them "criminals" in some typological way conceals those very real differences in causality.

A second problem some behavioral geneticists face, aside from the mere complexity and multivariate basis of many human-behaviors, is the subjectivity involved in making and applying definitions, what I call the "Robin Hood Problem." That is, should Robin Hood be classified as a hero or a criminal? This depends on the perspective of the person doing the classifying: in this case, the poor of rural England or the sheriff of Nottingham, respectively. Psychologists and psychiatrists have struggled with the definitional problem for generations, as reflected in the changing classification of various psychological conditions (including removal of some and addition of others) in their *Diagnostic and Statistical Manual* (now in the second version of its fourth edition). Geneticist Thomas Hunt Morgan stated this problem most succinctly in 1925 when examining then-current claims about the hereditary nature of feeblemindedness:

The case most often quoted is feeblemindedness that has been said to be inherited as a Mendelian recessive, but until some more satisfactory definition can be given as to where feeblemindedness begins and ends, and until it has been determined how many and what internal physical defects may produce a general condition of this sort, . . . it is extravagant to pretend to claim that there is a single Mendelian factor for this condition.[4]

If a particular phenotypic trait or category cannot be readily recognized by independent observers, it is impossible to carry out a genetic study on that trait with reliable outcomes.

3. *Biased population sample.* Sample populations are often not matched for age, sex, socioeconomic status, or environmental inputs such as diet, exercise, and home or workplace stress. In some cases, as in a certain twin study in Minnesota, subjects are volunteers who have quickly surmised that if they report a majority of characteristics that differ from their identical twin, they might be dropped from the study (for many subjects being in the study has its exciting and pleasurable side). Kamin reports that in *Crime and Human Nature*, James Q. Wilson and Richard Herrnstein quote an older study by Sheldon and Eleanor Glueck that attempted to correlate body morphology with criminality.[5] Comparing five hundred juvenile delinquents in Boston with a matched population of five hundred nondelinquents, the Gluecks concluded that a tendency toward crime was associated with a square-muscular body type (mesomorphic in the lingo of the trade). As it turned out,

however, the two populations were not carefully matched for age: Although the range of ages for both groups was ten to seventeen, the majority were ages fourteen or fifteen, and in more than half of these cases the delinquent was six to fourteen months older than the nondelinquent. During early and middle adolescence such age differences have enormous effects on body structure (another study found a sample of Princeton students to be more mesomorphic than the Boston delinquents). Choosing study groups and matching controls is extremely difficult in human populations where so many variables are at work.

4. *Results that cannot be replicated.* Studies done on one population in many cases cannot be repeated in another population. For example, an original study by Kenneth Kidd et al. that purported to find a linkage between a section of chromosome 11 and familial manic depression was based on data collected in an old-order Amish population in Pennsylvania and could not be replicated in an Icelandic population where manic depression was also common.[6] A finding in a study by Hamer et al.,[7] showing an association between male homosexuality and a marker on the X chromosome, although found in a weaker association in a second study by the same researchers,[8] could not be confirmed at all by a Canadian team using a completely separate set of families.[9] Similar problems have also been found with studies linking the dopamine D_2 receptor gene and alcoholism and with studies purporting to have identified a gene for "novelty seeking." Failure of others to replicate the findings of a scientific inquiry seriously undermines the validity of claims resulting from that scientific inquiry.

5. *Misuse of statistics (especially those regarding heritability).* Although statistics can be valuable tools in scientific research, they can also be misused in ways that can give erroneous impressions about the validity of any data set. For example, in human-behavior genetics the concepts of *heritability* and *analysis of variance* (on which heritability is based) have been so consistently misused that some researchers have abandoned them altogether.[10] Heritability and analysis of variance are concepts introduced and developed by British biometrician and eugenicist R. A. Fisher between 1918 and 1932 as an aid to practical breeders. They provide an indirect way to distinguish the genetic from the environmental components of traits. Heritability calculations are a substitute for actual breeding results and can legitimately be used only (1) within a specified population, (2) when genetic relationships among members of the population are clearly known (such as which individual is the parent of which set of offspring) and (3) when it can be reasonably assumed that all

individuals in the population have been subjected to the same environmental conditions. For human-behavior genetics it is often questionable whether the last assumption prevails for all members of a study population. For example, Berkeley psychologist Arthur Jensen's conclusion in the 1960s that the persistent difference in IQ scores between blacks and whites in the United States was due to genetics was based upon heritability data. However, the conclusions were invalidated because Jensen assumed both populations shared the same environment (educational, cognitive, dietary, socioeconomic).[11] Heritability studies done on one population cannot be extrapolated to another.

Another problem with heritability estimates is that they apply only to populations, not individuals. Even if it could be reliably established that intelligence or criminality had a high heritability in a given population, it would say nothing about *any given individual* within that population. Thus as a predictor of individual behavior, which is the only legitimate use to which such studies could be directed, heritability estimates are of no value. These sorts of limitations in the use of heritability estimates are seldom discussed in any detail in either the scientific or popular literature when high heritabilities for certain traits are quoted.

6. *Conflation of biological differences with genetic differences.* Many behavior genetics studies conflate measurable biological differences (for example, neurotransmitter or enzyme levels) among individuals with a difference in genetic constitution. Neurophysiologists and other researchers have found that such biological differences are often the result of different experiences to which the organism has been subjected and may have nothing to do with genetics, as in the poetry example used earlier. On a more empirical level, for example, neurobiologists have shown that in primates and other social animals, various neurotransmitter levels, such as 5-hydroxytryptamine (serotonin), can change *as a result of* a change in the animal's social rank or other behavioral activities. Neurotransmitter levels may be thus as much or more a product of changed environments as of differences in the genetic makeup of the individual.

Plasticity of the Genotype-Phenotype Relationship

One of the lynchpins of genetic-determinist theory is that there is a regular, predictable relationship between genotype and phenotype. After all, the ultimate value of determinist theories is their ability to predict the phenotype of offspring, and thus their use in reproductive decisions. Retaining a fetus to term or aborting it is, under these circumstances, a choice made on the basis of genetic information that makes a reliable choice possible. Today, however, after a generation or more of molecular and biochemical genetics, biologists realize that there is no one-to-one correspondence between genotype and phenotype—a view emphasized by the concept of norm of reaction discussed earlier in the chapter.

To illustrate this point, let me turn now to one current example of how complex the picture is even when the genetic components of a system are extremely well understood. Cystic fibrosis (CF) is a devastating degenerative disease that is fatal in many people. It is a genetic condition caused by mutations in the gene coding for a protein called cystic fibrosis transmembrane regulator (CFTR). CFTR functions as a channel in the membranes of many types of epithelial (lining) cells, regulating the outflow of chloride ions from the cell. The CF gene has been mapped and sequenced and has been found to have well over eight hundred site mutations within the gene itself. In Caucasians the most common mutation is Δ F 508; an individual who inherits two copies of that gene (i.e., in genetic terms a homozygote) can produce a severe set of symptoms that can be very debilitating and shorten their life span. The mutant gene prevents or greatly reduces the outflow of chloride in almost all cells. As a result, water tends to remain in the cells with the chloride, causing the cell surface to become dried out. In lung tissue, the dry surface becomes encrusted with mucus, thus restricting air flow.

The effects on other tissues, such as the pancreas, intestines and vas deferens (in males) can also be severe. The CF gene thus shows what geneticists call *pleitropy*, meaning that the gene has multiple sites of action. For example, various mutations within the CF gene affect the ability of the pancreas to secrete its digestive enzymes. In males, mutations within the gene cause a developmental failure of the bilateral vas deferens (which transports sperm from the testes to the urethra) to develop, thus leading to sterility. In contrast to the effects on lung tissue, in many individuals with the CF gene, chloride secretion from sweat glands is *increased*.

Although CF mutations have a wide range of effects, researchers have found that the effects on different organs within the same individuals, and in the same organ among different individuals, vary enormously (figure 13.3). To the extent that there are data on the cause of these variations, the degree of expression appears to depend on which part of the gene was mutated, on other genes present in cells (i.e., genetic background), and on aspects of the individual's environment such as diet, exercise, and smoking (at least with regard to effects on lung tissue). The *black box* in which

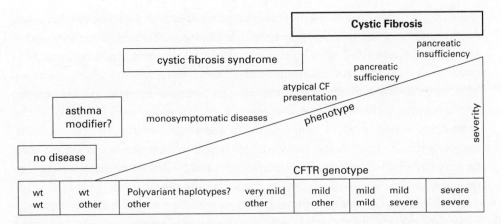

Figure 13.3
Range of phenotypic traits associated with various genotypic combinations of the cystic fibrosis gene

genotype is converted into phenotype is thus an extremely complex one that defies prediction from knowing the genetics alone. According to a recent report:

Inheritance of CFTR mutations and acquiring the CF phenotype are merely [the] beginning and ending in the succession of a series of events leading to CF [phenotype]. These intermediary events include only partially known processes at the molecular, cellular and organ levels. A CFTR genotype constitutes only a potential (predisposition) for CF disease, which will be to various degrees (penetrance) expressed and translated into CF pathophysiology. As shown by [many] studies, the process of genotype realization is a complex and variable one; even inheritance of the same mutations can result in remarkably variable manifestations of disease. . . . This is especially true for the pulmonary component of the CF phenotype, which is the most variable and least reliably predicted solely on the basis of genotype.[12]

Sweat gland chloride levels, traditionally the easiest way to test clinically for CF, are also highly variable and are thus not as reliable an indicator of the presence of a genetic defect as was originally thought. The point I want to stress here is that even in a case in which we know so much about a particular gene and in which the clinical manifestations of a particular phenotype (when they are present) are clearly recognizable (not fuzzy, subjective categories like "criminality" or "alcoholism"), the path between geno- and phenotype is not a straightforward, deterministic one. Natural selection has evolved a developmental process that is both complex and highly flexible to meet changing conditions of the external environment and the individual's genetic background. A review of the literature on the genetics of CF makes it clear that various researchers have recognized that environmental compo-nents must play a role in expression of the CF mutations. Yet surprisingly, the major review articles examined offer no evidence that researchers ever collected and ana-lyzed data regarding any environmental factors—not even the obvious one of whether or not the individuals in the various studies were smokers![13] Such extreme developmental blindness is one consequence of the widespread influence of the genetic-determinist model. Although the influence of environment is explicitly acknowledged, environmental factors are subsequently ignored. As a result, no data on gene-environment interactions are available, and by default, the gene emerges as the most important causative agent in producing the phenotype.

If this kind of variability between genotype and phenotype exists for such rela-tively definable conditions as CF, what are the prospects for predicting, from fetal analysis, such highly complex traits as "criminality", "alcoholism", or violence-prone behavior? The answer, it seems to me, is "not very high." Yet behavior geneti-cists and their financial backers, such as the National Institutes of Mental Health (NIMH), are proceeding to carry out studies that attempt to make the predictive link between genotype and phenotype for exactly those kinds of conditions.

The Dangers of Behavior Genetics: A Lesson from History

It may be all well and good to point out the limitations of present genetic methods for any rigorous account of how genes and environment interact to produce a phe-notype, but we might ask seriously, "Who cares?" Is it only a relatively small group of biologists and historians of science who are concerned about such extravagant claims? Or are there more serious social and political as well as biological reasons why the issue is important, especially with respect to the legal system? In my view it *is* an important issue, and one on which history can shed some light. In the early twentieth century (roughly 1900–1940) a widespread movement in the United States and Europe, known as *eugenics*, was making similar strong claims about the genetic basis of human behavioral and personality traits—mostly those traits considered deleterious, like criminality or feeblemindedness. Eugenicists based their hereditar-ian claims on the then-new and exciting science of Mendelian genetics, which like molecular genetics today was making great strides in advancing understanding of basic genetic mechanisms (in those days, how genes were transmitted and recom-bined in subsequent generations). Eugenicists' claims had a far-reaching impact on legislation in a number of countries, including the United States, Scandinavia, and most of all Germany after the Nazi takeover in 1933. The historical development of the eugenics movement can provide some useful lessons for us today. We need not walk the path our predecessors did in their enthusiasm to apply the findings of a new science to the solution of long-standing social problems.

Eugenics was a term coined in 1883 by Francis Galton, geographer, statistician, and cousin of Charles Darwin. It referred to "the right to be well-born," or in the words of Galton's foremost American disciple, Charles B. Davenport, the "science of human improvement by better breeding."[14] Eugenics dominated much of the social-reform thinking that abounded in the first four decades of the last century. Eugenicists argued that many social problems could be eliminated by discouraging or preventing the reproduction of individuals deemed genetically unfit (negative eugenics), whereas desirable social traits could be increased by encouraging reproduction among those deemed most genetically fit (positive eugenics). Eugenicists thought of themselves as bringing the latest scientific research to bear on old and previously unsolved social problems, among the most prominent of which were criminality and violent behavior.

Many eugenicists, especially those carrying out research work, had an interest in, or experience with, agricultural breeding and thought of their work as extending the knowledge of animal husbandry to the improvement of the human species in much the same way as a breeder improves a flock or herd. "The most progressive revolution in history could be achieved," Davenport wrote in a 1923 letter, "if in some way or other human matings could be placed on the same high plane as . . . horse breeding."[15] Indeed, as historian of science Barbara Kimmelman has shown, the first organized eugenics group in the United States was founded in 1906 as the "Eugenics Committee" of the American Breeders' Association, headed by David Starr Jordan, then president of Stanford University.[16] Like the breeder, the eugenicist used pedigree analysis to determine the hereditary makeup of family lines; but unlike the breeder, the eugenicist could not use controlled mating experiments to test conclusions drawn from pedigree analysis. Hence, methodologically, social transmission and biological transmission were conflated. Nonetheless, eugenicists put forth numerous claims for inheritance of a wide variety of behaviors, including pauperism, scholastic ability, feeblemindedness, manic depression, pellagra, criminality, and thalassophilia (love of the sea). Moreover, they relied on and extended late-nineteenth- and early-twentieth-century family studies, such as those of the infamous Juke and Kallikak families, which supposedly documented in a dramatic way the ultimate outcome of hereditary degeneracy (figure 13.4).

Figure 13.4
The "effects" of good and bad heredity on the descendants of Martin Kallikak

Much of the research work was carried out or organized through the Eugenics Record Office (ERO) at Cold Spring Harbor on Long Island. The ERO was the institutional nerve center of North American eugenics; it was directed by Davenport and funded by the Harriman family of New York until 1916. At that time it was taken over by the Carnegie Institution of Washington, which maintained it until its closure in 1940. The ERO was managed by Davenport's enthusiastic minion Harry Hamilton Laughlin, whom he had recruited in 1910 from a teaching position at an agricultural and teacher-training school in northeastern Missouri.[17] Laughlin served eugenics in a number of capacities: superintendent of the ERO (1910–1940), propagandist in state legislatures, "expert eugenics witness" to the House Committee on Immigration and Naturalization (1921–1924), tireless organizer of meetings, author of newsletters and articles on eugenics, and head of a series of summer training sessions for eugenics field workers held at the ERO and funded by John D. Rockefeller Jr. The ERO boasted a distinguished board of scientific advisors in the early years of its existence, including such important figures as W. E. Castle (mammalian geneticist) at Harvard; David Starr Jordan (ichthyologist and evolutionary biologist), president of Stanford University; Irving Fisher (economist) at Yale; Thomas Hunt Morgan (at the time just beginning the work with *Drosophila* that would earn him a Nobel Prize in 1933) at Columbia; and Alexander Graham Bell, who had a long-standing interest in hereditary deafness, which ran in his family. Besides the ERO, many other eugenics organizations existed in the United States, including state branches of the nationwide American Eugenics Society, the Race Betterment Foundation (funded by the Kellogg cereal family in Battle Creek, Michigan), and the Human Betterment Foundation in Pasadena, California.

Beyond research, eugenicists were also interested in social action, including education and popularization of eugenics, and in working to pass laws that would promote eugenic goals. In the former category (popularization) eugenicists wrote books and magazine articles, promoted exhibits, delivered eugenic sermons and held Fitter Family contests at state fairs, and even produced eugenic movies. Eugenics became incorporated into most major high school textbooks from the 1920s well into the 1950s.[18] The picture that emerged for even the most casual reader was that eugenics represented the cutting edge of modern science, the application of rational scientific principles to the solution of what had been seen as intractable social problems. Gone were the ineffective charity and social-work programs that eugenicists were convinced only perpetuated pauperism, criminality, and alcoholism, because they did not touch the source of the problem: bad genes. Indeed, charity and public handouts, according to eugenics literature, only increased the problem by allowing the degenerate segments of the population to have more children.

Eugenicists were especially active in the United States in areas of immigration restriction (1921, 1924) and in the enactment of state eugenic sterilization laws. On the immigration issue, eugenicists were convinced that the newer immigrants coming to the United States after 1880, mostly from central and southern Europe, the Balkans, Russia, and Poland, were biologically inferior (the "dregs of humanity," as one eugenic pamphlet put it) to the older Anglo-Saxon and Nordic stocks whose immigration had flourished in the first half of the century. Laughlin and others carried out studies purporting to show the high rates of pauperism, feeblemindedness, criminality, and other deleterious traits—claimed to be genetic in origin—that existed in various immigrant groups. Laughlin took his findings to Congress, where he appeared as the official "expert eugenics witness" to the House Committee on Immigration and Naturalization, whose chairman, Representative Albert Johnson of Washington state, was an enthusiastic eugenicist who several years prior had been appointed honorary president of the Eugenics Research Association. Laughlin's data, such as his comparison of rates of incarceration for criminal behavior among different national groups (figure 13.5), were designed to convince the House committee that scientific evidence, not ethnic bias or political expediency, made such immigrant groups a bad risk. The objective cover of science had considerable political appeal to the legislators. The Johnson Act, or Immigration Restriction Act, passed both houses of Congress in 1924 and was signed into law by President Calvin Coolidge, acting on his earlier assertion that the country "cannot have too many inhabitants of the right kind."[19] The Johnson Act had drastic consequences. Among others, boats bringing refugees from Nazi Germany in the mid- and late 1930s were turned back because of the "quota" established by the Johnson Act. We can only wonder about the fate of their passengers.

Eugenicists were also instrumental in lobbying for the passage of compulsory sterilization laws at the state level. Articles in newspapers and popular magazines emphasized the cost to the average citizen of maintaining degenerate and inferior people *and their children* at state expense. Laughlin drew up a Model Sterilization Law that was sent to all state legislatures. The results were successful: By 1935 thirty states had enacted laws that allowed inmates of state institutions (prisons, insane asylums, sanitariums, and mental hospitals) to be forcibly sterilized after examination by a "eugenics committee."[20] "Habitual criminality," "sexual perversion," "low moral sense," "hereditary feeblemindedness," and epilepsy were all categories

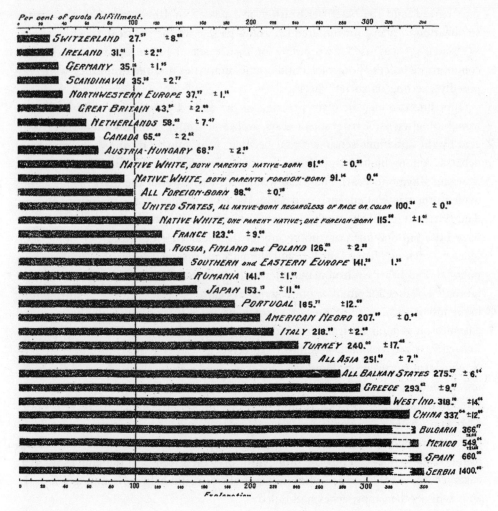

Figure 13.5
Chart presented by Harry Laughlin before the House Committee on Immigration and Naturalization purporting to show rates of incarceration among different national groups

that could lead to compulsory sterilization. By 1935 over twenty-one thousand eugenically motivated sterilizations had been performed, and by the early 1960s it has been estimated that over sixty-four thousand people had been sterilized in the United States alone.[21] Sweden carried out almost the same number over the same time period, and the Nazi sterilization law, passed in 1933, eventually led to the sterilization of over four hundred thousand people. In the political arena, eugenics, as "science," was used to promote or justify social policies that conformed to common prejudices about racial and ethnic minorities and the drain they were supposedly exerting on society at large.

Opposition to eugenic claims started in the early 1920s. Some objections came from biologists, some from sociologists, and some from journalists and writers bothered by the antiethnic sentiment that became so prominent during the immigration debates. Among biologists, protozoologist Herbert Spencer Jennings and geneticists Morgan, Raymond Pearl, and H. J. Muller all wrote about the extravagant claims made in the name of eugenics and about the lack of rigor in the analysis of eugenic data (virtually all of the methodological objections discussed earlier in the chapter were raised in one form or another about the older eugenics research). Some sociologists, such as Henry Ward, noted the lack of any real discussion of economic, political, and other environmental factors in the writings of many eugenicists. And journalist Walter Lippman wrote a series of scathing attacks in the *New Republic* in the fall of 1922 on the claims of a genetic basis for IQ.[22] Many Catholics opposed eugenics on general doctrinal grounds, and in 1930 Pope Pius XI put forward the Encyclical *Casti connubi*, specifically directed at the eugenics movement and its emphasis on sterilization. However, this was seen, even by those opposed to eugenics, as theological and doctrinal, not rational and scientific, opposition. Except for Lippman and Pearl, who each published one major attack on eugenics in H. L. Mencken's widely circulated *American Mercury*,[23] most of the criticisms from scientists were published in more scholarly journals and did not become well known to the reading public. Thus the impression prevailed well into the late 1930s that eugenics was a valid science whose social policies could help solve a range of problems where other approaches had failed.

Although the old-style eugenics claims from the 1910s through the 1930s did decline in popularity and visibility by the start of World War II, the reasons for this are not altogether clear. It was distinctly not because of widespread public disbelief in eugenic claims or because geneticists undermined its scientific validity. Increasing public awareness of Nazi racial policies, as reported in U.S. newspapers, may have

played some role, though the full horrors of the Holocaust and its eugenic justification were not revealed until after the war. It is most likely that in the United States,
at any rate, the withdrawal by 1940 of support by the patrons of eugenics, including the Rockefeller Foundation and Carnegie Institution of Washington, may have
sent the old-style eugenics movement into decline. The wealthy elites had used
eugenic "science" to oppose aspects of unrestricted immigration and to build ethnic
prejudices (whether intended or not) against immigrant workers, who were actively
organizing militant unions, many overtly against the large Carnegie and Rockefeller
interests.[24] Eugenics arose and flourished in a context of considerable economic,
political, and social turbulence, an age dominated, in one historian's term, by "the
search for order."[25]

Eugenicists most certainly did not invent the whole raft of social problems to
which their genetic solutions were directed. The period in which eugenics thrived
was one of great social upheaval and change in the United States—and with certain
differences in time frame, in most countries of western Europe as well—concomitant with massive urbanization, industrialization, and increasingly unstable economic processes, including depressions every ten to fifteen years, the "labor wars"
as one historian has characterized the period,[26] and massive unemployment. This
was also the era of the Bolshevik revolution in Russia, militant Industrial Workers
of the World ("Wobbly") agitation in the mining and lumber industries in the Pacific
Northwest, the anti-immigrant hysteria of the Sacco and Vanzetti case (in which
two Italian radicals in Massachusetts were accused of murder in 1921 and sentenced
to death), and the Seattle general strike of 1919. Eugenicists argued that their
approach was the most efficient way to solve such recurrent problems and bring
order into the chaotic economic and social arena. The logic of eugenics was compelling: If the increasing number and extent of social problems were due largely to
an increasing number of genetically defective people in American society, then the
most efficient and lasting way to solve the problem was to attack it at the source:
that is, to prevent the reproduction of the defectives themselves. And of course,
those deemed defective were usually the poor and ethnic and racial minorities, the
very people least able to defend themselves. As author Allan Chase succinctly put
it, the eugenicists' policies were "aimed directly at the gonads of the poor."[27] But
national efficiency was a major issue in the 1920s and 1930s, not only in the United
States but also in Europe, and in this country it and eugenics were incorporated
particularly well into the ideology of the progressive era. One headline from a British
newspaper found in Laughlin's archive summed up the reasoning behind eugenics:

"Rationalizing Mankind: 'Big Business' Methods in Evolution; Eugenic Reform." Efficiency—"Taylorism" was its industrial name—brought about by the use of technically trained experts was an effective argument in a period in which inflation was rampant and, after the Depression, joblessness was high. Historian Diane Paul has pointed out that biologists and others who were opposed to, or at least skeptical about, compulsory eugenical sterilization before 1929 were considerably more favorable after the stock market crash of that year.[28] Eugenicists and their supporters played on concerns about livelihood, taxes, safety, and social chaos to build support for supposedly scientific solutions to social problems.

Conclusions: Lessons for Today

To turn to the second set of questions posed at the outset of this chapter—How can current knowledge of human-behavior genetics be of use in the criminal justice system?—there are now several levels of response that can be given.

To the question of whether current evidence allows us to predict, from various biological indicators early in life (including prenatal tests), whether a given individual will display a propensity for criminal or violent behavior, I think the answer is clearly "no." No genes for criminality or even for aggression have ever been identified, and no physical or physiological markers for such behavior have shown any strong or reliable correlation. Despite this, a current study in New York's Washington Park (Manhattan) neighborhood, sponsored by NIMH, is gathering data on the younger siblings of boys held in juvenile detention to determine whether these younger sibs share any biological characteristics in common (with their older brothers and with each other). The study has raised many ethical questions, such as making available to the researchers the names of families with children who are in prison, performing a battery of physiological and psychological tests on quite young children (down to six months of age) that requires an overnight hospital stay, suspension of any regular medications, and a rigorously controlled diet during the testing period. That such studies are seen as producing valid data for associating biology with criminal behavior is itself disturbing. That the results could be used to stigmatize young boys as "potential criminals" and thus become a self-fulfilling prophecy has dark overtones. From what I have tried to suggest in earlier parts of this chapter, such studies, past and present, almost uniformly overlook the obvious environmental factors that might affect criminal and aggressive behavior. The NIMH study is no exception. Although the grant proposal notes that socioeconomic factors play a role, no data have been or are being collected on these factors or on the effects of home environment on the study subjects. In short, genetic blindness has once again focused attention only on biology.

Unfortunately, new human-behavior genetics claims and large-scale programs based on them are continuing to be put forward today. Headlines still continue to inform us that there are genes for "anxiety," "coyness," "family conflict resolution" (based on studies in mice), and athletic prowess (especially related to people of African American descent). Of particular interest in the criminal justice community are the ongoing claims that criminal, violent, or other forms of antisocial behavior are significantly determined by genes. A case in point is a recent report in *USA Today* that describes studies in Oregon showing that crime runs in families, with the implication that genetics lies at the heart of the problem.[29] Great Britain is currently about to launch an ambitious program to examine eighty thousand people and their relatives to determine the roles of genes, environment, and their interactions in the etiology of disease.[30] At least six other countries are preparing to follow suit, with Iceland already in the lead with a comprehensive genetic survey of its entire population. A 2002 report in *The New Scientist*, claiming that a person's physical appearance can be determined from a readout of his or her DNA,[31] has garnered considerable interest and enthusiasm from police and other investigative agencies, though critics, biologists among them, argue that the method is too crude to produce any very specifically useful images. As with earlier cases, most of these claims are being propagated through popular or semipopular sources, leaving the distinct impression in the public mind that specific genes are already known, or will eventually be found, that profoundly influence complex traits such as criminal behavior. The smoke screen effect continues to obscure the very real socioeconomic factors that even the strongest genetic determinists acknowledge play a role in the development of antisocial or other supposedly pathological behaviors. But where does the *real* illness lie? Might it not be more pathological for children of lower socioeconomic families to respond with apathy and passivity to the degrading circumstances in which they are raised than to respond with anger and violent behavior? Even if there are genes to be triggered, all sides of these debates acknowledge that certain environments are more likely to provide the trigger than others. This is just another way of saying that the more we can work to provide good environments for *all* people, the less likely it is that undesirable behaviors will arise. In most cases, the genetic argument, even if it were valid, is largely irrelevant in determining the origins of criminal or antisocial behavior.

Even if valid biochemical or genetic markers made accurate predictions about such behavior possible, and even if environmental factors could be shown to be negligible, how would results of something like the NIMH study be used? Gene therapy is a long way down the road even if a true gene or genes for criminality were to be identified. The only viable intervention at this point is administration of drugs—Ritalin, Prozac, or other behavior-modifying agents—a practice that raises a whole spectrum of ethical and legal questions. To place young children on long-term (possibly lifetime?) drug use is chilling enough even when they have displayed truly pathological behavior. To place them on drugs because they *might* exhibit such behavior seems ethically and legally reprehensible.

As to whether behavior genetic evidence could (legitimately) be introduced in a trial as a means of exonerating someone involved in criminal activity, or lightening the sentence imposed, I think the answer is very much the same as above. The kind of data that exist at present simply do not allow us to draw any valid conclusions about a genetic influence in criminal behavior. There is no reliable genetic evidence that suggests we are puppets responding to strings pulled by our genes. Although genetic evidence has supposedly been introduced in trials for the purpose of absolving the defendant of some degree of responsibility (a 1994 article in the "Marketplace" section of the *Wall Street Journal* details such a case),[32] from what I can tell it has not been taken seriously by the legal community.

Let me conclude with a qualification and a warning. The qualification is that if and when we ever develop truly reliable evidence about a largely genetic, environmentally nonmodifiable cause for criminal behavior, the way in which it is used in the criminal justice system will have to be evaluated in the same way we have traditionally evaluated other kinds of technical information, such as psychiatric data. The current debates about the execution of mentally retarded criminals on death row is a prime example. Most forms of mental retardation are readily diagnosed by experts. Some are truly genetic (Down syndrome, for example), whereas others are congenital (such as fetal alcohol syndrome or cerebral palsy), but in neither case is the retardation the fault of the individual. The criminal justice system must allow for such evidence in its ponderings. Yet the evidence must be agreed upon by experts, and as we have seen, in the case of claims about a genetic basis of crime, there is clearly no consensus at the moment.

The warning is to avoid accepting at face value every new claim about a genetic basis for some complex human behavior, especially in the case of behaviors that are likely to involve claims of criminality and forms of antisocial behavior that could affect decisions within the criminal justice system. Scanty, misinterpreted data are worse than no data at all, and as the adage tells us, "a little knowledge"—

especially, as in this case, circumstantial and unverified knowledge—"can be a dangerous thing."

Notes

1. "Spectre at the Feast," *Science* (November 1995): 35.

2. Richard C. Strohman, "Human Genome Project: Where Is the Program?" (unpublished manuscript, University of California, Berkeley, 1998).

3. Richard C. Lewontin, *The Triple Helix: Gene, Organism and Environment* (Cambridge, Mass.: Harvard University Press, 2000); Steven Rose, "The Rise of Neurogenetic Determinism," *Nature* 373 (1995): 380–382; Richard C. Strohman, "Ancient Genomes, Wise Bodies, Unhealthy People: Limits to a Genetic Paradigm in Biology and Medicine," *Perspectives in Biology and Medicine* 37 (1993): 112–145; Douglas Wahlsten, "The Objectives of Human Behavior Genetics," *European Bulletin of Congnitive Psychology* 10 (1990): 696–703; Douglas Wahlsten, "Insensitivity of the Analysis of Variance to Heredity-Environment Interaction," *Behavior and Brain Sciences* 13 (1990): 109–161.

4. Thomas Hunt Morgan, *Evolution and Genetics* (Princeton: Princeton University Press, 1925), 200–201.

5. Leon J. Kamin, "Is Crime in the Genes? The Answer May Depend on Who Chooses What Evidence" (review of Wilson and Herrstein's *Crime and Human Nature*), *Scientific American* 254 (1986): 22–27; James Q. Wilson and Edward Herrnstein, *Crime and Human Nature* (New York: Simon and Schuster, 1985); Sheldon Glueck and Eleanor T. Glueck, *Physique and Delinquency* (New York: Harper, 1956).

6. Miranda Robertson, "False Start on Manic Depression," *Nature* 342 (1989): 222.

7. Dean Hamer et al., "A Linkage between DNA Markers on the X Chromosome and Male Sexual Orientation," *Science* 261 (1993): 321–327.

8. Stella Hu et al., "Linkage between Sexual Orientation and Chromosome Xq28 in Males but not in Females," *Nature Genetics* 11 (1995): 248–256.

9. Erica Goode, "Study Questions Gene Influence on Male Homosexuality," *New York Times*, April 23, 1999, A19.

10. Douglas Wahlsten, "Insensitivity of the Analysis of Variance to Heredity-Environment Interaction," 109–161; Wahlsten, "The Objectives of Human Behavior Genetics," 696–703.

11. Jerry Hirsch, Terry R. McGuire, and Atam Vetta, "Concepts of Behavior Genetics and Misapplication to Humans," in *The Evolution of Human Social Behavior*, ed. Joan S. Lockard (New York: Elsevier, 1980), 215–238; Richard C. Lewontin, "Race and Intelligence," *Bulletin of the Atomic Scientist* 26 (July–August 1970): 2–8.

12. Julian Zielenski, "Genotype and Phenotype in Cystic Fibrosis," *Respiration* 67 (2000):127–128.

13. John E. Mickle and Garry R. Cutting, "Genotype-Phenotype Relationships in Cystic Fibrosis," *Medical Clinics of North America* 84 (2000): 597–607; Zielenski, "Genotype and Phenotype in Cystic Fibrosis," 117–133; Eitan Kerem and Batsheva Kerem, "The

Relationship between Genotype and Phenotype in Cystic Fibrosis," *Current Opinion in Pulmonary Medicine* 1 (1995): 450–456. A similar point is made about mortality rates in E. F. McKone, S. S. Emerson, and K. L. Edwards, "Effect of Genotype and Mortality in Cystic Fibrosis: A Retrospective Cohort Study," *The Lancet* 361 (2003), and a similar lack of clear correlation with regard to pulmonary function is reported in A. Hamosh, "Correlation between Genotype and Phenotype in Patients with Cystic Fibrosis," *New England Journal of Medicine* 330 (1994).

14. Charles B. Davenport, *Eugenics* (New York: Henry Holt, 1910).

15. Charles C. Davenport, letter to W. P. Draper, March 23, 1923; Charles B. Davenport Papers, American Philosophical Society, Philadelphia.

16. Barbara A. Kimmelman, "The American Breeders Association: Genetics and Eugenics in an Agricultural Context," *Social Studies of Science* 13 (1983).

17. Garland E. Allen, "The Eugenics Record Office at Cold Spring Harbor, 1910–1940: An Essay in Institutional History," *Osiris* 2 (second series, 1986): 225–264; Frances Hassencahl, "Harry H. Laughlin, 'Expert Eugenics Agent' for the House Committee on Immigration and Naturalization, 1921–1931" (Ph.D. diss., Case Western Reserve University, 1970).

18. Steven Selden, *Inheriting Shame: The Story of Eugenics and Racism in America* (New York: Columbia University Teachers College Press, 1999).

19. Calvin Coolidge, "Whose Country Is This?" *Good Housekeeping*, February 1921, 13–14, 106, 109.

20. Kenneth Ludmerer, *Genetics and American Society: A Historical Appraisal* (Baltimore: Johns Hopkins University Press, 1972).

21. Jonas Robitshcer, *Eugenic Sterilization* (Springfield, Ill.: Thomas, 1973).

22. Leila Zenderland, *Measuring Minds: Henry Herbert Goddard and the Origins of American Intelligence Testing* (Cambridge: Cambridge University Press, 1998), 312–315.

23. Raymond Pearl, "The Biology of Superiority," *American Mercury* 1 (1927): 257–266.

24. Sidney Lens, *The Labor Wars* (New York: Doubleday, 1973).

25. Robert Wiebe, *The Search for Order, 1877–1920* (New York: Hill and Wang, 1967).

26. Lens, *The Labor Wars*.

27. Allan Chase, *The Legacy of Malthus* (New York: Knopf, 1977), 134.

28. Diane Paul, *Controlling Human Heredity: 1865 to the Present* (Atlantic Highlands, N.J.: Humanities Press International, 1995), 134.

29. John Ritter, "A Town Wonders: Does Crime Run in Families?" *USA Today*, September 5, 2002.

30. Gwen Kinkead, "To Study Disease, Britain Plans a Genetic Census," *New York Times*, December 31, 2002.

31. Clare Wilson, "Ready for Your Close-Up? Working Out What Someone Looks Like from Only a DNA Sample is No Longer Science Fiction; You'd Be Surprised What Forensics Experts Can Already Do," *New Scientist*, July 20, 2002.

32. Fox Butterfield, "Man's Genes Made Him Kill, Lawyers Say," *Wall Street Journal*, November 15, 1994, B1.

14

Selective Arrests, an Ever-Expanding DNA Forensic Database, and the Specter of an Early-Twenty-First-Century Equivalent of Phrenology

Troy Duster

We can all celebrate the use of DNA technology to free more than 140 wrongly convicted prisoners, some of whom were on death row, and others who served decades for rapes they did not commit.[1] Similarly, when law enforcement can score a cold hit and catch a rapist because his DNA is on file, there are reasons to applaud. The use of this technology in high-profile cases has led to a full set of arguments for widening the net of the DNA database, so that more and more samples can be included, ranging from those from convicted felons to those from arrestees—from those of suspects to those of the whole population.[2] There are currently about 1.5 million profiles in the national database, but in early 2002, the attorney general of the United States ordered the FBI to generate a plan that is supposed to expand this to 50 million profiles. What more objective way could there be of exculpating the innocent and convicting the guilty? However, such an argument conflates three quite distinct strategies and practices of the criminal justice system that need to be separated and analyzed for their disparate impact on different populations.

The first is the use of DNA in postconviction cases to determine whether there has been a wrongful conviction, the kind of situation that would help to free the innocent. The second is the collection of DNA from suspects or arrestees in pretrial circumstances to increase the DNA database, which in turn is designed to help law enforcement determine whether there are matches between the DNA samples of those suspects or arrestees and tissue samples left at some unsolved crime: the net to catch the guilty. The third is the advocacy of increasing the collection of DNA from a wider and wider band of felons and misdemeanants in the postconviction period, so that there is a record of their DNA profile on file in the event of recidivism. Much like the current situation in which police can stop a driver and determine whether he or she has outstanding warrants or traffic ticket violations that have piled up, the new technology would permit authorities to see if the DNA of the person stopped and arrested matches the DNA on file for someone at an unsolved crime scene.

This is not just hypothetical. In early 2000 the New York City Police Department began a pilot project experimenting with portable DNA laboratories.[3] The police take a buccal swab—some saliva from inside the cheek—of a person stopped for a traffic or other violation and place it on a chip the size of a credit card. They then put this chip through a machine no larger than a handheld compact disc player, which reads the DNA via a laser in two minutes, isolating about thirteen DNA markers to create a profile of the individual. When this task is completed, the police can then transmit these data to a central database, where it currently requires about twelve minutes to determine whether the profile matches that from any crime scene sample on file.

Who could possibly be opposed to the use of these technologies for such crime-fighting purposes? The answer is a bit complex, but it has to do with (1) some hidden social forces that create a patterned bias determining that certain populations will be more likely subjected to DNA profiling and (2) the resuscitation of some old and dangerously regressive ideas about how to explain criminal behavior.

It is now commonplace to laugh at the science of phrenology, a once widely respected and popular research program in the late nineteenth century that attempted to explain crime by measuring the shapes of the heads and faces of criminals. Yet the idea that researchers *begin with a population that is incarcerated*, and then use correlational data from their bodies in an attempt to explain their behavior, is very much alive and well as a theoretical and methodological strategy in the contemporary world. When researchers deploy computer-generated DNA profiles or markers and correlate them with the crimes of those caught in the grip of the criminal justice system, the findings take on the imprimatur of the authority of human molecular genetics.[4] Despite the off-chanted mantra that correlation is not causation, the volatile social and political context of such correlations will require persistent vigilance and close monitoring if we are to avoid the mistakes of the past.

To provide the context for this chapter's discussion of expanding DNA databases, I begin by pointing out yet again the systematic bias, by race, of a full range of behaviors displayed across the criminal justice system, from the decisions by police at the point of stop, search, and arrest, through the sentencing guidelines and practices, to the rates of incarceration. I then turn to empirical evidence that documents recent developments in the literature of forensic science that claim to be able to predict "ethnic affiliation" from population-specific allele frequencies. It is the relationship between these two developments that is the source of my final point: the looming danger of easily crafted DNA-based research programs with the consequent misattribution of genetic causes of crime. I conclude that such research could easily segue into the moral equivalent of a new phrenology for the twenty-first century, something we need to acknowledge, intercept, and avert.

Phenotypical Expression at the Point of Arrest: The Selective Aim of the Artillery in the War on Drugs

In the last three decades, the war on drugs has produced a remarkable transformation of the U.S. prison population. If we turn the clock back no more than sixty years or so, whites constituted approximately 77 percent of all prisoners in America, and blacks accounted for only 22 percent.[5] This provides a context for reviewing Figure 14.1 and the astonishing pattern it reveals in the evolution of general prison incarceration rates by race in recent history. Note the striking increase over the last half century in the incarceration rate for African Americans in relation to that for whites as shown in figure 14.2. In 1933, blacks were incarcerated at a rate

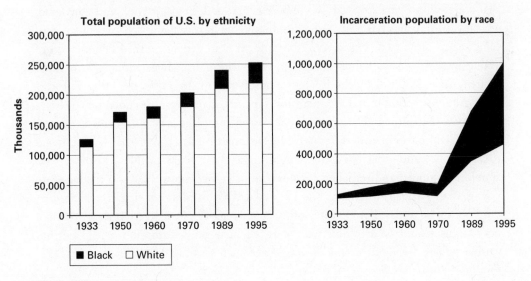

Figure 14.1
Population versus incarceration rate

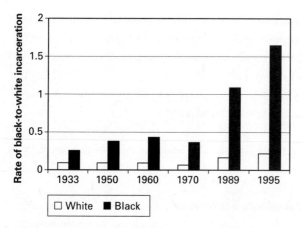

Figure 14.2
Incarceration rate by race

approximately three times that of whites (table 14.1). In 1950, the ratio had increased to approximately four times; in 1960, it was five times; in 1970, it was six times; and in 1989, it was seven times that of whites. These figures are dramatic, yet incarceration is but one end of the long continuum of the criminal justice system that starts with being stopped by the police, arrested, held for trial, and convicted.

The war on drugs has played the dominant role in this story. Whereas racial profiling seems often to be characterized as a local police practice, the phenomenon of young minority males being "just stopped by the police" was actually a national strategy first deployed by the Reagan administration. In 1986, the Drug Enforcement Administration initiated Operation Pipeline, a program designed in Washington, D.C., that ultimately trained twenty-seven thousand law enforcement officers in forty-eight participating states over the ensuing decade. The project was designed to alert police and other law enforcement officials to "likely profiles" of those who should be stopped and searched for possible drug violations. High on the list were young, male African Americans and Latinos driving in cars that signaled that something might be amiss. For example, a nineteen-year-old African American driving a new Lexus would be an "obvious" alert, because the assumption would be that neither he nor his family could have afforded such a car, and the driver must therefore be "into drugs."

According to the government's own statistics, during the height of the intensity of the drug war, blacks accounted for only 15–20 percent of the nation's drug users,[6]

Table 14.1
Incarceration rates by race

Year	Population[a]			Incarceration[b]			Rate (%)[c]			Approximate ratio
	Total	White	Black	Total	White	Black	Total	White	Black	Black to White
1933	125,579	112,815	12,764	137,997	102,118	31,739	.11	.09	.25	2½:1
1950	151,684	135,814	15,870	178,065	115,742	60,542	.12	.09	.38	4:1
1960	180,671	160,023	19,006	226,065	138,070	83,747	.13	.09	.44	5:1
1970	204,879	179,491	22,787	198,831	115,322	81,520	.10	.06	.36	6:1
1989	248,240	208,961	30,660	712,563	343,550	334,952	.29	.16	1.09	7:1
1995	263,168	218,149	33,095	1,126,287	454,961	546,005	.43	.21	1.65	8:1

Sources: For population: "Series A 23–28: Annual Estimates of the Population, by Sex and Race: 1900–1970," in *Historical Statistics of the United States, 1976* (Washington, D.C.: Bureau of the Census, Department of Commerce, 1976), pp. 9–28; "No. 19: Resident Population—Selected Characteristics: 1790–1989," in *Statistical Abstract of the United States 1991*, 111th ed. (Washington, D.C.: Bureau of the Census, Department of commerce, 1999), p. 17, and in *Statistical abstract of the United States 1997*, 117th ed. (Washington, D.C.: Bureau of the Census, Department of commerce, 1997), pp. 9, 19. For incarceration: "Characteristics of Persons in State and Federal Prisons," in *Historical Corrections Statistics in the United States* (Washington, D.C.: Bureau of Prison Statistics, Department of Justice, 1986), p. 65, and in *Correctional Population in the U.S., 1995* (Washington, D.C.: Bureau of Justice Statistics, Department of Justice, 1997), p. 91.
[a] Total population of the United States by ethnicity (in thousands).
[b] Total number of prison population by ethnicity (estimated).
[c] Percentage of total population, white population, and black population incarcerated.

but in most urban areas, they constituted half to two-thirds of those arrested for drug offenses. Indeed, in New York City, African Americans and Latinos constituted 92 percent of all those arrested for drug offenses.[7] In Florida, the annual admissions rate of blacks to the state prison system nearly tripled between 1983 and 1989, from 14,301 to nearly 40,000.[8] This was a direct consequence of the war on drugs, since well over two-thirds of the crimes of which these Florida blacks were convicted were drug-related. The nation gasped at national statistics reported by the Sentencing Project in 1990 that revealed that nearly one-fourth of all young black males twenty to twenty-nine years of age were either in prison, in jail, on probation or on parole on any given day in the summer of 1989.[9] This figure has been recited so often that (relatively) a collective yawn greeted an announcement in mid-1992, that a study had revealed that *56 percent of Baltimore's young black males were under some form of criminal justice sanction on any given day* in 1991.[10] Indeed, of the nearly thirteen thousand individuals arrested on drug charges in Baltimore during 1991, more than eleven thousand were African Americans.

The explanation for this extraordinary imbalance between patterns of drug consumption by race and arrest statistics derived from the point of the sales transaction is not difficult to find. It is the selective aim of the artillery in the drug war. Interviews in 1989 with public defenders in both the San Francisco Bay Area and Atlanta revealed that over half of their caseload involved young, overwhelmingly black males arrested through "buy-and-bust transactions" by the police.[11] *Most of these transactions involved quantities of cocaine valued at less than seventy-five dollars.* In contrast, even at the height of the drug war, drug sales in fraternity houses or "in the suites" routinely escaped the net of the criminal justice system.[12] It is the street sales of drugs that are most vulnerable to the way in which the criminal justice apparatus is currently constituted and employed. Some judges began to throw out cases in which there was obvious racial bias in administering drug laws so unevenly across the population. A white Manhattan judge allowed crucial evidence to be suppressed in a drug arrest case at the New York Port Authority bus terminal on the grounds that drug enforcement efforts in the terminal were aimed exclusively at minorities.[13] It is a well-known and accepted police practice in many areas to intercept citizens who fit a "profile" of a likely offender. That profile increasingly took on an overwhelmingly racial dimension as the war on drugs escalated. When a superior court judge in Los Angeles was informed in 1990 that 80 percent of all illegal drug transactions involved whites rather than blacks or other minorities, he replied in astonishment that he thought it was exactly the opposite.[14]

The drug war affected the races quite differently with regard to their respective prison incarceration rates. The most striking figure showing this is the shift in the racial composition of prisoners in Virginia: In 1983, approximately 63 percent of the new prison commitments for drugs were white, with the rest, 37 percent, minority. Just six years later, in 1989, the situation had reversed, with only 34 percent of the new drug commitments being whites, and 65 percent minority. It is not just the higher rate of incarceration, but the way in which the full net of the criminal justice system all the way through mandatory sentencing falls selectively on blacks. For example, powder cocaine is most likely to be sold and consumed by whites, whereas blacks are more likely to sell and consume crack.[15] Moreover—and I would argue, not coincidentally—federal law is not race neutral on these two very much related chemical substances: Possession with intent to distribute five grams of powdered cocaine brings a variable sentence of ten to thirty-seven months, but, possession with intent to distribute five grams of crack cocaine brings a mandatory minimum five-year sentence.[16]

A study by the Federal Judicial Center revealed that the mandatory minimum sentencing in drug cases enacted as part of the war on drugs has had a dramatically greater impact on blacks than on whites.[17] In 1986, before the mandatory minimum sentences became effective, for crack offenses, the average sentence for drug-related offenses was 6 percent higher nationally for blacks than for whites. Just four years later, in 1990, the average sentence was 93 percent higher for blacks.[18] Although the figures for crack are the most shocking, the shift toward longer sentences for blacks also includes other drugs. In the same time period, from 1986 to 1990, the average sentence for blacks vis-à-vis whites (for offenses related to powder cocaine, marijuana, and opiates) increased from 11 percent greater for blacks to 49 percent greater.[19]

The charge of police profiling by race those that they subject to stops and searches has now reached the highest circles of government. Attorney General John Ashcroft, no crusading hero of civil liberties, has gone on record as opposing the practice, and has promised to root it out and end it as he uncovers and discovers remnants of racial-profiling policies. But some still contest that there has ever really been something called "racial profiling" (related to the "offense" of "driving while black"). So it is instructive to present some compelling data on the topic gathered by the Maryland State Police Department. The data reflect the way in which the Maryland State Police stopped drivers, by race, along the Interstate 95 corridor in that state, from January 1995 to September 1996. Note that although drivers in all

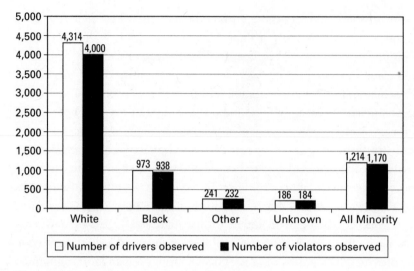

Figure 14.3
Number of traffic violations observed, by race

categories have a high percentage of violations that could be the source of being asked to pull over (from lane changing without signaling to speeding), as shown in figure 14.3, minority drivers were stopped at much higher rates, as shown in figure 14.4, with the difference certainly pronounced enough to support a reasonable conclusion of selective profiling.[20]

Background to "Ethnic-Affiliation Markers" at the DNA Level

At the level of DNA, we have now been told repeatedly by the mappers and sequencers of the Human Genome Project that all humans are 99.9 percent alike. However, there is an unacknowledged eight-hundred-pound gorilla hovering around the FBI's national DNA database for forensic investigation. That gorilla has a name, "race" (although it has recently applied for and received a name change and now prefers to be called, more politely, "ethnic estimation based upon allele frequency variation"). The official line from the disciplines of molecular biology, physical anthropology, hematology, the neurosciences, and a dozen other scientific fields is that "the concept of race has no scientific meaning, and no scientific utility."[21] On the surface, this is of course correct. There are no biological processes (circulation of the blood, patterns of neurotransmission) that map along any system for classi-

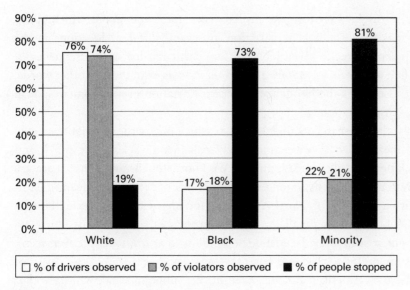

Figure 14.4
Percentage of drivers stopped, by race

fying humans that we can dredge up from the past or invoke from the present, and as I shall show, the future belongs to a whole newly evolving nomenclature.

But if humans are 99.9 percent alike and "race" is purportedly a concept with no scientific utility, what are we to make of a series of articles that have appeared in the scientific literature over the last decade, looking for genetic markers of population groups that coincide with commonsense, lay renditions of ethnic and racial phenotypes? It is the forensic applications of such markers, if they can be shown to exist, that have generated much of this interest. Devlin and Risch made the following statement in "Ethnic Differentiation at VNTR Loci, with Specific Reference to Forensic Applications," a research report that appeared prominently in the *American Journal of Human Genetics*:

The presence of null alleles leads to a large excess of single-band phenotypes for blacks at D17S79.[22] . . . This phenomenon is less important for the Caucasian and Hispanic populations, which have fewer alleles with a small number of repeats. . . .

 [I]t appears that the FBI's data base is representative of the Caucasian population. Results for the Hispanic ethnic groups, for the D17S79 locus, again suggest that the data bases are derived from nearly identical populations, when both similarities and expected biases are considered. . . . For the allele frequency distributions derived from the black population, there may be small differences in the populations from which the data bases are derived, as the expected bias is .05.[23]

When genetic researchers try to make probabilistic statements about which group a person belongs to, they look at variation at several different locations in the DNA—usually from three to seven loci. For any particular locus, the frequency of a particular allele *at that locus, and for that population*, is examined. In other words, what is being assessed is the frequency of genetic variation at a particular spot in the DNA in each population.

Occasionally, these researchers find a locus at which one of the populations being observed and measured has, for example (let's call them) alleles H, I, and J, and another population has alleles H, I, and K. We know, for instance, that there are alleles that are found primarily among subpopulations of North American Indians. When comparing a group of North American Indians with a group of Finnish people, one might find a single allele that was present in some Indians but in no Finns (or present at such a low frequency in the Finns that it is rarely, if ever, seen). However, it is important to note and reiterate—again and again—that this does not mean that all North American Indians, even in this subpopulation, will have that allele.[24] Rather, we are referring to the probability of the appearance of that allele in the subpopulation. Indeed, it is inevitable that some North American Indians will have a different set of alleles, and that *many of them will be the same alleles as some of the Finns*. Also, if comparing North American Indians from Arizona to North American Caucasians from Arizona, we would probably find at least some level—probably a very low one—of the "Indian allele" in the so-called Caucasians, because there has been "interbreeding." Which leads to the next point.

It is possible to make arbitrary groupings of populations (geographic, linguistic, self-identified by faith, identified by others by physiognamy, etc.) and still find statistically significant allelic variations among those groupings. For example, we could simply pick all of the people in Chicago, and all in Los Angeles, and find statistically significant differences in allele frequency at *some* loci. Of course, at many loci, even most loci, we would not find statistically significant differences. When researchers claim to be able to assign people to groups based on allele frequency at a certain number of loci, they have chosen loci that show differences between the groups they are trying to distinguish. The work of Devlin and Risch, Evett et al., Lowe et al., and others suggests that only about 10 percent of DNA sites are "useful" for making such distinctions.[25] This means that at the other 90 percent of the sites, the allele frequencies do not vary between groups such as "Afro-Caribbean people in England" and "Scottish people in England." Even though we cannot find a single site at which allele frequency matches some phenotype that we are trying to identify (for forensic purposes, we should be reminded), it does not follow that no grouping (of four, six, seven) can be found that will be effective, for the purposes of aiding the FBI, Scotland Yard, or the criminal justice systems around the globe in making highly probabilistic statements about suspects and the likely ethnic, racial, or cultural populations from which they can be identified—statistically.

So when molecular biologists assert that "race has no validity as a scientific concept," there is an apparent contradiction with the practical applicability of research on allele frequencies in specific populations. It is possible to sort out and make sense of this, and even to explain and resolve the apparent contradiction—but only if we keep in mind the difference between using a taxonomic system with sharp, discrete, definitively bounded categories and using one with categories that show patterns (with some overlap) that may prove to be empirically or practically useful. When representative spokespersons from the biological sciences say that "there is no such thing as race," they mean, correctly, that there are no discrete categories of "race" that come to a discrete beginning and end, that there is nothing mutually exclusive about our current (or past) categories of "race," and that there is more genetic variation within categories of "race" than among them. All this is true. However, when Scotland Yard, or the Birmingham, England, police force, or the New York police force wants to narrow the list of suspects in a crime, it is not primarily concerned with tight taxonomic systems of classification with no overlapping categories. That is the stuff of theoretical physics and logic in philosophy, not the practical stuff of helping to solve crime or the practical application of molecular genetics to health delivery via genetic screening—and all the messy overlapping categories that will inevitably be involved with such enterprises. That is, some African Americans have cystic fibrosis, even though the likelihood is far greater among Americans of North European descent, and in a parallel if not symmetrical way, some American whites have sickle cell anemia even though the likelihood is far greater among Americans of West African descent. But in the world of cost-effective decision making, genetic screening for these disorders is routinely done based on commonsense versions of the phenotype. The same is true for the quite practical matter of naming suspects.

The July 8, 1995, issue of *New Scientist*, entitled "Genes in Black and White," makes some extraordinary claims about what it is possible to learn about socially defined categories of race from reviewing information gathered using new molecular genetic technology. In 1993, a British forensic scientist published what is perhaps the first DNA test explicitly acknowledged to provide "intelligence information" along "ethnic" lines for "investigators of unsolved crimes." Ian Evett, of the Home Office's forensic science laboratory in Birmingham, and his colleagues in the Birmingham Metropolitan Police, claimed that they had developed a DNA test could distinguish between "Caucasians" and "Afro-Caribbeans" in nearly 85 percent of the cases.

Evett's work, published in the *Journal of Forensic Science Society*, draws on apparent genetic differences in three sections of human DNA. Like most stretches of human DNA used for forensic typing, each of these three regions differs widely from person to person, irrespective of race. But by looking at all three, Evett and his fellow researchers claimed that under select circumstances, it is possible to estimate the probability that someone belongs to a particular racial group. The implications of this for determining, for practical purposes, who is and who is not "officially" a member of some racial or ethnic category are profound.

A year after the publication of a statement by the United Nations Educational, Scientific, and Cultural Organization purportedly buried the concept of "race" for the purposes of scientific inquiry and analysis,[26] and during the same time period that the American Anthropological Association was deliberating on and generating a parallel statement, an article appeared in the *American Journal of Human Genetics*, authored by Evett and his associates, summarized in the article's abstract as follows:

Before the introduction of a four-locus multiplex short-tandem-repeat (STR) system into casework, an extensive series of tests were carried out to determine robust procedures for assessing the evidential value of a match between crime and suspect samples. Twelve databases were analyzed from the three main ethnic groups encountered in casework in the United Kingdom: Caucasians, Afro-Caribbeans, and Asians from the Indian subcontinent. Independence tests resulted in a number of significant results, and the impact that these might have on forensic casework was investigated. It is demonstrated that previously published methods provide a similar procedure for correcting allele frequencies—and that this leads to conservative casework estimates of evidential value.[27]

In more recent years, the technology has moved along, and forensic scientists are now using VNTR loci, and investigating twelve to fifteen segments of the DNA, not just the earlier three to seven. Recall that in the opening section of the chapter I referred to a pilot program of the New York City Police Department, employing thirteen loci for identification purposes. The forensic research conducted by Evett and his colleagues occurred before the current computer chip revolution, which will permit research on a specific population to develop a SNP profile of that group.[28]

Deploying DNA technology in this fashion can be dangerously seductive. Computers will inevitably be able to find some patterns in the DNA within a group of, say, three thousand burglars. But this is a mere correlation of markers, and it is far from anything but a spurious correlation that will explain nothing—but it will have the seductive imprimatur of molecular genetic precision.

The Dangerous Intersection of "Allele Frequencies in Special Populations" and "Police Profiling via Phenotype"

The conventional wisdom is that DNA fingerprinting is just a better way of getting a fingerprint. That "wisdom" is wrong. The traditional physical imprint of one's finger or thumb provides only that specific identifying mark, and it is attached to one individual and one individual alone.[29] Quite unlike an actual fingerprint, DNA contains information about many other things that go beyond simple identification. It contains information about potential or existing genetic diseases or genetic susceptibilities one may have and also information about one's family. These can involve data of interest to one's employer and of course, to insurance companies. For these reasons, law enforcement officials claim that they are interested only in that part of a DNA profile that provides identifying markers that are not in coding regions. Coding regions account for only 10 percent of the DNA in a DNA sample, and it is in these regions that the nucleotides code for proteins that might relate to a full range of matters of concern to researchers, from cancer or heart disease to neurotransmission and thus, for some, to *possible "coding" for "impulsivity" or biochemical outcomes that might relate to violence.* Although the FBI and local and state law enforcement officials tell us that they are looking only at genetic markers in the noncoding region of the DNA samples they take, twenty-nine states now require that tissue samples be retained in their DNA data banks after profiling is complete.[30] Only one state, Wisconsin, requires the destruction of a tissue samples once the DNA profile has been extracted.

States are the primary venues for the prosecution of violations of the criminal law, and their autonomy has generated considerable variation in the use of DNA data banks and storage of DNA samples. Even as late as the mid-1980s, most states were collecting DNA samples only from sexual offenders. The times have changed quite rapidly. All fifty states now contribute to CODIS. Moreover, there has been rapid change in the interlinking of state DNA databases. In just two years, the CODIS database went from a total of nine states cross-linking "a little over 100,000 offender profiles and 5,000 forensic profiles" to thirty-two states, the FBI, and the U.S. Army now linking "nearly 400,000 offender profiles, and close to 20,000 forensic profiles."[31] States are now uploading an average of three thousand offender profiles every month. If this sounds staggering, recall that computer technology is increasingly efficient and extraordinarily fast. It now takes only five hundred microseconds to search a database of one hundred thousand profiles.[32]

As we increase the number of profiles in DNA databases, there will be researchers proposing to provide SNP profiles of specific offender populations. Twenty states authorize the use of data banks for research on forensic techniques. Based on the statutory language in several of those states, this could easily mean assaying genes or loci that contain predictive information. Tom Callaghan, program manager of the FBI's Federal Convicted Offender Program, has refused to rule out such possible uses by behavioral geneticists seeking a possible profile for a particular allele among specific offender populations, including especially violent offenders and sexual offenders.[33] It is useful to note here that SNP profiles of violent and sexual offenders are the wedge, and then the expansion via "function creep" (see chapter 9) to other crimes and even misdemeanors. Indeed, Louisiana became, in 1999, the first state to pass a law permitting the taking of a DNA sample for all merely arrested for a felony.

Thirty states now require DNA data banking on *all* felons, including those convicted of white-collar felonies. In the fall of 1998, New York Governor George Pataki proposed that the state include white-collar convicts in the DNA database, but the state legislative assembly balked and forced him to jettison the idea. Perhaps they were concerned that some saliva might be left on the cigars in those backrooms where price-fixing and security-exchange fraud occur. Today, nearly half the states include those convicted of certain misdemeanors in the DNA databank. So we can now see that what started as DNA collection from "sex offenders" has now graduated to collection from misdemeanants and arrestees. Although thirty-nine states permit expungement of profiles from DNA databases if charges are dropped, almost all of those states place the burden on the individual to initiate expungement.

Population-Wide DNA Database

It is now relatively common for scholars to acknowledge the considerable and documented racial and ethnic bias in police procedures, prosecutorial discretion, jury selection, and sentencing practices—of which racial profiling is but the tip of the iceberg.[34] Indeed, racial disparities penetrate the whole system and are suffused throughout it, all the way up to and through racial disparities in seeking the death penalty for the same crime. If the DNA database is primarily composed of those who have been touched by the criminal justice system, and that system has engaged in practices that routinely select more from one group that from others, there will be an obvious skew or bias toward this group in the database. David Kaye and Michael Smith take the position in chapter 12 that the way to handle the racial bias in the DNA database is to include everyone. But this does not address the far more fundamental problem of the bias that generates the configuration and content of the criminal (or suspect) database. If the lens of the criminal justice system is focused almost entirely on one part of the population for a certain kind of activity (drug-related street crime) and ignores a parallel kind of crime (fraternity cocaine sales a few miles away), then even if the fraternity members' DNA is in the data bank, they will not be subject to the same level of matching, or of subsequent allele-frequency-profiling research to "help explain" their behavior. *That behavior will not have been recorded.* That is, if the police are not stopping to arrest the fraternity members, it does not matter whether their DNA is in a national database, because they are not *criminalized* by the selective aim of the artillery of the criminal justice system.

Thus it is imperative that we separate arguments about bias in the criminal justice system at the point of contact with select parts of the population from "solutions" to bias in cold hits. It is certainly true that if a member of one of those same fraternities committed a rape, left tissue samples at the scene, and—because he was in a national DNA database—the police could nab him with a cold hit, that would be the source of the justifiable applause with which I opened this chapter. But my point here is that by ignoring powder cocaine and emphasizing street sales of cocaine in the African American community, the mark of criminality thereby generated is not altered by having a population-wide DNA database. However, the surface fiction of objectivity will lead to a research agenda regarding the DNA database about which I would now like to issue a warning.

There is a serious threat of how new DNA technologies are about to be deployed that is masked by the apparent global objectivity of a population-wide DNA database. I am referring to the prospects for SNP profiling of offenders. As noted, even if everyone's DNA profile were in the national database, this would not deter the impulse of some to do specific and focused research on the select population that has been convicted, or who are, in Amitai Etzioni's phrase, "legitimate suspects" (see chapter 10).

An article in the *American Journal of Human Genetics* in 1997 made the following claim:

[W]e have identified a panel of population-specific genetic markers that enable robust ethnic affiliation estimation for major U.S. resident populations. In this report, we identify these loci and present their levels of allele-frequency differential between ethnically defined samples, and we demonstrate, using log-likelihood analysis, that this panel of markers provides significant statistical power for ethnic affiliation estimation.[35]

As in the earlier work by Devlin and Risch,[36] one of the expressed purposes of this research is its "use in forensic ethnic affiliation estimation."[37] Such a research agenda is likely to produce a significant challenge to the communitarian claim of a common public-safety interest in maintaining a DNA database.

DNA Profiling and the Fracture of "Community"

Chapter 10 of this volume is written by the leading figure in the communitarian movement, Amitai Etzioni. Perhaps the central thesis of chapter 10, if not of the communitarian movement, is that we need to strike a better balance between individual rights and community interests. That is a laudable goal when it is possible to determine a consensus of community interest based on the common health, the commonweal(th), and the common interest. Normally, public health is just such an issue. The right of an individual to remain in a community while he or she has a contagious disease such as smallpox or tuberculosis is trumped by the state's right to protect the public health of the general citizenry. But molecular biology has played a powerful role in fracturing the public-health consensus. Whereas we could all agree that it was in our common interest to rid us (more or less) of cholera, yellow fever, tuberculosis, infectious meningitis, and smallpox, this type of communitarian consensus about public-health issues has been dramatically undermined as we have learned that some groups are at higher risk for particular genetic disorders than others. Cystic fibrosis is a genetic disorder that can affect the upper respiratory system in a life-threatening manner, but only those from North European ancestry are at significant risk for developing the disorder. Beta-thalassemia is a blood disorder primarily associated with persons with ancestors from the southern Mediterranean region. Sickle cell anemia is primarily associated, in the United States, with Americans of West African descent. And so it goes. In the 1970s, the public-health consensus about general health screening was disrupted by this development, as group interests began to emerge to demand more funding for research and genetic testing of the gene disorder most associated with "their group."[38]

If molecular genetics and the emergence of group-based research agendas fractured the country's public-health consensus, we can expect an even more dramatic parallel development when it comes to discussions of the public safety. It is almost inevitable that a research agenda will surface to try to find patterns of allele frequencies, DNA markers, and genetic profiles of different types of criminals. One could do a SNP profile of rapists and sex offenders and find some markers that they putatively share. As noted above, "ethnic-affiliation estimations of allele frequencies" is high on the research agenda in forensic science. In the abstract, there is a public consensus about the desirability of reducing crime. However, when it comes to the routine practices of the criminal justice system, a demonstration of systematic bias has eroded (and will further erode) the public consensus on how this is best achieved. The war on drugs began with a broad consensus, but the consensus fractured when the practices briefly outlined earlier in the chapter, and thoroughly documented in the literature, came to light.[39] This fracture in the public consensus will be exacerbated by the inevitable search for genetic markers and seductive ease into genetic explanations of crime.

But like phrenology in the nineteenth century, these markers will be precisely that, "markers," and not explanatory of "the causes" of violent crime. Even if the many causes of criminal violence (or any human behaviors) are embedded in the full range of forces that begin with protein coding, there is interaction at every level, from the cellular environment, all the way up through embryological development, to the ways in which the criminal justice system focuses on one part of the town and not another when making drug busts. We are bemused today about tales of nineteenth-century scientists who sought answers to criminal behavior by measuring the sizes and shapes of the heads of convicted felons. The newest IBM computers can make 7.5 trillion calculations per second for biological chip analysis. These are sirens beckoning researchers who wish to do parallel correlational studies of "population-based allele frequencies" with "ethnic estimations" and groupings of felons—a recurring seduction to a false precision. A higher and more determined vigilance of these and similar developments is necessary if we are to avoid repeating the mistakes of the late nineteenth century.

Notes

1. Jim Dwyer, Peter Neufeld, and Barry Scheck, *Actual Innocence: Five Days to Execution and Other Dispatches from the Wrongly Convicted* (New York: Doubleday, 2000). At the time of Dwyer's report, the number was less than one hundred, but in the last two years there have been a number of additions.

2. Aaron P. Stevens, "Arresting Crime: Expanding the Scope of DNA Databases in America," *Texas Law Review* 24 (March 2001); Allison M. Puri, "An International DNA Database: Balancing Hope, Privacy, and Scientific Error," *Boston College International and Comparative Law Review* 24 (2001).

3. Kevin Flynn, "Fighting Crime with Ingenuity, 007 Style: Gee-Whiz Police Gadgets Get a Trial Run in New York," *New York Times*, March 7, 2000, A21.

4. Dorothy M. Nelkin and Susan Lindee, *The DNA Mystique: The Gene as Cultural Icon* (New York: Freeman, 1995).

5. Andrew Hacker, *Two Nations: Black and White, Separate, Hostile, Unequal* (New York: Scribner's, 1992), 197.

6. Timothy J. Flanagan and Kathleen Maguire, eds., *Sourcebook of Criminal Justice Statistics 1989* (Washington, D.C.: U. S. Government Printing Office, 1990).

7. Edna McConnell Clark Foundation, *Americans behind Bars* (New York: 1992).

8. James S. Austin and Aaron David McVey, *The N.C.C.D. Prison Population Forecast: The Impact of the War on Drugs (F.O.C.U.S.)* (San Francisco: National Council on Crime and Delinquency, 1989), 1–7.

9. Reported in *The New York Times*, February 27, 1990.

10. Jerome G. Miller, *Hobbling a Generation: Young African American Males in the Criminal Justice System of America's Cities: Baltimore, Maryland* (Alexandria, Va.: National Center on Institutions and Alternatives, 1992).

11. Author's interviews with several public defenders in the San Francisco Bay area and Atlanta regarding their caseload involving drug charges, 1989.

12. When the police conducted a raid on a fraternity house in Virginia in 1989, it was national news . . . almost a "man bites dog" story.

13. Ronald Sullivan, "Judge Finds Bias in Bus Terminal Search," *New York Times*, April 25, 1990, B3.

14. Ron Harris, "War on Drugs Is Charged as War on Black America," *Los Angeles Times*, April 22, 1990.

15. Flanagan and Maguire, *Sourcebook of Criminal Justice Statistics 1989*.

16. 21 U.S.C. § 841 (a).

17. Barbara S. Meierhoefer, *The General Effect of Mandatory Minimum Prison Terms: A Longitudinal Study of Federal Sentences Imposed* (Washington, D.C.: Federal Judicial Center, 1992).

18. Those who defend disparate sentencing policies for crack and cocaine argue that crack produces a more violent environment. For a full discussion of these issues, see Craig

Reinarman and Harry G. Levine, *Crack in America: Demon Drugs and Social Justice* (Berkeley and Los Angeles: University of California Press, 1997).

19. Meierhoefer, *The General Effect of Mandatory Minimum Prison Terms.*

20. For a full account of the methodology used in the Maryland State Police Study, see http://www.aclu.profiling/report/index/html.

21. Solomon H. Katz, "Is Race a Legitimate Concept for Science?" in *The AAPA Revised Statement on Race: A Brief Analysis and Commentary* (Philadelphia: University of Pennsy Lvania, 1995); Luigi Luca Sforza-Cavalli, "Race Difference: Genetic Evidence," in *Plain Talk about the Human Genome Project,* ed. Edward Smith and Walter Sapp (Tuskegee, Ala.: Tuskegee University, 1997), 51–58.

22. B. Devlin and Neil Risch, "A Note on the Hardy-Weinberg Equilibrium of VNTR Data by Using the Federal Bureau of Investigation's Fixed-Bin Method," *American Journal of Human Genetics* 51 (1992): 549–553. As predicted in B. Budowle et al., "Fixed-Bin Analysis for Statist Evaluation of Continuous Distributions of Allelic Data from VNTR Loci, for Use in Forensic Comparisons," *American Journal of Human Genetics* 48, no. 5 (May 1991): 841–855.

23. B. Devlin and Neil Risch, "Ethnic Differentiation at VNTR Loci, with Specific Reference to Forensic Applications," *American Journal of Human Genetics* 51 (1992): 540, 546.

24. This is a major point that is being made by two sets of statements about race, one from UNESCO and the other from the American Anthropological Association, and it cannot be repeated too often.

25. Devlin and Risch, "Ethnic Differentiation at VNTR Loci"; Devlin and Risch, "A Note on the Hardy-Weinberg Equilibrium of V.N.T.R. Data"; I. W. Evett et al., "The Evidential Value of DNA Profiles," *Journal of the Forensic Science Society* 33, no. 4 (1993): 243–244; I. W. Evett et al., "Establishing the Robustness of Short-Tandem-Repeat Statistics for Forensic Application," *American Journal of Human Genetics* 58 (1996): 398–407; Alex L. Lowe et al., "Inferring Ethnic Origin by Means of an S.T.R. Profile," *Forensic Science International* 119 (2001): 17–22.

26. Katz, "Is Race a Legitimate Concept for Science?"

27. Evett et al., "Establishing the Robustness of Short-Tandem-Repeat Statistics for Forensic Application," 398.

28. Hisham Hamadeh and Cynthia A. Afshari, "Gene Chips and Functional Genomics," *American Scientist* 88 (2000): 508–515.

29. Simon Cole has just published a book challenging some of the long-held beliefs about the infallibility of the physical fingerprint, but that is another story. Simon A. Cole, *Suspect Identities: A History of Fingerprinting and Criminal Identification* (Cambridge, Mass.: Harvard University Press, 2001); see also chapter 4 of this volume.

30. Jonathan Kimmelman, "Risking Ethical Insolvency: A Survey of Trends in Criminal DNA Databanking," *Journal of Law, Medicine and Ethics* 28 (2000): 211.

31. Barry Brown, statement for panel ("DNA and the Criminal Justice System") conference, John F. Kennedy School of Government, Harvard University, Cambridge, Mass., November 20, 2000.

32. Ibid.

33. Kimmelman, "Risking Ethical Insolvency."

34. Marc Mauer, *Race to Incarcerate* (New York: New Press, distributed by Norton, 1999).

35. Mark D. Shriver et al., "Ethnic Affiliation Estimation by Use of Population-Specific DNA Markers," *American Journal of Human Genetics* 60 (1997).

36. Devlin and Risch, "Ethnic Differentiation at VNTR Loci."

37. Shriver et al., "Ethnic Affiliation Estimation by Use of Population-Specific DNA Markers," 957; see also Lowe et al., "Inferring Ethnic Origin by Means of an STR Profile."

38. Troy Duster, *Backdoor to Eugenics*, 2nd ed. (New York: Routledge, 2003).

39. Reinarman and Levine, *Crack in America*; Mauer, *Race to Incarcerate*; Jerome G. Miller, *Search and Destroy: African-American Males in the Criminal Justice System* (New York: Cambridge University Press, 1996); David Cole, *No Equal Justice: Race and Class in the American Criminal Justice System* (New York: New Press, 1999).

IV

Defining the Discourse

15

DNA's Identity Crisis

Sheila Jasanoff

Introduction

Major technological innovations by their very nature entail seismic changes in social organization, behavior, and beliefs. The printing press, the light bulb, the automobile, the atomic bomb, the personal computer—and most recently our ability to cut and splice the genes of plants and animals—all brought with them profound shifts in the ways that individuals and communities think, act, and conduct their relations with one another. While these observations are uncontroversial, the relationship between technological and social change continues to occupy social scientists and has significant implications for public policy. The theory of technological determinism, which held that technological change has its own internal logic and drives social transformation, has long since been discredited as too simplistic.[1] Instead, analysts of technology now recognize that human agency shapes machines and material artifacts just as deeply as these, in turn, affect human needs, wants, and capabilities. To capture the interactivity of the human and the mechanical, the material and the social, one often speaks of a technological *system* or *network*—a heterogeneous assemblage whose elements complement and remain in play with one another over time.[2] As these systems evolve, their composition, their ties to other elements in society, and what they mean to people both within and outside the system undergo significant modifications. The history of technology thus is a history of adaptation in both structure and action, and in ideas as well as in material instruments and social capacity.

The new genetic technologies of the late twentieth century offer at once a site for studying a revolutionary technological system in the making and an opportunity for policymakers to reflect on how to use these novel techniques to further human welfare. DNA, often called the building block of life, has been a part of our cultural vocabulary since the discovery of its double-helical structure by James Watson and Francis Crick in 1953, a half century ago. Unraveling the molecular structure of DNA, easily the most important scientific discovery since the breakthroughs that characterized the internal makeup of the atom, has enabled changes, both real and imagined, in a wide variety of human practices—in agriculture, medicine, environmental management, human reproduction, and, most important for our purposes, criminal justice. Yet in each of these domains DNA remains a wayward, partially understood entity, an adolescent, we might say, if this complex molecule possessed human identity. Not only do we only imperfectly comprehend its behavior and potential, but we are unsure what rules should be crafted to socialize DNA as a responsible participant in our technological culture. To borrow a term that the eminent psychologist Erik Erikson invented to describe human development, DNA seems still to be undergoing a kind of "identity crisis" as it establishes its claim on our consciousness. As new applications of genetic manipulation emerge, we are forced to rethink which of DNA's possible guises we should welcome, which we should question or regulate, and which we should reject in the interests of our physical and moral well-being.

How should such fundamental choices about the management of a major technological innovation be addressed in a democratic society? How can we be sure that the answers we arrive at are both analytically sound and well deliberated, so that they gain the confidence of citizens? One sophisticated instrument that modern societies have devised for this purpose is the expert advisory committee, a body whose form and function are designed to produce balanced and reasoned decision making on issues that have a substantial scientific or technological component. In this chapter, I consider the role of expert commissions in helping to manage a specific aspect of DNA's adolescent growing pains: the use and accommodation of DNA tests within the criminal justice system. We are still in a state of flux not only with respect to the appropriate role of the tests themselves (how should they be administered and how should we manage the information they generate?), but also with respect to the social technology of advice giving (what roles should expert advisers play and through what mechanisms?). Experts of many kinds will participate in the scientific and social exploration that determines how effectively we master this potent instrument of social control. How should they conceptualize their task, and how should their specialist knowledges be integrated with other relevant perspectives and considerations? This chapter offers a framework for addressing these questions.

A Molecular Arbiter of Justice

On Monday, July 2, 2001, Supreme Court Justice Sandra Day O'Connor surprised many in the law enforcement community by seeming to line up with anti–death penalty forces in a speech she made to a group of women lawyers in Minneapolis. "If statistics are any indication," she said, "the system may well be allowing some innocent defendants to be executed."[3] This was a remarkable concession from a jurist whose support for the death penalty had rarely wavered in her twenty years on the high court and who had written in a 1989 majority opinion that there was "insufficient evidence of a national consensus against executing mentally retarded people convicted of capital offenses."[4] Among the developments responsible for her apparent change of heart was the observation that, since 1973, some ninety death row inmates had been exonerated by the discovery of new evidence, some just hours before their scheduled executions. O'Connor noted that a powerful tool, DNA testing, was now available to make convictions more reliable, but that access to these tests, and to adequate legal services, remained an insurmountable bar for the poorest, least competent defendants.

O'Connor's comments offered compelling evidence of a shift in the role of DNA testing within the criminal justice system. A technique cultivated for fifteen years as the most effective tool for identifying criminals and putting them securely behind bars had gained a second identity: as a liberator of the innocent, a friend of the wrongly incarcerated, and possibly even a lever to move America's political center from its almost unshakable commitment to capital punishment. This, however, was only a further twist in the history of DNA's relatively brief but turbulent entanglement with law enforcement.

In one of the earliest American uses of DNA evidence, Tommy Lee Andrews was convicted of rape by a Florida court in 1987 when DNA from his blood was found to match the DNA in semen taken from the rape victim.[5] Witnesses for the prosecution made much of the extreme accuracy of DNA-based identification, and over the next few years many dozens of cases were decided on the strength of DNA tests. But serious questions about the reliability of this evidence surfaced in the 1989 New York case of *People v. Castro*[6] and soon thereafter in the Minnesota case of *Schwartz v. State*.[7] The courts' refusal to admit some DNA test results in these cases called attention to deficiencies in existing testing methods and disclosure practices, especially in private laboratories. DNA typing suddenly lost its aura of infallibility. To restore the technique's credibility, a group of federal agencies called upon the

National Research Council (NRC), an arm of the prestigious National Academy of Sciences, to examine the unresolved issues surrounding DNA testing and recommend guidelines for its effective and beneficial use. In 1992, the NRC issued its first report on forensic DNA,[8] but controversies surrounding the report prompted a second look by another NRC committee, constituted in 1993 under a different chair, with only two members continuing from the earlier committee. Unexpectedly, the new committee's work took place in parallel with another, vastly more public assessment of the credibility of forensic DNA testing.

In June 1994, the former football star and media celebrity O. J. Simpson was charged in Los Angeles with the brutal double murder of his ex-wife Nicole Brown Simpson and her friend Ron Goldman. By the time his massively publicized trial began in January 1995, prosecutorial confidence in DNA evidence had risen to a high point. In the months before the trial, two well-known scientific experts, Eric S. Lander of the Massachusetts Institute of Technology and Bruce Budowle of the FBI, coauthored an article on forensic DNA typing in the leading scientific journal *Nature*. They claimed that the technical problems affecting the test used for DNA typing had been resolved and that there was no longer any scientific reason to doubt its accuracy.[9] The fact that Lander and Budowle had previously clashed in the debate over the reliability of DNA testing gave their pronouncement added authority.

Meanwhile, in the Simpson trial, blood stains formed the centerpiece of the prosecution's case. Spots and flecks of blood created an allegedly incontrovertible trail from the crime scene into the defendant's now-famous Ford Bronco, his private compound, his driveway, and finally his bedroom. Backed up by DNA tests, these samples, the prosecution argued, linked Simpson to the murder scene beyond reasonable doubt. Yet the prosecution's apparently watertight case developed leaks as cross-examination by the talented defense lawyer Barry Scheck revealed serious defects in the Los Angeles Police Department's handling of the DNA samples in the case. Laboratory evidence proved insufficient to neutralize the jury's suspicion that evidence had been planted at the crime scene, and Simpson was acquitted in October 1995 after only a few hours of jury deliberation. Only the publication of the National Research Council's second DNA report (from the reconstituted committee) in 1996 put to rest the controversies over how to process DNA samples and statistically interpret test results.[10]

While testing laboratories and federal agencies were scrambling to standardize pretrial testing techniques, Scheck and his partner, the attorney Peter Neufeld, were positioning DNA as a remedy for the wrongly convicted. In 1992, they established, at Yeshiva University's Benjamin N. Cardozo School of Law, the Innocence Project, a clinical program to review the cases of prisoners claiming to have been incorrectly identified as perpetrators of crimes they had not committed.[11] The project aimed to secure postconviction DNA testing in deserving cases and by the end of the decade had succeeded in exonerating some forty persons on the basis of such tests. To the surprise of both project directors, test results turned out to clear more than half the people whose cases were sent on to laboratories for follow-up testing. Within a few years, the results from the Innocence Project began to attract national attention not only in the news media, but also within federal law enforcement.

In 1996, the U.S. Department of Justice issued a report that significantly paved the way for Justice O'Connor's second thoughts about capital punishment. Entitled *Convicted by Juries, Exonerated by Science*, the report reviewed twenty-eight cases in which individuals who had served an average of seven years in prison had successfully challenged their convictions using DNA evidence.[12] A prefatory message from Attorney General Janet Reno acknowledged that DNA now had a new identity in the "search for truth": as a tool for exonerating the innocent in addition to its older role as a device for establishing the guilt of defendants. Reno noted the need for exacting standards in handling DNA:

Among the tasks ahead are the following: maintaining the highest standards for the collection and preservation of DNA evidence; ensuring that the DNA testing methodology meets rigorous scientific criteria for reliability and accuracy; and ensuring proficiency and credibility of forensic scientists so that their results and testimony are of the highest caliber and are capable of withstanding exacting scrutiny.[13]

In 1998, at Reno's request, the National Institute of Justice appointed a National Commission on the Future of DNA Evidence (hereafter, the "National Commission"). The commission's task was to recommend ways to improve the use of DNA as an investigative tool and more broadly "in the operation of the criminal justice system, from the crime scene to the courtroom."[14] Spurred by the discoveries of false convictions, Reno, a humane and principled official, automatically appealed to better science as a plausible solution to law enforcers' problems. The issue for her was how to institutionalize the best possible technical inputs into the criminal process so as to make it more reliable, and the mechanism she chose, not surprisingly, was the time-tested social technology of the expert advisory commission.

A breaking story in April 2001 supported the attorney general's worries about standards, as well as Justice O'Connor's uncharacteristic concern about capital punishment for possibly innocent defendants. While media attention concentrated on the impending execution of Timothy McVeigh, the man convicted of bombing the Alfred P. Murrah Federal Building in Oklahoma City in April 1995, that city's police department came under another kind of scrutiny. Oklahoma Governor Frank Keating suddenly and unexpectedly ordered a far-reaching investigation of the work of Joyce Gilchrist, a police chemist employed by Oklahoma City from 1980 to 1993. Earlier that month, an FBI report had charged Gilchrist with having misidentified evidence or given improper testimony in at least five cases reviewed by the agency. Gilchrist's work had figured in about three thousand cases. Her testimony had helped win convictions in some twenty-three trials for capital offenses; eleven of the convicted defendants had been executed, one immediately following the FBI's disclosure.[15] Days later, defects in Gilchrist's DNA analysis of some hair samples led to the release of Jeffrey Pierce, who had been in prison for sixteen years following a conviction for rape.

Granting that high standards are a sine qua non for the responsible use of DNA tests does not, of course, amount to saying that technical standards are the only issue of concern in relation to this infant technology. Indeed, in a speech to a symposium at Harvard University in the fall of 2000, Reno herself struck a deeper, more humanistic note, saying that the challenge is to learn how to govern, rather than be governed by, the power of DNA.[16] If the problem is the broad one of governance, not simply the narrower one of standard setting, what role should experts expect to play in that process? A growing body of scholarship on the work of expert advisory committees in the regulatory process suggests some answers.

Experts between Truth and Power

By the middle of the twentieth century, experts were engaged in public policymaking in sufficient numbers and in varied enough roles to attract the attention of political analysts. Early observers saw the expert's role in policymaking as that of linking scientific and technical knowledge to political decisions and worried mainly about experts' accountability in a democratic system. On the whole, democratic theorists were persuaded that the very nature of technical analysis would adequately check the power of experts. Writing in the 1960s, for example, Harvard's Don K. Price situated experts on "the spectrum from truth to power." He viewed science, lying at one end of the spectrum, as concerned with truth and hence basically apolitical, whereas politics, at the other end, served power, not truth. Because of the apparent lack of interdependence between the two institutions, Price believed that each could be governed by its own criteria of legitimation: "(1) the more an institution or function is concerned with truth, the more it deserves freedom from political control; (2) the more an institution or function is concerned with the exercise of power, the more it should be controlled by the processes of responsibility to elected authorities and ultimately to the electorate."[17] Experts as Price conceived of them mediate between truth and power but are bound by, and accountable to, the regime of "truth." Accordingly, they should be able to offer impartial advice to politicians, unhampered by political controls on their autonomy. Politicians for their part are periodically held accountable by the electorate for their exercise of power; actions for which they can be judged at the polls presumably include their wise use of expert advice.

This picture of the relationship between experts and policymakers has come to be recognized as misleadingly simple in light of research on the practices of advisory bodies. Little of the "truth-to-power" model holds up when we look closely at the empirical record of advice giving. To begin with, the stark fact-value distinction on which the model is founded is hard to sustain. It assumes that issues of power play no part in the assessment of technical questions for public policy. In reality, politics and values enter into the deliberations of expert committees at many levels: in the selection of members, the definition of their charge, the extent of their fact-finding powers, the formal and informal constraints on their deliberative processes, and their relationship to the ultimate decision maker. Frequently, too, the very framing of an advisory body's charge in technical terms reflects an underlying decision to treat a politically sensitive issue *as if* it could be resolved through expert analysis. For example, Congress has repeatedly called upon the National Academy of Sciences to evaluate the scientific adequacy of the Environmental Protection Agency's risk assessment practices; yet the motivation in each case has been the ongoing national debate about the appropriate cost and stringency of environmental standards.[18] Not surprisingly, the dynamic of turning to science for "solutions" is every bit as central to the American political process as the underlying conflicts over the right way to govern.

Second, the truth-to-power model assumes that expert advisers are engaged in something close enough to ordinary scientific activity for their work to be characterized as a search for truth. Yet as studies of regulatory science have consistently shown, the information and advice imparted by experts to policymakers seldom has the definitive quality of scientific facts. From an institutional standpoint, the conditions under which policy-relevant scientific analysis is conducted are significantly different from the conditions that give rise to normal scientific findings. Experts derive their questions from the policy world rather than from existing bodies of scientific knowledge. This means that their work is often carried out in domains in which there are as yet no well-defined standard methodologies, as, for instance, in the early deliberations concerning DNA typing. Policy experts operate under different, often more rigid constraints of time, money, and resources from scientists working in institutions whose sole or primary function is basic research. Expert advisers are also accountable to more heterogeneous communities of critics—for example, courts or congressional committees—whose standards of evidence and proof may be dictated by legal or policy considerations rather than by a simple desire for the truth.[19]

Third, contrary to one of the basic presumptions of the truth-to-power model, the question of where science or technical analysis stops and politics or power begins is seldom cleanly established or knowable in advance. Many of the issues that experts find themselves debating lie in a gray zone that is, at the outset, neither clearly science nor clearly politics. Which disciplines or bodies of knowledge are relevant to the problem being considered? When is a method, instrument, or set of observations reliable enough to be used as a basis for setting standards? How much evidence is enough to support a change in policy, especially when such a move may entail substantial costs or have negative distributive consequences? Which uncertainties are worth trying to assess before changing policy, which suggest a need for precautionary action, and which should be dismissed as speculative? Answering these sorts of questions inevitably requires a mix of different analytic perspectives, not only technical, but also pragmatic, political, and ethical. In practice, expert committees often exercise all these different kinds of judgment, even though the end result of their decision making may be labeled "science."[20]

A close look at the work of scientific and technical experts suggests, then, that their role is not so much to assess the truth in an isolated domain of "pure" facts, as Price and his contemporaries imagined, but rather to create and maintain plausible separations between what counts as impartial, rational analysis (relatively speaking), to be delegated to experts, and what counts as the exercise of preference or power, to be validated by conventional democratic processes. Expert advisory bodies, in other words, perform a complicated kind of social work, one output of which is a community's shared sense of the role of expertise in policy making. Three dimensions of this work deserve comment as having particular bearing on the future of DNA evidence.

The first of these dimensions is *framing*. In a seminal 1974 work, the sociologist Erving Goffman called attention to the fact that people make sense of experience not in random ways, but in accordance with "frames" or basic "principles of organization that govern events—at least social ones—and our subjective involvement in them."[21] Framing occurs not only at the level of individual human perception, but also at the metalevel of culture. For example, research in science and technology studies has underscored the U.S. policy culture's tendency to frame disputed questions in terms that can be answered by science (that is, as scientific or expert problems), preferably amenable to quantitative analysis.[22] In this context, it is interesting to note that Reno initially framed the National Commission's task in technical terms, as a matter of defining standards and maintaining scientific rigor. Put in these terms, her comments arguably underplayed the role of both nonscientific experts, such as law enforcement officials, and lay citizens in determining appropriate standards in DNA testing. Yet as the unplanned social experiment of the O. J. Simpson trial demonstrated, mere scientific rigor may not be sufficient to ensure the persuasiveness of evidence unless it also conforms to other professional (e.g., of police criminalists) and lay standards of credibility.

The second important dimension of expert bodies' efforts is what sociologists call *boundary work*, a kind of categorical line drawing between different types of human activity or experience. This work is essential to the functioning of complex societies because it helps assign and define social roles, underwrites the credibility of specialist institutions, and promotes the creation of relevant forms of expertise. The boundary between science and other forms of authority has acquired particular social and moral significance in contemporary societies because scientific knowledge has such extraordinary importance as both a cognitive and political resource in policymaking.[23] It is a boundary which, among other things, carves out activities on one side of it—that of scientific expertise—as requiring different safeguards from those required in politics. Indeed, the designation "scientifically valid" derives much of its legitimating power precisely from its apparent denial of the influence of politics. Producing the science-politics boundary thus emerges as a salient achievement of expert advisers.

The third dimension of the work that expert bodies perform is *negotiation*. In technologically advanced, modern societies, people often come to the policy table holding markedly different beliefs about both knowledge and power. While the need for debate and compromise on political questions has been acknowledged for centuries, there is much less recognition of a similar deliberative need in the domain of technical analysis. Yet the resolution of many questions that fall within what Price and others considered the realm of truth is now recognized as entailing values, preferences, and power. Settling apparently technical differences may require every bit as much horse trading as negotiating over more overtly political outcomes. Examples of hybrid fact-value issues that experts routinely negotiate over include the following: How much uncertainty surrounds a prediction and how should it be characterized or communicated? Which methods are appropriate for calculating uncertainty? When does it make sense to disaggregate at-risk populations and when not? When is a novel scientific method sufficiently robust to underwrite a policy decision? Who has relevant knowledge or expertise in a particular matter? Who is a credible expert? The answers in each case reflect as much a society's normative judgments about tolerable forms and levels of risk as they do the knowledge of its experts.

Bounded Democratization

As empirical support for the truth-to-power model of expert advice has worn thin, a more nuanced view of the role of expert bodies in technology policy has grown up to take its place. Instead of being seen as guardians of "the truth," expert commissions can now be viewed as playing a more democratically accountable role in society's gradual accommodation of technology. In effect, such bodies can serve as sites of deliberation in which framing, boundary work, and negotiation take place in an integrated fashion, making room for lay as well as expert inputs. We can call this model "bounded democratization": It is *democratic* because it looks at alternative sociotechnical trajectories and is open to multiple viewpoints; it is *bounded* because deliberations of this sort are necessarily constrained by the scientific and technical resources available to society at a given moment. This model differs from that of "speaking truth to power" because it does not presume that there is a pre-existing demarcation between these two poles of the decision-making spectrum, especially at the moment when thorny, hybrid sociotechnical questions are first laid at the experts' door. The separation of science from politics occurs, if at all, only as a result of the experts' successful boundary work. Unlike the earlier model, too, bounded democratization does not see the commingling of politics and expertise as a problem in itself;[24] rather, it recognizes that politicization of experts is to some degree a necessity if technically complex, factually uncertain areas of public policy are to remain answerable to citizens' wants and needs.

There are numerous precedents in U.S. policy for such bounded democratic approaches in relation to technological change, and two of these are especially germane to the case of DNA testing. An approach that proved popular in the 1970s was technology assessment. The Technology Assessment Act of 1972, which responded to growing protests against technology's harmful environmental and social impacts, created a new Office of Technology Assessment (OTA) to advise Congress on the positive and negative consequences of new technologies. For almost a quarter of a century, until its sudden elimination by a Republican Congress in 1995, OTA served as a forum in which options for technology policy were identified and evaluated. The agency's immediate impact on policy was slight,[25] and we can say in hindsight that the statutory framing of OTA's responsibilities was based on an exaggerated estimation of any expert body's ability to forecast future sociotechnical developments. From our standpoint, however, OTA played in many ways an invaluable role by revisiting issue areas as they developed (the series of OTA reports on biotechnology is a good example), building interdisciplinary networks of analysts and policymakers, and involving a wider range of opinion than was usual for the more staid and insulated committees of the National Academy of Sciences. OTA also performed an important piece of boundary work by generating reports that were seen as mostly technical, and hence relatively apolitical, even though they rested on a sophisticated negotiation of underlying political judgments.

A second example of bounded democratization that has recently gained prominence is in the work of ethics advisory bodies, of which a prime example is the National Bioethics Advisory Commission (NBAC) created by President Clinton's Executive Order 12975 of October 3, 1995. The proliferation of such bodies, including high-level national commissions like NBAC, reflects a growing uneasiness in modern societies about the moral ramifications of human interventions in nature. Groups like NBAC were formed in North America and Europe over a generation ago to address questions about the ethics of biomedical research, the appropriate uses of novel medical technologies, and the allocation of scarce resources in health care, from body parts to expensive life-prolonging therapies. More recently, these bodies have been sucked into the intensifying debate surrounding genetic technologies in biomedicine. Many national-level bioethics reports have been produced throughout the industrialized world on such issues as genetic screening and privacy, human cloning, and stem cell research. Like the more conventional technical advisory bodies attached to health, safety, and environmental agencies, bioethics bodies also wrestle with fuzzy issues, replete with uncertainties, which they clarify through a mixture of principled analysis, boundary work, and outright negotiation. When completed, their work commands respect as the judgment of experts; if a report is successful, the uncertainties that were surmounted and the everyday compromises that were made in order to achieve its seemingly principled conclusions are largely erased from view.[26]

DNA's Multiple Identities

The simple truth-to-power model of expert advice current in the 1960s remains applicable in the case of DNA testing so long as we think about such testing chiefly as a tool in law enforcement. From this standpoint, technical questions about the tool's adequacy for the job are the ones that come to the fore. The National Commission's charge was founded in part on just this kind of technocratic framing of the challenges posed by DNA: to recommend "courses of action to improve its use as a tool of investigation in the operation of the criminal justice system."[27] To deploy DNA tests responsibly, the commission needed to think through how to standardize them, how to validate the information they produce, how to assess new and emerging methodologies, and how to communicate conclusions about these issues in the form of policy advice. All these issues call for specialized competence, or expert judgment as conventionally defined.

Both the commission's membership and its early organizational choices, however, reflected a more complex understanding of its advisory mandate. To begin with, it was not constituted as a purely scientific body. The commission was chaired by Shirley Abrahamson, chief justice of the Wisconsin Supreme Court, and its nineteen commissioners represented a wide range of expertise not only in forensic science, but also in the domains of law enforcement, municipal politics, legal aid, victim advocacy, and academic law. This heterogeneous body constituted itself as five working groups reflecting its sense of the most urgent tasks ahead. Again, the group's choices went beyond mere technical standardization. The topics selected for further review were (1) research and development (to focus on evolving DNA technologies), (2) postconviction issues (to accelerate the process of exonerating wrongly convicted persons), (3) crime scene investigation (to improve and standardize the capacity of law enforcement officials), (4) legal issues (to examine barriers to admissibility and postconviction relief), and (5) laboratory funding (to study the costs of database backlogs).

This way of dividing up the commission's activities looks at one level like the pragmatic response of a criminal justice system caught between the hammer of rapid technological change and the anvil of existing institutional commitments. On the one hand, there is an urge to adopt DNA techniques more speedily, disseminate the information they produce more widely, and develop the capacity to use that information more uniformly. On the other hand, there are worries about striking the right balance between respect for the truth and the need for repose in an overburdened law enforcement process. Conceived in this way, the commission seems at best to be concocting, hastily and retroactively, the rules for a game already in progress—a game in which the stakes for some players could amount literally to life or death. This view of the commission's role makes it appear far from visionary and not nearly so ambitious in its objectives as traditional technology assessment, even though its work could be highly consequential for a few individuals.

Yet reading through transcripts of commission meetings, one is struck by repeated slippage into less immediate and pragmatic concerns. Commissioners and presenters convey the sense that DNA should be regarded as more than just a physical marker or identification tag, no different in principle from a bit of fiber, a shoe print, a voice recording, a piece of handwriting, or even that hoary staple of forensic science, the human fingerprint. Fleetingly in the record of commission deliberations one encounters other possible framings of DNA's identity: It is not only a tool but a source of information; when compiled from numerous sources, DNA evidence constitutes data. It identifies and classifies not just individuals, but groups who share genotypic or phenotypic traits of interest to society. It is a commodity that can be viewed as someone's property, or not. It can be used for purposes only tangentially connected with law enforcement, with divergent implications for public policy—most obviously, for example, in research on the genetic correlates of violent behavior. (Table 15.1 summarizes the possible identities of DNA and some of the significant policy issues associated with each.) Uncertainties regarding which of DNA's identities is at stake in a given policy context may be compounded by gaps and inconsistencies in the rules governing the use of DNA, especially in a federal system with competing legal jurisdictions.

The multiplicity of DNA's identities and the substantial policy issues that each raises point to a much more expansive role for expert bodies like the National Commission. Instead of functioning primarily like technical experts debating issues of interest only to specialists, commission members emerge as people in a position to inform, even shape, a wider public debate about the limits and uses of genetic

Table 15.1
DNA's multiple identities

DNA's identity	Issues for policy
Physical sample	Methods for collection, analysis, storage, etc. Rules for use, exchange, or destruction
Individual identifier	Privacy, postconviction relief, misuse of information
Group identifier	Racial bias, group stigmatization, misuse of information
Commodity/property	Ownership and control, exchange, disposal
Data	Anonymity and access, consent, misappropriation or misuse
Research tool	Research ethics, informed consent (by individuals and groups)

identification. Sorting through the complex of issues surrounding DNA involves not only technical analysis, but the assertion of values that are fundamental to the functioning of a democratic society, notably, liberty, privacy, and equality under the law. As the FBI's CODIS project manager, Steve Niezgoda, put it at the commission's inaugural meeting, "The big issues that I see facing this committee is balancing what is scientifically possible versus what we as a country find socially acceptable." Excerpts from the transcript of that first meeting (held March 18, 1998, in Washington, D.C.) illustrate that worries about social acceptability, associated with several of DNA's identities, were on the participants' minds from the very beginning:[28]

DNA as data:

Mr. Niezgoda (CODIS Program Manager, FBI): The population files contain DNA profiles. However, the source of that DNA was anonymous, so you can't track it back to an individual. And the idea being that the population file eventually finds its way into the population statistics calculations presented in court. So it's anonymous, anonymous. . . .

Dr. Reilly (Commissioner): If I may, I'd like to ask a question about the meaning of the word "anonymous." Would it be correct to interpret it as meaning it would be absolutely impossible for any individual—to do it with individuals to establish a connection between two data points?

Mr. Niezgoda: It is not absolutely anonymous.

DNA as physical sample:

Professor Scheck (Commissioner): [T]he certification provision that's in the Federal legislation here that says you have to certify that access will only be for these "law enforcement identification purposes," which are specifically defined. But that does not necessarily cover, does it, the blood samples which are stored in each State? In other words, access to the blood samples themselves will be covered by State law, or do you read—or does the certification include within it some pledge by the State that access to the blood samples as opposed simply to the data that's been sent to the FBI and the data that the FBI will send back, that is, the actual DNA profilings, is limited in this fashion?

Do you understand my question?

Ms. Herkenham (Chief, Forensic Science Systems Unit, Laboratory Division, FBI): I understand what you're getting at. This certification that I described is specifically limited to DNA records and analysis, so the scope of the Federal certification would not reach the samples, which I think is what you're asking.

DNA as group classifier:

Mr. Niezgoda: And I'd also mention just of interest that there is currently a case pending in Massachusetts. They had recently enacted a law and had begun the collection of samples from their population that was out on supervised release, and a group of those offenders brought an action to enjoin the collection, and the court did grant the preliminary injunction on the grounds that the Massachusetts State Police had failed to issue regulations on the collection process. Those regulations have been issued as emergency regulations and they are now awaiting a final decision on the merits by the court.

Each of these observations and exchanges illustrates the intertwined character of social and technical questions surrounding DNA testing and its possible applications. Specialized approaches to collection methods, storage systems, and techniques of anonymization are inseparably bound up with concerns about privacy, stigmatization, and inappropriate surveillance. Together, the quoted excerpts also underscore the fact that DNA is not a simple, single-purpose tool, but rather a many-faceted, evolving entity still in search of appropriate and acceptable niches within the criminal justice system.

Conclusion: Democratic Expertise

Like an unruly adolescent, DNA has imprinted itself on our consciousness over the past fifty years. Through incessant demands on our attention, it is transforming the conceptualization of human nature and identity and the social behaviors that are conditioned on new understandings of personhood. One of DNA's most powerful manifestations has been as an aid to society's persistent efforts to control or eliminate the dangerous human elements that threaten our collective security. The identification of criminals using technological means is not new; the search for better instruments of detection has been a preoccupation of Western societies since at least the late nineteenth century.[29] The appropriation of DNA techniques, first to identify criminals and more recently to exonerate the wrongly convicted, is only the most recent episode in the long history of technologically assisted law enforcement.

More than most devices in the tool kit of forensic science, however, DNA testing opens the door to a range of uses and abuses, and associated policy questions, that extend far beyond the core objectives of criminal justice. The reason for DNA's greater instrumental potential is that it can be "read" for much more than the immediate markers that link a particular individual to the perpetration of a particular crime. A DNA database can be mined for information about a suspect individual that has little or nothing to do with the offense for which a sample was originally taken (kinship, disease propensities, other physical or mental characteristics); it can also be used for information on various social groupings, including the perennially volatile categories of race and ethnicity. It is no wonder, then, that the idea of vast masses of DNA information lodged in the control of law enforcement agencies gives rise to more than a frisson of anxiety in even the most law-abiding citizens.

Expert commissions representing a range of specialized knowledge and experience can, as I have suggested, play an important part in subordinating the power of new DNA techniques to effective social control. In a word, they can help to ensure DNA's accountability. But for their deliberations to achieve desired goals, these bodies themselves need to be more reflexively aware of the nature of the task delegated to them. In particular, it is important for expert committees like the National Commission to recognize that they are not mere technical specialists "speaking truth to power." They are instead sites of deliberation, more limited in the scope of their duties than a parliament or an executive agency, but no less important in the nature of their undertaking than the historically recognized major branches of a democratic government. Indeed, as technology becomes an ever more salient presence in contemporary life, expert bodies, as agents of bounded democratization, may have more relevance to people's workaday concerns than do the more elevated institutions of national power strung along Washington's majestic avenues.

This vision of the expert committee's role in resolving the issues surrounding DNA testing carries numerous consequences for the ways in which such bodies should be constituted and carry out their duties. It is worth explicitly noting three of these implications. There is, to begin with, the issue of membership. The National Commission, as originally constituted, was reasonably broadly representative, but it was still constrained by the criminal justice frame within which questions of DNA evidence were first broached. Accordingly, the commission did not specifically include religious experts, historians, political theorists, or social analysts of science and technology—in short, experts who might have helped situate the group's deliberations within a wider context of normative and critical reflection. Second, there is the issue of linkage to other technology assessment activities related to DNA. Interestingly, for example, the National Commission, through its first two years of operation, had no contact with the Human Genome Project at the National Institutes of Health, even though the two programs shared interests in such areas as privacy, access, group identification, consent, and misuse of genetic information.[30] Finally, there is the procedural framework in which the commission conducted its deliberations. Although it conformed to the requirements of federal law, this process was less interactive with society at large than one would hope and expect from an important agent of democratization.

The National Commission's formal work ended in November 2000 with the presentation of its final report to Attorney General Janet Reno at a special conference hosted by Harvard University. But DNA's growing pains will continue for some time, both within and outside the justice system's institutional boundaries. We need expert bodies like the commission to help us understand and mediate our relations with DNA-based techniques. In turn, the experts must learn to see their role as integral to democratic governance in what scientists have termed the age of genetics—and to conduct their affairs accordingly.

Notes

I am indebted to Elisabeth Palladino for invaluable background research for this article and to David Lazer for offering me the opportunity to develop my ideas on this topic.

1. Merritt Roe Smith and Leo Marx, *Does Technology Drive History?* (Cambridge, Mass.: MIT Press, 1994).

2. For contemporary theories of technological systems, see in particular Wiebe Bijker, Thomas Hughes, and Trevor Pinch, eds., *The Social Construction of Technological Systems* (Cambridge, Mass.: MIT Press, 1987); Sheila Jasanoff et al., eds., *Handbook of Science and Technology Studies* (Thousand Oaks, Calif.: Sage, 1996).

3. "Justice O'Connor on Executions," *New York Times*, July 5, 2001, A16.

4. *Penry v. Lynaugh*, 492 U.S. 302, at 334 (1989).

5. *State v. Andrews*, 533 So.2d 841 (Dist. Ct. App. 1989).

6. *People v. Castro*, 545 N.Y.S.2d 985 (Sup. Ct. 1989).

7. *Schwartz v. State*, 447 N.W.2d 422 (1989).

8. Committee on DNA Technology in Forensic Science, *DNA Technology in Forensic Science* (Washington, D.C.: National Academies Press, 1992).

9. Eric S. Lander and Bruce Budowle, "DNA Fingerprinting Dispute Laid to Rest," *Nature* 371 (1994): 735–738.

10. Committee on DNA Technology in Forensic Science: An Update, *The Evaluation of Forensic DNA Evidence* (Washington, D.C.: National Academies Press, 1996).

11. Jim Dwyer, Peter Neufeld, and Barry Scheck, *Actual Innocence: Five Days to Execution and Other Dispatches from the Wrongly Convicted* (New York: Doubleday, 2000).

12. Edward Connors et al., *Convicted by Juries, Exonerated by Science: Case Studies in the Use of DNA Evidence to Establish Innocence after Trial* (Washington, D.C.: National Institute of Justice, 1996).

13. Ibid., iii.

14. www.ojp.usdoj.gov/nij/dna/welcome.html.

15. Jim Yardly, "Inquiry Focuses on Scientist Employed by Prosecutors," *New York Times*, May 2, 2001, A14.

16. Janet Reno, "Recognition of Commission Members" (speech, "DNA and the Criminal Justice System" symposium, John F. Kennedy School of Government, Harvard University, Cambridge, Mass., November 19–21, 2000).

17. Don K. Price, *The Scientific Estate* (Cambridge, Mass.: Harvard University Press, 1965), 191.

18. Significant reports that have resulted from such exercises include National Research Council, *Risk Assessment in the Federal Government: Managing the Process* (Washington, D.C.: National Academies Press, 1983); National Research Council, *Science and Judgment in Risk Assessment* (Washington, D.C.: National Academies Press, 1994); National Research Council, *Research Priorities for Airborne Particulate Matter*, vol. 1, *Immediate Priorities and a Long-Range Research Portfolio* (Washington, D.C.: National Academies Press, 1998).

19. The influential physicist and science administrator Alvin Weinberg observed as early as 1972 that expert advisers are asked to answer questions that can be framed in scientific terms and yet are not answerable by science. He called the gray zone in which experts operate "trans-science." Alvin Weinberg, "Science and Trans-Science," *Minerva* 10 (1972): 209–222. Subsequent work in the sociology of science has established that a more productive way to look at the differences between research science and regulatory science is in terms of their different institutional and social contexts. These differing contexts influence the content as well as the credibility of the knowledge that is produced in each setting. See, in particular, Sheila Jasanoff, *The Fifth Branch: Science Advisers as Policymakers* (Cambridge, Mass.: Harvard University Press, 1990).

20. For illustrative cases, see Jasanoff, *The Fifth Branch*.

21. Erving Goffman, *Frame Analysis: An Essay on the Organization of Experience* (Cambridge, Mass.: Harvard University Press, 1974), 10–11. The importance of framing has also been discussed by policy analysts. See Donald A. Schon and Martin Rein, *Frame/ Reflection: Toward the Resolution of Intractable Policy Controversies* (New York: Basic Books, 1994).

22. Theodore Porter, *Trust in Numbers: The Pursuit of Objectivity in Science and Public Life* (Princeton: Princeton University Press, 1995); Sheila Jasanoff, *Risk Management and Political Culture* (New York: Russell Sage Foundation, 1986).

23. Thomas Gieryn, *Cultural Boundaries of Science: Credibility on the Line* (Chicago: University of Chicago Press, 1999). On the role of science in legitimating democratic politics, see Yaron Ezrahi, *The Descent of Icarus* (Cambridge, Mass.: Harvard University Press, 1990).

24. Politicization of experts is usually represented as a problem by political scientists. See, for example, Bruce Bimber, *The Politics of Expertise in Congress* (Albany: State University of New York Press, 1996).

25. Ibid., 93–95.

26. For a sociological analysis of how such erasure happens in the work of experts, see Stephen Hilgartner, *Science on Stage: Expert Advice as Public Drama* (Palo Alto: Stanford University Press, 2000).

27. www.ojp.usdoj.gov/nij/dna/welcome.html.

28. www.ojp.usdoj.gov/nij/dna/frstmtg.htm.

29. Simon A. Cole, *Suspect Identities: A History of Fingerprinting and Criminal Identification* (Cambridge, Mass.: Harvard University Press, 2001); see also Michel Foucault, *Discipline and Punish: The Birth of the Prison* (New York: Pantheon, 1977).

30. A review of the commission's meeting transcripts, for instance, yields no references to the presidentially appointed National Bioethics Advisory Council.

16

DNA and the Criminal Justice System: Consensus and Debate

David Lazer and Michelle N. Meyer

In the last decade, DNA analysis has become a mainstay of the criminal justice system—the gold standard for identification. Following Stephen Breyer's and Sheila Jasanoff's discussions, in chapters 2 and 15, respectively, of the role of deliberation in the integration of technology and society, this concluding chapter examines where we, as a society, have reached a consensus—or should reach a consensus—on the use of DNA in the justice system and also points to the unsettled areas of debate in which there remains room for reasonable disagreement.

As Edward Imwinkelried discusses in chapter 5, DNA technology has been integrated rapidly and fairly easily into the courtroom; its integration into the pre- and posttrial areas of the judicial process has been slower and more complex. Nevertheless, some broad areas of agreement exist, or should exist, in these areas, including that some level of postconviction relief is warranted, and that some form of DNA databases are effective and appropriate investigatory tools. Beyond the broad consensus in those two areas, however, exists a sometimes vociferous debate about how extensive postconviction and database programs should be and the institutions and rules that should govern them. In the following, we first summarize the areas of consensus, then analyze the remaining areas of disagreement. We conclude by discussing deeper questions at the nexus of law, science, and society.

Areas of Consensus

There are two broad areas of consensus regarding the role of DNA in the criminal justice system. The first is that DNA changes the meaning of time in the justice system. From this principle follow a number of subsidiary points: that DNA evidence must be preserved, that there should be statutory criteria for postconviction access and review of evidence, and that statutes of limitations barring the presentation of new DNA evidence should be lengthened or abolished. The second area of consensus is that DNA databases—in some form, at least—are legitimate and effective investigatory tools.

DNA Changes the Meaning of Time for Justice

As Imwinkelried and Margaret Berger both demonstrate (in chapters 5 and 6, respectively), time has been deeply programmed into justice, both preconviction, with respect to statutes of limitation, and postconviction, in limitations on bringing new evidence to bear. DNA has undermined this fundamental tenet of the justice system, and a consensus has developed that the rules of the system must be altered to reflect this.

Few individuals disagree with the principle that unambiguous evidence of innocence should be grounds for exoneration. (The extent of this consensus can be illustrated by an exception to the rule: As Assistant State Attorney General Frank A. Jung tried to block a death row inmate from having his conviction reopened on the basis of new evidence, Missouri Supreme Court Judge Laura Denvir Stith asked him, "Are you suggesting that even if we find Mr. Amrine is actually innocent, he should be executed?" Jung answered, "That's correct, your honor." Judge Michael A. Wolff asked again: "To make sure we are clear on this, if we find in a particular case that DNA evidence absolutely excludes somebody as the murderer, then we must execute them anyway if we can't find an underlying constitutional violation at their trial?" Again, Jung said yes.[1]) Instead of viewing a court's judgment as infallible or otherwise unimpeachable, the principle of finality has traditionally been thought to foster trust in the system and to allow all participants in crimes and their prosecution, especially the victims, to gain closure. Moreover, most evidence deteriorates over time. Old evidence, even if newly discovered, is likely to be unreliable. And new evidence would be unfairly compared to the old, deteriorated evidence in the original record, putting the prosecution at a disadvantage. In addition, one piece of new evidence, whether deteriorated or not, typically cannot alter the balance of evidence against a defendant; reopening a case with every newly found piece of evidence would be unproductive and needlessly disruptive. Finally, limitations on prosecution and postconviction relief, as well as the principle of double jeopardy, encourage counsel to try their case correctly the first time by investigating any evidence while it is fresh and offering such evidence at the original trial.

Yet the 143 (as of May 2004) DNA-based postconviction exonerations have fundamentally changed the terms of the debate about finality and the criminal justice system. Most would now agree that DNA constitutes an exception to the principle of finality. As both Imwinkelried and Berger note, DNA is unique among identifying evidence in both its durability and its degree of reliability. DNA's degree of certainty is so high that under some circumstances it is likely to outweigh all other evidence in the original record. And although the judicial system should not be structured so as to encourage sloppy counsel, in many past cases, DNA testing was not discoverable at the time of trial because the technology did not exist. Even in more recent cases in which the defense could, with due diligence, have discovered exculpatory DNA evidence, it seems unjust to punish a potentially innocent convict for the errors of his lawyer. Finally, there is little evidence that increased access to postconviction testing would drain resources from the criminal justice system. In those states that have enacted postconviction testing statutes, relatively few convicts have requested testing,[2] and exonerations actually save the state money, since housing an inmate costs anywhere from $16,000 to $25,000 annually, while testing costs from $50 to $5,000 per case, including materials and personnel expenses.[3]

From the principle that DNA constitutes a legitimate exception to the rule of finality follow two corollaries: that evidence from old cases must be preserved and categorized, and that there must be an established, fair, and timely mechanism for negotiating requests for access to evidence and postconviction review.

Evidence Must Be Preserved   Any policy debate over how to manage inmate access to DNA testing must logically assume that the evidence to be tested exists and is locatable. Yet in many cases, such evidence has been lost, destroyed, contaminated, or allowed to deteriorate. In 75 percent of the cases in which the Innocence Project has determined that a DNA test on some piece of biological evidence would be determinative of guilt or innocence, the evidence is reported either lost or destroyed;[4] overall, adequate DNA material for testing is available in only one in five past and present felony cases.[5] Police and prosecutors in each jurisdiction have their own policies for managing and disposing of the evidence that they retain after investigations and trials. The obvious policy solution to this problem is the enactment of laws that standardize the management of physical evidence and require it to be retained for later retrieval. The central concern about this solution is the logistics of storing all evidence indefinitely. Compromise policies thus might make distinctions among the types of evidence to be preserved, the length of its required preservation, or both.[6]

Negotiating Access and Postconviction Review   Assuming that the evidence is available, the most basic—and often the most difficult—obstacle that inmates face in attempting to secure postconviction DNA testing is obtaining physical access to the evidence. The most basic policy questions, in turn, are, Who controls this physical access, and by what criteria do these gatekeepers grant or deny access? Currently, the answers to these questions for any individual convict depend on whether he is imprisoned in a state with a statute that specifically addresses postconviction testing.[7]

About one-third of all states currently lack statutes that provide a procedural mechanism for addressing convict requests for postconviction testing. Convicts in these states have three options: (1) appealing informally to police and prosecutors; (2) appealing to elected officials for clemency; or (3) litigating before a judge for the right to test (often claiming newly discovered evidence).

The experience to date suggests unambiguously that each of these routes is deeply flawed and that the odds that a given convict will be granted access to evidence through one of them are slim. Regardless of which route a convict chooses, for instance, convict requests for DNA testing typically occur in a postconviction relief setting in which the convict has no right to the legal representation necessary to search for physical evidence or apply for the permission to test or for a new trial.[8]

The current policy is that police departments effectively "own" evidence not used at trial, and prosecutors "own" evidence used at trial. A convict's first step, then, is often, through his counsel (if he has any), to informally ask the prosecutor of his case for permission to test evidence. Yet relying on prosecutorial discretion is asking an institution designed for one purpose—to make the case against someone suspected of a crime—to perform exactly the opposite function. Postconviction cases divert resources from the district attorney's office's primary organizational mission of convicting criminals and undermine the credibility of the office. They also threaten existing relationships with law enforcement and do not achieve the political imperative of being tough on crime—costs that governors, to whom convicts might appeal for clemency,[9] share with prosecutors. While individual prosecutors and elected officials sometimes rise above these institutional pressures, the experience to date (the Criner case discussed in chapter 1 is an exemplar) indicates that it is unreasonable to ask prosecutors as a class to take on this function.

If appealing to individual prosecutors[10] or other elected officials fails, convicts imprisoned in states without postconviction testing statutes might attempt the third option of litigation. The Innocence Project claims that those who do face an average delay of four and a half years in obtaining access to evidence, increasing the likelihood that the evidence will be lost or destroyed.[11] Moreover, convicts are faced with the daunting task of forcing the square peg of potentially exculpatory DNA evidence into the round hole of existing rules governing postconviction relief. Because no clear precedent regarding postconviction DNA testing exists in states without specific statutes addressing such testing, courts, no less than prosecutors and governors, tend to rule on a case-by-case basis and rulings within states, much less among them, are not always consistent. Moreover, many judges, too, face reelection by a public that often expects them to demonstrate their commitment to punishing crime. Finally, and perhaps most importantly, convicts face various time restrictions. In thirty-three states, for instance, inmates have six months or less to file a motion based on new evidence.[12] Convicts also face the recent trend of states' enacting statutes of limitations that bar postconviction relief for any reason after a certain point beyond conviction. The number of states with such statutes increased from three in 1972 to twenty-eight as of 2002. Only fifteen states permit a convicted felon to request a motion for a new trial based on newly discovered evidence more than three years after judgment in the case.[13] In the absence of state statutes that permit specific exceptions to these limitations for DNA-based cases, those convicted either prior to the introduction or admissibility of DNA evidence, or before advancements in the scientific analysis of DNA, are procedurally barred from receiving postconviction relief.[14]

Given the flaws in each of these three alternatives, it is clear that some mechanism must be established that is designed especially for negotiating access to evidence and postconviction review. One option is for states to enact statutes that permit testing in certain situations when convicts request it. At the time this book went to press, thirty-nine states and the District of Columbia had enacted specific statutes to address convict access to postconviction DNA testing, up from only two states in 1999;[15] another three states and the federal government had legislation pending. By taking decisions about who should have access to evidence out of the hands of individual district attorneys, these laws, in theory, provide a less arbitrary, more effective standard for negotiating postconviction access to evidence. Indeed, in 2000, most exonerations resulting from DNA testing came from New York and Illinois, the only two states that had enacted such statutes at that time.[16]

Yet state statutes vary widely in their criteria for granting postconviction review (see subsequent discussion); the narrowest of these statutes arguably provide no better access than the avenues just discussed that are used by convicts in states without statutes. Another option, then, is to enact a single federal statute with the effect of forcing sufficient convict access at the state level.[17] Denying an individual access to potentially exculpatory evidence is arguably unconstitutional, nothing short of a civil rights violation; from this perspective, postconviction testing (at least in some circumstances) is a fundamental right that should trump something as arbitrary as the state in which a particular individual happens to have been convicted.[18] Another argument in favor of federal legislation harkens back to the flaws inherent in allowing individual prosecutors to determine whether to grant review. Just as prosecutors have an interest in avoiding a critique of their own work and that of their colleagues in law enforcement, individual state legislatures (which are often composed of many former prosecutors) arguably have similar interests in appearing tough on crime and in conveying an image of their state law enforcement as competent.

Statutes of Limitations Must Be Adjusted to Take into Account DNA Evidence
The logic for supporting extensions on prosecutorial statutes of limitations is identical to the logic for increasing the time permitted to apply for postconviction relief: DNA evidence can be powerfully probative many years after a crime. DNA can identify a perpetrator (or exclude a convict) with a high degree of probability that, in turn, effectively removes the doubt that ordinarily surrounds the prosecution of an old crime. There has even been serious contemplation abroad of making exceptions to the rule of double jeopardy in cases of new DNA evidence.[19]

DNA Databases Are an Effective Investigative Tool   Experience in the United Kingdom and the United States indicates unambiguously that DNA databases are an effective investigative tool, having aided many thousands of investigations. In the United Kingdom, the Forensic Science Service (FSS) reports that approximately one in ten adult males is now in the country's DNA database, and that there is a 40 percent chance that probative biological evidence from any given crime scene will result in a hit to the database.[20] In the United States, all fifty states have passed statutes authorizing the creation of DNA databases, and although the fraction of the population that is in the database is considerably smaller than in the United Kingdom, the number of entries is rapidly growing. With the significant exception of *United States v. Kincade*, in which a three-judge panel from the 9th Circuit Court ruled that collection of DNA from a parolee violated the Fourth Amendment, DNA databases have withstood constitutional challenge. The 9th Circuit is reconsidering that decision en banc.

Areas of Disagreement

As we move from broad principles regarding whether and in what ways DNA should be used in the criminal justice system to the specifics of how DNA use should be governed, consensus gives way to disagreement. The first set of questions that provoke such dissent focuses on the design of postconviction institutions: Who should be the gatekeepers of postconviction review? What should the criteria for postconviction review be? How should the system respond when the results from postconviction testing return? And are there systemic flaws in the criminal justice system, and if so, how should we address them? The second set of questions that give rise to substantial disagreement focuses on the DNA databases: Who should be in the database? Should the database be searched for "near misses"? How should the database be regulated?

Disagreements in the Area of Postconviction Review

Who Should Be the Gatekeepers of Postconviction Review?   There is considerable variation among states as to which parties play the role of the gatekeepers of postconviction review. In states without postconviction statutes, individual prosecutors, governors, and judges act as such gatekeepers. In states that have enacted statutes governing postconviction review, state legislators who create the relevant law, combined with the judges who interpret and apply it, act as gate-keepers. A third option is to create commissions that are independent of the criminal justice system to review cases for possible testing. Instead of petitioning a judge under a statute, for instance, convicts might seek permission to test from a DNA panel whose members represent a variety of interests (e.g., prosecutors, defense lawyers, victims' rights advocates). All of the above options rely on individual convicts to initiate the process of review. Placing the burden on the convict is probably both sufficient and efficient in most cases; some convicts who lack education or who have significant intellectual deficits, however, might fall through the cracks. A final option, then, used in conjunction with one of the above, is to establish a mechanism (perhaps independent committees) through which society reviews convictions.

What Should the Criteria for Postconviction Review Be?   As Berger highlights in chapter 6, a second set of policy decisions concerns the *criteria* that these gatekeepers, whoever they are, ought to use in determining who is given postconviction access to evidence. Existing state statutes provide a good starting point for exploring the range of policy options on who should be granted access.

The first step in gaining access to postconviction DNA testing under a state statute is to qualify as a petitioner. By setting various standards for who qualifies as a legitimate petitioner, states reasonably seek to control the number of access requests with which the judicial system must deal[21] and in particular to discourage frivolous requests that waste resources and needlessly subject victims to painful memories. For example, must the conviction in question be of a certain kind? Although state positions on this question range from no restriction on who may be granted access to testing[22] to permitting testing only for capital convictions,[23] the most common position among state statutes is to grant access to testing only to prisoners who have been convicted of a felony.[24] Similarly, must the petitioner have received a sentence of a certain length? Again, some states impose no minimum sentence requirements on those requesting DNA testing,[25] whereas others limit testing to those sentenced to life imprisonment or even death.[26] Although such conviction and sentence limitations are successful in stemming the flow of postconviction requests, they have the significant disadvantage of possessing no relationship to the ethical or legal merits of review. An innocent person who is sentenced to fifteen years for a lesser crime is just as wrongfully imprisoned as one sentenced to life imprisonment for murder.

Should postconviction testing be subject to statutes of limitations? Some postconviction testing statutes require that the petition for such testing be filed within a certain time limit after conviction or sentencing.[27] Others establish an expiration date after which the statute will no longer exist.[28] Still others restrict review to cases in which convictions were entered before a certain time (usually the mid-1990s, when DNA evidence became a routine presence in the courtroom).[29] On the one hand, such restrictions successfully limit the number of potentially reviewable cases by attempting to isolate those that are most likely to have been mishandled and/or to benefit from DNA analysis. On the other hand, they tend to assume a limited cause of wrongful conviction (e.g., prior unavailability of DNA testing), such that a brief window of review will suffice to identify and correct all wrongful convictions. Yet these restrictions would exclude a variety of cases of potential wrongful conviction, such as those in which the evidence to be tested took years to locate, or in which DNA testing was available during trial but not pursued by incompetent defense counsel, or in which there was false or purposefully deceptive testimony.

Moreover, new technologies are on the horizon that will play an analogous role to that of DNA; mtDNA analysis, for instance, is likely to produce a second wave of postconviction cases by questioning convictions based largely on hair analysis.

Finally, should a convict requesting postconviction DNA testing have consistently maintained his innocence, and should he have been convicted as a result of a guilty verdict at trial, rather than by entering a plea of guilty or nolo contendere? Applying such criteria prevents potential frivolous petitions, but it would also have excluded from review several men who have now been exonerated but who "confessed" to various crimes or pled guilty as part of a plea bargain.

After setting the criteria for defining a legitimate petitioner, statutes determine how a convict must show a credible prima facie case that DNA testing is potentially exonerative. Here, states almost unanimously agree that the evidence in question must have been subject to a demonstrable chain of custody but disagree significantly on nearly every other matter. They are divided, first, on whether a petitioner must show that his conviction turned on the identity of the perpetrator of the crime should play in assessing a convict's request, and most either specifically require such a showing or do not. Those that require a showing argue that if the verdict in the convict's original trial turned on the victim's or accused's state of mind, for instance, rather than on the perpetrator's identity, a DNA test would be irrelevant.

More controversial are crimes in which multiple persons may have participated. Some argue that whenever there were multiple perpetrators, or it is uncertain whether a rapist ejaculated or the victim had consensual sex prior to being raped, the absence of the appellant's DNA at the crime scene is meaningless.[30] Others counter that if two rapists were involved in a particular assault, for instance, and DNA tests reveal the presence of semen from two individuals, neither of whom is the defendant, then the test is exculpatory. Similarly, results of DNA testing could be suggestive, if not definitive, if crime scene DNA was found to match that of a known criminal in the DNA database. Others note that in some cases, identity should have been an issue at trial but was not, perhaps because eyewitness testimony seemed definitive.[31] California accommodates this concern by requiring prisoners to show "why the identity of the perpetrator was, *or should have been*, a significant issue in the case."[32]

In part, these different approaches to the question of identity reflect different approaches to a second question, that of the standard of proof required for postconviction testing to be granted.[33] Those postconviction review statutes that do not require a showing that identity was at issue during trial, for example, often do not require that test results be able to demonstrate actual innocence, but rather only that "a reasonable probability exists that the petitioner would not have been prosecuted or convicted if exculpatory results had been obtained through DNA analysis."[34] An even weaker standard of proof is that first established in 1994 by New York's statute, which denies postconviction testing to a petitioner who fails to show that "if the results had been admitted in the trial resulting in the judgment, there exists a reasonable probability that the verdict would have been more favorable to the defendant."[35] Other states distinguish between the reasonable probability of a more favorable verdict or sentence and the reasonable probability that the petitioner would not have been prosecuted or convicted.[36] The strongest standards, on the other hand, require that results of DNA testing be able to prove actual innocence. Slightly less strong is the requirement that the results be able to significantly advance a convict's claim of actual innocence—in other words, that they be able to raise a reasonable probability that the convict is actually innocent.[37]

What Should Happen When the DNA Results Come Back?   The next set of policy decisions concerns what happens when the results from a DNA test are returned. When results are not exculpatory, for instance, what should be done? Ought only the original conviction stand, or ought we to criminalize convict requests for tests that turn out to confirm guilt?[38] Conversely, when results are exculpatory, what should happen? Although relief is the clear goal of those who pursue postconviction testing, some state statutes enacted expressly for the purpose of negotiating this testing nevertheless fail to specify the remedy for exculpatory results.[39] Currently, in some cases, the defense moves for a new trial, the prosecutors decline to retry the case, and the defendant is released. In others, prosecutors decide to pursue a second trial.[40] Or should courts have the authority to vacate a judgment, as is the case in New York?[41]

Are There Systemic Flaws in the Criminal Justice System, and If So, What Should Be Done about Them?   The single biggest issue raised by the introduction of DNA into the criminal justice system actually does not have to do with cases that involve DNA testing. Instead, the question is whether DNA-based exonerations tell us about the vast majority of cases that do not involve DNA evidence. The fact that there have been hundreds of exonerations does not tell us that we have a badly flawed criminal justice system. Given a system where many millions have been convicted of crimes since the first DNA-based exoneration fifteen years ago, a few hundred exonerations over the same period by itself does not constitute prima facie evidence that the system is flawed.

The question then becomes whether these exonerations tell us whether there are systematic patterns in where those errors occur. It is clear, in fact, that they do. This is manifested by the very success of the Innocence Project. Imagine, for a moment, that there are no systematic errors in the criminal justice system. For those cases where DNA evidence is available and highly probative, what would the likelihood be that that evidence would either (a) confirm the guilt of the convict, or (b) exonerate the convict? Even if one selected the weakest cases where there were convictions, that probability should be quite small—"beyond a shadow of a doubt." That is, to find a wrongful conviction would truly be searching for a needle in a haystack. What is the actual probability? The Innocence Project reports that in 50 percent of its cases in which evidence exists and is tested, the results exonerate the convict. This tells us that a set of experts on where the system gets it wrong can pick out a set of cases where the system gets it wrong *about half the time.*

The most exhaustive study of postconviction exonerations (including 145 individuals cleared by DNA evidence, and 183 cleared by other means) during the period 1989–2004, by Samuel Gross and colleagues at the University of Michigan, points to some of the cracks in the system.[42] They found a number of overlapping factors underlying false conviction: (1) *eyewitness misidentification:* 64 percent of the cases involved at least one misidentification;[43] (2) *perjury:* 44 percent of the cases involved perjury; (3) *false confessions:* 15 percent of the cases involved false confessions, largely among juveniles and those with mentally disabilities;[44] (4) *race:* in the rape cases, in 75 percent of the cases where the perpetrator was black and the race of the victim could be identified, the victim was white—despite the fact that most rapes are within racial groups;[45] (5) *race and age:* despite the fact that the majority of teenagers arrested for rape or murder are white, only 10 percent of those exonerated were white.[46]

If the criminal justice system does make *systematic* errors, then DNA technology is a woefully inadequate after-the-fact fix that has the potential to correct erroneous convictions only in the relatively small fraction of cases in which testable evidence is available. There are three reasons why DNA is an inadequate fix for such systematic errors. First, most crimes, other than rape, do not involve DNA evidence that is so compelling as to prove innocence or guilt. Assuming that any systematic errors exist just as often for cases in which there is no compelling DNA evidence as they appear to for cases that do, the Innocence Project's hundred-plus exonerations represent simply the tip of the iceberg of criminal justice system failures. Second, for most crimes that were committed before the common use of DNA analysis, the evidence has been discarded. There are almost certainly innocent people in jail convicted of crimes for which DNA evidence that might have exonerated them has been discarded or misplaced. Third, if systematic errors exist, those biases remain even in cases in which DNA evidence is used. As Frederick Bieber notes in chapter 3, the most DNA technology can do is reliably match two samples. It is up to the prosecution and defense to construct competing narratives as to why two samples do or do not match and up to judges and juries to weigh those competing narratives. If there is a flaw in any step of the process, the system will make mistakes, no matter what technology it uses.

Thus, while DNA evidence's exoneration of over one hundred convicts is tremendously important, the illumination of systematic errors in the criminal justice system is more important. It would be misguided of our society to view this period of DNA exonerations as a temporary aberration and ignore the larger lessons that these experiences potentially have to offer us. The illumination of any systematic errors that DNA exonerations may reveal would create the possibilities of (1) opening up other old cases based on those errors and (2) correcting these errors as we move forward. Official evaluations of fault lines in the system have already occurred to a limited extent: for example, the National Institute of Justice report *Convicted by Juries, Exonerated by Science*[47] examined some of the common denominators in twenty-eight wrongful convictions; in Canada, the Ontario government did a thorough self-examination of its system after DNA revealed the wrongful conviction of Guy Paul Morin (the Kaufman Commission);[48] in the United Kingdom, England has created a standing commission to reevaluate cases postconviction (the Criminal Cases Review Commission).[49]

These efforts at self-reflection have had an impact. For example, New Jersey recently changed how it conducts photo lineups based on a combination of cognitive psychological studies about accurate recalls and the National Institute of Justice report.[50] A few states attempt to ensure fair questioning of suspects by videotaping interrogations, including any confessions that may occur during them.[51]

Postconviction DNA exonerations have also changed the terms of the debate around capital punishment. Although the presence of systematic errors in the criminal justice system is a concern at all levels of severity of crime, it is a particular concern in capital cases, because the finality of the death penalty removes the possibility of postconviction correction. The exonerations of inmates on death row, as well as studies that indicate a substantial error rate in the handling of capital cases,[52] certainly undermine the case for capital punishment, especially in the absence of repairs to the system. It is this set of reasons that persuaded Illinois Governor George Ryan and Maryland Governor Parris Glendenning to place a moratorium on capital punishment and later led Ryan to commute the sentences of all 167 inmates who remained on death row in his state.[53] In Massachusetts, where Governor Mitt Romney is proposing to reinstitute the capital punishment, he appointed a commission that focused on the source of these exonerations. This commission produced a set of proposals for a very narrowly applied death penalty aimed at excluding those classes of convictions that are relatively more likely to be inaccurate (most notably, those relying largely on eyewitness testimony).[54]

However, so far, the impact of these efforts has been quite limited, and a critical question that needs to be addressed is how to use the information that exonerations provide to improve the justice system. Should there be a standing commission, as in the United Kingdom? Or alternatively, as Barry Scheck has proposed, should a blue-ribbon commission along the lines of the Kaufman Commission be formed to conduct an investigation every time there is an exoneration?[55]

The possibility of systemic flaws in the system also raises another question about the criteria for postconviction review: Should postconviction review be limited to DNA-based cases? On the one hand, again, there is a need to limit the scope of potential cases that can be reviewed. Yet there is no reason to think that the errors (and intentional misconduct) that lead to wrongful convictions are limited to those cases in which DNA testing is possible, and such a restriction would make most of these other cases unreviewable.

It is arguable that in addition to increasing access to postconviction review and bringing about the formation of commissions to study systemic patterns of error, DNA data banks, though established with the primary end of prosecution, will also help exonerate the wrongfully convicted as well as prevent wrongful convictions in the first place. When DNA samples from a crime scene not only fail to match the person convicted of the crime but instead match a known offender, the convict's case for postconviction relief becomes that much stronger. Similarly, as crime scene samples achieve immediate cold hits, police and prosecutors will be diverted from attention they might otherwise have paid to innocent suspects. These effects presumably increasingly accrue as the database grows.[56] It is to the policy issues that concern this other broad use of DNA in the criminal justice system that we now turn.

Disagreements in the Area of DNA Databases

Who Should Be in the Database?   Recent years have seen a clear trend toward expanding the criteria for inclusion in DNA databases. Two main factors have driven this trend: the economics of the database and lessons learned from leaders in the development of convict databases. The economics of the database are simple: Once the system is in place, adding individuals to the database is cheap—the cost of processing a sample is $50–100.[57] Processing of convict samples can also be outsourced efficiently, as compared to samples from cases, because the convict samples are standardized.

The lesson that has been learned from early adopters of DNA technology—the United Kingdom, Florida, and Virginia—is that a bigger offender database is much more effective than a smaller database. That is, for example, Florida and Virginia now claim that most of their convict-to-case cold hits now involve convicts who have been convicted only of property crimes. As a result, there has been a national move toward all-felon databases. There is also an incipient move toward including arrestees for included crimes in the database (e.g., Virginia and Louisiana), and there have been cases as well in which exclusion samples collected from suspects (sometimes relatives and friends of the victim) have been searched against the database.[58] Finally, there is substantial disagreement over whether juveniles should be included in the database: Should an individual be under lifetime surveillance because of something he or she did as a minor? Table 16.1 summarizes the criteria for inclusion in the database across the fifty states. It is important to note, however, that there have been no independent evaluations of the relationship between the scope of the criteria for inclusion in DNA databases and those databases' efficiency.

The scope of inclusion in significant part must be based on interpretations of what it means to collect a DNA sample from an individual. Jasanoff argues in chapter 15 that DNA has an "identity crisis." The critical question as we move forward with DNA databases is how we view what DNA samples "really" are. At a minimum, DNA is an identifier, and because we shed our DNA, a tool for surveillance. It allows the matching of biological samples collected from some location (e.g., a crime scene) to an individual. The critical questions are, What individuals and what locations? As discussed earlier, there is great variation in the choices of states along these dimensions. The critical issue from a privacy perspective is what justifies this level of state surveillance of an individual? For instance, if DNA molecules are viewed as miniature medical records, then a databank of tissue samples is itself essentially a database of intimate details regarding the individuals whose tissue is in the databank, awaiting the appropriate technology to be applied to withdraw that information. Under this view, the holding of DNA by the state becomes a substantial intrusion on the individual.

In chapter 9, Barry Steinhardt asserts that the set of people whom it is justifiable to monitor in this fashion is very small: that inclusion in the database should be limited to those who have committed the most egregious crimes (and, preferably, not even them). Viktor Mayer-Schönberger and Amitai Etzioni, with very different emphases, argue (in chapters 11 and 10, respectively) that a balancing of individual rights and societal interests is necessary, with Mayer-Schönberger emphasizing the former, and Etzioni the latter. D. H. Kaye and Michael Smith, finally, argue in chapter 12 that there is no individual right against *just* identification by society, and that therefore there is no logical limit on who should be included in DNA databases.

Should the Offender Database Be Searched for "Near Misses"?   DNA also may reveal to whom an individual is related. This is especially likely in parent-child and full-sibling relationships. In principle, a DNA database can be searched to examine who is related to whom, as well as used to examine who is not related to whom. This is a particular challenge for the possibility of a universal database, as Kaye and Smith advocate in chapter 12.[59] It would be possible to use such a database to find out whether an individual had any "unreported" children, or to trace whether "reported" children were, in fact, genetically related to that individual.[60]

The fact that DNA may be used to identify close relatives is relevant not just when both individuals are in the *offender* database. DNA may be used to identify whether someone in the offender database is related to an individual who was the source of DNA from a particular crime scene, logged in the other half of the database. This will be the single biggest challenge to the development of DNA databases over the coming decade. As Bieber discusses in chapter 3, one can currently conduct a "low-stringency" search of the offender database that would, with rather high probability, result in near misses of any sources of DNA who were siblings, parents, and children of a convict. In the future it might be possible to develop less discriminating tests based on Y-chromosome loci and mtDNA sequences that would reveal distant relatives of a convict. In fact, this indirect approach has been taken on a large scale in identifying remains from the 2001 attacks on the World Trade Center (as well as on other mass disasters): a database has been set up using DNA of close relatives of victims to produce matches through low-stringency searches.

Table 16.1
DNA database laws

State	Sex	Other violent	Property crimes	All felonies	Arrestee	Suspects	Destroy sample	Research	Expunge	Juveniles included	Penalties
Alabama	Yes	Yes	No	Yes	No	No	No	Yes	Yes	Yes	Yes
Alaska	Yes	Yes	No	No	No	No	No	Yes	Yes	Yes	Yes
Arizona	Yes	Yes	Yes	Yes	No	No	No	No	Yes	Yes	No
Arkansas	Yes	Yes	Yes	Yes	No	Yes	No	Yes	Yes	Yes	Yes
California	Yes	Yes	No	No	No	No	No	No	No	Yes	Yes
Colorado	Yes	Yes	Yes	Yes	No	No	No	Yes	Yes	No	No
Connecticut	Yes	Yes	No	Yes	No	No	No	Yes	Yes	No	Yes
Delaware	Yes	Yes	Yes	Yes	No	No	No	Yes	No	No	No
Florida	Yes	Yes	Yes	Yes	No	No	No	Yes	Yes	Yes	Yes
Georgia	Yes	Yes	Yes	Yes	No	No	No	Yes	No	No	Yes
Hawaii	Yes	Yes	No	No	No	No	No	No	Yes	No	No
Idaho	Yes	Yes	Yes	No	No	No	No	Yes	Yes	No	Yes
Illinois	Yes	Yes	Yes	Yes	No	No	No	Yes	Yes	Yes	Yes
Indiana	Yes	Yes	Yes	No	No	No	No	Yes	No	No	No
Iowa	Yes	Yes	Yes	Yes	No	No	No	No	No	No	No
Kansas	Yes	Yes	No	Yes	No	No	No	No	No	Yes	Yes
Kentucky	Yes	Yes	No	No	No	No	No	Yes	Yes	Yes	Yes
Louisiana	Yes	Yes	No	Yes	Yes	No	No	Yes	Yes	Yes	No
Maine	Yes	Yes	Yes	No	No	No	No	Yes	Yes	Yes	Yes
Maryland	Yes	Yes	No	No	No	No	No	Yes	Yes	No	No
Massachusetts	Yes	Yes	Yes	Yes	No	No	No	Yes	Yes	Yes	Yes
Michigan	Yes	Yes	No	Yes	No	No	No	No	Yes	Yes	No
Minnesota	Yes	Yes	Yes	Yes	No	No	No	No	Yes	Yes	No
Mississippi	Yes	Yes	No	Yes	No	No	No	No	No	No	No
Missouri	Yes	Yes	No	Yes	No	No	No	Yes	Yes	No	No
Montana	Yes	Yes	Yes	Yes	No	No	No	Yes	Yes	Yes	Yes
Nebraska	Yes	Yes	No	No	No	No	No	Yes	Yes	No	Yes
Nevada	Yes	Yes	Yes	No	No	No	No	No	No	No	No
New Hampshire	Yes	Yes	Yes	No	No	No	No	Yes	Yes	Yes	Yes
New Jersey	Yes	Yes	No	Yes	No	No	No	Yes	Yes	Yes	No
New Mexico	Yes	Yes	Yes	Yes	No	No	No	Yes	Yes	No	Yes

Table 16.1
(continued)

State	Sex	Other violent	Property crimes	All felonies	Arrestee	Suspects	Destroy sample	Research	Expunge	Juveniles included	Penalties
New York	Yes	Yes	Yes	No	No	No	No	Yes	Yes	No	Yes
North Carolina	Yes	Yes	Yes	Yes	No	No	No	Yes	Yes	No	Yes
North Dakota	Yes	Yes	Yes	No	No	No	No	Yes	Yes	No	Yes
Ohio	Yes	Yes	Yes	No	No	No	No	Yes	No	Yes	Yes
Oklahoma	Yes	Yes	Yes	No	No	No	No	Yes	No	No	No
Oregon	Yes	Yes	Yes	Yes	No	No	No	Yes	Yes	Yes	No
Pennsylvania	Yes	Yes	Yes	No	No	No	No	Yes	Yes	Yes	Yes
Rhode Island	Yes	Yes	No	No	No	No	No	Yes	Yes	No	Yes
South Carolina	Yes	Yes	Yes	Yes	No	No	No	Yes	Yes	Yes	Yes
South Dakota	Yes	Yes	Yes	Yes	No	No	No	Yes	Yes	Yes	Yes
Tennessee	Yes	Yes	Yes	Yes	No	No	No	No	No	Yes	No
Texas	Yes	Yes	Yes	Yes	Yes	No	No	Yes	Yes	Yes	No
Utah	Yes	Yes	Yes	Yes	No	No	No	Yes	Yes	Yes	No
Vermont	Yes	Yes	No	No	No	No	No	No	Yes	No	Yes
Virginia	Yes	Yes	Yes	Yes	Yes	No	No	No	Yes	Yes	Yes
Washington	Yes	Yes	Yes	Yes	No	No	No	No	No	Yes	Yes
West Virginia	Yes	Yes	Yes	Yes	No	No	No	Yes	No	No	Yes
Wisconsin	Yes	Yes	Yes	Yes	No	No	Yes	No	Yes	Yes	Yes
Wyoming	Yes	Yes	Yes	Yes	No	No	No	Yes	Yes	No	Yes

Key: A "Yes" entry for a particular state means the following things, by column:

"Sex": Those convicted of sexual-based offenses are included in the state's database.

"Other violent": Those convicted of at least some other violent crimes besides rape are included in the state's database.

"Property crimes": Those convicted of at least some property crimes are included in the state's database.

"All felonies": Anyone convicted of a felony is included in the state's database.

"Arrestee": At least some people who are arrested are included in the state's database, even if they have not been convicted.

"Suspects": At least some suspects are checked against the state's database.

"Destroy sample": The authorizing statute in the state includes provisions for destroying samples after they have been typed.

"Research": The authorizing statute in the state allows research on samples that have been collected from convicts.

"Expunge": The authorizing statute in the state includes provisions for expunging data concerning individuals who are acquitted or cleared of the conviction that resulted in the placement of their DNA in the database.

"Juveniles included": Juveniles are included in the state's database.

"Penalties": There are penalties for unauthorized access to the state's database.

A partial profile "match" may not be precise enough to use as evidence in court, since a partial profile might result in multiple matches. From an investigative perspective, however, narrowing a list of suspects in a particular crime to a handful of individuals, one of whom, the investigator is nearly certain, is the perpetrator, may be almost as good as a direct hit. The Forensic Science Service (FSS) of the United Kingdom, in fact, has begun offering "familial searching" to police to assist in identifying suspects. Its potential effectiveness was demonstrated in the Lynnette White case. Lynette White has been murdered in 1988. Three men who had been convicted of her murder in 1990 were later cleared, prompting the police to revisit the crime scene, where they found a few spots of blood on the skirting board that they had missed in their original search. A search of the national database did not reveal a match. However, one of the alleles from the sample was particularly rare, facilitating a search for near misses in the database. Eventually they narrowed their search around one particularly near miss—notably, that of a teenager born *after* the murder took place. The DNA of an uncle of this teenager, Jeffrey Gafoor, matched the DNA from the crime scene; Gafoor subsequently confessed to the crime.[61]

The Gafoor case, and a couple of others in the United Kingdom,[62] illustrates the potential for close relatives of someone in the data to be undre almost as much surveillance as those individuals in the database. In fact, that is still likely potential—since even in that case investigators had to sift through hundreds of near misses (with no guarantee that any of them was a useful lead). It is unlikely that such leads could be followed in more routine cases. However, if the databases are expanded to include more data on each individual in the database, the number of near misses could shrink dramatically, and familial searching would then likely become a routine part of investigations. It is possible to imagine scenarios in which searching a database in this fashion would be irresistible, and not searching perhaps even unconscionable, such as in the case of a murder or a rape involving biological evidence that would likely be linked to the murderer.

However, it is notable that the number of people "indirectly" included in the DNA database because they are closely related to someone who is in the database is potentially much larger than the number of offenders in the database. The potential efficacy of low-stringency searches is also accentuated to the extent that those convicted of crimes are related to each other at a rate greater than chance, as a recent Department of Justice study suggests.[63] Low-stringency searches would also multiply the uneven coverage of the DNA database across demographic groups. For example, each year approximately 1.2 percent of the African American population is convicted of a felony (as compared to 0.25 percent of Caucasians).[64] A calculation of the percentage of African Americans who would either directly or indirectly be "in the database" would require detailed and unavailable knowledge of the total number of living offenders, as well as the relationship between offenses and familial ties—but it is certainly conceivable that *most* African Americans would either directly or indirectly be in the database if very low-stringency searches were conducted.

Finally, low-stringency searches will create the peculiar situation, as in the case of Gafoor's nephew, in which the database yields a low-stringency "hit" of an offender who could not possibly have committed the crime—for example, in an extreme case, because the offender had died years earlier (there are few if any provisions in state database laws for expunging from databases data from deceased convicts). That is, a convict's genes might continue to implicate his close relatives for many years after his death.

While the architecture of CODIS allows low-stringency searches (they require only the development of the appropriate search algorithm, which would take only a short time, and the patience to wait a few extra seconds for a more time-consuming search), the FBI has not set standards for low-stringency searches of CODIS, and no state database laws have set policy with respect to whether such searches should be done. As Breyer mentions in chapter 2, the legal and policy question is, What is the basis for low-stringency searches?

If the theory underlying DNA databases is that convicts forfeit certain rights, as Etzioni argues in chapter 11, and if low-stringency searches similarly systematically and exclusively infringe on the rights of individuals who have not forfeited those rights, then low-stringency searches should not be allowed.

If, on the other hand, inclusion in the database (and de facto intrusion) does *not* constitute an intrusion on an individual's rights, and the rationale for inclusion of convicts is that recidivism makes it cost effective to include them, then the rationale for doing low-stringency searches for matches against crime scene evidence would be that the cost is essentially zero. Such an "opportunistic" logic, as the cost of typing samples drops toward zero, however, could also support the typing of any easily available databanks of genetic material (indeed, there was a recent proposal in Congress to create a database for crime fighting from the samples collected from the military).

This logic, as Kaye and Smith argue in chapter 12, potentially leads to a universal database. The costs of creating such a database would not be large and are likely to drop substantially in coming years. The benefits are easily quantifiable: The

FSS reports that in the United Kingdom, which has the largest convict DNA database in the world, 40 percent of cases result in a match to the convict database.[65] With a universal database, this number would (theoretically) approach 100 percent.

Low-stringency searches thus pose a distinctive mix of ethical, legal, and political challenges for the growth of DNA databases. Notably, none of the state or federal statutes dealing with DNA databases addresses low-stringency searches. The political logic underlying the expansion of DNA databases is simple: They are effective at catching criminals, and they impinge largely on the rights of offenders. As a general matter, few state legislators have lost office voting for legislation that embodies these values—hence the fact that all 50 states have passed database legislation. The inclusion of arrestees and suspects in the database erodes the political premise of database legislation to a limited extent—but the wholesale inclusion, directly or indirectly, of millions of nonconvicts means that the rights of nonconvicts/nonarrestees/nonsuspects must be weighed against public safety.

There are four distinct paths we might go down: first, including only individuals convicted of certain crimes in the DNA database and conducting only high-stringency searches of the database; second, including only those individuals, but conducting low-stringency searches of the database; third, opportunistically searching any database that is available; and fourth, developing a universal database. If low-stringency searches are allowed and some limits on such searches are required, the database will need some level of regulation, the next question that we visit.

How Should the Database Be Regulated?   As noted earlier, part of the question surrounding the scope of DNA databases turns on the extent to which inclusion in such a database is intrusive. There is intrusive, in fact, substantial potential for intrusion beyond the objective of surveillance. Genes will be able to reveal an increasing amount of information about an individual, most notably the individual's likelihood of getting certain diseases and perhaps of exhibiting certain behaviors (see subsequent discussion). In chapter 7, George Annas likens the DNA molecule to a miniature medical record about an individual that requires special protection. In fact, as R. Alta Charo discusses in chapter 8, very rigorous protocols have been (and are still being) developed for informing individuals of the risks of participating in federally funded research and for protecting information collected from individuals. The collection of convict samples generally does not involve either providing information about possible uses of the DNA material (other than for matching against crime scenes) or obtaining the consent of the convicts.[66] The protocols Charo discusses have not been applied to the convict samples collected for CODIS, and state statutes vary enormously in their internal regulation of the DNA samples that state law enforcement personnel collect. Thus, some states prohibit research on the samples, whereas others allow just anonymous research on population statistics, and yet others (such as Alabama) mandate research "to assist in other humanitarian endeavors, including but not limited to educational research or medical research or development."

Database DNA also provides information about those not in the database who are genetically tied to someone who is. It follows from the discussion in the preceding section that information uncovered about an included individual's likelihood of developing a genetic disease or condition may also convey information about the same tendency in that individual's relatives. For example, if an individual has the abnormal allele for Huntington's disease, there is a 50 percent chance that each of that individual's full siblings has the allele and a 100 percent chance that at least one of that person's biological parents has the marker.

The critical question that we are left with is what privacy protections are necessary for CODIS. Again, we might take care of several distinct paths: first, allowing research on the DNA samples of those included in the database if identities can reasonably be cloaked; second, developing and implementing an informed-consent protocol for convicts, in which they either consent or do not consent to having their tissue samples used for research; third (Etzioni, chapter 10), conducting no research on the samples but retaining them (e.g., for quality assurance purposes); fourth (Steinhardt, chapter 9; Mayer-Schönberger, chapter 11), destroying the samples once the information from the thirteen loci used for identification in criminal investigations has been extracted.

In each of these paths, part of the equation is the construction of a regulatory regime to guard the integrity of the data collected. How easily should data in the database be able to be accessed and by whom? What punishments should be meted out if the data are improperly accessed? Should DNA samples be discarded or retained? These are questions that have, at best, been incompletely addressed by the various state statutes authorizing the creation of offender databases.

Questions at the Nexus of Law, Science, and Society

The most obvious role of science in the criminal justice system is in the area of forensics. What is less clear is how forensic science should be organizationally positioned within the criminal justice system. In most U.S. states, forensic DNA tests are conducted by state-, county-, or city-run crime labs. This is in stark contrast to the corresponding structure in the United Kingdom, for example, where the FSS is independent of law enforcement. The institutional position of DNA testing in the United States raises several interrelated concerns, the first of which is that the labs that conduct the tests are usually dependent on and controlled by the law enforcement community, which has a vested interest in the lab results. This concern is reinforced by the drumbeat in recent years of cases of crime lab errors, the vast majority of which seem to favor the prosecution.[67] Although actual cases of bias are surely the exception to the rule, combined with the organizational dependency of forensic science on law enforcement, they produce an additional *perception* of bias, which is itself harmful in undermining public confidence in the criminal justice system and in the science of DNA analysis.

Anecdotal evidence suggests that unintentional error is also a factor in some forensic cases.[68] Many forensic techniques used by the criminal justice system—including fingerprint analysis, hair and fiber analysis, and analysis of eyewitness testimony—are essentially scientific in nature. Yet they have never been subjected to the same level of scientific scrutiny as DNA analysis. Although cases of misconduct and error have often been uncovered through the application of DNA analysis postconviction, DNA analysts themselves have not been immune to either errors or accusations of pro-prosecution biases.[69]

Although the defense in a criminal case has an opportunity at trial to present evidence of either intentional bias or unintentional error, reliance on the adversarial process is problematic in part because the defense often does not have the resources to effectively challenge the state's experts, whose imprimatur can be powerfully persuasive to juries. Further, severe limits have been placed on defendants seeking discovery of testing data, which might then allow them to challenge either the admissibility of the results in a pretrial hearing or, failing that, their weight during trial. Crime labs have resisted such discovery, often successfully.[70]

Cases of bias and error in DNA testing and analysis raise the issue of whether the relationship between law enforcement and science needs to be reengineered, somehow insulating forensic laboratories from the law enforcement community and its interests by bringing forensics more squarely within the scientific community. In such a scenario, all forensic labs would be completely independent of both the prosecution and the defense, and both sides would have equal access to the lab's process of data analysis. That process, furthermore, would be subject to stronger regulation and oversight than is currently in place. For instance, accreditation by the American Society of Crime Laboratory Directors Laboratory Accreditation Board (ASCLD/LAB) should be mandatory for all forensic labs, not voluntary, as is currently the case.

Science has other crucial roles to play in the criminal justice system beyond forensics. For instance, researchers who are impartial and free from conflicts of interest can contribute helpfully to the debates discussed in this volume by providing independent empirical research about the criminal justice system. Indeed, as noted earlier in the chapter, the scientific community has already done so in the form of various reports on exonerations and psychological studies of eyewitness testimony. More such empirical studies are needed. Although the policy issues we face concern questions of values, the answers to these ethical questions, in turn, often depend, in part, on empirical data. The legitimacy of expanding DNA databases, for instance, hinges on their effectiveness in punishing and preventing crime—a value that must be balanced against others, such as individual privacy. As noted earlier, however, no independent data exist on the extent to which expanding DNA databases from, say, including some felons to including all felons, or from including felons to including arrestees, results in an increase in the number of suspects identified through cold hits.

Similarly, there are no data on how many suspects who are identified by cold hits are then convicted, nor is there at present any easy way to compile these data, because the outcomes of cold hit cases are not recorded. For instance, a 2001 study of New York's first 102 cold hits found that four hits had resulted in convictions and that charges were pending in fourteen others; in two-thirds of the cases, however, no information on the outcome of the cold hit was available.[71]

Other proposed scientific studies involving the justice system are less clearly appropriate. As noted in the preface, for example, an investigation to find a Louisiana serial killer that had already been notable for achieving many controversial law enforcement "firsts"[72] also became the first known investigation in the United States to predict a suspect's race from DNA left at the crime scenes. Because most serial killers are white, police had been searching for a white man, until investigators sent a sample from one of the crime scenes to DNAPrint Genomics, which typed the sample as being from someone of 85 percent African and 15 percent American Indian ancestry. The suspect arrested in the killings is black; it is not known if he has any American Indian ancestors.[73]

Britain has had an active interest in phenotypic profiles of suspects based on an analysis of their DNA—which British investigators call DNA "photofits"—and the technology has already helped police there solve crimes. Currently, DNA analysis can reveal ethnic appearance as well as red hair and eye color, and researchers are attempting to find genetic links to other physical traits, such as jaw shape, although some scientists feel the task is so complex that much further progress in this area is not likely.[74] From the perspective of criminal investigators, being able to reliably predict the appearance of a suspect in a given case is useful (and stands to be more so if the technology improves) when, as in the Louisiana case, when crime scene DNA fails to match any database samples and when there is no suspect to test.

Yet whatever its benefits in individual cases, the *practice* of what we might call "genetic racial profiling" raises complex issues. The science of "photofitting" has developed largely as a result of giving researchers access to police databases.[75] Such research raises a variety of potential issues. First, many genes involved in physical appearance are also connected to inherited diseases; for example, pigmentation genes are involved in skin cancers, and mutated versions of facial genes could cause congenital abnormalities. As Troy Duster (chapter 14) and Garland Allen (chapter 13) note, there are also scientific questions about the meaningfulness of correlational research that extrapolates from a population that is already weighted toward certain racial and ethnic groups. Moreover, if Duster and others are correct that the justice system engages in systemic racial bias that results in certain racial groups' being far more represented than others in DNA databases, then the fact that the results of research conducted on tissue samples from the databases could be used to stigmatize those in the database (and fellow members of their racial or ethnic group, including their families) as "potential criminals" seems to add insult to injury.

But as Allen and Duster both note, perhaps the biggest concern about genetic tests that claim to predict race from DNA is that it would make behavioral genetic research much easier. What role, if any, should our knowledge of the relationship between behavior and genetics play in the justice system? This is the major debate on the horizon, and the positions in such a debate have not yet fully crystallized. Increased claims about the relationships between our behavior and our genes combined with behavior-based genetic surveillance make it inevitable that a debate on this matter will come, however. Should claims about genetically determined behavior enter into decisions about guilt, innocence, and potential for rehabilitation? Will such claims stigmatize some members of our society as genetically programmed to be criminals? Could increased understanding of the causes of behavior yield therapeutic interventions that might, for example, *prevent* criminal behavior?

Conclusion

DNA analysis has rapidly become one of the pillars of the criminal justice system. As a society, we have reached a consensus on particular applications of DNA technology in the areas of postconviction relief and convict DNA databases. As noted in chapter 1, it is less clear whether we have followed through on that consensus. In the postconviction area, several states have not taken even the most minimal steps to create statutory rights to review, and in many of the remaining states, either the statute securing postconviction review is an unfunded mandate, no legislation or resources ensure the preservation and categorization of evidence, or the criteria for qualifying under the statute are unreasonably narrow. DNA databases have received more support, but too often resources have been slow to follow the mandate. Yet however difficult such reallocations of resources and changes of routine have been for the criminal justice system to achieve, the next generation of questions will present an even more daunting challenge.

Notes

1. Adam Liptak, "Prosecutors See Limits to Doubt," *New York Times*, February 24, 2003.

2. When San Diego County prosecutors, became the first in the country, in 2000, to offer free DNA tests to some inmates, they had few takers. In Broward County, Florida, only three of twenty-nine death row inmates have accepted offers to be tested. Finally, a New Jersey program that offered free tests to felons was actually suspended because so *few* convicts (fewer than twelve) applied. R. Willing, "Few Inmates Seek Exonerations with Free DNA Tests," *USA Today*, July 30, 2002, 1A. One suggested reason for the low uptake is convict fears that tests will confirm their guilt, thus making pardon or parole more difficult, or that by taking the tests, they will be linked to other crimes. Another is the likelihood that those many cases of wrongful conviction have already been pursued by defense lawyers who specialize in DNA-related exonerations. See also Honorable William D. Delahunt, statement to the House Judiciary Committee on Crime, *The Innocence Protection Act of 2000: Hearings on H.R. 4167*, 106th Cong., 2nd sess., June 20, 2000, which discusses states that have adopted postconviction statutes without experiencing the dreaded "floodgate" effect.

3. For instance, according to South Dakota Republican Senator Kermit Staggers, the main sponsor of a postconviction measure that was killed in the South Dakota House of Representatives, tests cost about $100 plus administrative expenses, whereas "it costs thousands of dollars a year to house an inmate." C. Brokaw, "House Committee Kills Plan to Help Convicts Get DNA Tests," *Associated Press State & Local Wire*, February 13, 2002. According to the Arizona Department of Corrections, the average cost of keeping one individual in prison in that state is $45.49 per day. Brokaw, "House Committee Kills Plan to Help Convicts Get DNA Tests." According to Barry Scheck, costs for housing an inmate at an average state prison run from $20,000 to $25,000 a year. B. Alpert, "DNA Tests Cost Less Than

Housing Inmate; Case of L.A. Man Cleared in Rape Drives Push for Law," *Times-Picayune* (New Orleans, La.), February 28, 2000. Texas officials estimate that the state's postconviction statute will generate up to fifty cases of court-ordered DNA testing or retesting each year, at an annual cost to the state of about $73,000. J. B. Elizondo Jr., "Governor Signs DNA Testing Bill; Under New Law, State Will Pay For," *Austin American-Statesman*, April 6, 2001.

4. The Innocence Project adds that although evidence is reported lost or destroyed in 75 percent of the cases they accept, "it takes years to determine if that's really the case." See Peter Neufeld and Barry Scheck, statements to the House Committee on Crime, *The Innocence Protection Act of 2000: Hearings on H.R. 4167*, 106th Cong., 2nd sess., 2000.

5. "A Pandora's Box," *Economist*, December 14, 2002.

6. Illinois' postconviction statute, for instance, requires the preservation of evidence permanently for homicide conviction, for twenty-five years for severe felonies as defined in the criminal code, and for seven years for any other felonies, unless the court is petitioned by the state and grants permission for disposal of the evidence. 725 Ill. Comp. Stat. § 5/116-3 (1997).

7. For a discussion of the inconsistent approaches to postconviction DNA testing among jurisdictions, see B. A. Masters, "DNA Testing in Old Cases Is Disputed; Lack of National Policy Raises Fairness Issue," *Washington Post*, September 10, 2000, A1, A5.

8. B. Barrouquere, "Despite Law, DNA Test Fund Empty," *Advocate* (Baton Rouge, La.), December 13, 2002.

9. In addition, in some states, laws and court rulings do not allow the governor to consider pardons even when DNA evidence casts doubt on a conviction. R. A. Oppel Jr., "States Move toward Easing Obstacles to DNA Testing," *New York Times*, June 10, 2000.

10. Note that opting for litigation does not completely avoid the need for prosecutorial consent, because few judges are willing to order DNA testing for a habeas petition without the consent of the prosecutors. J. Autrey and R. Rodriguez, "Access an Issue in DNA Testing," *Fort Worth Star-Telegram*, July 20, 2000, 1.

11. See Peter Neufeld, statement to the Senate Judiciary Committee, *The Innocence Protection Act of 2000: Hearings on S. 2073*, 106th Cong., 2nd sess., June 13, 2000.

12. Oppel, "States Move toward Easing Obstacles to DNA Testing." In Minnesota, for example, a defendant must bring a motion for a new trial based on newly discovered evidence within fifteen days of the verdict. Minn. R. Crim. P. 26.04 (West 2000).

13. Many states have even shorter statutes of limitations for appealing death penalty cases than they have for other convictions. Donald E. Wilkes, *State Postconviction Remedies and Relief* (Norcross, Ga.: Harrison Company, 1996), 27.

14. See National Commission on the Future of DNA Evidence, *The Future of Forensic DNA Testing: Predictions of the Research and Development Working Group* (Washington, D.C.: National Institute of Justice, U.S. Department of Justice, 2000), 9; C. Bryant, "When One Man's DNA is Another's Exonerating Evidence: Compelling Consensual Sexual Partners of Rape Victims to Provide DNA Samples to Post-conviction Petitioners," *Columbia Journal of Law and Social Policy* 33 (2000): 123.

15. R. Bailey, "Guilt Trip: Prosecutors Who Believe in Justice Should Be Clamoring for DNA Testing," United Press International, November 7, 2002; see www.dnapolicy.net for examples of postconviction statutes.

16. Illinois produced fourteen exonerations; New York produced seven. Alpert, "DNA Tests Cost Less Than Housing Inmate."

17. For example, the Innocence Protection Act, independently introduced in Congress in 2000, and most recently reintroduced in the Senate and House on October 1, 2003, as Title III of the proposed Advancing Justice Through DNA Technology Act of 2003, would give those convicted of a federal crime access to postconviction testing in certain circumstances (§ 311), and it would reserve federal funds for DNA training and education of law enforcement (§ 203), DNA research and development (§ 205), DNA identification of missing persons (§ 207), and postconviction DNA testing (§ 312) for "states that have adopted adequate procedures for providing post-conviction DNA testing and preserving biological evidence for this purpose" (§ 313). See www.leahy.senate.gov/press/200310/100103b.html. The act (HR 3214) passed the House by a vote of 357 to 67 and, at the time this book went to press, was pending in the Senate.

18. Indeed, some courts (e.g., *Summerville v. Warden*, 641 A.2d 1356 (Conn. 1994)) have ruled that convicts have a constitutional right to demonstrate their actual innocence through habeas corpus review, under either the Eighth Amendment's protection against cruel or unusual punishment or the Due Process Clause of the Fourteenth Amendment. Other courts (e.g., *Sewell v. State*, 592 N.E.2d 705 (Ind. App. 1992); *Commonwealth v. Brison*, 618 A.2d 420 (Pa. Super. Ct. 1992); *Dabbs v. Vergari*, 570 N.Y.S.2d 765 (N.Y. 1990)) have, citing fundamental principles of fairness and justice, confirmed a right to testing under *Brady v. Maryland* 373 U.S. 83 (1963), in which the U.S. Supreme Court held that a defendant has a constitutional right to be informed of exculpatory evidence. The court in *Dabbs v. Vergari*, for instance, ruled that "[n]otwithstanding the absence of a statutory right to post-conviction discovery, a defendant has a constitutional right to be informed of exculpatory information known by the state" (767). See J. Boemer, "Other Rising Legal Issues: In the Interest of Justice; Granting Post-conviction Deoxyribonucleic Acid (DNA) Testing to Inmates," *William Mitchell Law Review* 27 (2001): 1979–1980; R. L. Haller, "The Innocence Protection Act: Why Federal Measures Requiring Post-conviction DNA Testing and Preservation of Evidence Are Needed in Order to Reduce the Risk of Wrongful Executions," *New York Law School Journal of Human Rights* 18 (2001).

19. Both Australia and Great Britain are considering exceptions to double jeopardy in cases in which compelling new evidence has emerged, such as DNA test results not available at the time of acquittal. The Law Commission of England has recommended an exemption in murder cases in which compelling and reliable new evidence emerges. The former chief justice of Australia's High Court, Sir Anthony Mason, has similarly called for an exemption. M. Owen-Brown, "Remove Double-Jeopardy Rule, Says Ex–Chief Justice," *Advertiser* (Cessnock, New South Wales, Australia), December 23, 2002, 11; T. Richissin, "Britain Considers Judicial Reforms; Double Jeopardy Allowed under Broad Plan by Blair," *Baltimore Sun*, December 2, 2002, 1A; N. Cowdery, "In Compelling Cases, A Retrial Makes Sense," *Australian* (Sydney), December 16, 2002.

20. "Police Furious over Forensics Sell-Off Plans," *Observer* (London), January 19, 2003.

21. The extent to which these restrictions are necessary to protect the system from a deluge of requests is discussed below.

22. E.g., California.

23. E.g., Kentucky.

24. E.g., Arizona. Indiana is even stricter, making testing available only to those convicted of murder or a class A, B, or C felony. Ind. Code Ann. §§ 35-38-7-1, 35-38-7-5 (Michie Supp. 2001). Tennessee specifies the crimes of which a person must have been convicted in order to petition the court for forensic DNA analysis, including first-degree murder, second-degree murder, aggravated rape, rape, aggravated sexual battery or rape of a child, attempted commission of any of these offenses, or any lesser offense included in these offenses. Tenn. Code Ann. § 40-30-403 (Supp. 2001).

25. Louisiana's statute, for instance, covers anyone in custody. 2001 La. Acts 1020 (2001).

26. Maine, for instance, limits requests for testing to convictions that carry "the potential punishment of imprisonment of at least 20 years," and petitioners must be serving the sentence at the time of petition. Me. Rev. Stat. Ann. tit. 15, § 2137 (West Supp. 2001).

27. Idaho's statute provides that capital-case review will be granted only if petitioner files within forty-two days from the day of judgment or by July 1, 2002 (whichever is later). For other cases, petitioner must file within one year of the day of judgment or by July 1, 2002 (whichever is later). Idaho Code §19-4902 (b) (2001).

28. For example, New Mexico requires the petition to have been filed prior to July 1, 2002, and states explicitly that "[t]he district court shall not accept any petitions after that date." N.M. Stat. Ann. § 31-1A-1(H) (Michie Supp. 2001). Oregon's statute requires all cases to be filed within four years of the enactment of the statute. 2001 Or. Laws 697 (2001). Washington state allows prisoners who are or were convicted on or before December 31, 2004, to submit a request to the county prosecutor for DNA testing; "[o]n and after January 1, 2005, a person must raise the DNA issues at trial or on appeal." Wash. Rev. Code Ann. § 10.73.170(1) (West Supp. 2002).

29. New York's statute, for instance, contains no statute of limitations but restricts legitimate petitioners to those convicted of a crime before January 1, 1996. N.Y. Crim Proc. Law §440.30 (1–a). The Virginia legislature took something of a middle route. Instead of placing a deadline on prisoners' requests for testing, the legislature instructed courts to use their discretion in considering, when evaluating motions for testing, any unreasonable delays in filing of the petition "after the evidence or the test for the evidence became available at the Division of Forensic Science." See Va. Code Ann. § 19.2–327.1(A)(v) (Michie Supp. 2001).

30. St. Louis Circuit Attorney Jennifer Joyce, for instance, has repeatedly refused to permit testing of rape evidence in such cases. T. Bryant, "Tests of Convicts Have Only Just Begun," *St. Louis Post-Dispatch*, August 4, 2002, B4. In one case in Texas, a convict was given access to testing, and the exculpatory results of that testing were then deemed irrelevant to his innocence. Roy Wayne Criner was denied a new trial on his rape conviction after DNA tests showed he was not the source of semen found in the victim. The judge ruling on Criner's request for retrial reasoned that he could have committed the rape and worn a condom. Two years later, more DNA tests showed Criner's innocence, and after ten years in prison, then Governor George W. Bush pardoned him. S. Cohen and P. Shepard, "DNA Test Clears Scores of Felons," *Minneapolis Star Tribune*, October 8, 2000, A29.

31. Two Pennsylvania Superior Court decisions wisely granted DNA testing when the conviction was based largely or primarily on identification testimony but denied testing when a confession or other form of evidence was relied on. S. P. Duffy, "DNA Test Could Offer Exculpatory Evidence," *The Legal Intelligencer* (Philadelphia, Penn.), August 30, 2001.

32. Cal. Penal Code § 1405(c)(1)(A), emphasis added.

33. Sometimes there is even confusion over the required standard of proof in states with enacted statutes that specify this. In Texas, for example, a court ruled that the defense in a particular case must meet a reasonable-probability-of-innocence standard, despite wording in the statute that specified a lower standard, that of a reasonable probability that the defendant would not have been prosecuted or convicted. E. Timms and D. Jennings, "Ruling Sets DNA Test Rights," *Dallas Morning News*, April 18, 2002.

34. Tenn. Code Ann. § 40-30-404 (Supp. 2001).

35. N.Y. Crim. Proc. Law § 440.30 (1–a) (McKinney 1994 and Supp. 2002).

36. For example, when a reasonable probability exists that a more favorable verdict or sentence would have been the result, Arizona instructs courts that they *may* order the testing; but where there is a reasonable likelihood that the petitioner would not have been prosecuted or convicted, Arizona directs courts that they shall order the testing. Ariz. Rev. Stat. Ann. § 13-4240(B)(1), (C)(1)(a).

37. For a fuller discussion of the various claims of innocence and their relation to postconviction DNA testing and relief, see R. Schaffer, *Texas Lawyer*, November 12, 2001, 1. See also chapter 6 of this volume.

38. St. Louis Circuit Attorney Jennifer Joyce is now drafting legislation that would criminalize inmates whose DNA tests confirmed guilt by charging the cost of failed tests to prison accounts, adding six months to such prisoners' sentences, and requiring the attempts to be considered at parole hearings. Liptak, "Prosecutors See Limits to Doubt"; see also Bryant, "Tests of Convicts Have Only Just Begun."

39. After his first chance at exoneration failed when the sample was consumed by a state crime lab, John Douglas Waller successfully petitioned, under Chapter 64 of the Texas Code of Criminal Procedure, for permission to test hairs found at the scene of the crime of which he was convicted. Waller was paroled in 1993, but he wants to either be granted a new trial or have an appellate court overturn his conviction so that his name will be cleared and he'll no longer be on parole. However, while the trial court found the results of the mtDNA testing favorable to Waller, Chapter 64 does not specify what relief is required after an exculpatory test. See J. Council, "Right without a Remedy? Law Silent on What Happens If DNA Test Is Favorable to Defendant," *Texas Lawyer*, December 10, 2001, 6. The most likely avenue to relief in cases like Waller's is for the convicted individual to petition the court of criminal appeals for a writ of habeas corpus that would, if successful, result in a new trial for the convicted person. Meanwhile, prosecutors continue to resist Waller's attempt at exoneration. In April 2003, a Texas appeals court dismissed for want of jurisdiction the State's appeal of the trial court's finding that DNA results were favorable to Waller. *State v. Waller*, 104 S.W.3d 307.

40. Boemer, "Other Rising Legal Issues," 1989.

41. N.Y. Crim. Proc. L. 440.10(1)(g) (McKinney 1995); *People v. Dabbs*, 587 N.Y.S.2d 90, 92 (1991).

42. Samuel Gross et al., "Exonerations in the United States: 1989–2003." Working paper, April 19, 2004.

43. Gross et al., "Exonerations in the United States," 21.

44. Gross et al., "Exonerations in the United States," 23.

45. Gross et al., "Exonerations in the United States," 26.

46. Gross et al., "Exonerations in the United States," 28.

47. E. Connors et al., *Convicted by Juries, Exonerated by Science: Case Studies in the Use of DNA Evidence to Establish Innocence after Trial* (Washington, D.C.: National Institute of Justice, 1996).

48. Fred Kaufman, *Report of the Kaufman Commission on Proceedings Involving Guy Paul Morin* (Toronto, Ontario, Canada: Ministry of the Attorney General, Government of Ontario, 1998). Available at www.attorneygeneral.jus.gov.on.ca/english/about/pubs/morin.

49. See www.ccrc.gov.uk.

50. The Innocence Project found that in 84 percent of its first seventy exonerations, the original conviction involved an eyewitness identification that turned out to be mistaken. Of the project's first eighty-two convicts to be exonerated by DNA, 73 percent were convicted based on such mistaken witness testimony. See www.innocenceproject.org. Because the Innocence Project accepts a select group of cases (of which their successful exonerations are even more select), the percentages they report of mistaken testimony are likely to be much higher than the general rate of mistaken eyewitness identification. Still, the inherent difficulties of eyewitness/victim identification, as well as those measures that can mitigate these difficulties, are well documented.

51. This policy is law in Minnesota, Alaska, and the United Kingdom.

52. J. S. Liebman et al., "Symposium: Restructuring Federal Courts; Habeas. Capital Attrition: Error Rates in Capital Cases, 1973–1995," *Texas Law Review* 78 (2000): 1864.

53. D. Babwin, "Gov. George Ryan Grants Blanket Clemency for Death Row Inmates," Associated Press State & Local Wire, January 11, 2003. Glendenning's moratorium was also based on a Maryland survey that concluded that state prosecutors are far more likely to seek the death penalty for black suspects charged with killing white victims than in other cases. C. O'Clery, "US Death Penalty 'Has Racial Bias,' " *Irish Times*, January 9, 2003.

54. *Governor's Council on Capital Punishment Final Report*, May 3, 2004.

55. Scheck proposed this during the roundtable on "Postconviction Relief," "DNA and the Criminal Justice System" conference, John F. Kennedy School of Government, Harvard University, Cambridge, Mass., November 20, 2000.

56. See, however, our discussion below of the need for more empirical research on the effectiveness of databases.

57. This understates the cost of collection, however. For example, the administrative costs of collecting DNA from parolees and probationers are likely considerably greater than this. In addition, analysis of DNA from cases is dramatically more expensive—on the order of $2,000 or more per sample.

58. The Ohio Bureau of Criminal Identification and Investigation, for example, keeps the DNA profiles of suspects and compares them with evidence collected in unsolved crimes.

"DNA Database of Suspects Draws Support, Criticism," Associated Press State & Local Wire, August 8, 2002. See also *Damon Smith v. State of Indiana*, 744 N.E.2d 437 (2001), in which police got a cold hit in a rape case from a sample that was collected from the defendant in a separate rape trial and kept in the database even though the defendant was acquitted. The trial court denied the defense's motion to suppress the DNA evidence, and the denial was upheld on appeal.

59. As Kaye acknowledged during the roundtable on "Privacy: Processes and Structures," "DNA and the Criminal Justice System" conference, John F. Kennedy School of Government, Harvard University, Cambridge, Mass., November 21, 2000.

60. This is a concern with respect to the current databases as well, but less so, since these issues come up only when both individuals whose genetic connection one is studying are in the database.

61. "How the Police Found Gafoor," *BBC News*, July 4, 2003, available at www.bbc.co.uk/crime/caseclosed/opmagnum.shtml.

62. In April 2004, Craig Harman was convicted of manslaughter; a "familial search" matched his brother and led to Harman (see "World First for Police as Relative's DNA Traps Lorry Driver's Killer," *Telegraph*, April 20, 2004, available at www.telegraph.co.uk/news/main.jhtml?xml=/news/2004/04/20/nharm20.xml; see also the posthumous identification of Joseph Kappen as the likely perpetrator of three murders from 1973, available at www.bbc.co.uk/crime/caseclosed/opmagnum.shtml).

63. Unpublished data received via personal communication from Allen Beck, from the "1997 Survey of Inmates in State and Federal Correctional Facilities." Overall, 47 percent of state and 39 percent of federal inmates report at least one close relative (parent, spouse, sibling, or child) being incarcerated.

64. According to Matthew Durose and Patrick Langan, *State Court Sentencing of Convicted Felons, 2000 Statistical Tables*, 924,700 individuals were convicted of felonies in 2000 (Bureau of Justice Statistics, 2003). For those for whom there were data, 53 percent (about 500,000) were identified as Caucasian, and 44 percent (about 400,000) were identified as African American. As of the 2000 census, there were between 34,658,000 and 36,419,000 African Americans and between 211,460,000 and 216,930,000 Caucasians in the United States.

65. The National DNA Database: Annual Report 2002–2003, Forensic Science Service, 3.

66. In principle, states, coupled with an informed-consent process, could give convicts the option of "donating" their DNA samples toward research.

67. Fred Zain, former director of the Division of Public Safety's serology division at the West Virginia state police crime laboratory, was indicted on charges of perjury, accused of lying for years on the witness stand to favor prosecutions. Zain died of cancer in 2002 before his case was retried after the first trial ended in a hung jury. See *In re Investigation of the W. Va. State Police Crime Lab., Serology Div.*, 438 S.E.2d 501, 503 (W. Va. 1993).

   In 2001, Oklahoma City police chemist Joyce Gilchrist was fired after an FBI report found that she did poor work and provided false or misleading testimony. B. Bohrer, "Scientist's Cases under Review in 2 States after DNA Clears Man of Rape," Associated Press, December 15, 2002.

In Illinois, three men who served fourteen years in prison, and a fourth, who served six and a half, were exonerated in 2001 of the rape and murder of medical student Lori Roscetti. A DNA expert found that the analyst at the original trial, who had said semen found at the crime scene could be that of the men, gave testimony that amounted to "scientific fraud." The same analyst had testified at two 1986 sexual-assault trials and at the trial of an accused serial rapist; all three convictions were later overturned. D. K. Baker, "When 'Justice Delayed' is 'Non-existent Justice,'" *N'DIGO* (Chicago, Ill.), December 13, 2001, 10.

Similarly, Arnold Melnikoff, the former director of Montana's state crime laboratory for almost two decades and for the past thirteen years forensic scientist for the Washington State Police, was placed on paid leave while both states conduct reviews of about one hundred of his cases. The audits come after DNA evidence cleared a Montana man who spent fifteen years in prison for rape based on Melnikoff's testimony about head and pubic hair samples. Melnikoff had testified that the chances that either set of hairs found at the scene of the rape were not those of the defendant were one in one hundred, and that since head and pubic hairs look different, "it's a multiplying effect, it would be 1 chance in 10,000." An FBI report concluded that the hairs were microscopically dissimilar from those of the defendant's and that the head hair was similar to that of the victim. Other experts argued that the testimony was "totally fallacious" and "without any scientific basis" and suggested that intentional bias might have been present. Owen-Brown, "Remove Double-Jeopardy Rule, Says Ex-Chief Justice."

Most recently, FBI scientist Kathleen Lundy admitted knowingly giving false testimony about her specialty, bullet analysis. J. Solomon, "F.B.I. Scientist Admitted False Testimony," *Boston Globe*, Thursday, April 17, 2003.

68. For instance, retired FBI metallurgist William Tobin has questioned the bureau's science on bullet analysis, prompting the FBI to request a review of its methodology by the National Academy of Sciences. Solomon, "F.B.I. Scientist Admitted False Testimony."

69. In the San Francisco crime lab, a court noted in 1999 that the lab's head at the time, Alan Keel, demonstrated an unacceptable degree of bias in favor of the prosecution. The court, in declaring his DNA evidence inadmissible, described Keel's declaration in opposition to defense discovery as "beyond advocacy—it indicated a critical attitude toward the defense function in a criminal case." See *People v. Bokin*, No. 168461, slip op. at 15 (Cal. Super. Ct. May 5, 1999).

Police officials suspended DNA testing at the Houston police crime laboratory after a December 2002 audit found various problems with the lab's methods, including poor calibration and maintenance of equipment, improper record keeping, and a lack of safeguards against contamination of samples. In response, the district attorney's office ordered a review of all convictions based on DNA evidence tested by the police laboratory, the lab was shut down, and it has been banned from entering DNA profiles into CODIS. See N. Madigan, "Houston's Troubled DNA Crime Lab Faces Scrutiny," *New York Times*, February 9, 2003; Solomon, "F.B.I. Scientist Admitted False Testimony." The Houston lab has also been accused of intentional bias. A lab employee offered evidence in a rape trial to suggest that a DNA sample recovered by investigators was a precise match for the defendant, but other DNA experts disagreed, arguing that the sample was in fact a mixture of DNA from at least two people and that the lab testimony amounted to "outright misrepresentations of scientific findings." See Madigan, "Houston's Troubled DNA Crime Lab Faces Scrutiny."

FBI lab technician Jacqueline Blake resigned after a spring 2001 investigation by the Justice Department's inspector general found that she failed to follow proper procedure during her analysis in at least 103 DNA cases. Blake is accused of failing to compare the DNA evidence with control samples, which is required to obtain accurate results. Solomon, "F.B.I. Scientist Admitted False Testimony."

The Las Vegas police forensics lab mistakenly switched the DNA profiles of two suspects in its computer, which resulted in two false cold hits. The error caused an innocent man to spend nearly a year in jail on sexual-assault charges, for which he faced life imprisonment. Discovery of the error prompted an audit of all the DNA analyses ever done by that lab, as well as an internal investigation that revealed that safeguards aimed at catching such mistakes had failed, primarily because they do not review for text or transcriptional errors. G. Puit, "Police Forensics: DNA Mix-Up Prompts Audit at Lab," *Las Vegas Review-Journal*, April 19, 2002, 1B; G. Puit, "Changes Proposed in DNA Handling," *Las Vegas Review-Journal*, May 15, 2002, 1B. It was unclear whether the suspect whose DNA profile actually matched the crime scene sample would be prosecuted, since the victim of one of the sexual assaults had already made an (erroneous) identification of the innocent man as her attacker in court.

A judge in Los Angeles dismissed drunken-driving charges against a twenty-year-old college student in 2002 after DNA testing paid for by his parents showed Los Angeles police had tested the wrong blood sample in the case. The same police department has faced questions of its handling of blood evidence before, including during the O. J. Simpson murder trial. "Judge Dismisses DUI Case after DNA Shows LAPD Tested Wrong Sample," *Associated Press*, December 15, 2002.

Cellmark, a British company that specializes in DNA identification, made a false positive DNA match in 1987 that could have led to the execution of an innocent man; the company further attempted a cover-up of the error until it was revealed by an external investigation. W. Hodgkinson, "DNA in the Dock," *Observer* (London), November 30, 2002, 83.

70. For a discussion of the efforts of prosecutors, the FBI, and private forensic laboratories to resist defense discovery, see W. C. Thompson, "Evaluating the Admissibility of New Genetic Identification Tests: Lessons from the 'DNA War,'" *Journal of Criminal Law and Criminology* 84 (Spring 1993): 22–104. With respect to the success of such resistance, since there is no nationally recognized right of access to the data underlying DNA tests, defendants must utilize existing rules of discovery embedded in state and federal statutes and in court rulings. Courts, however, have applied these rules to the data underlying DNA tests in a variety of ways, and such rules thus entail a tenuous path, at best, for a defendant seeking access to the data. For an overview of the relevant rules of discovery and various court reactions to them in the context of DNA data, as well as arguments used by commercial labs in resisting discovery, see J. N. Mellon, "Note: Manufacturing Convictions; Why Defendants Are Entitled to the Data Underlying Forensic DNA Kits," *Duke Law Journal* 51 (December 2001): 1097–1137.

71. R. Willing, "DNA Testing Fails to Live Up to Potential," *USA Today*, October 7, 2002.

72. The investigation was controversial first for launching one of the largest DNA dragnets in the United States, and for allegedly using coercive tactics in some cases to procure the more than one thousand "voluntary" samples. Concern about the dragnet only heightened when the state crime lab announced that it would eventually return the excluded samples

and profiles to police who, though they could not place them in either the state or federal databases, which restricts profiles to arrestees and convicts, respectively, would nevertheless retain them to be searched by hand in future investigations. Melissa Moore, "Use of DNA Tests in Killings Raises Rights Questions," *Sunday Advocate* (Baton Rouge, La.), November 24, 2002.

73. DNAPrint Genomics is a Sarasota, Florida, company that owns the rights to a test developed by Mark Shriver, a Pennsylvania State University geneticist, that predicts race from DNA. (It is Shriver's 1997 *American Journal of Human Genetics* article announcing this test that Duster discusses near the end of chapter 14.) The test uses markers that are more often found in people from one continent than another, allowing investigators to predict "with reasonably high confidence" to which major continental race or races—African, Caucasian, East Asian, or American Indian—an individual belongs. Police sent twenty samples and did not tell the lab which one was from the crime scene. Nicholas Wade, "Unusual Use of DNA Aids in Serial Killer Search," *New York Times*, June 3, 2003.

74. C. Wilson, "Ready for Your Close-Up? Working Out What Someone Looks Like from Only a DNA Sample Is No Longer Science Fiction; You'd Be Surprised What Forensics Experts Can Already Do," *New Scientist*, July 20, 2002.

75. Britain's advances in this technology, for instance, were largely the result of a March 1996 FSS analysis of the entire National DNA Database.

Contributors

Garland Allen, Washington University
George Annas, Boston University Law School
Frederick R. Bieber, Harvard Medical School
Margaret A. Berger, Brooklyn Law School, New York City
Stephen Breyer, United States Supreme Court
R. Alta Charo, University of Wisconsin
Simon A. Cole, University of California at Davis
Troy Duster, University of California, Berkeley
Amitai Etzioni, George Washington University
Edward J. Imwinkelried, University of California at Davis
Sheila Jasanoff, Kennedy School of Government, Harvard University
D. H. Kaye, Arizona State University
David Lazer, Kennedy School of Government, Harvard University
Viktor Mayer-Schönberger, Kennedy School of Government, Harvard University
Michelle M. Meyer, Kennedy School of Government, Harvard University
Michael E. Smith, University of Wisconsin
Barry Steinhardt, American Civil Liberties Union

Index